CALIFORNIA GOLD-RUSH PLAYS

THE AMERICAN DRAMA LIBRARY

The American Drama Library is an ongoing series of American plays in anthology format, in which we plan to emphasize nineteenth and early twentieth century plays. Each volume will be edited by a specialist in the field, with the purpose of revisioning a particular genre, historical perspective, or individual playwright. The greater portion of the plays will be those which are previously unpublished, out-of-print, or difficult to find.

Much of our dramatic past has been ignored, belittled, or misunderstood, with the result that dramatic literature as a genre has not taken its rightful place in American letters. A serious loss in the study of American drama is the unavailability of published plays, and the commentary on them by which an art form and its audience interrogates itself and its responses to social and artistic change, from an historical point of view. This is the all-important process by which a field of study matures in relationship to the new ideas of any age. It is also the basis from which a dramatic repertoire grows.

The American Drama Library will, we believe, bring many more plays, new interpretations of dramatic form and cultural history, and reconsideration of literary reputations to our readers. Perhaps in the reflection of American experience this new material gives back to us, we may see in greater detail how, as a society, we give form to our feelings in the art of drama.

The Publishers

Other books in the American Drama Library Series:

American Melodrama / Edited by Daniel C. Gerould

American Popular Entertainments / Edited by Brooks McNamara

CALIFORNIA GOLD-RUSH PLAYS

JOAQUIN MURIETA DE CASTILLO
Charles E. B. Howe

A LIVE WOMAN IN THE MINES
Alonzo Delano

TWO MEN OF SANDY BAR
Bret Harte

Edited, with an Introduction, by
GLENN LONEY

PERFORMING ARTS JOURNAL PUBLICATIONS
NEW YORK

General Editors of The American Drama Library series:

Bonnie Marranca and Gautam Dasgupta

© 1983 Copyright by Performing Arts Journal Publications

First Edition
 For information, write to Performing Arts Journal Publications, 325 Spring Street, Room 318, New York, N.Y. 10013.

Library of Congress Cataloging in Publication Data
California Gold-Rush Plays
CONTENTS: *Joaquin Murieta de Castillo, A Live Woman in the Mines, Two Men of Sandy Bar.*
Library of Congress Catalog Card No.: 83-61191
ISBN: 0-933826-34-6 (cloth)
ISBN: 0-933826-35-4 (paper)

Graphic Design: Gautam Dasgupta

Printed in the United States of America

Publication of this book has been made possible in part by grants received from the National Endowment for the Arts, Washington, D.C., a federal agency, and the New York State Council on the Arts.

CONTENTS

Introduction   7

JOAQUIN MURIETA DE CASTILLO   21
Charles E. B. Howe

A LIVE WOMAN IN THE MINES   65
Alonzo Delano

TWO MEN OF SANDY BAR   103
Bret Harte

A Brief Chronology of California History   177

Bibliography: Selected Works   179

ACKNOWLEDGEMENTS

This edition of these forgotten plays, depicting an exciting, troubling, and mercurial time in California's transformation from a Spanish-Mexican territory into an American State, is affectionately dedicated to Celeste Ashley, who did much of the initial research on this project—which once was to have been an anthology of Pioneer Drama of the West.

The editor is deeply grateful to the curators and research librarians who have made reference materials, originals and copies of the plays, and other valuable documentation available. Among the libraries, collections, and organizations which have helped are the California Historical Society, the San Francisco Public Library, and the San Francisco Archives of the Performing Arts, all in San Francisco; the Bancroft Library of the University of California, Berkeley; the Stanford University Libraries, Stanford; the California State Library, Sacramento; the Henry E. Huntington Library, San Marino; the New York Public Library, and the Billy Rose Theatre Collection of the Lincoln Center Library of the Performing Arts in Manhattan.

INTRODUCTION

"Westward the course of empire takes its way," wrote Bishop Berkeley, in tracing the development of the American nation. Today, some are pained to think of the conquest of Western America as empire-building, but now that's very much what it seems to have been. Just over a week before Mexico was to cede the territory to the United States, in the aftermath of the lost Mexican War, gold was discovered in California. That was in 1848, and it sparked one of the greatest human migrations the world has ever seen. Not only by Americans from the East, the South, and the Midwest, but also by fortune-seekers from the British Isles, from France, Germany, and Sweden, from South America, and even from China. The Irish fled a fatal famine. Germans ran from poverty and a failed revolution. Between 1848 and 1852, in fact, the population of California—which was primarily Indian and Mexican before the influx of Forty-Niners—rose dramatically from 15,000 to 250,000.

In that brief period, some $200 million in gold was found in the placer mines, by digging, panning, and sluicing brown California dirt for nuggets and gold-flakes. These were indeed exciting times, stirring the imaginations of journalists, novelists, and dramatists, both at home and abroad. One of the first plays which purported to deal with life in the mines, *Cockneys in California*, was merely an exercise in fantasy, however. It was written in distant England by J. Stirling Coyne, an adept creator of farces, for a London production of 1849. Considering the numbers of highly educated men—doctors, lawyers, teachers—who rushed to the goldfields, hoping to make a strike which would transform them into millionaires, it is surprising that the great California Gold Rush didn't spawn more impressive and authentic dramas than this awkward, trivial piece and similar efforts seen on Eastern American and British stages. Even with writers of the stature of Bret Harte and Mark Twain honing their skills in the West as journalists, the San Francisco stage of the 1850s had no premieres of western dramas by these observant, witty men. Those were to come later, when both Harte and Twain had been lionized in the

East—and not without a real loss in force and verity.

As George MacMinn wrote in his 1941 study, *The Theatre in the Golden Era in California*: "It might be expected, however, that before long the argonauts [the goldseekers were popularly equated with Jason and his followers, seeking the Golden Fleece] themselves would produce a playwright, a competent amateur if not a professional, whose sense of comedy—or of serious drama—would not preposterously distort the truth about life on the Gold Coast. The fact is that such talent was exceedingly scarce. Nothing in the form of a regular, full-length play was actually printed in the new state until 1856."

Completing my doctorate at Stanford University, I did research in American theatre history and dramatic literature which aroused my interest in forgotten plays, especially those of the Old West, written by people who were actually in the places depicted in the plays at the time of their actions. A student colleague, Celeste Ashley, who was to help develop an impressive Theatre Collection—unfortunately later dispersed—for the Stanford Library, shared my interest. We planned to prepare an edition of Western or Pioneer Dramas, especially of those dealing with the California experience. [Celeste Ashley has since retired from her Stanford University post, but she has continued to support my efforts to publish at least some of the plays we located—so this is also her book.]

My first exposure to such works had been sparked by my discovery, as a UC/Berkeley undergraduate, of a forgotten Gold Rush play by one of the founders of my hometown in the Sierra foothills. The town is Grass Valley, which has a twin-city, Nevada City, home of the 1865 Nevada Theatre. This playhouse is considered by its valiant preservers as the oldest California theatre still being used for that purpose. Grass Valley's founder-playwright was Alonzo Delano. Since theatre activity began in Nevada City as early as 1850, Delano had professional models close at hand. An experienced writer, he was also a correspondent from the Far West for newspapers in the Midwest, the South, and the East. He wittily reported on life in the mines. Delano was familiar with the theatre of the East, as well as with that which was just getting started in Sacramento and in San Francisco—which was to become and remain for many, many years a thriving theatre center.

Alonzo Delano's *A Live Woman in the Mines; or, Pike County Ahead!* seemed not only an interesting picture of the rough-and-ready Forty-Niners—especially with its novelty of the arrival of the first woman in the mines, among a host of lonely men—but it also appeared to be a stage-worthy comedy-melodrama. Undaunted by my lack of directorial experience, I staged this unknown, forgotten work in William Randolph Hearst's Greek Theatre on the Berkeley campus as one of the annual "Sophomore Farces" of the late 1940s. It's all a bit hazy now, but I do recall our efforts to confine the performance of the relatively small cast to the central portion of that vast stage, which once had resounded to the art of Bernhardt and Pavlova. We did burst out, however, in a "Dream Sequence" of Mary arriving in the mines, to the unconfined joy of the eager miners. The immediate inspiration was Agnes de Mille's dream ballet in *Oklahoma!*, of course, but the actual choreography was devised by Durevol Quitzow, who derived his skills—also as leading dancer—from his family, who were disciples and students of San Francisco's own Isadora Duncan. The production was aptly labeled the "Sophomore Farce," for that's more or less how it turned out. Nonetheless, it was fun to do, and I still long to see this unusual historical-dramatic artifact given a really imaginative professional production.

Another fellow-student of theatre at Stanford, Stuart Wallace Hyde, completed an impressive Ph.D. dissertation, *The Representation of the West in American Drama from 1849 to 1917*, with an accompanying playlist of equally impressive length. Using this and other sources, Celeste Ashley and I began to draw up rosters of possible plays for an anthology of Western Drama. We soon found out that, for some earlier American historians and playwrights, the West seemed to have begun just across the Hudson River from New York City. There was a time, of course, when Kentucky and Ohio were really pioneer territory, areas of westward expansion. Such dramas as *Davy Crockett* and *The Lion of the West*, which drew their inspirations from bold personalities or vital events in the taming of the Midwest and the South, had already been rescued from obscurity by the *America's Lost Plays* series. So Ashley and I decided to focus on dramas of the Far West, especially those dealing with the Gold Rush in California and its immediate aftermath. We made lists. We crossed off those plays which had vanished without a trace. We eliminated those scripts which were really London or New York plots, reworked with a western setting. We also avoided those melodramas and farces about the Far West which seemed to have been written by bored actors during a tour of the English Midlands. An unusual number of these, as it happened, were concerned with the marital affairs of the Mormons in Salt Lake City, a subject which apparently both appalled and intrigued theatre-goers in Queen Victoria's England.

It used to be a commonplace of Hollywood Westerns that, possibly by right of Eminent Domain, the American West was there only waiting to be "won" by the hardy overland pioneers. Indeed, one U.S. Army World War II training-film—a patchwork of great film-clips—showed pioneers, cowboys, and U.S. Cavalrymen energetically slaughtering Indians to the accompaniment of a fruity narration along these lines: "And so, Americans moved constantly Westward, conscious that a Nation *had* to be born!" This was obviously not a consciousness shared by the Indians. In California, the scene of all three plays in this collection, not only the native Indians, but also the Spanish and Mexican settlers had to give way to the masses of Americans and other foreigners who came flooding into California. By the thousands, they were bound for the goldfields of the Mother Lode—in the Southern Mines—and for the riches of the Northern Mines. Unfortunately, many earlier settlers, who held large Mexican land grants, rapidly found themselves displaced by these emigrants. They often acted as "squatters," but they were protected by new American laws and property deeds. Captain John Sutter, builder of Sutter's Fort in Sacramento, saw his large landholdings overrun and seized by prospectors, staking their claims for the golden riches. On 24 January 1848, gold had been discovered at Sutter's Mill, in Coloma, news of which launched the Gold Rush. Sutter was driven out of California—a son murdered by a mob—to die in poverty and bitterness in the East. For those readers unfamiliar with the saga of the Conquest of California, there is a chronology of major events, from 1542 to 1882, in the Appendix. This not only provides a brief survey of the history of what came to be called "The Golden State," but it also can be useful in reading the plays. It helps explain the attitudes and actions—depicted in the dramas—of the new American settlers and prospectors regarding the Californians they found already on the land.

With the first stirrings of the Gold Rush, San Francisco became California's theatre center, a hub of producing activity, thanks both to relocated Easterners and to touring players—such as the aging Junius Brutus Booth, Sr., and his solicitous teenage son, Edwin Booth. One of his other sons, Junius Brutus, Jr., was to be a San Francisco regular in the theatre of the 1850s. One of the most interesting pioneers of San Francisco Gold Rush theatre, however, was David G. ("Doc" or "Yankee") Robinson. He was born in East Monmouth, Maine, and was, it was said, associated for a time with the great Phineas Taylor Barnum. Robinson's *The Life and Adventures of the Reformed Inebriate* was published in 1846 in Boston. The following year he opened a drugstore in San Francisco's Portsmouth Square, giving added import to the name of "Doc" Robinson. The stage soon lured him. His first drop-curtain was painted with curry and mustard powder, so primitive then were circumstances and supplies. His second stage was the Robinson and Everard Dramatic Museum—a name possibly borrowed from Barnum—on California Street, below Kearny.

Among the San Francisco-oriented plays credited to Doc Robinson in the early 1850s are *The Dashaways, Seeing the Elephant,* and *The Past, Present, and Future of San Francisco*. Even in its early days, San Francisco offered scope for the socially active; *The Dashaways* satirized this. (Its title is similar to that of a Victorian social spoof, *The Never-at-homes*.) "Seeing the elephant" apparently derived its initial currency from the curiosity and excitement generated by the exhibition of a large pachyderm. Some relate it to Barnum's ballyhoo for his specimen; others give it an earlier London origin. In the West, however, it took on more bitter overtones. Going to the mines with high expectations and having them harshly dashed was also described as "seeing the elephant." Later, jocular San Franciscans would use the phrase to indicate a projected tour of local landmarks, wonders, and night-spots.

Unfortunately, none of Doc Robinson's San Francisco play-manuscripts has survived. In an unpublished 1937 Federal Theatre study by Lois Foster, *Annals of the San Francisco Stage, 1850-1880*, Robinson's San Francisco career is reviewed. Apparently, he thought there might be interested audiences on the East Coast for his Gold Rush dramas, so he set out, leaving behind his wife and his son, Charles Dorman Robinson, later to become a noted painter of western scenes. He became gravely ill on shipboard and died in port in Alabama. It's reported that all his plays were stolen, including his epic survey of San Francisco history and his script of *The Reformed Drunkard*, which was, it has been alleged, stolen and rewritten as the enduringly successful temperance melodrama, *Ten Nights in a Barroom*. Since the Boston version of this Doc Robinson fable was already in print as a novel, this explanation of the origin of *Ten Nights in a Barroom*, while intriguing, may not be correct.

What did survive of Doc Robinson's antic stage humor and satiric wit are a number of his "Comic Songs," used in his various plays about San Francisco. They were published in that city in 1853, with the subtitle of *Hits at San Francisco*, "sung by him at the San Francisco Theatre." This is a pun, for they were, as reviewed by local newspapers, certainly hits with Doc Robinson's audiences, but they also were often sharply critical "hits" at corrupt local politicians and entrepreneurs, with their many odd or devious schemes. Pretensions of notable San

Franciscans and their distinguished visitors were mocked as well. One visitor to San Francisco who did not escape was the notorious European adventuress, Lola Montez. It has been said that she initially lodged with the Robinson family, and Mrs. Robinson sewed the spiders on her costume for her celebrated "Spider Dance." Lola Montez, who had been the mistress of King Ludwig I of Bavaria—not to mention Franz Liszt and others—had been created Countess of Landsfeld by the aged monarch. Robinson wrote a burlesque—*Who's Got the Countess?*—about Lola and her dance, which was performed with great success by a local comedienne, Caroline Chapman. The highlight was Chapman as Montez in the "Spy-Dear Dance." Tom Maguire, who was to be a major theatre-builder and producer in San Francisco for years, had bid for Montez's talents, but John Lewis Baker bid higher, so she opened 26 May 1853 at Baker's American Theatre. Her first-night box-office was reported at $4,500, but knowing local critics scoffed at her dancing. There were some San Franciscans, however, who were entranced by Montez and wrote poems about her to the newspapers.

Doc Robinson wrote his own poem about Lola Montez and set it to music for his audiences. It gives an idea of the topics and treatment favored by this early San Francisco playwright-satirist—as well as the tastes of Gold Rush theatre-goers. There are some references in the song which may be unclear today—these are foot-noted immediately below the text:

Oh, have you heard the news of late
Of what happened in our State?—
There has arrived a monarch[1] mate,
   Imported from Bavaria!
If you would like to see the sight,
And aint afraid the crittur'll bite,
Just pay five dollars any night,
And Baker'll[2] get the show up right!
She'll glance you with those sparkling eyes,
And other means she will devise
To make you puff her to the skies,
While she the spiders will surprise!
And all the Bakers in the town
Will find the Countess does it Brown,
When with the dust[3] they must come down—
   To the Countess of Bavaria!

A Baker once, as I am told,
Became so fond of shining gold
That he at public auction sold—[4]
   The Countess of Bavaria!
Altho' he got but small advance,
Yet he went in and stood his chance,
Relying on that Spider Dance[5]
To put the public in a trance;

But when to see her they did go
The ladies thought, but didn't know,
The Countess lacked some calico,[6]
Which would improve the classic show!
Altho' some men were fairly sold,[7]
Yet Lola thanks them for their gold;
Her dancing knocks all dancing cold—
    She learned it in Bavaria!

That classic play-house[8] down below,
To which all moral people go,
Requires no trump of fame to blow—
    The Countess of Bavaria!
Altho' her fame was often told,
The morning that her tickets sold
She did poor Baker curse and scold
Because they brought so little gold!
While frightened Lewis[9] did protest
That with them he had done his best,
For all his soups he had well dress'd,
And they had each out-bid the rest!
But all his efforts were in vain,
And as his nose, to him 'twas plain,
That gold would not be showered like rain—
    On the Countess of Bavaria!

But people's tastes so disagree,
That what suits one may not suit me,
So you had better go and see—
    The Countess of Bavaria!
And if she deigns to you a chance
To see her classic Spider Dance,
Which did that Alta[10] man entrance
And fixed him with that killing glance!
But what increases our surprise
Is that our heroes, who despise
To shoot, yet like a martyr dies
A victim to a lady's eyes!
And thus in life 'twill ever be
We always find some foolish plea,
And you'll find one to go and see
    The Countess of Bavaria!

---

1. Ludwig I of Bavaria. 2. Theatre-manager John Lewis Baker. 3. Gold dust. 4. Opening-night tickets were auctioned. 5. Montez's specialty, in which spiders seemed to infest her costume. 6. Her costume was too scanty. 7. Cheated; "sold a bill of goods." 8. The American Theatre was a rival to Robinson's playhouse. 9. Manager Baker. 10. One of Montez's conquests.

Despite some hostile reviews and Doc Robinson's mockery, Lola Montez continued playing her repertory until the end of June. Her most popular attraction was a dramatic survey of her life and loves. After her San Francisco engagement, she retired for some months to that Sierra mining-town Alonzo Delano helped found—Grass Valley. She had taken and discarded a husband; she'd also acquired a pet bear, which she led around on a silver chain to the astonishment of the locals. It was said she had horsewhipped an editor who derided her talents. In short, she was a woman of some interest to the miners, whom she complimented on occasion by herself wearing miner's garb. During her stay in Grass Valley, tradition has it that Montez taught the little girl next door to dance. That child was Lotta Crabtree, who is reputed to have danced for the miners on a blacksmith's anvil, earning "pokes" or bags of gold dust. Later, as "The Darling of the Forty-Niners," she went on to a long career as one of America's first musical theatre stars. Grass Valley was also the birthplace of the distinguished Harvard philosopher, Josiah Royce, so the historic old town had an affinity for the arts and humanities in its earliest days. For Lola Montez, after Grass Valley her career was a downhill slide. She died in poverty and obscurity—an almost obligatory end for notorious women in the moral fiction of the time—and she lies buried in Brooklyn's Green Wood Cemetery as "Mrs. Eliza Gilbert." *Sic transit Lola.*

Doc Robinson obviously was no respecter of persons. If Montez was annoyed, that was as nothing to the anger of city councilmen and others who were his regular satiric targets. One of Doc Robinson's most popular numbers was a forlorn ditty to the tune of "A Used-Up Man." He called the song "Life in California," but he retained the "used-up man" phrase in all the refrains. Here are two verses to provide a sample of this early San Francisco entertainment:

I lives 'way down in Maine, where I heard about the diggings;
So I shipped aboard a darned old barque, commanded by Joe Higgins;
I sold my little farm, and from wife and children parted,
And off to California sailed, and left 'em broken-hearted.
  But here's a used-up man, a perfect used-up man,
  And if I ever get home again, I'll stay there if I can.
O I han't got no home, nor nothing else, I 'spose;
Misfortune seems to follow me wherever I goes;
I come to California with a heart both stout and bold,
And have been up to the diggings, there to get some lumps of gold.
  But I'm a used-up man, etc.

Doc Robinson delighted his audiences with this—updated from time to time with references to new San Francisco scandals and events—appearing in his Yankee guise, sporting a broken umbrella. A resourceful theatre-man, Doc Robinson instituted an early form of "Bank Night," with prizes for the audience. He also favored that popular nineteenth century stage attraction, the gradually unrolling scenic-panorama. His *Panorama of Venice* was a 2,956-foot wonder, costing $10,000 to construct and paint. He also showed a panorama of the "Antediluvian World," that is, the earth before the biblical flood. Someday, perhaps, Doc Robinson's stolen San Francisco plays will be found again. In the meantime, we have

some musical specimens of his humor, this Yankee comedian, touched with Gold
Rush brashness.

Two California plays from the 1850s are included in this volume, along with one
from the 1870s, which recreates its author's own experiences and observations of
the 1850s. The three plays are Charles E. B. Howe's romantic melodrama, *Joaquin
Murieta de Castillo, the Celebrated California Bandit* (1858); Alonzo "Old Block"
Delano's sentimental melodrama *A Live Woman in the Mines; or, Pike County
Ahead!* (1857), and Bret Harte's adventure melodrama, *Two Men of Sandy Bar*,
which was premiered in New York in 1876, and in San Francisco in 1878, following a national tour. It is unfortunate that there's no room in this volume for Warren
Baer's jolly musical satire on Gold Rush mining swindlers, *The Duke of California*
(1856). Or for Joseph Nunes's *Fast Folks; or The Early Days of California*—with a
dedication to William H. Seward, the man who later bought Alaska for the United
States. Nunes's comedy-melodrama was produced in 1858, at San Francisco's
American Theatre. It's a West Coast equivalent to Anna Cora Mowatt's *Fashion*
and owes its inspiration to the same playwright Mowatt echoed—Richard Brinsley
Sheridan. Nor has it been possible to include either of Joaquin Miller's most in-
teresting dramas of the West: *The Danites* and *Forty-Nine—An Idyll Drama of the
Sierras*. Both were effective staples of the repertory of McKee Rankin and his wife,
Kitty Blanchard, popular nineteenth century American touring players. Levi
Damon Phillips has written a definitive doctoral dissertation on Rankin's *Danites*
production for UC/Davis, where he is a Special Collections librarian. Perhaps the
most famous of all melodramas about the Far West and the Gold Rush is David
Belasco's *The Girl of the Golden West*. San Francisco-born in the midst of the
Golden Era in 1853, Belasco experienced at first-hand what he put on stage so
many years later, in 1905. Early involved in theatre, Belasco was once nearly hanged by vigilantes when he was mistaken for a horse-thief in Virginia City, Nevada.
He was acting at Piper's Opera House during the great Comstock Lode boom.
There are two reasons his notable melodrama is not in this volume: 1) its 1905 date,
despite its authentic sources, puts it too far beyond the period of the Gold Rush,
and, 2) it is already included in *American Melodrama* which Daniel Gerould
edited for The American Drama Library Series of which this volume is part.

After a thorough search of the annals compiled in San Francisco under WPA
auspices by Federal Theatre researchers and writers in 1937-38, there appeared to
be no record of a professional production of either of the first two plays chosen for
this collection. This, even though Alonzo Delano was a well-known personality
and a respected writer. That doesn't rule out forgotten amateur productions. One
volume of the Federal Theatre San Francisco histories is even devoted to records of
amateur stagings, but neither *Joaquin Murieta de Castillo* or *A Live Woman in the
Mines* is listed. It's entirely possible that the Federal Theatre researchers may have
overlooked some newspaper reports of amateur shows in the late 1850s or in the
1860s. Or that amateur mountings of these plays occurred but were not, in fact,
reported at all. In any case, Delano's affectionate, slightly comic exercise in
nostalgia for the goldfields of 1849 was not published in San Francisco, but in New
York, by Samuel French, as part of its popular series of "Minor Drama." These

were plays sold for productions by stock-companies, amateur troupes, and schools, so it is likely that *A Live Woman in the Mines* in its day had its share of non-professional stagings.

It would be tempting to link Charles E. B. Howe, the dramatist of *Joaquin Murieta de Castillo*, with Julia Ward Howe, poet of "The Battle Hymn of the Republic," both because of their last names and their pronounced Union sentiments. Thus far, no relationship can be verified. In fact, aside from listings in local records as a resident of San Francisco, no important biographical information about Charles Howe has come to light. Possibly he intended his play for reading only, as a closet-drama. It was published in San Francisco in 1858, by the Commercial Book and Job Steam Printing Establishment. There are no records of productions or reprintings. But Howe did write some other plays, shorter and less ambitious. One of these, *Signing the Declaration of Independence; or, Scenes in Congress, July 4th, 1776*, was published by Samuel French, circa 1887. It was actually produced in San Francisco much earlier—in 1863, and, appropriately enough, in July at Maguire's Opera House. Living in the Far West had obviously left its mark on playwright Howe. Outside Independence Hall in Philadelphia, a patriot is made to say by the dramatist: ". . . you are a cowboy and a traitor. Such as you are as unfit for freedom as a rattlesnake would be to play with children. A tory and a cowboy!" Charles E. B. Howe's play about the notorious California bandit, Joaquin Murieta, depicts this legendary scourge of the West from Spring 1851 to 24 July 1853, when he was captured and killed by a posse led by Captain Harry Love, just as recorded in the drama. That the play is partly based on history is not so remarkable. There are, according to Francis Farquhar, who has made an extensive study of the Murieta literature, at least 20 versions of the Joaquin Murieta story. It has been retold in verse, reportage, drama, and fiction. Howe's version is especially interesting because it comes so soon—only five years—after the bandit's death. It is, in fact, one of the earliest attempts to characterize this daring bandit. The play appeared not long after the 1854 account by "Yellow Bird," or John David Ridge. This was the first version of Murieta's tale, part fact, part fiction, called *The Life and Adventures of Joaquin Murieta, the Celebrated California Bandit*. It had its first installment in May 1854, in the *Pacific Police Gazette*, but that first issue was also the last. A full ten installments appeared later in 1859, the year after Howe's play was published, in the *California Police Gazette*.

Since that time, versions have appeared in English and in Spanish. Joaquin Murieta has passed over into California legend; from a murderous desperado, he has been transformed into an Hispanic Robin Hood. The historian Joseph Henry Jackson, although he has admitted that there was a Murieta, doubted the many exploits attributed to him. Legend or truth, Murieta's image was and is a potent one. In the 1930s, near Grass Valley no less, people still pointed out the cave on Pilot's Peak, where Murieta was said to have hidden out after a foray in a Sacramento Valley town. Murieta's nemesis, Captain Harry Love, proved that the bandit had breathed his last. After the capture, Murieta's severed head and the pickled hand of his lieutenant, Three-Fingered Jack, were publicly exhibited. Indeed, many years later, the grisly trophies were still to be seen in carnival sideshows; at least the pitchmen assured customers that they were authentic. Nonetheless, there were those who said that Joaquin Murieta had escaped, a romantic but lethal Mexican anti-hero, who lived on to enjoy his ill-gotten gains far from California. The legend has been artistically enhanced by no less a modern talent than Chile's Nobel Prize-winner, Pablo Neruda. His poetic fantasy-drama, *Splendor and Death of Joaquin Murieta* (1966), insists often that Murieta was a Chilean. It also shows him as a man outraged by the Americanos who look down on him and mistreat his people. In the light of developing attitudes about the historic relationships between Americans and Hispanics, Neruda's vision of Murieta and his opponents could be viewed as a seminal literary comment.

And yet consider how much Charles E. B. Howe anticipated this time of polarization of attitudes. When Howe wrote his play, Murieta was widely considered a bloodthirsty Mexican thief, a dangerous, thoughtless murderer. His supposed Mexican origins certainly did not enhance him in the eyes of those immigrant Americans who feared him alive and could not forget him dead. He became a legend for his fearlessness, his daring. If murderous, he was still a brave desperado, one who was, however grudgingly, admired. But Charles Howe didn't depict a vicious, blood-crazed Mexican monster in his play at all. He created a poetic Joaquin Murieta, a real aristocrat, a natural leader, robbed of his patrimony—as were his fellow Mexicans of their lands and goods by the incoming Americans, who treated California as though it were their own and not a Mexican territory. Considering the condescension and often outright hostility with which the Eastern emigrant settlers treated the native Mexicans, Howe's portrait of Murieta as a valiant, intelligent, sensitive man, driven to a life of vengeful crime by deep wrongs done him, may be something of an American *mea culpa*. It is most unusual to find it so early in California history, not to mention American drama. Howe even allows Murieta moments of Robin Hood bravado and courtesy, when he protects some decent American settlers. Howe's play, no matter how high-flown its language or how devious the villainous plots of the bad priest, Gonzalles, is still an interesting testimony and document of life and attitudes in California in the 1850s.

That is even more the case with Alonzo Delano's *A Live Woman in the Mines*, published in 1858 in New York by Samuel French. Born in 1802 or 1806 in Aurora, New York, a third cousin twice removed from Franklin Delano Roosevelt, Delano (d. 1874) moved to the Midwest at 15, eventually dealing in drygoods and produce in South Bend, Indiana. On 19 April 1849, he and a small party of migrants began the 2,000-mile overland trek from St. Joseph, Missouri, to the California goldfields. Delano, it has been said, earned his living more with his pen than with his pan—that is, his mining pan. As "Old Block," he was soon providing newspapers such as the *New Orleans True Delta* and even the *New York Times* with his witty, but occasionally pathetic, accounts of life in California. Among his books are: *Pen—Knife Sketches; or, Chips of the Old Block* (1853), *Life in the Plains and Among the Diggings* (1854), *Old Block's Sketch-Book* (1856), and *A Sojourn With Royalty*, reprinted in 1936. In San Francisco, he had a produce business, but one of that city's disastrous fires incinerated that. Some measure of the man may be taken from the fact that, in the Panic of 1855, he permitted depositors of the bank he ran in Grass Valley to take their money out, even though he had telegraphic orders to close the bank and seal the safe.

Alonzo Delano was a remarkable man, and it shows in his unusual play. As George MacMinn says, in *The Theatre of the Golden Era in California*: "It came from the pen of a genuine California pioneer; it presented authentic and significant characters; its dialogue, full of flavor, was consistently realistic, and the whole was suffused with true atmosphere. That it failed to be adequately appreciated in California itself may be attributable to the fact that the local critics were generally disposed, by 1857, to assume the airs of sophisticates in all matters." One San Francisco book reviewer recommended it to miners. MacMinn admits that the play has never been accepted as a "possible contribution to American literature," yet he views it as "the most distinctively Californian of the plays produced by the golden era." Despite its formulary debts to standard stage melodrama of the day, Delano's play is amazingly fresh and direct, nowhere more so than in its portraits of the rough but good-natured prospectors of the goldfields, longing for homes and families left behind in the East, or even farther away, in England and in Europe.

Of the three plays in this collection, *Two Men of Sandy Bar* is the only one known to have professional productions of record. The drama's New York City premiere took place at the Union Square Theatre on 28 August 1876. Francis Bret Harte (1836-1902), its author, had made his name in the Far West as an especially apt observer of life in the mines, with a gift for translating those unusual scenes and characters into fiction. Actually, the name he made was his pen-name: Bret Harte. As editor of the *Overland Monthly*, he was able to share his own tales and those of other western writers with a fascinated, discriminating eastern audience, eager for insights into the life of adventure in the West. A number of his stories and poems, such as *The Outcasts of Poker Flat*, *Tennessee's Partner*, *The Luck of Roaring Camp*, *The Heathen Chinese*, *Salomey Jane's Kiss*, and *M'liss* became classics in their own time. Well into the twentieth century, they were still required reading for high school students of American literature. Born, like Delano, in New York State, Harte moved from Brooklyn to San Francisco in 1854. He learned the trades of printer, journalist, and editor, and later schooled his sometime colleague and friend, Samuel Clemens (Mark Twain). Although Harte held the sinecure of Secretary of the California Mint and, later, a professorship in "recent literature" at the University of California at Berkeley, as well as editorship of the *Overland Monthly*, he ran up debts and incurred other obligations. So he decided to move East, where his writings had already conquered—as they also had abroad, as far afield as Britain, France, and Germany. Unfortunately, also in the East, he was careless about repaying what he owed and awkward in dealing with others—even abrasive. Removed from the land and people which had given him his initial inspiration, his later work was either unconvincing invention or a faded reworking of his California triumphs.

Bret Harte's *M'liss*, adapted in San Francisco by Clay M. Greene, with Katy Mahew in the title role, at the California Theatre on 6 August 1877, had been well received. It would be again adapted, next time by John E. McDonough, as *M'liss, an Idyll of Red Mountain*. (As recently as 1976, it was seen off-Broadway in Manhattan as a musical.) Considering the great and continuing popularity of his California short-stories, Harte must have thought he was well advised to take some characters and situations from several of those classics, such as *Tennessee's Partner* and *The Outcasts of Poker Flat*, and rework them into a romantic melodrama of the Old West. The more serious aspects would be lightened with comic moments, partly supplied by a Chinese character, Hop Sing, played by C. T. Parsloe. Parsloe was to be much admired for his Oriental stereotypes, even in the subsequent—and disastrous—Bret Harte and Mark Twain collaboration, the western comedy-melodrama, *Ah Sin*, which premiered in New York on 31 July 1877. That play was the cause of an irrevocable break between the two writers.

It's curious that other writers have been, at least in terms of crafting acceptable stage-vehicles, far more successful with Harte's tales than he himself was. One interesting example is *Salomey Jane*, made into a popular play by Paul Armstrong, and later into a 1914 film, featuring Beatriz Michelena. And there were other Harte adaptations which pleased the audiences of their day. In *Two Men of Sandy Bar*, Harte preserved some of his most admired characters from various tales, but at the cost of distorting their initial freshness and reality. This he did by forcing them into a melodramatic plot of romance, mistaken identity, dubious relationships, gratuitous comedy, exotic locales, manipulated suspense, fortuitous actions inconsistent with character, and other devices dear to the nineteenth century melodramatist. Inexperienced playwright that he was, Harte didn't bring it off as well as the professionals. Nonetheless, there are in the play distinctive vestiges of Harte's vision of the Old West which are rewarding, if not especially demanding of stage-production. Despite its poor reviews in performance, the play pleased Harte well enough for him to include it in his *Collected Works*.

Perhaps it should be remembered that 1876 was America's Centennial Year. At the great Exhibition in Philadelphia, the huge Corliss Steam-Engine was on display; in New York, the Rev. Henry Ward Beecher was embarrassingly in court, and, in the West, General George Custer was making forays against the Sioux. Harte's westerners of the 1850s were by that time no novelty to eastern audiences. Harte didn't yet realize it, but his time had passed. The actor Stuart Robson had paid him $3,000—plus a $20 royalty each night until the sum reached an additional $3,000—to craft this drama from his famous stories. Opening-night critics in New York were not kind. The anonymous reviewer from the *Herald* was excoriating: "As an 'American drama,' it is an absolute outrage upon the intellectual reputation of the country." This judgment was modified by the critic's admission that there were, in fact, worse dramas than *Two Men of Sandy Bar* currently on the boards, but, in his opinion, none of them had such distinguished origin. Perusal of other plays then popular shows them not much of an improvement over Harte's play, in terms of reality of character, plausibility of action, and inventiveness of dialogue. But other writers raised fewer expectations than Harte had—and they managed the melodrama formulas better. There was more to this hostile critical reaction than cavils about Harte's craftsmanship. Other New York critics echoed the reservations of the *Herald*'s reviewer, but he said it more forcefully: "Ever since he left California, Mr. Harte has lived on his reputation and failed in his performances." A celestial metaphor was invoked: "He has reversed the path of the sun. He rose splendidly in the West and has set in darkness in the East."

The play had been tried out in Chicago by Stuart Robson, who initially played Harte's swaggering, pretentious Col. Starbottle. In New York, this was considered a minor, even unnecessary, role and an odd choice for the actor who had commissioned the play. Over a year later, having toured this play and others in his repertory across the country, Robson and his troupe opened *Two Men of Sandy Bar* in San Francisco. By this time, Robson had given up the colonel for the central role of

Sandy. After the 23 September 1878 opening, the *San Francisco Bulletin's* critic thought the part was "quite out of his line, but not a bad performance." Bret Harte apparently still had some friends in San Francisco, if not in New York, for the *Bulletin's* nameless reviewer suggested that the play's mechanical faults weren't entirely the playwright's. The play, he noted, had been undergoing changes at the hands of Robson and his troupe for two years. The critic from the *San Francisco Chronicle* preferred Harte's play as a closet-drama, to be read, as he said, with frequent pleasure. On stage, the play had, in his opinion, "a certain idyllic grace, a quiet pictorial quality, and an unobtrusive study of character." Unfortunately, those fine qualities were not enough, he said, to "violently stimulate the imagination or satisfy the dramatic desire." Fortunately, on both coasts, the scenery was found to be natural and pleasing. Thus, *Two Men of Sandy Bar* was seen as an ineffective stage work.

When one reads the play now, it's easy to see Harte's technical awkwardnesses as a dramatist, but it isn't so very much different in quality from Joaquin Miller's *The Danites*, which was generally approved by the critics of that time. Perhaps, as has been suggested, so very much more was expected of Bret Harte than of the run-of-the-mill melodramatists. One reviewer even negatively compared Harte's plotting with that of the ever popular Dion Boucicault—but Boucicault was a seasoned playwright-actor-manager. Bret Harte was a beginner in the theatre. Accounts of actual performances in New York make it clear that the Manhattan cast was inexperienced, awkward, uneven, and in some cases untalented. Tasteless minstrelsy was interpolated in the last act to get laughs. A Spanish dance by supers was critically derided. Later, in San Francisco, the dance was found "very pretty," but reviews indicate that the ensemble's performances on the long tour had become even more farcical and coarse. Bret Harte's drama was a novice's effort; his misfortune as a playwright was to give it to a company which could only cheapen it, rather than develop it and emphasize its special appeal as Harte's picture of the Far West in the Gold Rush era. Now, perhaps, readers can savor its nostalgia more indulgently.

Glenn Loney

A DRAMATIC PLAY

ENTITLED

JOAQUIN MURIETA DE CASTILLO

THE CELEBRATED

CALIFORNIA BANDIT

IN FIVE ACTS

BY

CHARLES E. B. HOWE

Dedicated to
P. Q. VROOM, Esq.
of Monroe County, New York,
for His Gentlemanly Worth
and Scholastic Attainments,
by His Friend,
The Author

CHARACTERS

Joaquin Murieta de Castillo
Garcia, Three-Fingered Jack
Gonzalles, a priest
Ignacious, a monastic scholar
Roderiguez, a renegade priest
Pedro, Jose, Juan,
Gale, Knox, Bill Harvey,
Jo, Missouri, San Antone,
Texas Bill, Zeke, Harry Love,
Henderson, Bill Byrnes, White,
Bill, Mike, Squire Brown,
Tennessee, Jack, Pitch,

WOMEN

Belloro
Rosa
Bonita
Mrs. Gale
Mary Gale

ACT I

SCENE I: *Two Priests conversing under the walls of a monastery. Time—Evening.*

(Enter Gonzalles and Ignacious.)

GONZALLES: 'Tis well we have met here, for those rude walls have ears within that might cause us to lose our own, if they should hear what I have to say; therefore this appointment, but the sound of our voices dies ere it reaches yonder grating, and the fire-fly's lamp is far preferable to the oil sconce light of the monastery's aisles, for the utterance of my thoughts.

IGNACIOUS: Most true, reverend father—the free air of heaven for conversing on worldly matters, while the monastery's cells, with beads and rosary, or the altar and shrine, are the only fitting places for silent worship. Yet of late I have often been lost in revery on wickedness—worldly wickedness; for your language has recalled to memory scenes long since forgotten. Mountains, brooks, trees and extensive plains, once familiar to my eyes, have again passed in panorama form athwart my dreamy vision, and voluntarily I have bowed my knees in prayer, saying, At last I have found the true spot to worship the true God. I fear it was sinful, reverend father.

GONZALLES: What the heart wishes for, the waking or dreaming thoughts will seek. Now I have a view of worldly scenes that I wish to lay before you, but listen, and you may profit by the result. By disposition you are romantic, and young blood heeds its soothings. Yet how could it be otherwise? for the hot Moorish blood of old Castile in your veins has not lost ardor by long study and close confinement within Santa Cruz Monastery, and you, sir, are prone to lean towards its promptings. *(Aside.)*—Ignacious is clay, and I will mould him to my purpose as the potter moulds the tile to shed winter rains. *(To Ignacious.)*—Ignacious, dost thou ever dream of thy boyhood home 'mid the hills of dear old Spain? and how more fair is their sweet verdure than in this land of the wiley

Aztec. In Spain the vine-clad hills o'ertop the romantic villages, in which there are many romantic homes; the trees wear a greener dress; the sky is more serene in its loveliness; the people are more happy, and the voluptuous swell of music rises on the soft twilight of the evening air, echoed by the lips of beauties, whose blood shines through their transparent skin with a rosy tinge; and the warm hearted Spaniard will ever bid a welcome. Unlike all we meet here. What a pity!

IGNACIOUS: What a pity! Reverend father, I am no voluptuary; yet, Spain, dear old Spain; how I long to see it once more, as I saw it in childhood, but—(*A noise.*)

GONZALLES: But—Speak out, Ignacious; we are all confidence.

IGNACIOUS: I heard a noise; I fear a listener.

GONZALLES: It was but an owl or bat leaving its nest in yonder eaves; and the stones are loose from decay and are easily displaced. Speak on.

IGNACIOUS: But, I am poor, and a novice in a monastery is seldom rich.

GONZALLES: It is what I would have said. We are poor; therefore, what a pity!

IGNACIOUS: Then you, too, reverend father, have dreamed of—of travelling.

GONZALLES: Yes, and if I had wealth, I would renounce my vows. At least I will get a dispensation to travel.

IGNACIOUS: Reverend father! holy horror! Sante Christo protect us. Sacrilege! (*Crosses himself.*) Renounce your vows? oh, no! A dispensation would be far better.

GONZALLES: Yes, I think it would be. I still retain a dispensation. I obtained it through the Bishop of Mexico and used it during the American war,[1] where I earned the soubriquet of "the fighting priest"; I roamed with as brave a guerrilla band as ever harassed *Los Americanos*. *Caramba!* I can fight, swear, or serve at high mass. Ignacious, would you become rich, powerful, adored—and that, too, in thy own native land, beneath the lovely ethereal skies of thy own dear native Spain?

IGNACIOUS: Why should I ask, how is this to be? For it is impossible. You do but tempt me through my wishes.

GONZALLES: No, I do not wish to tempt you—I swear it; yet I will tell you all. Within yonder walls there is a young man, who was reared and fostered there. He is thy senior classmate, and he is heir, sole heir, to titles and wealth, broad lands, and villages, and vine-clad hills that are in old Spain, besides plantations in Cuba. I alone possess the secret and proofs of his birth and heirship. I want one to personate him and divide with me the wealth. The one who so personates him shall have the titles for so doing. Is it worth the trial? Do you understand me?

IGNACIOUS: My head is in a blaze; all the blood in my body has rushed there. Reverend father, this is so new to me that I know not what to say. But yet—what of him? who is he?

GONZALLES: He is a forward, impetuous devil; one, I think, you like not; dictatorial in his ways and haughty in his manners. He was left on the roads when an infant, by an aged servitor, who died from inhaling, on a warm day, the dead winds of the Sierra Madre. I discovered him and possessed myself of the old man's papers, and they shall now become of some value, by being used.

IGNACIOUS: It is Joaquin.

GONZALLES: Yes, "Joaquin Murieta de Castillo," son of the former Governor-General of Cuba, and now within yonder walls of Santa Cruz Monastery, and the only heir to a dukedom.

IGNACIOUS: Ah, 'tis now I see the cause of his proud overbearing assumption. 'Twas born with him, and for it I like him less. Thou art very shrewd, Father Gonzalles; how shall we proceed? And what of Joaquin?

GONZALLES: Leave that to me. Keep your own counsel; be secret, and abide my time. He will probably die; he is too good to live.

IGNACIOUS: How terrible you look! You would not—(*An owl screams; Ignacious starts.*)

GONZALLES: Never mind, 'tis but an owl. Now to prayers, for there's the vesper bell. (*Bell sounds.*) Of this we will speak anon. To prayers for our success.

IGNACIOUS: To prayers! (*Exit.*)

GONZALLES: Ignacious, I fear, is too honest; yet he seems inclined to favor this. Why not? Who ever knew honesty or virtue to stand a severer temptation, when the body that inherits it leans incliningly towards the seduction; and this is pictured to his imagination by a descriptive mind. Religion is also a component of his disposition; yet I shall entirely destroy the promptings of his heart and turn him to my will, and until all my desires are gained, I say, conscience, lie thee still! (*Exit.*)

SCENE II: *A Guerrilla Camp in sight at the walls of a Monastery; saddles, men, and women lying on serapes;*[2] *camp-fire; kettles, etc. strewed around. Garcia walking uneasily about; Pedro looking at him; Juan, Roderiguez, Belloro, Bonita, Rosa, etc.*

GARCIA: *Caramba! Maldeta; Ladrones,*[3] *Los Americanos!*

PEDRO: In one of your old moods, Senor Garcia. What is to come next? Silver trains are scarce, and the rancheros are as poor as a friar's dog; for this damned American war, just ended, has shut up the mines, impoverished the people, and our trade has gone to the devil.

GARCIA: Our trade has gone to the devil, and there we shall have to go and find it; and if our luck lies next to the gates of hell's dominions, we must make an onset to pay for this delay. Since that last affray near the City of Mexico, where I received this (*holds up his hand with thumb and forefinger gone*[4]) from that cursed American officer, we have not had a single peso to turn a card for. *Caramba! Maldeta, Los Americanos!*

PEDRO: What say you, Garcia, to a church or two, and then for California; there are churches on the way that have escaped the war and are yet rich.

GARCIA: Any deed to get hold of gold. A good idea! California is a new field, and the Americans are flocking there by thousands; gold has been found in abundance, and if the Americans work as well as they fight, they will be angels of gold, and we will be the devils to take it from them.

PEDRO: We will pay a visit to the Church of Dolores in Sonora, which is on the way to California, and there is plenty of silver in vessels, altar railings, images, and money, to load five of our stoutest mules, besides gold enough to load another; and Father Novo I hate, as the devil hates holy water. I'll take his gown for my pay, and the spoils shall be divided among the band.

GARCIA: One less leaves ten; and your share as informer would be three times as much as either of the boys would receive. Now that's liberal; let's hear what the boys have to say. Ho, you lazy ladrones, leave the women to their cigaritos; a word with you all! (*Band gathers around Garcia.*) Boys, Mexico, Chihuahua [Che-wa-wa], Sinaloa, Guadalajara [Gau-da-la-hair-ah],[5] and almost the whole republic has been travelled over in vain. We have not found one, from bullion dealer to peon, worth lassooing; not a paso have we had for months, and now I say it is time we used our escopets [shotguns] and knives. What say you all for California; there is plenty of gold to be had and there is a church on the road that Pedro has put a red cross on, which he says is rich. What say you all?

GUERRILLAS ALL: For the church—lead us on! Yes, yes, lead us on!

JUAN: Lead us on! has been the cry too long already. Since you, Senor Garcia, saw the color of your own blood, you have quit your actions and drooped your head like a sick paroquet.

GARCIA: Hound of an exiled family, dare you taunt me?

JUAN: Taunt you! Why you have become a cheto[6] in camp at day, and at night steal cattle, for fear you'll forget your old trade. An honorable guerrilla would look only to the road for pay at daylight, and at night the shade of the Sierras would be his spot of safety, in place of playing gipsy under the walls of a monastery.

GARCIA: Hell![7] Have I not led where no one of you would follow? Have I not made streams of blood that sickened you all? Have I not killed more in one night than all the band have since you joined us? Have I not brought more booty into camp than any other guerrilla in the Sierra Madre? Have you forgotten all?

JUAN: Forgotten all? No! We all remember one brave act of Three-Fingered Jack's.

GARCIA: Where and when? if you remember so well.

JUAN: The time you killed your former master's only child, down in Chihuahua, to reach her patron the bullion dealer. She was a lovely girl; Cary was a playmate of mine; and damned foul work you made.

GARCIA: (*Draws his pistol.*) Hell and hell's furies! Take this and follow her! (*Fires at Juan.*) Curse the hand that served my fingers such a trick. I never missed before.

JUAN: (*Pulls his pistol and aims at Garcia.*) 'Twas well meant, but badly directed; the ball grazed my locks. No more shooting, Three-Fingered Jack, or I'll make sure work of you if I commence.

GARCIA: No more taunts about dead ones, or by the eternal shades, you'll wake such a hell in me that every saint in the calendar will swear that I am ten Judases thrice damned.

RODERIGUEZ: (*A renegade priest.*) Put up your pistols! Fools, is it your trade to kill each other? Talk business, not fight among yourselves, like a pack of hungry wolves; for the flesh of neither would make a meal, nor buy a bottle of aguadiente [whiskey]. (*They put up their pistols.*)

PEDRO: Father Roderiguez, Senor Garcia and myself were speaking of California. Los Americanos are filling every canyon, ravine, and river in that State in search of gold; and we would be in damned bad luck if we, as proud a guerrilla band as ever straddled mustangs, could not lessen their numbers, and load our purses with oro.[8]

RODERIGUEZ: True, my children; those cursed heretics of Americans have robbed poor Mexico by the war, and now there is a chance to regain at least part of what we have lost. My blessing on your undertaking.

ALL: Ho for California!

JUAN: I also say, For California!

BAND: And I, and I, etc.

GARCIA: Pass the gourd bags; then, Juan, your pretty sister can sing us our evening song, which will be sweeter than the music of a pistol-shot.

JUAN: No more shooting, Garcia.

GARCIA: No more taunts, Juan. Let us drink. (*Drinks.*) Pass the gourd, boys. (*Hands it to Juan. All drink.*)

JUAN: Bell, will you sing us "Our Home is Mexico"; and then we will retire; for we want to be on our journey before the sun rises.—Boys, join the chorus.

BELLORO: (*Takes a guitar and sings.*)

OUR HOME IS MEXICO

Air—"The Watcher"

We're a brave guerrilla band, as free as light we are,
And take our tribute on the land wherever we may be;
Our homes are the Sierras' shade, 'mid the chapparel so wild;
No wealth have we to boast of, like the lordly pampered child.

Chorus
We roam from summer vales to hills of eternal snow;
Whate'er the change may be, our home is Mexico! (*Repeat.*)

We levy tribute on the rich, and make them pay it down;
And good fare we receive from them of the litany and gown;[9]
And when the fray and prayer is o'er, we seek a quiet vale,
As to God above, to the maid we love we repeat th' exciting tale.

Chorus
We roam from summer vales to hills of eternal snow;
Whate'er the change may be, our home is Mexico! (*Repeat.*)

When the golden sun is shining from out the distant west,
And the humming-bird is seeking its downy pendant nest,
And the vesper bells are sounding on the mellow evening air,
Our hearts grow light with music and dancing with the fair.

Chorus
We roam from summer vales to hills of eternal snow;
Whate'er the change may be, our home is Mexico! (*Repeat.*)

SCENE III: *A Road.*

(*Enter Garcia.*)

GARCIA: This is lonely work. There is nothing but peones[10] out as late as this, and I have not met one that's worth a peso; ah! here comes a priest, and I will try the butt of my pistol on his head and see if that will make him remember where he left his last winnings at monte; for who ever knew a priest to lose. No! it's worth as much as the winner's soul to cheat a priest at cards. (*Enter Gonzalles, with a cowl over his face.*) Stop, Reverend Father! I want your purse; I care not how few ounces it contains, but the more the better, for my conscience's sake.

GONZALLES: Yes, Senor Garcia, a purse full, if you will earn them.

GARCIA: (*Draws his pistol.*) Off with your cowl, or I'll blow it from your face; who are you that knows me in the dark. (*Cocks his pistol; priest throws back his cowl.*) Gonzalles! the fighting priest! Ha, ha, ha. (*Laughs, and puts up his pistol.*) A very nice hombre to get money from particularly on the road; I would stand a better show to get it from a stone. Well, tradesmen often meet, for their wares bring them in contact. On the same errand? ah, you old hell-hound.

GONZALLES: No, you thrible-headed dog of the devil; but I have a job that will suit you, there being a purse of gold for every thrust of your dagger.

GARCIA: Then you must want only one blow to be struck, or your cell must contain at least a mule load of onzas;[11] for I would fill the skin of Santa Anna[12] in the president's chair so full of holes at that price, that there would not be room for another. What work is it?

GONZALLES: Strike as often as you think necessary to do the work. It's only a boy; he is in yonder monastery, and I want you to spirit him away. Leave his body outside the walls, so that it will seem as if it was the work of woman's jealousy.

GARCIA: Lead on! I know you; your word is good for the job. Show me his cell, and I will send his soul to heaven or hell! (*Exit both.*)

SCENE IV: *A room in a monastery; chair, table and lamp. Joaquin sitting at the table reading; rises and walks.*

JOAQUIN: Oh, how gloomy these walls have become. They are hateful to my sight; for their darksome shadow finds a reflection in my thoughts, and makes me sick at heart. What is there to cure this despondency? What thought, of all I have read, will aid to dispel these fancies of a home and a mother? I never knew what it was to have maternal care; yet how precious is the very sound of such a name as mother; and when connected with the name of home, oh how much more dear it sounds! There's a charm in the words that thrills through me as if they were electricity. Mother and Home! From all that I have heard of them, I have learned to long for their existence; yet I know them only by name. The blessed of this world are those who have a mother to counsel with and guide them, and the roof-tree to shelter them in hours as dark as mine. Mother and Home! I never tire repeating them. Then again, in my dark visions I see a fairy form that lights up and adds the glory of loveliness to my musings. That could not be my mother, for I have watched the wild blast of the hurricane and trembled, and that same form would glide before me, and all seemed pleasant—even the dread havoc that the wild wind caused seemed less fearful in its destruction. I have watched the stars, until my eyes grew weary with grazing on their twinkling orbs, and this form has passed, and I have forgot myself in her invisible presence. I have walked amid the flowers, and their rich blossoms gave forth no perfume, until her image crossed my path, and then I bemoaned, because the humming bird intercepted their odor. What fairy can this be? Is there a reality for these wild fancies? Yes; it is possible there is some place in this world inhabited by my vision; then why not leave these walls and go forth into the world and seek her? But what do I know of the world or its people? for I have not seen much of its surface, or associated with them. Yet I wish I was free, to act, to do for myself. I will—yes, I will be free! I am a prisoner here. This night I will leave this cell, and forever! What words? I am surprised at the very thought, and more so at their utterance. But shall I endure this serfdom? tremble when the Superior comes, to show him that I am a peon—a slave? observe his humor, and play the puppet to conciliate his favor? Oh, I have crouched at his look as a sloth hound does under the lash of his master. And to continue thus for days, weeks, months to come; no! I would rather be transformed to a monkey, and play in freedom on the boughs of a tree, than submit to confinement within these walls another space marked by a day. I want freedom; yet I tremble at the uncertainty before me. But I will be free; and this night, though the venom of my dagger's sting pierces a body more precious than the Pope's. (*A noise without.*) Psst! What noise is that? Who should invade the secrecy of my cell at this hour of the night? I will extinguish the light and use my dark lantern[13] for I fear, I know not what; for this is an untimely visit.

(*Enter Garcia, groping about with a knife in his hand.*)

GARCIA: He said, "His bed is on the left as you enter the door." I will find it and ease the sleeper.

JOAQUIN: What does that man want here? I see the glitter of a dagger. It is my life he seeks. Heaven, who have I harmed? Courage; a little light will do. (*Sets the dark lantern open on the table, springs behind Garcia's back and draws his dagger, as Garcia leans over the bed, lays his hand on his neck and holds him down.*) Move and I will kill thee, vile reptile. What art thou doing within these walls at this hour? Dost thou know thy doom? It is death!

GARCIA: Are you Joaquin?

JOAQUIN: I am.

GARCIA: Spare me!

JOAQUIN: Who are you?

GARCIA: I am Garcia.

JOAQUIN: Garcia, the fiend, the terror of Mexico? Why are you here?

GARCIA: To kill you!

JOAQUIN: To kill me! What for? and who employed you?

GARCIA: I know not—I came for pay.

JOAQUIN: Give me your knife. (*He hands it to Joaquin and rises.*) Then you are

Garcia, the murderer of the innocent. To do Justice a kind act, I would kill you. (*Motions towards Garcia.*)

GARCIA: Spare me, Joaquin, and I will be your friend in all you may ask.

JOAQUIN: (*Aside.*) My hands shall never be stained with human blood. (*To Garcia.*) Lead me from this place; I wish to leave it.

GARCIA: I will, but where to, then?

JOAQUIN: Any place; for I am sick of this abode.

GARCIA: Follow us! To-night our band starts for California, and before the morning dawns, many leagues will be placed between us and this spot.

JOAQUIN: Will you swear to be my friend in all things?

GARCIA: Yes; if you will not see too much for our safety; for our band are guerrillas.

JOAQUIN: Agreed; if you will befriend me until I reach a place of safety.

GARCIA: I will! I never break a promise.

JOAQUIN: Kneel then, and swear on this cross as I dictate. (*Garcia kneels and repeats after Joaquin.*)—I solemnly swear that I will be the true friend to Joaquin Murieta, until he is safe from harm. As I fail to keep my vow, so punish me, my patron saint, in this world and in the world to come.

GARCIA: I swear! (*Kisses the cross.*)

END OF ACT I

ACT II

SCENE I: *Emigrant's camp; women cooking; men playing cards; cattle in the distance; wagons, etc.; river in sight.*

GALE: Knox, it's your night to stand guard, I reckon. We needn't be scared of the Injins, for we're out of their range; for at this season they don't come so low down on the Gila[14] as this. Bill Harvey, you and Jo, go and hobble old Brindle, and stake out the roan colt; for the mustang is wild yet, and this bottom looks like the Mosquito Creek, where he was foaled, and he may take a likeness to stray. Mary, what is you and Bill Harvey perting about? 'Tend to getting supper ready.

MRS. GALE: Daddy, Bill Harvey's getting right pert lately after Moll and putting darn queer notions into her head. She can't do anything now-a-days, unless Bill's somewars to watch her. Bill, I reckon you'd better look to Jim Simese's darter[15] that's ahead of us in old Ike's train.

BILL HARVEY: Look yer, mamme; I reckon I know what's what—Jim Simese's darter Sal is a good gal enough, but she's no more account to Mary than a calf is to old Brindle. Sal can't mend clo's; she can't make bread, ride a hoss, or shoot a rifle, like Mary can. I'll bet my rifle agin a jack-knife, I can whip any man that come from Texas, this year, that says she can; dog-on my skin, if I don't.

MRS. GALE: Yer dreadful bold when there's nothing to be afeared on. A yaller-skin or Greaser[16] would run a hull rigiment jest like you.

MARY: Dog-on it! Do let Bill alone; he's sorter snarly now. I've been pestering him most to death all day; and I reckon it's hard enough for one of the family to pester Bill at a time. (*Takes up a tea canister.*) Mamme, I reckon we'd better have sassafras teas to-night; the boys are all tuckered out, and drinking saline water makes them awful thirsty. Shall we have long sweetening or short sweetening?[17] (*Bill stands up behind and kisses her.*)

MRS. GALE: Long sweetening. Bill, jest let Mary alone, I tell yer.

GALE: Bill Harvey, why don't you and the boys go and tend to them cattle? I reck-on by this time you'll find 'em way down the bottom. Case, you go along with the boys, too. Take along your rifles—you mount jump up[18] some game. (*Bill Harvey, Jo, and Case shoulder their rifles.*)

BILL HARVEY: Daddy Gale is right pert to-night. He's socked himself down on that old saddle reading the Bible agin. I swar I believe he'll take to preaching Meth-odism as he used to, when we git to California; dog-on my skin if I don't. Mamme, too, is cross as Satan. Them old buckskin breeches she's mending must be tough as a bull's hide to git a needle through. (*To Mary, patting her on the cheek.*)—You ain't cross, are you, honey?

MARY: Clear out, Bill, or I'll—

BILL: You bet; I'm going. Come boys! (*Exit Bill, Jo, and Case.*)

MRS. GALE: Daddy, how long do you reckon it will take us to git to the diggins?

GALE: Nigh on to two weeks; for when we reach the settlements, I reckon we'd bet-ter stop and recruit the cattle, for they're powerfully tuckered out; and a few day's delay, I take on, wouldn't injure any of us. Mamme, I thought we would done better to take the Salt Lake route, but the Lord seemed willing it should be otherwise; and as we are all well and safe, we needn't complain; for it was all for the best.

MRS. GALE: Thank the Lord; for this trip has been powerful weakening. Saline water and the hot sun pulls a mortal down powerful fast, I reckon.

MARY: Shall I git supper ready?

MRS. GALE: No; I reckon you'd better wait till the boys come back.

MARY: Then I wish they'd hurry. Bill Harvey is the slowest mortal in the world. (*Aside.*)—He's as slow as the laziest critter in the train; I b'lieve he'd court me till doomsday, unless I pop the question; and you bet I'll take the chances; dog-on me if I don't. (*Firing outside—Gale and Mrs. Gale arise.*) Oh, Lord! what is that?

GALE: There's something wrong; there was several shots fired in quick succession. What in the world can it be? I must go and see. (*Mrs. Gale and Mary hold him fast.*)

MRS. GALE: Don't go and leave us all alone.

(*Enter Bill Harvey, wounded, a pistol in his hand.*)

HARVEY: Jo and Case are shot by the Guerrillas! Oh, God! I am wounded. (*Falls insensible; Mary goes to him.*)

MARY: Water, water! Give me some water, mother! (*Mrs. Gale hands Mary some water.*)

(*Enter Garcia, with a knife in his hand.*)

GARCIA: Caramba! Los Americanos! Death to the Americans!

(*Enter Guerrilla Band; Joaquin follows with drawn pistol.*)

JOAQUIN: Back I say! Back, or death to some of you! I swear I will kill the first who raises a hand against these defenseless people. Remember, Garcia, remember your oath! Those people never harmed you or yours, and why should you murder them? I did not think you loved blood so well. Is the current of life's stream so cheap, that you must wash in it?

PEDRO: Heed him not, Garcia.

JOAQUIN: I warn you, another move, and some of you die! Have gray hairs on the brow of age no respect from your fiendish hearts? Have not youth and innocence a charm that would repel the dastard acts of a coward from your souls? Go, go to your camp; and if harm befall one of these that's here, I will murder you all; I swear it. (*Exit band.*)

GARCIA: Damn that oath! (*Exit.*)

GALE: How can we thank you, our noble preserver; and how can I repay you for your timely protection to my family? I know you are good as you are wildly beautiful. (*Joaquin puts up his pistol and takes off his hat.*) Honor and nobleness are stamped on thy brow.

JOAQUIN: I need no thanks—much less pay. How is our wounded friend?

HARVEY: The wound is painful, but I do not think it is serious.

MARY: I thank you, noble sir, for your protection, and Mary Gale will always remember you.

JOAQUIN: No thanks, lady. A dishonest act I never committed, much less a murder; to protect you with my life was but my duty as a man, and I follow its directions. The least of God's creatures should not receive harm if I could prevent it.

MARY: What is your name, kind sir? Tell us, so that we can remember you and pray for you.

GALE: And I will beseech the throne of grace, in my daily prayers, to spare and protect you.

JOAQUIN: Thank you, good friends; I may need your prayers, for this world is new to me. My name is Joaquin—Joaquin Murieta.

(*Gale extends his hand; Joaquin kneels on one knee.*)

GALE: May Heaven's blessings go and abide with thee, and may the blessing of a father and mother follow thee for this act, and goodness attend thee for ever and ever. Amen.

SCENE II: *A road; mountains; river.*

(*Enter Garcia.*)

GARCIA: Joaquin has dared to interfere between the wolf and its victims. Hell's curse! That I should hold that oath so binding, when to cut his throat would release me from all promises. What is one life? Have I not taken twenty—aye, fifty—better, far better than his; and for less gold than old Gonzalles offered? To say I will kill Joaquin is easier said than done. I have seen him asleep close by my side, as unconscious as if he were in no danger; yet it seemed to me that whenever I approached him, with that thought on my mind, he would move uneasily in his sleep, and his eyes would open, as if his very eyes and ears did nothing but spy my acts and learn the fall of my footsteps. I hate him! No; I do not love him; then by hell and its furies, I fear him. A boy! caramba! I may just as well say I have found a master; Curse the name! I once had a master. Hell! how my blood boils! That master was my father; my mother his slave, and I born his peon. How I have seen that man whip my mother. Large scars showed their hideousness all over her once beautiful face. She said she was once beautiful—and I believe her. That master whipped my mother once too often. It was in a by-place; I heard the lash falling on the back of one begging for mercy; I hurried to the spot—it was my mother, bleeding at every blow; I felled the hound of hell to the earth—my master, my father—I plucked his eyes out; and then he begged for what he had refused to give, Mercy. I cut limb from limb of his body; his heart I trampled under my feet. I was blood—all I saw was blood. And then my mother embraced me and called me her child—(*laughs*)—and I became a fiend. When I think of that first act, I could drink blood. The Past—the awful Past—I cannot think of it! What a hell is conscience!

(*Enter Pedro and Jose.*)

PEDRO: Why, Garcia, you look as if some devil had frightened you. What's the matter, man?

GARCIA: Hell and the devil, both! My bosom is the hell, and my conscience the devil.

PEDRO: Only one of your old moods. Garcia, we must leave here. The interference of Joaquin is liable to give us trouble; for if another train of emigrants should come up, our skins would have to be bullet-proof to escape the Americans.

JOSE: Jesus Christo! I want to kill that refuse of a priest. Let me once get the chance! (*Clutches his knife.*)

PEDRO: Well, well, some other time. Our safety first—Joaquin after.

GARCIA: No! hell! no, never! Harm a hair of Joaquin's head, and I'll cut you in pieces; and I'll make yard meat of your body if ever you speak of it again.

PEDRO: There, talk no more of Joaquin. Garcia, I say, let us move from this place. Yonder is their camp-fire; two of whom fell by our shots this night. (*Laughs.*) A bad place for them to camp in! Garcia, the church of Dolores is three leagues from here, and I feel as if to-night is the very time to settle with old Father Nivo.

GARCIA: We'll go, Jose. Tell the boys to bring up the mules. Let Juan and Joaquin follow with the women, and tell them to meet us at the mission of San Gabriel, in California. Go, Jose! Meet us at the spring, for I will not go to camp. (*Exit Jose.*) Pedro, if the church of Dolores is as rich as you say, we'll have no reason to complain of this night's work. Ho, for crime! My blood is up, and this night I am a fiend again!

PEDRO: You will find all as I tell you, Senor Garcia; and I feel eager for revenge; for my star is on the rise, and before to-morrow's dawn old Father Nivo dies. (*Exeunt.*)

SCENE III: *A river; train of wagons in the distance.*

(*Gale, Mrs. Gale, Mary, and Harvey discovered.*)

GALE: Death has entered our train and in a sudden manner. Coming so unexpected, the shock has fallen more severe. Yonder is two graves, and the cross we have
placed above them will soon decay, and their sleeping place will be forgotten.

MARY: Poor Jo and Case!

MRS. GALE: They'll never see California, I reckon.

GALE: God's judgment will overtake their murderers; for blood will cry from the
ground for revenge, and the judgment will be terrible. The wicked have their
day, but the works of the good endures forever.

HARVEY: It's right hard to think that these devils escaped so easy. If we'd kept with
any of the trains, Jo and Case would been alive now. I reckon these devils will
catch it yet for this. My side is right sore, and every stitch of pain they have put
on me shall be paid 'em some day or other.

GALE: We must say farewell to this spot and go on our way; but sad will be the remembrance of last night's work; yet as this noble poet says—(*reads from a
book*)—we should "So live, that when the summons comes to join the innumerable caravan that moves to the pale realms of shade, where each shall take his
chamber in the silent halls of death, thou go not like the quarry slave at night,
scourged to his dungeon, but sustained and soothed by an unfaltering trust, approach thy grave like one who wraps the drapery of his couch about him and lies
down to pleasant dreams."[19] (*Exeunt.*)

SCENE IV: *Room in a Mission.*

(*Joaquin and Belloro dressed for a bridal.*)

BELLORO: Dear Joaquin, think you that Garcia will not meet us here, as he appointed on the night of his sudden departure from the camp on the Gila River?

JOAQUIN: Yes, dearest, I think he will, and I suppose he will have a bloody tale to
tell; for I have no doubt that the massacre at Dolores Church was the work of
his mutilated hand. The old priest with his skull cleaved open and his gray locks
mingled with his gore; the woman, his servant, killed by a shot in the brain; the
two men-servants, cut in many places, lying dead beside the altar which the
profane hand of the robbers had despoiled—all was horrible. And I was happy
to think you, dear Belloro, escaped the sight of such a heart-rending scene. I felt
my blood running like hot lava through my veins, for revenge on the sacreligious
monster murderers, when I gazed on their victims.

BELLORO: Dear Joaquin, I shudder at the sight of that man Garcia; for his appearance recalls to my mind the hooded cobra. But let us forget the past—for
God will punish them for their wickedness; and now that we are in a land of civilization, we must part from their company. Brother Juan is heartily sick of
them, and, as it is your own wish and Juan's also, I feel that I will have a double
protection in a husband and a brother; and you that I love—oh, how dearly my
heart and God alone knows! (*Bows on Joaquin's breast.*)

JOAQUIN: Forgive me (*embraces her*), my own, my dear Belloro—my golden Bell
—that I should recall the past, wherein lie sad memories, and on such a day as
this, but the music of your voice echoes like the sound of a merry chime on my
heart-strings and dispels all that's rude. To-day, dear Belloro, you become my
wife; and oh, with what anticipated pleasure I have looked forward to the hour
when the indissoluble knot will be tied that makes us one on earth; and in heaven I feel that we will not be parted. Oh, the ecstatic thrill of joy that bounds
thro' every fibre of my body, as I repeat the words, *My own sweet wife!* Dearest, they hang on my lips and leave a taste almost as sweet as honey. Oh, the vast
space that once was void in my heart is filled with thy presence, my wife. The
love I bear thee will be shown while life holds its seat within my brain; and all
will be paid me ten thousand fold by thy love, my own sweet wife. At midnight,
when the silent earth was undisturbed by busy life, I have dreamed of thee. I
have gazed on the starry dome in a mood which hung on my mind like a thun-
dercloud in a summer sky; and thy lovely form would glide into my musings,
and all the darkness was dispelled; the flowers that bloomed in my pathway
seemed to inhale their fragrance from thy invisible presence. Thou art of myself
a part. How else should I have known that you, my golden Bell, did exist before my eyes beheld thee? And now, to become my wife! My heart bounds with
an ecstasy of joy it never knew before.

BELLORO: There is a fatality in this, dear Joaquin; an invisible direction of the
Omnipotent for our good. The death of my father left my brother Juan and myself alone and friendless, and we joined that guerrilla band for protection, as
they travelled in the direction of Sonora, where we expected to meet an uncle;
but, alas, we were disappointed, and yet how happy will be the result. Your
sudden resolve to leave that gloomy monastery—the entrance of Garcia to take
your life, and your power to overcome him and make him befriend you—your
joining us, and the preservation of that old man's family from Garcia's bloody
hand—all, all was guided by invisible spirits that hover over us and guide us as
they will. But Joaquin, I never thought that I could meet with one who would
become so dear as thou art and take such complete mastery of my heart.

JOAQUIN: God bless thee, Bell; bless thee! (*Kisses her.*)

(*Enter Juan.*)

JUAN: Have you forgotten your brother? Come, love-makers, there is time enough
to talk and act lovingly after an important ceremony has been gone through
with. The priest awaits you.

BELLORO: Juan, you are cruel.

JUAN: Not half so cruel as you are, Miss Belloro—and this is the last chance I will
have to call you Miss, for you have chosen another protector besides your dear
brother. (*Aside.*)—And if I had my choice and Mexico's Republic to pick from
among her people for a husband for my sister, I would have said, *Joaquin, take
her!* Yet he cannot love her more than I do.

JOAQUIN: So soon! Well, Juan, Time is a rapid messenger when the heart is filled
with joy.

JUAN: (*Taking Joaquin's hand.*)—But when the heart is parting with all it holds dear on earth, then minutes seem weeks, and hours centuries; 'twas thus we parted with our father. Love her, Joaquin, and protect her! But you will not watch her happiness with more vigilance than I. Come; the priest is at the altar, and Bonita, Rosa, and our friends, are waiting to accompany you to the church. Come! (*Exeunt.*)

SCENE V: *Altar in an old church; music playing; boy swinging a censer; priest dressed in wedding robes; music stops; priest chants from a book which he holds in his hand.*

PRIEST: Beatus Vir qui timet Dominum in mandatis ejus volet nimis. Potens in terra erit semen ejus: Generatio recotrum benedicetur. Gloria et divitia in domo ejus; et justicia ejus manet in saeculum saeculi. Jucundus homo qui miseretus et commodat, disponent sermones suos in judicio: quia in aeternum non commovebitur.[20]

(*Enter procession; music; stops in front of the altar; priest stoops and whispers; then speaks aloud.*)

PRIEST: And you take this woman to be your lawful wedded wife; to love, honor and obey; to cherish in sickness and in health.
JOAQUIN: I do!
PRIEST: And you take this man to be your husband; to love, honor and obey; to cherish in sickness and in health. (*Belloro bows.*) Then in the name of the Holy Church I pronounce you man and wife; and what God has joined together, let no man put asunder. (*Music plays; Priest chants.*) In memoria aeterna erit justus: ab auditione mala non timebit. Paratum est cor ejus sperare in Domino; confirmatum est cor ejus; non commovebitur donec despiciat inimicos suos. Dispersit, dedit pauperibus; justicia ejus manen in saeculum saeculi; cornu ejus exaltabitur in gloria. Peccator videbit, et irascetur; dentibus suis femet et tabescet; desiderium peccatorum peribit. Gloria Patri Deo.

(*Enter Garcia, followed by his band.*)

GARCIA: Stop, damned priest! Stop this mummery! Stop! Curse you, I forbid it!
PRIEST: Sacreligious dog! How dare you interfere in that which concerns you not?
GARCIA: It does; it does! Belloro shall be my wife.
PRIEST: You are too late; she is married.
GARCIA: Married! Oh, God! The only being I ever loved on earth! (*Staggers and falls to the floor.*)

END OF ACT II

ACT III

SCENE 1: *A creek. Arrival of Joaquin, Belloro, Juan, Bonita, Rosa, and others.*

JUAN: This tedious journey is ended, and I am glad. We have reached the placers[21] in health; the miners are all taking out plenty of oro, and this is the place to make the ounces; for our chances are as good as any. Why, this is a pleasant country!

BELLORO: Truly, this is a pleasant place, and I really love this kind of scenery; there is something so noble and grand in the tall pine, with its long arms projecting from its sides, and something that's homelike in the chirping of those little birds. Unlike Mexico, to be sure; there are no palms here, with their tall trunks and leaves like wings—no orange, with its fragrant blossoms—or lime trees, with their deep green shade—or birds of gay plumage—or other sights that resemble our native place; yet I feel a sense of contentment; for it will be our home, will it not, Joaquin? And here we will be free from troubles and turmoils, such as harrass our people.

JOAQUIN: True, dear wife; and I hope that among the Americans we will find friends; for all that I have seen of them has been noble, generous, and kind. At first, we will be obliged to stay with some of our country people; but as soon as I can find a vacant casa,[22] we will take possession of our first home.

ROSA: Did you notice how those men stared at us as we passed them?

JUAN: Who? what men?

ROSA: Those men that were mining, down yonder, on the creek.

BONITA: Why shouldn't they, pray? I suppose they were pleased to see us; for 'tis said there are not many women in the mines.

ROSA: A very good reason, and a very good chance to get an adorer. Oh, I like that!

JUAN: You minx, envious of Bell! I suppose you begin to think of getting married.

ROSA: Why should I not? for Bell is the happiest mortal alive; and so would I be, if I had just another such a man as Joaquin for a husband!

BELLORO: Pshaw, how many Joaquins would you have in this world? One is enough. (*Juan, Bonita, and Rosa laugh.*)

JUAN: Hold me up, Joaquin, for God's sake! Belloro is jealous because Rosa wants a man like you.

JOAQUIN: I am the more happy at this, for Love shows itself in a jealous out-burst. Oh, you elf! you could love me more than I adore thyself.

BONITA: Come, Juan; do not stand there teasing Bell, but seek some place where we can rest. We will have plenty of time to see all we wish after we get settled and rested from the fatigues of this journey.

JUAN: I see a Mexican flag on yonder house, and no doubt there we can get entertainment and find some of our people. Come! (*Exeunt.*)

(*Enter Garcia.*)

GARCIA: From my hiding-place in that clump of bushes, I heard and saw all. Jesus Christo! how my heart aches! I never knew that I possessed such a soft piece of stuff until I saw her, the golden Bell! Sacramento! I cannot live and see her in possession of Joaquin. Why didn't I kill him? What shall I do for revenge? Hell! that I had the devil for a counsellor! What, is it possible that there comes Gonzalles? He is after me and my spirited coarse Joaquin, whose body I was to have outside the walls of a monastery. (*Laughs.*) Well, a purse of onzas now will put me in a good humor and save a dead man or two.

(*Enter Gonzalles.*)

GARCIA: Good day, old renegade! Where to, so fast?

GONZALLES: Good day, imp of darkness! I have not far to go. I was in hopes you had gone home.

GARCIA: Home! Where is my home, good fighting priest?

GONZALLES: In hell! What other home do you expect to have?

GARCIA: Very kind of you, and that job of yours is not yet done.

GONZALLES: By my patron saint, you have caused me a long journey. Your word is not as good as a rotten pine-apple, for that at least keeps its perfume.

GARCIA: I have thought that you set a trap for my good cabeza.[23] In place of my making holes in his skin, if I had not begged and swore like a *commandante*, he would have made holes in mine.

GONZALLES: No doubt you swore and begged; for you never would forget that part of your trade.

GARCIA: Joaquin made me swear on the cross.

GONZALLES: On the cross! You can swear well. To what purpose?

GARCIA: Simply to see him safe out of Mexico.

GONZALLES: You promised, and you have done it.

GARCIA: Yes, damn him!

GONZALLES: Where is he now?

GARCIA: In that tent up yonder, I think, by this time.

GONZALLES: How, by this time?

GARCIA: Why he was married at San Gabriel Mission, two weeks ago, and has just arrived.

GONZALLES: I did not stop at San Gabriel, or I would have heard of this; for the love of God, who is he married to?

GARCIA: To—to Belloro—the sister of Juan.

GONZALLES: I have seen her. She's a beautiful girl, I believe. Ah! I see you like it not—this marriage?

GARCIA: No, no; I like—hell's fire! how my bosom burns!

GONZALLES: (*Aside.*) It is better than I thought. Garcia, does Joaquin love his wife?

GARCIA: Yes; why, by the eternal shades! shouldn't he? Is she not all that's good and pure? Curse it; yes, they only live for each other.

GONZALLES: Then kill him through her, and, if you succeed, I will double the pay I promised you; here's a purse of gold—this work is worth more to me than all the wealth of these gold mines. (*Hands Garcia a purse, which he lets fall.*)

GARCIA: What! kill Joaquin, and Belloro, too? Curse you, foul priest, curse you! I wished for the devil, and you came; your foul carcass is worse than mine; the very buzzards would be poisoned by eating your flesh.

GONZALLES: Bah! parricide and murderer of a priest, robber of emigrants and desecrator of churches, bah!

GARCIA: (*Attempts to draw a knife.*)—I'll—I'll cut you in pieces!

GONZALLES: Not quite so fast; this stings. (*Exhibits a pistol.*) Garcia, I want you to do as I tell you, or I will have you hung by the miners to the highest limb on these trees. Do you understand me?

GARCIA: I do.

GONZALLES: I want you to keep at your trade. Travel over the State, and at every place you get a chance, do some deed that will excite the people, and be sure to leave the name of Joaquin for the bounty; and, by the time you return, I will have the train so arranged that Joaquin will fall a victim. Take part of your guerrilla band with you, and occasionally leave the name of Three-Fingered Jack with Joaquin's and after a short space of time, your names will be a weapon to meet an army of *Los Americanos*. Get all the wealth you can, and I will double the sum when we return to Mexico.

GARCIA: Is that all, good master?

GONZALLES: No sneering at me, Garcia. I swear I will hang you if you do not do as I bid you. You will never follow any other trade but that of a guerrilla, and I am advising you for your own good; follow my directions, and all shall end well. Pick up that purse (*picks up the purse*) for I suppose you want money. I want you to start to-day, or, at least, as soon as possible, for if you remain where Belloro is, you will lose what little sense you have got left. I will keep track of you and send you word from time to time, as I want you to hear from me. Obey the directions I give you, and all will end well.

GARCIA: And every step I take carries me nearer hell; I'll go, for it suits me, but this plot of yours—

GONZALLES: You know; no matter, so you are well paid.

GARCIA: I would like to go to that fandango to-night, but—

GONZALLES: Joaquin, Juan, Rosa, Bonita, and—Belloro, will be there; I believe that is his party.

GARCIA: Curse it! yes. No, no; I'll not go; the dance would be worse than the wedding scene at church; such feelings are new to me.

GONZALLES: Well, do as I bid you, do not go to the dance. I see you are impatient to be off; you can easily find me; I want to see you to-night.

GARCIA: I will meet you. (*Exit.*)

GONZALLES: A dance to-night? I will attend; it's no strange sight to see a priest at a Spanish dance. (*Exit.*)

SCENE II: *Night; a room; men and women; Spanish gentleman playing music; men and women dancing a fandango. After the dance, enters a party of drunken miners: Texas Bill, Missouri, San Antone, and Zeke.*

MISSOURI: Go in, old gals; you're some on a break-down, ain't you, Dolly? (*Pulls Rosa.*)

TEXAS BILL: Rip it to 'em, old yaller skins! Come here, my greaser love; you're right pert, and the dogondest purtyest gal I've seen since I left Texas. (*Tries to kiss Belloro.*)

JOAQUIN: Back, sir! (*Throws Texas Bill away.*) That woman is my wife, sir. (*Miners laugh at Bill.*)

MISSOURI: Got hell that time, Texas Bill; try again; these greasers ain't worth much, any how.

SAN ANTONE: (*Slaps Gonzalles on the back.*) I say, old mutton taller, who ever heard of a greaser having a wife?

GONZALLES: If you mean a Mexican, I have, sir; and many of them. That woman is his wife. (*Miners laugh.*)

MISSOURI: What if she is, you old liar? To kiss her won't hurt her any.

GONZALLES: You're a disgrace to the name of Americans.

MISSOURI: Leave here, you old ghost of the devil! or I'll batter that head of yours to a jelly. Vamose[24] the ranch! (*Takes Gonzalles by the shoulders and puts him out of doors.*)

SAN ANTONE: Good for you, Missouri. Now, boys, let's put in for the gals! (*Women all run back in fear.*)

MISSOURI: Hold on, till I get the rest of the boys; they are close by. (*Exit Missouri.*)

ZEKE: Neow, I say, boys, these 'ere gals are fresh ones from Mexico; I swow we'll have a rousen time; won't we, San Antone? (*Slaps him familiarly.*) For this 'ere is something like it, I swow. Let's have some licker; come up, boys!

MISSOURI: (*Outside.*) Murder! Murder! (*Enters.*) Boys, I'm cut by a damned greaser; oh! God Almighty! he has killed me. (*Falls.*)

TEXAS BILL: Who cut you? (*Goes to Missouri.*) Missouri, who was he?

MISSOURI: Oh, Lord! he—said—"So much—for Joaquin"—as he—stabbed me. Oh, Lord! (*Dies. All stand astonished, as scene closes.*)

SCENE III: *A creek, day time.*

(*Enter Gonzalles.*)

GONZALLES: Last night Garcia made the first move towards the accomplishment of my designs on Joaquin. If I had not so large a fortune to use my wits for, I would put an end to this by killing Joaquin myself, but there is Father Roderi-guez, who is suspicious of my actions, and he keeps a vigilant watch over all I do. I must be wary, for he may possibly know something of my object in coming here, and that prevents me from accomplishing my plans more speedily. What I do, must be done quietly, for Garcia will only act against Joaquin indirectly, and I cannot trust any of the others even for money. Ah! I have it; tell those of the Americans I come in contact with that Belloro is all right—that she is in-clined to be a good soul—kind and easy—not adverse to strangers—and get rid of her, and Joaquin will be at my mercy. For with some men, the hopes of this life dies with the loss of their wives, and Joaquin is one of these. Even now, all Mexico is being searched for him, and that mark of the house of Castillo—a Maltese cross on his breast—might betray all. No matter at what cost, this prize shall be mine, and a Cardinal's hat I will buy—in time. (*Exit.*)

SCENE IV: *Interior of a rude house; chairs, table, picture of a saint over the fire-place; Joaquin and Belloro standing, Joaquin's arm around Belloro's waist.*

JOAQUIN: Why do you hang your head with such a sorrowful look, my own sweet wife? Why, your cheek is pale! Is it because I am going to be absent for a few days? Oh, my dearest Bell, cheer up; for a desponding look from you would un-man and tie me for ever at home.

BELLORO: Has this not been a happy home?

JOAQUIN: Why, yes; to be sure it has; and may the merry voice of my Golden Bell be left for years to come and sound as merrily as in the few months that are past.

BELLORO: I find happiness in every thing with thee, Joaquin. The music of thy footsteps, when you return from your labor of the day, gives me happiness; this room seems more pleasant when you are here; the day begins with your presence and ends with your return, and then I forget the weary hours that have past.

JOAQUIN: I know it, and feel it in every act, that my presence is necessary to your happiness. But, my dear wife, I will not be away from you but a few days—three, at most. Juan and his partner are on the claim at the flat, and they are anxious that I should come over, for they say it is a rich one.

BELLORO: I know there is not an hour you would be absent, if it was not for our welfare, but, oh, dear Joaquin, the heart of your Golden Bell counts the hours of your absence, and the hours seem so long; I feel a sense of fear when you are away, for our love is too holy, too sincere to last.

JOAQUIN: 'Tis but the tone of an anxious heart, which would divert all evil from its idol. Dear wife, I must start if I would get there before sunset, for it's a long ride and the day is nearly over. One kiss for fortune's smiles (*kisses her*) so, and I'll not be long from thee. (*Exit.*)

BELLORO: He has gone. It is the first time he has left me to be absent for a day. (*Cries.*) 'Tis not that I think he loves me less, for that would kill me, but absence of those we love afflicts the heart. Am I not a woman? and the love I bear my husband will sustain me. But when he knows that I am to become a mother, his joy will be increased a thousand fold. (*Walks in front of the picture of a saint.*) Oh, thou Mother of Mercy! sustain me, and protect my husband with thy merci-ful hand. (*Kneels down, kissing a cross as if in prayer.*)

SCENE V: *Grocery on a road; notice on the tent.*

(Enter San Antone and Texas Bill.)

SAN ANTONE: Look 'ere, Bill; what this ere notice say? I hain't no book larning, and yer right pert at readin; come and diskiver what it ses.

TEXAS BILL: *(Looks at the notice.)* Well, I'll be cussed if there ain't a going to be a meeting; this 'ere what it ses. *(Spells.)* "N-O-T-I-C-E, Notice.—There will be a meeting of the Miners of Woods' Creek at this place, this evening, September 19th, for the purpose of taking measures to drive all the Spanish population out of the county. All favorable are requested to attend.—MANY MINERS." I'll be dog-oned if I ain't in, sure.

SAN ANTONE: Look 'ere, Bill, that just suits me; I'm in for that, certain. Bill, who do you suppose killed Missouri t'other night at the fandango?

TEXAS BILL: Why, Joaquin, to a dead certainty; didn't Missouri say so after he got cut?

SAN ANTONE: Who is Joaquin?

TEXAS BILL: Some of them greasers, you can just bet, and an ugly cuss he is, too, for he killed almost a dozen that I've heard of.

SAN ANTONE: Bill, let's take a taste at that bottle, I'm cussed dry. *(Both drink from a bottle.)* That's good old rye, you can jest bet your buttons.

TEXAS BILL: Yonder comes the boys! and we'll just see if them 'ere greasers is a going to have all the good diggins or not; and besides, they ought to be driven out cause they kill and steal every chance they get.

(Enter Miners.)

SAN ANTONE: A pretty big party! Now who's a going to be spokesman. Zeke, let's hear what you have got to say about these greasers.

ALL: Zeke! Zeke! Zeke!

ZEKE: *(Gets a chair, and gets upon it.)* Neow, folks, this 'ere meeting has been called to hear what you got to say about putting all the greaser folks out of the county. They're a darned infernal set, and that's so, by golly! There's no mining where they are, for they get all the good diggings, and we don't stand any more show than a chicken does in the claws of a hawk. *(Cries of Good!)* That's so too, by Perkins! If we get a claim and take out an ounce, they get one and take out pounds; but that ain't the worst on't, for they're all thieves, and just as lieves kill a feller as not, and more especially if he has any money. Hain't they killed lots of the boys, all around here? and didn't Joaquin kill Missouri t'other night. *(Cries of Hang the Greasers.)*[25] Boys, by Jehosaphat! I wish we could hang 'em all, but I swow there are too many of 'em. Let's drive 'em from the county, I calculate that would be a damned sight better, I do, by gewilikins!

TEXAS BILL: That's the way to do it, drive 'em out. Do as we have done in Texas. Put up notices for these 'ere greasers to vamose; and them as don't go, we'll hang.

ZEKE: And don't let us buy any thing of a store-keeper that'll sell to a greaser. *(We won't, we won't.)*

SAN ANTONE: Go in, Yank, you'll do to bet on, for you're a dog-on good talker.

ZEKE: Here's some resolutions I've drawn up (*takes out a paper*) for the consideration of the meeting. Neow, I'll read 'em—Resolved. That every greaser found in
this county after ten days' notice, shall be hanged by Judge Lynch[26] as soon as
found. Resolved. That we are Judge Lynch, and hold ourselves responsible to
the Court. Resolved. That every murder, theft, and horse stealing, which has
been done in this county, was done by greasers. Them is my sentiments, and I do
believe they are good ones, I do, by gracious! (*Cries of Good, Good.*)

TEXAS BILL: I make a motion that the people of this 'ere meeting tell every greaser
they see of our resolution, and that one post up notices on the trees, warning
them to leave.

ZEKE: Boys! you heered the motion; all in favor of it, will say aye. (*All: Aye.*) Mag-
nanimously carried! The meeting is adjourned.

TEXAS BILL: Now, them as don't go, I'll swear, we make go. Come, boys; let's all
go and licker up. (*Cries of Good! Good! All enter the grocery.*)

(*Enter Gonzalles.*)

GONZALLES: How little kindles a fire, and what superhuman efforts it takes to
subdue it! So with the human passions. That notice I posted upon the house, has
kindled a flame that will help me to the accomplishment of my full designs. My
plot is yet small, but deep; and it will cause many to mourn and weep. (*Exit.*)

SCENE VI: *Mining scene. Juan, Joaquin, and a friend at work.*

(*Enter several citizens.*)

JACK: Who claims that horse staked out down yonder?

JOAQUIN: I do, sir.

JACK: Where did you get him?

JOAQUIN: I bought him, at Woods' Creek.

JACK: You lie! You stole him, you damned greaser thief!

JOAQUIN: I have got a bill of sale from the person I purchased from.

PITCH: I'll bet you're a liar. Hang the damned thief!

JOAQUIN: Gentlemen, I can soon satisfy you that I am an honest man, and that I
paid my money for that animal.

JACK: How much did you pay for him.

JOAQUIN: Six ounces.

PITCH: Now I know you lie! for that horse is worth twenty ounces, and he was
stole from old Daylor's ranch.

JUAN: Gentlemen, I know that he purchased him, but of course he will have to give
him up.

JACK: You shut up! Nobody is talking to you; 'tain't your put!

PITCH: Oh, you don't get off so easy. (*Two grab Joaquin, with cries of hang him!*)
No, boys, whip the damned greaser!

JACK: Yes, give him a hundred lashes; that will cure him of horse stealing!

(*Enter Gale.*)

GALE: What is the matter here? (*They commence tying Joaquin to a tree.*)

JACK: We're going to whip this horse thief.

GALE: How do you come to know he stole a horse.

PITCH: Why, he says he owns old Daylor's horse, and Daylor has offered a reward for the horse.

GALE: He may be innocent; he don't look like yer thieves.

JUAN: I know he is innocent of theft.

GALE: Boys, don't be too hasty!

JACK: You're an old Methodist rascal, if you want to take a greaser's part.

GALE: I am an honest hard-working man, as you all know, I reckon; and look yer, I say, find out if he stole the horse first, before you whip him!

JOAQUIN: Gentlemen, I am innocent!

JACK: You're a liar! Give it to him good. (*Commence to whip him.*)

GALE: For God's sake, are you men? Stop whipping him!

JACK: Shut up, you old rascal (*pulls his pistol*), or I'll blow the top of your head off. (*They continue to whip Joaquin, and count the blows.*)

PITCH: 95, 96, 97, 98, 99, 100. One more for full count! There, that will do for his meat; let him down. (*They loose Joaquin, who falls insensible at the foot of the tree.*) Now you and your tribe leave here by dark, or, damn you, we'll hang you all. (*Gale goes to Joaquin, and supports his head.*)

JACK: Who is he, anyway?

GALE: Oh, God! this man saved me and my family from being murdered on the Gila River. Noble, generous boy! What an outrage is this? Poor Joaquin! (*Supports his head.*)

ALL: Joaquin!

PITCH: Boys, we ought to hung him!

END OF ACT III

ACT IV

SCENE I: *Joaquin in front of his home, pale, haggard, and fatigued.*

JOAQUIN: Is it possible I am still alive, and before the door of the only home I ever possessed, with a heart degraded by unjust punishment? A home, oh, God! where I expected to find so much of this world's happiness; a home where I have experienced all the joys of heaven. Now, now degraded by the lash of unfeeling men; oh, what tale shall I tell to conceal the depth of my misery from my dear wife? What shall I say to her? That I have received a hundred lashes? Ah, no; for they would fall more heavily on her heart than on my innocent back. God! that man should have so little faith in man! Those men fell upon me and called me "thief" and lashed me as if I was some refractory peone. Why should I suffer this, without having revenge? I will—I will suffer all for thy dear sake, my wife; I will bear all and not complain. How will I break this sad news to her? God give thee, my wife, strength to bear this first sad affliction. That good old man paid me the ransom of a hundred lives by his kindness, and I feel that I yet have friends who will pity me. How I need thy consoling voice, dear wife, to heal the wounds which are on my heart and body; for thy sympathy is a balm, and thy voice is an antidote for all my sorrows. My own sweet wife, I come, and by thy side I will forget all harm that has been done. (*Enters the door.*)

SCENE II: *Joaquin's home. Rosa, Bonita, and Juan; Joaquin kneeling at the bedside of Belloro.*

BELLORO: Touch me not, Joaquin; I am polluted! Oh, the misery of this day!
JOAQUIN: What strange words! You are sick; I am by thy side, my own sweet wife. How dreadfully pale you are. (*Aside.*)—Oh God, can it be that the disgrace I have received has been told her, and has caused this? Dear wife, do not hate me, for it would kill me; I am innocent; I am yet thy Joaquin. Do not turn from me!

Ah, I know thy loving heart too well to think that you will not forgive me.

BELLORO: Touch me not, Joaquin! (*Rises in bed.*) I tell thee I am foul—polluted— a being not fit to live, nor yet prepared to die!

JOAQUIN: Say not so; talk not of dying; for my heart is bursting with its sorrow. You die? No, no!

BELLORO: Joaquin, the priest has been here. I am dying, and you heed not what I say!

JOAQUIN: Spare my wife, oh God! No, no, you will not die! Do not take to heart what punishment I received; it was nothing, for I am innocent.

BELLORO: I too am innocent! Joaquin, you are as dear to me as ever. But—I am dying!

JOAQUIN: No, no! oh, God, no!

BELLORO: Hear me, Joaquin. But a few hours since, some men came rushing into this room and said you was hung—that you was dead. I fell in a swoon upon the floor, and when I awoke, Rosa stood over me—but I was your wife no more!

JOAQUIN: Am I not by thy side! Talk not thus; 'tis but a wild dream; you are only a little unwell, dear wife.

BELLORO: Dear Joaquin, listen to me for a few moments, for I feel that my life is ebbing fast. Listen, and forgive me.

JOAQUIN: I will—I will!

BELLORO: Dear Joaquin, I am happy—you are here. Those men took more than my life—they destroyed my virtue! My heart is broken! Bless your Bell, Joaquin; think of Bell sometimes! My husband—my Joaq——. (*Falls back dead; Juan and women kneel.*)

JOAQUIN: (*Takes her hand.*) Dead! (*Gives a scream and falls to the floor. Scene slowly closes.*)

SCENE III: *A forest scene. Enter Gonzalles.*

GONZALLES: Garcia, the three-fingered devil, has exceeded my expectations, from what I hear of his exploits, and even my own acts have produced effects I did not anticipate. It is over a year since Garcia started, and well has he followed my directions. From Los Angeles to Mount Shasta, the name of Joaquin and Three-Fingered Jack ring like a death-knell on the ears of the traveler. Seven men were killed in four days at Marysville; five killed and robbed at Bidwell's Bar; besides many others; and the northern country may well be in arms. Captain Wilson and General Bean were killed at Los Angeles; besides, cattle drovers, jew-peddlers, and Chinamen innumerable. It's time Garcia returned, for I wish to see him. After the use that mutilated hand has been put too, I think he will find a way to use it on Joaquin; and now that Belloro is dead, he will do so the more readily.

(*Enter Pedro.*)

PEDRO: Father Gonzalles—the very man I wanted to see.

GONZALLES: Welcome back, Pedro. (*Shakes hands.*) Where is Garcia?

PEDRO: Coming this way, for there was a house burnt in the lower country a few nights since, and every soul murdered as they came out—men, women, and children, and I think that must be Three-Fingered Jack's work, and no other's. (*Throws off his serape.*)

GONZALLES: I see you have made it pay; the richness of your clothing shows success.

PEDRO: Yes; our purses are not empty, but it has been hot work for our party.

GONZALLES: Why, how is that?

PEDRO: Harry Love, the Deputy Sheriff of Los Angeles, played the devil among us. He captured Claudio, and Mountain Jim started to overtake them, and Love, seeing that he could not escape with Claudio, and Claudio shouting for the boys to come on, Love drew his pistol and shot Claudio, leaving him on the road dead as a stone post. Harry Love is an awful man to contend against, for he does not fear the devil, and he is the worst enemy we have in the State.

GONZALLES: (*Aside.*) Claudio was a cowardly murderer, and Harry Love saved the county some trouble and money by shooting him. Pedro, peace to Claudio's soul; an *Ave* or two, and he will rest well, I hope—(*aside*) in hell.

PEDRO: Where is Juan and Joaquin?

GONZALLES: Come with me and learn all. How I pity Joaquin; his wife, Belloro, is dead.

PEDRO: Sacramento![27] Bell dead!

GONZALLES: Yes, and to-day we bury her. There will be many a sad tale told for this, but come and learn all. (*Exeunt.*)

SCENE IV: *Mountain scene, with forest. Music. Enter funeral procession, led by Priest Gonzalles. Boy swinging censer. Coffin with bearers. Joaquin and friends.*

GONZALLES: (*Chants, with open book in his hand.*)
Tantum ergo Sacramentum
Veneremur ceruni
Et antiquum documentum
Novo cedat ritue
Presatit fides supplementum
Sensuum defectue.

(*Priest swings censer in the grave; body is lowered; priest chants.*)

Mers stupebit et natural
Cum resurget oreatura
Judicanti respondura.
Index ergo cum sedebit
Quidquid latet apparebit
Nil inultum nemanebit
Pio Jesu domine
Dona eis requieum.

(*Music. Exit of Gonzalles; Priest and censer-boy swinging burning incense; Joaquin kneels at the grave; Enter Garcia, stands surprised.*)

JOAQUIN: The grave of my wife; Oh, God! (*Bows his head; rises.*) The grave of all my fond anticipations—the burial spot of all my hopes of joy in this life. The chamber where the good will rest; the grave the portal opening into Paradise. But why should thy form be laid within the mold, food for worms? Yet this heart will bend, like the cypress, forever over this hallowed spot, last resting place of thee, my wife. Oh, Death, unholy curse of mortality, why have you robbed me? God of heaven, and men of earth, what have I done that I should be used thus? And thus afflicted, oh, what have I to live for now?

GARCIA: Revenge!

JOAQUIN: Revenge—deep revenge! 'Twill help to cure the sorrow of my soul, and I will have it. (*Kneels at grave.*) Oh, by thy sainted soul, dear wife, by every spot hallowed to mortality, I swear I will revenge thee! With thy body has gone down into the grave all that is good on earth of me! Revenge, with its unholy light, takes possession of my soul! Oh, thou furies of the eternal shades, aid me, that I may wreck a vengeance on mankind that will make devils laugh. Hecate, embitter my soul! I will not believe in celestial heat; and my soul and body will I give to thee, oh hell, when my vengeance is complete!

JUAN: And I, too, will aid thee. I swear it, by the dead body of my sister, who lies beneath this sod; I will have revenge!

GARCIA: And I! Hell! I have something to kill for now.

JOAQUIN: A thousand lives will be but a just revenge for my golden Bell, my own sweet wife. (*Rosa and Bonita kneel at the grave; Joaquin, Juan, and Garcia clasp hands, with the left hand raised above their heads.*)

ALL: We swear to revenge Belloro!

SCENE V: *Mountain scenery; a cave; band comes out of the cave. Pedro, Jose, Roderiguez, Gonzalles, women, etc.*

GONZALLES: All here, but Juan, Garcia, and Joaquin.

PEDRO: And Claudio, who has gone to—to the other world.

RODERIGUEZ: God rest his soul.

PEDRO: God rest our bodies. Now that Joaquin joins us, we will have work enough to do.

BAND: Welcome to Joaquin!

(*Enter Garcia.*)

GARCIA: Boys, the work has commenced! I never saw anybody so cool.

PEDRO: What is it, Garcia? Spit it out.

GARCIA: Joaquin has got his first blood.

RODERIGUEZ: Who was it?

GARCIA: The one who helped to whip Joaquin. It was so coolly done, it makes me laugh. (*Laughs.*) Juan, Joaquin, and myself were coming down the hill, and ahead of us on the trail was a man whom Joaquin recognized as one who helped whip him. Joaquin tapped him on the shoulder and said, "Good day, my very good friend." The man turned, and yelled out, "Joaquin, by God!"' and fell on his knees, and Lord, how he begged. "Have you got done begging," said Joaquin. "For if you have, pray; for you're the first of the score that I'm going to kill." The man prayed for the Lord knows who all—wife, children, father, mother, and every relation in the world that he could think of; and as he said Amen, Joaquin blew his brains out. Joaquin then put his pistol in his belt, and walked on, whistling "The Devil's Farrier." I searched the man's pocket, and got a purse full of oro.

ALL: Good for Joaquin!

GONZALLES: Boys, he would make a good patron for the band.

GARCIA: The coolest in action I ever knew.

RODERIGUEZ: I love Joaquin, for he is brave. Let's make him our leader.

GARCIA: I am willing!

OTHERS: And I—and I—I—I!

GONZALLES: Yonder comes Joaquin and Juan down the rocks. (*Cries of welcome to Joaquin!*)

(*Enter Joaquin and Juan.*)

JOAQUIN: Boys, I have come to join you, and as I only want revenge, I suppose I will be more welcomed.

GONZALLES: I take it upon myself to say for the band here that you are welcome, and Garcia and the boys say that you must be patron and leader of them.

RODERIGUEZ: That is what we all say.

ALL: Yes, yes.

JOAQUIN: Companeros, I have a large job before me. There are men that I would not have killed by any other hand than mine for their weight in gold. I want but one month to do it in, and then you can kill who you please. I want them that whipped me, and I want the ravishers of my wife—her murderers! By the eternal shades! I will allow no man to kill them but myself. We have not always been guerrillas. There is one I would not see come to harm—an old man named Gale; you remember him on the Gila river. Boys, he is a good man. Spare him and his family, for my sake—for the sake of Belloro. And by the eternal shades of hell! I will kill the first man that injures them. If I am to lead you, you must obey.

PEDRO: Joaquin, we all swear to obey you.

GONZALLES: Revenge for Joaquin! Swear for revenge! (*Holds up a cross. Band raises their right hands.*) We all swear to be true to Joaquin and aid him in his revenge.

ALL: We swear! (*Scene closes.*)

END OF ACT IV

ACT V

SCENE I: *Forest scene—Love's band.*

HARRY LOVE: Gentlemen, at last I have received my commission. (*shows a paper.*) It is dated May 17th, 1853. The bill was passed by the Senate and Assembly, and signed by John Bigler, Governor of California, the same day. The longest term they would give us is three months to capture Joaquin and his band. The pay is one hundred and fifty dollars per month; the time is short, and the pay is small. As we are already organized, we need lose no time. You will hold yourselves subject to the order of Lieutenant Byrnes.

WHITE: Ah, Harry, the people of San Joaquin County have offered five-thousand for Joaquin, dead or alive; and the Governor offers one-thousand more. Now, if Joaquin is captured by us, are we in on the rewards?

HENDERSON: To be sure we are. Do you think Captain Harry Love wants to make money out of us? No, sir; Harry will give each man his share of the rewards, certain, sure.

BYRNES: What do the rewards amount to? I go in for the fight, for all depends on us now. Joaquin and his band are our game.

HENDERSON: Joaquin dead or alive, that's the programme. Hain't Joaquin blotted out some of my old friends, and some of the best men in the State? There's Captain Wilson, Ruddel, and Jo. Lake, boys, I'd go my bottom dollar on. I'll get even if I once get a bead on any of Joaquin's band. Damn the rewards!

HARRY LOVE: The rewards shall be shared equally, and if we get the rewards, and the pay allowed, it will not more than pay expenses. The rewards are poor stuff. I want to pay Joaquin and Three-Fingered Jack in their own coin for killing General Bean and Captain Wilson.

WHITE: When do we start? Three months ain't much time to work in.

HARRY LOVE: To-day. Byrnes, take the boys and go to San Jose, and I will meet you there in a few days. Scout over the mountains and keep watch of the roads and find out all you can about Joaquin, and we'll give his band the benefit of all the proclamations before three months pass.

BYRNES: I have a plan that I think will carry us through. Does Joaquin or his band know you?

HARRY LOVE: His band all know me—more especially Three-Fingered Jack, for I sent a ball so near his head one day that he ducked, and I have since heard that he said it made his head ache for a week, but I never saw Joaquin to know him.

BYRNES: I know that renegade priest, Gonzalles, and I know Joaquin. I think I can buy Gonzalles to betray Joaquin.

HARRY LOVE: I wish you would try it. Pshaw! you'd only lose your head.

BYRNES: I'll take the chances.

HARRY LOVE: Well, try; but if they blot you out, I will have a deeper reckoning against Joaquin and his band.

HENDERSON: Harry, Byrnes is heavy on a scent after greasers.

HARRY LOVE: Byrnes, I want to see you off for San Jose, and then I will try my plan, and if you go on the scout, Henderson will take charge of the men until I join them at San Jose.

HENDERSON: When will that be?

HARRY LOVE: In a few days at most.

ALL: Go in, Harry!

WHITE: Time will try our mettle.

HARRY LOVE: Come, boys, I want to see you started. (*Exeunt.*)

SCENE II: *Mountain scene.*

GARCIA: Ho! boys, Joaquin's month is up! Hell! isn't he the worst man you ever saw?

PEDRO: He beats the devil, and he takes the worst chances in the world to kill his man. He has killed fifteen between Wood's Creek and Murphy's Flat, and every one in the day-time. He's lightning; he shoots faster than any man can count.

ROSA: And every time he fires, he says: Another for murdering my wife. Joaquin has revenged Belloro in every man he has killed. Dear Bell, how well he loved her!

(*Enter Joaquin.*)

JOAQUIN: All here, Garcia?

GARCIA: Yes.

JOAQUIN: Boys, I have killed all but one of my enemies, and if I knew where he was, I would follow him even into the infernal regions of the devil; or if he was dead, I would dig him up to put a ball through his brain. I now take a new stand. Garcia, how many horses have we got?

GARICA: About fifteen-hundred.

JOAQUIN: Our organization will be two-thousand men when all is completed, and they are in Mexico, Lower California, and in this State. So, you see that I have not been idle. With the money you had when I joined you, and that I have taken since, we have money in abundance. I found twenty-thousand dollars in the saddle-bags of one, fifteen-thousand with another, and all is deposited in a safe place, and now I intend to send one-hundred-thousand dollars to Mexico, and then equip fifteen-hundred men, and sweep this State from Mokelumne Hill to the Colorado. "I intend also to kill the Americans by wholesale, burn their villages and ranches, and run off all their property so fast that they will not be able to collect an opposing force, and that will finish our work, and my revenge will be completed. And then, my brothers, we will be paid, too, for some of the wrongs of poor Mexico. This is the reason I have kept you so busy collecting horses. We will then divide our gains, and my career will then be ended, and may the rest of our days be spent in peace."[28] Gonzalles, you we want to send to Mexico. We have a remittance of one-hundred-thousand dollars to place in your hands for safe delivery to our bankers at Sonora. This is the commencement of all that ends, and I hope we will live to enjoy it with our friends.

ALL: Joaquin forever!

GONZALLES: I will accept of this trust, for my mission is peace, and I am tired of this warfare. (*Aside.*)—If that hombre keeps his appointment, I will set a trap that will snare the hunter and free the game; then Joaquin's time will end, for Joaquin, *he* is doomed. Joaquin, you can depend on me for its safe delivery.

JOAQUIN: Prepare, Gonzalles, for within a month you shall be upon your road.

GONZALLES: I shall prepare. (*Exit.*)

PEDRO: Ho! Joaquin, what is this?

JOAQUIN: Reayes, with armed men! Men, prepare!

(*Enter Reayes with four men.*)

JOAQUIN: Who are you, and what business brings you here?

FIRST HUNTER: We are hunters, in search of bear and deer.

JOAQUIN: We are hunters, also. You have found us here, and I have no guarantee that you will not tell you have seen us, and if I tell you who I am, you will tell it the first opportunity; therefore, you must die.

BILL HARVEY: (*Steps forward and fronts Joaquin.*) I suspect who you are. You are Joaquin Murieta, and, sir, I know you to be a gentleman in spite of all they've said against you. We are hunters, and I pledge you my word we will not speak of you or your company for one month, if you will allow us to go.

ROSA: (*Steps to Joaquin.*) Oh! Joaquin, spare them!

JOAQUIN: (*To Bill Harvey.*) I believe you, for I met with you a long, long time ago. (*Aside.*)—Oh, God! it was when I was innocent; what a change a few short years make for weal or woe! I believe you, sir.

BILL HARVEY: Is this the noble Joaquin I met on the Gila? I was wounded then, and you saved us.

JOAQUIN: Yes; go, you and your company! You are safe. Speak not of the past; Joaquin is not the being he was. Go! (*Party shoulder their rifles.*)

BILL HARVEY: 'Tis a pity for so good a man—

JOAQUIN: Go, sir, go! I am not over-patient. Go! (*Party exit.*)

ROSA: (*Claps her hands.*) Good, Joaquin, good!

ALL: Good for Joaquin!

ROSA, BONITA, BAND: (*Sing.*)

When the golden sun is shining from out the distant west,
And the humming-bird is seeking its downy pendant nest,
And the vesper bells are sounding on the mellow evening air,
Our hearts grow light with music and dancing with the fair.

(*Chorus*)
We roam from summer vales to hills of eternal snow;
Whate'er the change may be, our home is Mexico! (*Repeat*)

SCENE III: *A wood—Enter Gonzalles.*

GONZALLES: What, not yet come! The time was set precisely. I detest a laggard, a procrastinator, a thief of others' hours. There is no faith to be put in such men. In my anxiety to be here, I may be before the time; the sun is yet some hours high above the horizon, and I will wait. How assiduously I have tracked Joaquin and plotted for his fall; yet I have struck no blow. But now all of my schemes are ready to fall upon him with their fatality, for I must win. I am known far and near as the Fighting Priest, yet I have never taken life but in self-defense; therefore, my conscience is easy. It is only he that takes life for pay, or revenge for insult, that is a murderer; but he who strikes a life-taking blow in self-defense, and without malice aforethought, should not be held guilty. To strike when a hand is raised to kill thee, why, thy soul cries for revenge, and as the life-blood oozes from the veins of the victim, it rather cries for mercy than bears hatred. So, then, I strike no blow; yet they will fall, and others doing the deed leaves me free from guilt of conscience. Wealth I must have; I said it more than once; and that, too, before many months. Hist! a foot-fall, a shadow; he comes! (*Whistle blows; Gonzalles replies; enter Byrnes.*)
BYRNES: Here at last!
GONZALLES: I have been waiting.
BYRNES: I have but little time to spare. To business! What of Joaquin?
GONZALLES: As we agreed. I think you have forgotten something.
BYRNES: What, Sir Priest? Ah, yes! the ounces; here they are, (*hands the priest a purse*) and every one good Spanish ounces; (*aside*)—and every one will buy a Spanish head.
GONZALLES: Here I have written all that will interest you. (*Hands Byrnes a paper.*) I will leave in one month, and then the band will all be gathered; that will be a good time to strike.
BYRNES: (*Looks at the paper.*) What! is it possible! Priest, I believe you are in earnest in this.
GONZALLES: I am, and to the death.
BYRNES: Will you tell me why?
GONZALLES: No, not until the last ounce is paid, and I am sure there is no escape.
BYRNES: And then—
GONZALLES: I will tell you. Adios! Remember, our next meeting is on the hill. Adios! (*Exit.*)
BYRNES: There is a reason for this, and I *will* know what it is. (*Exit.*)

SCENE IV: *Room in a rude house; a prisoner chained, sitting in a chair; a Court of Justice; table with papers; men sitting, standing, smoking, etc.*

JUSTICE BROWN: Dick, I am going to swear you about this case. Hold up your right hand. You solemnly swear you will tell the truth touching the murder of a person known as Germany, and nothing but the truth, so help you God! And if the prisoner is guilty, he dies within one hour.

DICK: I will tell the truth just as sure as you are born. I had been down to the store getting some grub and fixin's, and was on the road home, and I heard old Germany cry murder three times as loud as he could yell, and I started for his tent, and the first thing I saw was Germany lying across the floor with his throat cut from ear to ear. Ugh! you bet it was an ugly sight.

JUSTICE BROWN: Who else saw him?

DICK: Jim, Big Mike, Bill, and some other boys but I got to the door first.

BILL: Yes, we come up, and I seed old Germany's pockets was turned inside out, and then I knew he had been robbed.

MIKE: Squire Brown, I stand forenenst ye's, and I swear by the holy cross I seen two Mexican greasers whip round the tent, and jest break for the chapparel, and this heathen I believe was one of them.

SQUIRE BROWN: We do not want your testimony until it is called for; we can't believe what you say now, but under oath we will.

MIKE: Who are ye's any way? Ye's are only the judge, and we's the jury, the constable, and sheriff, and yer after doubting an honest man's word. Vat the divil does your honor take me for?[29]

JUSTICE BROWN: I only meant that your testimony was not legal unless you were sworn.

BILL: Sworn be damned! After the boys said they had seen the two greasers, that was enough; we pitched into the chapparel after them; I took down the road and the boys went up the road, and when I got down to Tennessee's store, this greaser come riding up, and then the boys come up and arrested him.

TENNESSEE: Squire Brown, that is the truth; this greaser come out of the bushes and he seemed frightened, for I saw him.

ALL: He's the man! hang him! hang him!

JUSTICE BROWN: Prisoner, what have you got to say?

PRISONER: Mas, yo no sabe para que tengo esta cadena. (*Rattles his chain.*) Yo no hablo el Americano. In poco tiempo el muy amigo viendra aqui. Der Dios, yo no entender alguna cosa de esto.[30]

MIKE: You lie, you damned greaser thief; ye's can talk American, so ye's can.

JUSTICE BROWN: Boys, let's talk this over for half an hour.

(*Cries of—Hang him! string him up! no talk! hang him! Enter Joaquin, dressed as an American; looks at Pedro.*)

JOAQUIN: (*Aside.*)—I was right; the rascal! to get drunk and stray away from us.

PRISONER: Muy gracias! muy gracias! mi patron.[31]

JUSTICE BROWN: Who are you, sir?

JOAQUIN: "My name, your honor, is Samuel Harrington. I am a packer from the town of San Jose, and I am just now on my return from the northern mines, where I have been packing flour and other provisions. I am encamped within five miles of this place, and having heard from a citizen of your town this morning that a dark-skinned man, with gray eyes, was in custody on a charge of murder, and that, although there was no positive proof against him, yet there was so strong a prejudice against Mexicans that there was great danger of his being hung by the infuriated populace. It just struck me that the prisoner might be one of my hired men, a Mexican, whom I sent to town last night, and who, much to my astonishment, did not return. I find that it is indeed the case. Your prisnoer is none other than my packer and consequently cannot be connected with any robbing or thieving band around here. He has been with me for four years, and no man ever sustained a better character. I shall wish, your honor, to testify in his behalf; but before I take my oath, I would like to prove my identity as Mr. Harrington of San Jose. Please examine these letters."[32] (*Hands Justice Brown a package of letters.*)

JUSTICE BROWN: (*Reads.*)—Mr. Samuel Harrington, San Jose. Two letters from San Francisco; also, from Marysville, Nevada, Sacramento, Stockton, and from the Atlantic States. Mr. Harrington, you have a family I see, as your wife's sister speaks very affectionately.

JOAQUIN: No—yes—that is, I had a family, but they are all dead.

JUSTICE BROWN: That is sad. Mr. Harrington, we will swear you, and your evidence will be taken without any scruples. (*Holds up his hand.*) Hold up your hand. You solemnly swear the statement you have made is true in every particular, so help you God.

JOAQUIN: I do.

JUSTICE BROWN: Boys, I believe what Mr. Harrington has said is the truth. What do you say?

DICK: I believe him.

ALL: And I, and I, and I.

MIKE: By the powers of Saint Patrick, may the divil catch me if I do.

JOAQUIN: Dare you doubt my word, sir?

MIKE: I dare that. (*Aside.*)—May the divil catch me but yer one of his imps.

JOAQUIN: You're a fool.

MIKE: There are many of them fornenst ye.

JUSTICE BROWN: Mr. Harrington, there is but one opinion, and that is, the prisoner is not guilty. Bill, take off his chains. There, he is free, and we are sorry to have detained him. (*Bill sets him free.*)

JOAQUIN: Thank you, your honor; yet caution is necessary these dangerous times. Come, Pedro, we will go. Good day, gentlemen. (*Exit Joaquin and Pedro.*)

MIKE: The divil catch them, for 'pon my word as an Irish Count, I belave ye've let two of the damndest villains go that walks on the earth unhung, and so I do.

(*Enter a man.*)

MAN: Squire Brown, here's a letter for you.

JUSTICE BROWN: (*Reads.*)—"Your prisoner is Pedro, the worst thief and murderer in Joaquin's band. Hang him if you would save your own lives. In haste, from

ONE WHO KNOWS." "TO SQUIRE BROWN."

MIKE: Oh, musha worra! Mr. Harrington was Joaquin—the divil! Did ye's mind the look he gave me? Boys, we'll catch the spalpeens yet. (*Scene closes.*)

SCENE V: *A mountain road.*

PEDRO: How, by all the saints, Joaquin, did you happen to come in such a good time. Ugh! I expected to be hung.

JOAQUIN: Our proverb says, The devil takes care of his chickens. I came back to camp last night unexpectedly, and I found that you and Garcia had gone out to try your hands, and shortly after Garcia came back and said that he had killed a man in that little canvas town, and they had arrested you for the murder. "So, I then thought of several plans to save you. I had in my possession those letters of Harrington's which, thanks to my good sense, I had preserved, and I soon form-ed the plan of passing off for a respectable merchant, and it worked to a charm. I always save such papers, for sometimes they can be put to good use."[33]

PEDRO: How did you come to get them?

JOAQUIN: Easy enough; I killed a man on the road the other day, and I found them in his pocket, and but damned little else.

PEDRO: Joaquin, you ought to be a California judge, for you are heavy on papers. That Sunday ride into Stockton, where five-thousand dollars reward was posted on the court-house door for Joaquin, dead or alive, which you generously offer-ed to increase ten-thousand more by signing you name to the document; then your letter to Governor Bigler, asking him to increase the State's offering to ten-thousand dollars in place of the small sum of one-thousand, which he so begrudgingly offered.[34]

JOAQUIN: I had an idea of sending him nine-thousand dollars to make up the sum, for my head is worth more than they have offered yet.

PEDRO: (*Laughs.*) And they will have a merry time before they get it. I am in a hurry to get to camp.

JOAQUIN: And so am I, for I am as dry as a squirrel hole, and as hungry as a coyote. Our horses are at the foot of the hill, and they soon carry us to camp. Come. (*Exeunt.*)

(*Enter Byrnes.*)

BYRNES: I was too cautious, or I might have heard all they said. "Ten-thousand dollars," "Joaquin," "John Bigler," "killed a man on the road." I wonder who they are. I know their faces, but I do not remember where I saw them before. I swear I believe they are some of Joaquin's band. I will know very soon if that priest keeps his appointment.

(*Enter Gonzalles.*)

GONZALLES: Good day, Senor Captain.

BYRNES: (*Surprised.*) What! are you here? You came as still as a fox. Who are those two men?—here—going there down the hill—see!—there, those two.

GONZALLES: (*Looks.*) Ah! what! (*Laughs.*) Pedro and —and—

BYRNES: Who?

GONZALLES: Dressed as an American! Ah, so, Joaquin Murieta! He has got Pedro free, and how, by the saints, I do not know.

BYRNES: Joaquin! Had I been sure that he was Joaquin, I would have sent a ball through his heart. They stood on this very spot, and talked of their villainies. I lay concealed in yonder bushes waiting your arrival, and overheard part of their conversation. Now, I know the meaning of their words. I will know them when I see them again.

GONZALLES: It is just as well, for within one week the band will be on their road to San Juan Mission, there to collect their gold for me to carry to Mexico, and Joaquin will collect his forces to sweep the southern portion of this State, and when the band reaches the coast range, they will be easily exterminated by your party.

BYRNES: Is this the last news you have to tell me?

GONZALLES: It is; here are my last memoranda. (*Hands Byrnes a paper.*)

BYRNES: You have earned your gold. (*Hands him a purse.*)

GONZALLES: All is truth so far; the future for success lies with yourself.

BYRNES: Sir Priest, tell me why you have betrayed Joaquin.

GONZALLES: Revenge and gain; in another land—

BYRNES: For what, Sir Priest?

GONZALLES: To gain wealth—titles—a dukedom. Adios! farewell forever! adios!

BYRNES: Titles and wealth in another land! a dukedom (*laughs*) in the wilds of California! The best wealth in this world is a free man 'mid the mountains, with his rifle for a companion; the best title to a dukedom, an honest heart, firm in its honest purposes.[35]

SCENE VI: *A wood.*

HARRY LOVE: Sad, sad news we hear from every quarter of the southern mines[36] of Joaquin's band. The accounts of many murders have reached us since we started. If Byrnes does not return very soon, we shall be obliged to go on without him, which I would most sincerely hate to do.

HENDERSON: Yes, it is time we met Joaquin's band, and a few shots at their dark skins will pay off some of them for their dark deeds.

WHITE: Well, it is time Lieutenant Byrnes came back, and if he is alive, I'll swear he has some secret that will put us on the right track.

HARRY LOVE: Byrnes has got them, I am sure, but our time is almost up, and if we would meet them, we must seek their den. If I go among them, they know what I come for; they know me as well as a hunter knows his game, and the least suspicion that leads them to think that Byrnes is on their trail will cause him to lose his head, as sure as I can hit that clump of bushes. (*Pulls his pistol and fires.*)

WHITE: You hit the bush for I saw it move; yet Byrnes has a risky job, but he knows how to carry out every plan he sets himself to do.

HARRY LOVE: I would rather be put in a den with a she-bear and two cubs than to try and track these greasers alone and spy out their acts. Give me a fair field, and I will fight six of them any time.

HENDERSON: I'll bet we will have enough to do when Byrnes comes back. (*Looks out.*) What! Byrnes, I'll swear! for I know the height the heels of his horse throws the dust.

HARRY LOVE: Byrnes, by the Immortal! Here he comes.

(*Enter Byrnes.*)

HARRY LOVE: Welcome, old boy! (*Shakes hands.*) We were all anxious to see you. What success? Spit it out, for we have lain in camp so long that we have got rusty. Let's hear the news.

BYRNES: Captain, we have got one dead besides the others, sure.

HARRY LOVE: Got one dead? How is that?

BYRNES: Who fired that pistol at those bushes across the ravine.

HARRY LOVE: I did. Why?

BYRNES: You have killed one of Joaquin's band, the Priest Gonzalles, better known as the Fighting Priest, Joaquin Gonzalles, and the man of all others that wanted to live to see Joaquin killed, and the traitor of Joaquin Murieta's band.

WHITE: Good! a lucky shot!

HARRY LOVE: What was he doing there, for God's sake?

BYRNES: I think he saw you, and was trying to hide from sight. As I rode past some bushes, I saw his horse, and a few feet further on, I found him lying upon his face on the ground. I dismounted and went to him, and I found he was shot through the head.

HENDERSON: The priest had his head in a damned bad place, that's all I've got to say.

HARRY LOVE: I am sorry—for it was entirely accidental.

WHITE: You are sorry! What, to kill a darned snake, a traitor, a murderer, a—

HARRY LOVE: No, but I would like to have given him a fight for his chances.

BYRNES: Harry, we have got the best of Joaquin's band, sure! (*All give three cheers.*)

HARRY LOVE: Byrnes, let us hear what you have done; for we are anxious to hear what the prospect is.

BYRNES: I went to Mokelumne Hill, to Sonora, to Mariposa, and to every Spanish place in the Southern mines. At last I heard of Joaquin's band being at Chapparel Hill, near San Andreas, and I went there, and fell in with a Spanish priest, and I soon learned from him that he hated Joaquin. Then, by plying him with wine, he acknowledged that he was one of the band, or at least knew all their secrets, and I bribed him.

WHITE: Did he tell you?

BYRNES: Yes, and agreed that if we would kill Joaquin certain, and all of his band if possible, that he would put me on their track. I consented, and to make it certain on my part, he only wanted fify ounces for full information.

HARRY LOVE: What, did you have to pay the black rascal eight hundred dollars?

BYRNES: Yes, every cent of it, and I have got his receipt in my purse. I had several meetings with the priest, and he always met me at the appointed time, but I had to watch him very closely, until I was certain that he was in earnest, and then I followed him through ravines, gulches and canyons, where no one but the devil or Joaquin would go, unless on the same errand I was. But I found everything true he had said. Once Joaquin passed within a few feet of me, and I did not know him; Pedro, one of his satellites, was with him; Joaquin had been to a small place on the Mokelumne River, and got Pedro free from a charge of murder, just as the people were going to hang him. Joaquin played himself off for a respectable packer and trader of San Jose; and the result was, Pedro was let go. I saw them as they came down the hill, and I hid in the bushes near a flat piece of ground, the spot where I had agreed to meet the priest. Joaquin and Pedro stopped directly opposite me and commenced laughing and talking, so that I heard part of their conversation, which was about themselves and the rewards offered. Soon after, the priest came, and he told me who they were.

WHITE: Great God! What a chance you lost!

BYRNES: Just so, White; yet it is far better as it is, for now we will get the full band at one sweep. In a few days, they will be on their road to San Juan, and they will go through Pacheco's Pass; and when we once get them in this coast range of hills, they are ours, sure. But the priest Gonzalles, who informed, is dead.

HARRY LOVE: I am glad I shot the cur, for a traitor is the worst enemy to God or man on the earth. We will go and bury the poor devil, and then to the saddles, and as we ride we can hear all your adventures.

BYRNES: Gonzalles met his end in an unexpected manner. Joaquin's gold will do him no good, for he was to meet Joaquin at the Mission and carry their gold to Mexico, and I suspect he was on his way to the rendezvous.

HARRY LOVE: Byrnes, I hope your plans are all well taken. I heartily approve of them, thus far. Come, after this priest is disposed of, we will complete our plans, and when completed, Joaquin is ours, or I am damned. (*Exeunt.*)

SCENE VII: *Mountain scene; rocks; men and women lying about; Joaquin's band all present.*

JOAQUIN: We are well on our journey, and before the sun sets we will reach the pass; from thence a day's journey will carry us to the rendezvous. Padre Gonzalles will be there, and all ready to start for Mexico. One month will prepare us for our final exploit, and then for Mexico and peace; you boys, to enjoy your wealth, and I to mourn over the loss of her whose dear form is ever before me, to count over the stripes upon my back, and think over the deep and deadly revenge I have taken.

GARCIA: Joaquin, are you satisfied at what has been done?

JOAQUIN: Yes, so far. Why?

GARCIA: I will tell you. Curse it! I will tell you. (*Rises.*) I loved Belloro as dearly as you did. I, too, have been revenging her. Damn them! I have paid Los Americanos well. Hell! how I have killed them. Old Gonzalles wanted me to kill you long ago, and I would not on account of Belloro. Gonzalles says your name is Joaquin Murieta de Castillo, and that you belong in old Spain. So, you had no right to Belloro. If she had been my wife—

JOAQUIN: Belloro had been your wife! You're full with liquor, fool. My name is De Castillo! Fool! you are a liar and a devil that speaks of angels!

GARCIA: I've told you the truth. Yes, by God! and if Belloro had lived, I would have possessed her.

JOAQUIN: (*Jumps up and draws his pistol.*) Damn you! Dare you talk thus to me? I will send you to eternal hell if you breathe her name again. Why should I be angry with a fool? Ah, my sainted wife! Why should not all that saw thee love thee? for you were all that was good on earth. (*Cries.*) Oh, God! you were all that was good on earth of me.

JUAN: Garcia, you are a damned fool.

ROSA: Yes, to talk thus to Joaquin; he would have been justified if he had shot you, for you know how the mention of her name affects him.

JOAQUIN: Let it pass; her name is a worthy name for a saint.

PEDRO: Look, Joaquin, here come some men.

JOAQUIN: Who can they be? Get ready boys, (*all rise*) but be careful.

(*Enter Love, Henderson, White, and others.*)

HARRY LOVE: Which way is this party travelling?

RODERIGUEZ: We are going to Los Angeles.

WHITE: (*To Pedro.*) Where are you going?

PEDRO: To the Mariposa.

JOAQUIN: No, we are going to Los Angeles. (*To Love.*) Sir, if you have any questions to ask, address yourself to me; I am the leader of this company.

HARRY LOVE: I will address who I please, sir. Who are you? (*Joaquin starts to go, looks hard at Love, but keeps moving.*) Stop, sir, or I will blow the top of your head off.

JOAQUIN: Boys, every one for himself—go! (*Exit; Love fires at him; Henderson follows Joaquin.*)

(*Enter Byrnes.*)

BYRNES: Shoot him, Henderson; that is Joaquin.

GARCIA: Shoot, boys, shoot! (*Garcia and others fire; Love shoots Garcia; Garcia and others fall; women exit; four are taken prisoners; Joaquin enters, followed by Henderson, and staggers as Henderson fires.*)

JOAQUIN: Don't shoot any more. My work is done. (*Falls.*) My wife—my Belloro— I—come. (*Dies.*)

HARRY LOVE: Crime brings its own reward, and the stern hand of justice deals out the weight of its punishment.

END

FOOTNOTES

[1]*American war*: the same conflict described by Americans as The Mexican War, concluded by the Treaty of Guadelupe Hidalgo (2 February 1848), in which California was ceded to the United States, among other concessions, since Mexico lost.

[2]*Serapes*: often colorful blankets or cloaks, worn over the shoulder or shoulders, as well as being used as bedding and cover.

[3]*Maldeta; Ladrones*: a curse (on them); thieves.

[4]*Thumb and forefinger gone*: hence Garcia's nick-name, "Three-Fingered Jack," by which he was best known to fearful Californians.

[5]*Gua-da-la-hair-ah*: playwright Howe's attempt at phonetic spelling of these Mexican States; *hair* should be *har*, in Spanish, but this probably represents then current California American pronunciation.

[6]*Cheto*: obscure; possibly a pet, or paper-tiger.

[7]*Hell!*: a strong oath for the stage at that time.

[8]*Oro*: gold.

[9]*Litany and gown*: the clergy.

[10]*Peones*: peons, peasants.

[11]*Onzas*: Spanish for ounces, but actually a gold coin then worth about $16.

[12]*Santa Anna*: President of Mexico, defeated in the Mexican War.

[13]*Dark lantern*: a metal lantern with no glass; the candlelight is disclosed only when a hinged door is opened.

[14]*Gila*: Gila River.

[15]*Darter*: daughter.

[16]*Yaller-skin or Greaser*: Western American expressions for Mexicans, based on stereotypes about skin-color and oily complexion.

[17]*Short sweetening*: suggested meaning: a lot or a little sugar, but this may refer to different kinds of sweeteners.

[18]*Mount jump up*: you might scare up, or flush out, some game.

[19]*Pleasant dreams*: this quote is a prose restatement of the thought in William Cullen Bryant's much-admired poem, *Thanatopsis*, but its actual author is at present unknown.

[20]*Commovebitur*: from the Roman Catholic liturgy.

[21]*Placers*: the California placer mines, where gold was recovered by panning or washing in sluices.

[22]*Casa*: house.

[23]*Cabeza*: head.

[24]*Vamose*: corruption of *vamos*, or "Let's go," but meaning "Get out of here."

[25]*Hang the Greasers*: advocating vigilante measures, in which American emigrants took the law into their own hands, often acting as judge, jury, and executioners.

[26]*Judge Lynch*: "Lynch-Law," judgment by lynching, or hanging without a legal trial, conviction, and sentence.

[27]*Sacramento!*: this is an oath—"By the Holy Sacrament!"—not a salute to California's state-capital.

[28]*Peace*: supposedly a quote from Joaquin Murieta; possibly from a popular account.

[29]*Take me for?*: despite the hint of the Germanic in "Vat" for "What," this is supposed to suggest an Irish brogue.

[30]*Cosa de esto*: "But I don't know why I'm chained. I don't speak American. In a little while, my friend will be here. By God, I don't understand anything of this."

[31]*Mi patron*: "Many thanks! Many thanks! My leader!"

[32]*These letters*: supposedly a Murieta quote.

[33]*Good use*: supposedly a Murieta quote.

[34]*Offered*: Joaquin Murieta's bravado and sense of humor, in the tradition of Robin Hood, is demonstrated here.

[35]*Honest purposes*: typical American republican sentiments of the period.

[36]*Southern mines*: this was the "Mother Lode" country, site of early gold-strikes of great wealth, including El Dorado, Amador, Calaveras, Tuolumne, and Mariposa Counties; there was also a Northern Mines area, site of later riches in "hard-rock" quartz goldmining.

A
LIVE WOMAN IN THE MINES

OR

PIKE COUNTY AHEAD

A LOCAL PLAY IN TWO ACTS

BY

"OLD BLOCK"[1]
ALONZO DELANO

NOTE

The plot of this play is founded on fact. The history of John and Mary Wilson is that of hundreds who have come to California—and their misfortunes and ultimate success is a type of what many others have experienced within the author's knowledge.

Pike County Jess[2] is only a type of an open, generous, off-hand, uneducated, south and western man—copied from a character I met in crossing the Plains in '49.

High Betty Martin is a specimen of a back-woods, western Amazonian, such as I have seen, not only in the West, but upon the Plains—who is indomitably persevering and brave under difficulties, but withal with woman's feelings when difficulty is over.

Old Swamp, the Judge, Stokes, Ned, and Joe were my companions in the mines; and their disposition to make the best of bad circumstances is a truthful illustration of my messmates. The scene of the petticoat is true in the main, only that the author was the speaker on the occasion. Jones is a veritable character in name, adventures, and vocation. He is at this moment a citizen of San Francisco, and by his own permission I introduce him. His turkey dinner is copied mainly from his own letter to the author.

The other characters are introduced to carry on the plot, but are each as were daily seen in 1850, as well as at the present day.

THE AUTHOR

CHARACTERS

Pike County Jess, The Poet and Philanthropist
John Wilson
Cash ⎫
       ⎬ Gamblers
Dice ⎭
Sluice, the Plucked Pigeon
Judge
Stokes
Joe
Ned
Old Swamp, the Sermonizer
Doctor
Jones, the Printer Man
Express Rider
Watchman
Postmaster
Chinaman
Miners
Mary Wilson, the Live Woman
High Betty Martin (Betsey)

Costume—Modern and Mining[3]

ACT I

SCENE I: *J. Street in Sacramento. Time—about August, 1850.*

(*Enter John and Mary.*)

JOHN: (*Embracing her.*) Ah! Mary! Mary! Is it thus we meet again? No hope—no encouragement?

MARY: Oh, John, I am tired almost to death. I have been walking all day, inquiring for a situation at every respectable house, without success. I offered to do anything: to wash—scrub—in short, to do the most menial service; but every vacancy was filled.

JOHN: How were you received?

MARY: Generally with kindness. Some seemed to pity me, and encourage me with hope; some kindly advised me to go to the Mines and set up a boarding-house, while others looked coldly on me as a suspicious thing, and rudely answered to go somewhere else, they did not want my services, while I occasionally met one who crushed my heart by base insinuations, which, while it brought the blush of shame to my cheek, excited my indignation, that poverty and misfortune should be a mark for rudeness, and that wealth should be entitled to such license.

JOHN: O that I had been with you then! I too have been unsuccessful. I offered to perform any service, no matter how low, if it was honest. I felt willing to engage in any employment suited to my capacities, but I found every place occupied, from the boot-black to the merchant's clerk; and now, without a dime to buy a crust of bread, or provide a simple lodging for her I love better than my own life, I feel as if all hope had fled, and that here in the land of gold, and amidst the splendor of wealth, we are indeed beggars.

MARY: It is hard, John, but I feel it not for myself. When I see your anxious brow, your cheek pale with exertion, scarcely recovered from the debilitating effect of Panama fever,[4] yet struggling manfully to provide something for our subsistence, I forget my own weakness, my own helplessness, and gather fresh courage, and hope against hope and feel from my very soul that we must, we will yet succeed.

JOHN: O, Mary, Mary, why would you leave the comfort of your father's house to share my misery? When our hopes were blasted by the dubious turns of mercantile speculations: when it became necessary for me to try my fortune again in the world, why should you cling to me in the darkest hour, share the perils of the sea, risk the sickness of the tropics, and now be reduced to beggary by my misfortunes? O, Mary, Mary, why did you not let me suffer and die alone?

MARY: (*With fervor.*) You little know the strength of a woman's love. Where her heart is, there is her heaven on earth. I will never leave you till death throws its dark mantle round me; "wither thou goest I will go, thy people shall be my people, and thy God my God."[5]

JOHN: (*Clasping her in his arms passionately.*) You are my guardian spirit—my guiding star. As we have lived together, so will we die. Faint and weary as I am, your words have given me new courage, and with the morning sun we will make one more effort. Surely our countrymen will not let us starve!

MARY: No; a crust will not be refused to honest poverty, and I feel at this moment as if our darkest days had come, and a light must soon glimmer on us. Talk not of death, John, for, till the breath is out of the body, nobody in California dies. Courage then for another effort—aye, another and another, if need be—we will succeed.

JOHN: I never dreamed that you had such resolution.

MARY: And I never knew that I had it till necessity prompted it. I am only like thousands of others who have come to California; who knew not their own strength till occasion developed it.

JOHN: And now for a shelter to pass the night in. If we can only find an empty shed —a vacant tent—(*Crosses.*)

MARY: And if not, the blue vault of heaven beneath the spreading canopy of some friendly oak, with the twinkling stars for lamps will suffice.

JOHN: O, Mary! Has it come to this?

MARY: Hush! my husband. (*They retire up the stage as if in search of a lodging-place.*)

(*Enter Cash and Dice.*)

CASH: How much did you pluck that goose?

DICE: A cool five-thousand.

CASH: Five-thousand! you are in capital luck. How did you come it over the greenhorn so nicely?

DICE: Why, the moment he came in I had my eye on him. I saw he was a green 'un, just from the Mines, and therefore proper game. I carelessly began talking with him and found out that he was on his way home; told me a long yarn about his father and mother; old man was crippled, and the old woman supported the family by washing and all that nonsense, and how he should surprise them when he got home, and that they shouldn't work any more, and all that sort of thing; let out that he had dug a pile by hard labor, and had the money in his belt.

Well, of course I rejoiced with him, commended him as a dutiful son, and to show him my appreciation of so much virtue, insisted on his drinking with me.

CASH: Ha! ha! ha! You're a perfect philanthropist—well—

DICE: At first he rather backed water,[6] but I would take no denial, and I finally succeeded in getting the first dose down him. A little while after, not to be mean, he offered to treat me.

CASH: Of course you was dry.

DICE: Dry as a contribution box. I winked at Tom, so he made Sluice Forks'[7] smash good and strong and somehow forgot to put any liquor in mine.

CASH: What monstrous partiality!

DICE: Directly he began to feel the second dose and grew friendly and confidential. Well, I offered to show him around among the girls, in the evening, with all the sights in town, and at the same time cautioned him against falling into bad hands, for he might be swindled or robbed by strangers.

CASH: Good fatherly adviser—ha! ha! ha!

DICE: Yes, and he grew grateful fast, for he insisted on my drinking with him.

CASH: Ah! that hurt your feelings.

DICE: I told him I seldom drank anything—

CASH: Only when you could get it, I s'pose?

DICE: As he would take no denial I—hem!—reluctantly consented and nodded to Tom, who flavored his glass with morphine and mine, particularly, with cold water.

CASH: You're a practical illustration of a California temperance society.

DICE: It wasn't long before he was the richest man in California, and a damned sight the smartest. Of course he was, so I invited him up to the table to see the boys play. He asked me if I ever played. I told him I seldom staked anything, but what I did I was sure to win, so I threw a dollar on the red.

CASH: And won, of course.

DICE: Of course. And then I proposed that he should try it. He demurred some, but I told him a dollar was nothing—if he lost I would share the loss—so he finally let a dollar slip on the red.

CASH: And won, of course.

DICE: To be sure; our Jake knows what he's about. Sluice Box was absolutely surprised when two dollars were pushed back to him. He then doubled his stakes and went on winning till he thought he had Fortune by the wings, when suddenly his luck changed, and he began to lose and became excited. It was my treat now, and that settled the matter, for he swore he would not leave the table till he had won the money back. So he staked his pile, and we fleeced him out of every dime, and a happier man than Sluice Box is at this moment does not exist.

CASH: How, at being robbed?

DICE: Not that exactly, but, by the time his money was gone he was so beastly drunk that Tim kicked him out of the Round Tent[8] into the gutter, where he now lays fast asleep, getting ready for another trip to the Mines, instead of helping his mother wash at home, and plastering up his father's sore shins.

CASH: Ha! ha! ha! the fools are not all dead. We'll go it while we're young. (*Sings.*) "O, Californy, the land for me."

DICE: Stay! look there; who are they? (*Pointing to John and Mary in the back-*

ground.)

CASH: A devilish fine woman! I say, Dice, there's game; I'm in.

DICE: Wonder who that feller is with her?

CASH: O, some fool of a husband, brother, or lover. What's the difference? It's game and we'll come down on the bank and take our chances.

DICE: Good; I go halves. (*John and Mary advance.*)

CASH: (*Inquiringly.*) Good evening. You are strangers?

JOHN: But recently arrived, sir.

DICE: Eh! looking for lodgings, perhaps?

JOHN: Rather in search of employment. Lodgings, however, are desirable at this hour.

CASH: What business do you wish to engage in?

JOHN: Any that is honorable. The truth is, my means are rather limited at present, and although I was bred a merchant, I am not above earning an honest living in any profitable way.

DICE: And the lady?

JOHN: Is my wife, sir.

CASH: Eh! oh! ah! I say, Mr. Dice, you want a clerk, and my family will afford asylum for the lady.

DICE: Exactly, I think you are just the man I want; good salary, no reference needed.

MARY: You are very kind, gentlemen. Certainly this is unexpected.

CASH: Tut! nothing for California, and—hark ye—there is something in a pretty face and bright eye that—

MARY: (*With reserve.*) Sir!

CASH: O, nothing, nothing—we make bargains in a hurry in Sacramento.

DICE: Well, sir—will you go with me? My business is urgent—I've no time to waste.

JOHN: Please give me your address; I will call in the morning.

DICE: Morning? No, my business is in the evening. Go with me now. Mr. Cash, take the lady to your family—*to your family*, Mr. Cash; I will conduct the gentleman to my office. Come, sir, (*to John*) my office is in the Round Tent.

CASH: Madam, I will conduct you.

JOHN: (*Aside to Mary.*) Mary, I don't half like these men; there is something strange in their manner.

MARY: And I don't like it at all. I will not go without you.

CASH: Come with me, Madam—I have no time to spare. (*Takes her rudely by the arm.*)

MARY: Let me go, sir! I shall not go without my husband.

DICE: He's engaged with me. Come, sir, this way! (*He endeavors to pull him along.*)

CASH: No ceremony in California. I shall introduce you to my family, and (*aside to her*) if a thousand dollars will make you happy, I am your man, my dear.

MARY: (*Struggles as he attempts to pull her along.*) Back, sir—you are a villain.

JOHN: (*Struggles to protect Mary.*) Stand off, sir! Villain, unhand my wife!

DICE: Go it, Cash—now's your time. Be quiet, fool (*to John*), it's a cool thousand; you'll never make money faster nor easier.

(*Mary screams as Cash endeavors to force her off; John struggles to reach her, but is overthrown by Dice, who suddenly draws a pistol, and presents it at him. Enter Pike, running.*)

PIKE: Hillo, mister! Whar ye gwine to with that ar' live woman? Open yer traps, I say, and let 'er go! no jumping another man's claim in these diggins.[9] You won't? (*Knocks Cash down and releases Mary.*) What a gang on 'em! I say, you varmint, pick up yer tools and *vamos*[10] these diggins. Don't undertake to jump a claim that's already prospected. (*Collars Dice and forces him off—Cash gets up and sneaks off.*) Thar, strangers, is a specimen of Pike county justice, and if I catch you in these diggins again, I'll grease yer ears and swaller you whole. (*To them as Cash goes off, left.*)

JOHN: My good fellow, we are under infinite obligations to you.

MARY: Those villains tried to entrap us.

PIKE: Tried to trap you, did they? Set their trap wrong there, for the spring caught their own fingers, anyhow. Who are ye? Whar d'ye come from? Whar ar ye gwine to? What ye doin here, strangers?

MARY: We have just come to California; my husband was sick on the Isthmus; we lost all our money; we have both been trying to get work, but without success. We do not know what to do, or where to go, and were wandering up and down in search of a shelter when those villains assailed us, and you came to our rescue.

PIKE: I hope I may never strike a lead ef you arn't the prettiest speciment of a live woman I've seen in Californy. Don't get mad; I'm only a rough miner, but my mother was a woman, my sister is a woman, Caroline Betsey is a woman, and the last letter she got writ she said she was comin to Californy on her own hook. Is that chap your husband?

MARY: Yes.

PIKE: Wal, old feller, I kind o' have a sneakin for you, jist for your gal's sake. Thar's my fist on it; what may I call your name, stranger?

JOHN: John Wilson, my good fellow.

PIKE: Wal, John Wilson, you're strapped, are you?

JOHN: It is too true; my cash account is rather easily balanced, just now.

PIKE: Don't know whar to roost, eh?

JOHN: Indeed I do not.

PIKE: Well, I live up in the mountains, where you have to dodge to keep out of the way of sunrise; so jist go with me to Stringtown,[11] and set up a boarding-house, or a store, with your gal thar—you'd make money.

JOHN: I really appreciate your kindness, but I have neither the means to get there, nor the money to begin with when I am there.

PIKE: Pshaw! I've got the dust. Say you'll go, and I'll plank down all you want till you can pay. Your gal will keep you honest. I drive three mules and a jackass; come down for supplies for the boys; take the back track to-morrow. Gal, what's your name?

MARY: Mary Wilson, sir. Ha! ha! something of an original.[12] (*To John.*)

PIKE: Wal, Mary Wilson, my gal's name is Carolina Betsey,[13] known at home as High Betty Martin. What do you say—will you go to Stringtown and prospect? Shan't cost you a dime; Old Swamp is thar, and he'll be a father to you, so will

I, and so will all the boys.

MARY: John!

JOHN: Mary!

MARY: Yes, my friend, we will go with you, and thank heaven for the rough diamond it has thrown in our path.

PIKE: Whoora! for a live woman in the mines. What'll the boys say? they'll peel out o' their skins for joy. A live female woman in the mines! wake snakes and dead niggers! turnpikes and railroads come next and steam engines! whoora for Pike county! wheat bread and chicken fixins now—hoe cakes and slapjacks be damned—whoora! I say. Come to my tent under the oak tree in J street, and turn in. By day-light I'll start three mules and a jackass, a greenhorn and a live woman for Stringtown. Injuns and grizzlies clar the track, or a young airthquake will swaller you. Don't be skeered, gal—don't get mad, John; I mean it all right, but it all comes out tail end foremust. A live woman in the mines! fol lol de lol—lol lol de ral. (*Exeunt, left.*)

SCENE II: *Sacramento, in front of the Round Tent, J Street. Time—morning. Sluice discovered lying asleep in the gutter. Enter Watchman, left.*

WATCHMAN: These eternal broils among rowdies, these infernal cases of drunk slightually, and drunk particularly, with the pleasant pastime of dirking,[14] shooting, grabbing, and stealing are enough to try the patience of any Christian watchman this side of Hangtown.[15] I would resign if it wasn't for the chances, now and then, of plucking a partridge, in the way of hush money. That pays slightually; better, too, than city script or corporation notes. It doesn't do to be too hard on a man who has plenty of money. No, no, he wouldn't look well in the station-house; and then I may as well take a good fee for letting them off, as to let the lawyers and judges get it all for letting them off under color of law—besides, it saves time. Poor devils who have no money, and can't pay, why, they're of no use to anybody, and in the station-house they're removed from temptation, and the county settles their bills. Think I won't resign yet awhile. (*Discovers Sluice.*) Ah! here's a subject of contemplation. (*Watches him.*)

SLUICE: (*Starting from sleep.*) I go it on the red—down—yes I'm down—shove it over here, rake her up, old fel—Dice, one brandy smash—two jarvies and a cocktail, plenty of sugar, boy. (*Rubs his eyes.*) Eh! where am I? O, I thought this was Sacramento. What a dream I had. Come boys, it's day-light, time to go to work; Bill, I'll tend the rocker[16] to-day—you pick and I'll wash. (*Getting awake.*) Why, this ain't the Mines. Where have I got to? I thought I was on my claim. (*Looks about.*) Why, this is Sacramento. I'm in Sacramento or Sacramento is in me, I don't exactly know which.

WATCH: Shouldn't be surprised if it was a leetle of both, my young covey. Oblivious, slightually. (*Aside.*)

SLUICE: (*Gets up.*) Is this me—or somebody else? I had a hat; there's none on my head. (*Feeling for it.*) My coat had a tail to it; there's none on this. I had a pair of boots on; somebody's leg has only one on. Somebody has made a devil of a mistake, somehow. I don't remember going to bed; I don't remember any bed going to me. I—I—I—(*feels around him*). Where's my money? Where's my—my dust—my—my—five—thousand—dollars that I had last night? (*Much alarmed.*)

WATCH: (*Aside.*) Five-thousand dollars! Wonder if the *gentleman* has it about him now. If he hasn't I'll take the *loafer* to the station-house.

SLUICE: (*In alarm.*) It's gone—it's gone—'taint here! My money's gone—I've been robbed! (*Frantically.*) My dust is gone! (*Recollecting.*) O, I know—I remember—I was drunk—I played—I—I—O, mother! mother! what have I done? O, father! Murder! murder! (*Shouts.*) Help! help! Thieves! Robbers!

WATCH: Hello! what's all this fuss about, youngster! Be quiet, will you?

SLUICE: I've been robbed! I've lost my money! Every dime is gone!

WATCH: Why then, you are a very poor devil.

SLUICE: I had started for home; I had made my pile; I only got into town yesterday; I went into the round tent; they took me in.

WATCH: You was a stranger, I suppose.

SLUICE: They got me drunk—made me play. The gamblers have got it all—I can't go home. O, mother! mother!—O, father! what will you do now? I can never look you in the face again. I want to die—I ain't fit to live! (*Bursts into tears.*)

WATCH: Look here, my lark, I've seen hundreds in the same fix. You are just the goose for the gamblers to pluck; they're always on the watch for greenhorns from the Mines, and have the little jokers always ready. If you hadn't went to the gambling house you wouldn't have been tempted; if you hadn't drank you would not have been drunk; if you had not got drunk you would not have played; if you had not played you would not have lost your money. Do you understand?

SLUICE: (*Agonized.*) Take me to a tree and hang me forty feet high; I ain't fit to live—I want to die.

WATCH: No; I don't think you are worth hanging, so I'll arrest you, and take you to the station-house. A few days in the prison brig or the chain-gang for being uproarous may bring you to your senses. I'll do what I can legally to comfort you.

(*Enter Betsey, left, in men's boots, with a large ox whip in her hand.*)

BETSEY: Mister, whar's the post-office?

WATCH: Corner K and Third streets.

BETSEY: Anan!

WATCH: Corner K and Third streets, madam.

BETSEY: How far away's that from Sacramento?

WATCH: Why, that's Sacramento, madam.

BETSEY: You don't go for to say them places are in Sacramento. It's the post-office I want. Got sich a thing here? a place whar letter is got out of.

WATCH: I believe here's another case of drunk. Where do you hail from, madam?

BETSEY: I don't neither hail, rain, or snow, mister. I want to find the post-office, I do, for I expect thar's a letter from Jess.

WATCH: Well, you must have dropped down from somewhere. The post-office is on the corner of K and Third streets.

BETSEY: Haven't you got a guide book? I had one coming across the Plains, but I threw it away at Hangtown. It was only a Mormon guide, printed at Salt Lake City, and didn't go only to Hangtown. Folks said the trail was plain from thar to Sac City.

WATCH: Ha! ha! you don't need a guide book to go through our streets. Just go through Second street to K, then turn up K to Third, and there is the post-office on the left.[17]

BETSEY: (*Addressing Sluice.*) Young man, you look as if you'd jist crossed the Plains and had larnt something. Won't you be my guide to the post-office?

SLUICE: Hum! Yes, I crossed the Plains in '49, but I never learned anything till last night in Sacramento. I know more now than I wish I did. (*Groans.*)

BETSEY: Well, show me the way; I'm a stranger in town.

SLUICE: They're bound to take you in, then. But I'll show you the way to the post-office first and die afterwards.

WATCH: Stay, young man, you're my prisoner.

SLUICE: Your prisoner—what for?

BETSEY: What's he done, mister?

WATCH: He got drunk last night and slept in the street but the worst is, he lost all his money, and that is crime enough to commit any man. Didn't play his cards well.

BETSEY: Ar that a fact? Was yer fool enough to gamble?

SLUICE: Alas! it is too true. I had made a pile, started for home, got into bad company, and like a fool, indeed, lost it all and can't go home. I want to die—I ain't fit to live.

BETSEY: Young man, you ar a fool—you was a fool to gamble, but you ar a bigger fool to cry when the egg is broke. When you was on the Plains, what did you do when your gun missed fire at a buffalo—sit down and cry over it?

SLUICE: No, I picked the priming and tried it again. Any man would do that.

BETSEY: Did yer cry because yer lost the buffalo?

SLUICE: No, I was ready for the next and blazed away.

BETSEY: Right! so don't be a fool, but once in Californy. Pick your priming, put on another cap, go to the Mines, and blaze away for another pile. You're only in a slough—dig out and keep out.

WATCH: She's a true California woman, grit to the back-bone.

SLUICE: She gives my heart ease. Perhaps I can make my pile again; there's hope, anyhow, and I'll try.

BETSEY: Mr. Constable, don't be hard on the man. What may I call your name, mister?

SLUICE: It used to be Bill Sluice when I was at home—'taint much of anything now.

BETSEY: Well, Mr. Constable, don't come it too savage on a broken Sluice. Let me have him; Uncle Jo is sick in my wagon, and I'm tired of driving. He don't play cards any more if my eye is on him. Let him go, I'll take care of him.

WATCH: Ha! ha! ha! Ah! madam, there's no resisting your insinuating manners. I never could resist the glance of the fair sex. Go, young man, and beware of round tents and gambling gentlemen. Can't make anything out of him, anyhow. (*Aside, and exit, right.*)

BETSEY: Well, Sluice, will you go with me?

SLUICE: Yes, I'll go anywhere—to the devil, if you will, so that I can hide from myself.

BETSEY: Well, take my whip and show me the way to the post-office. Up Second street, down Third street, through B street, across Q street. I wish I had a spellin book—I disremember all the letters.

SLUICE: (*Leading.*) This is the way to the round tent—eh! I mean to the post-office. (*Exeunt.*)

SCENE III: *K Street, corner Third. Enter Sluice and Betsey.*

SLUICE: There's the post-office.

BETSEY: Whar?

SLUICE: There! Don't you see the sign?

BETSEY: What, that little painted board with black letters?

SLUICE: Yes, that's the sign.

BETSEY: Humph! a mighty little sign for sich a big house. 'Taint a quarter as big as the sign on the starn of a Missouri steamboat, nor half so pretty. What does it spell?

SLUICE: Post-office.

BETSEY: Whar's the figger-head?

SLUICE: I don't think they have one any more than I have; if they have they've served it as the gamblers did me—took it in.

BETSEY: Wal, rap at the door. (*He raps gently two or three times, and no response.*) Lord! Sluice, sich raps wouldn't wake a snake under a sage bush. Give me the gad and stand from under. (*Raps furiously.*) Hello! the post-office.

POSTMASTER: (*Puts his head out of the window—his night cap on.*) Who's there, making all that noise?

BETSEY: Ha! ha! ha! I thought I'd raise a figure-head.

POSTMASTER: What do you want at this time in the morning?

BETSEY: Are you the post-office, mister?

POSTMASTER: I am the post*master*, madam. What do you want?

BETSEY: I want my letter—and be quick about it—I'm in a hurry.

POSTMASTER: Go to the devil.

BETSEY: I shan't do no sich thing. Give me my letter, and keep your sauce for them as wants it. I don't.

POSTMASTER: Office opens at eight o'clock—come then. (*Shuts the window.*)

BETSEY: Wal, ef that don't beat a black wolf for impudence. The varmint shows his teeth in your very face. Eight o'clock! Humph! By that time we'd be more'n eight miles out of town. Now, my letter I will have; so thar! I'll have that figger-head out agin, or know the reason why. (*Raps furiously.*) Come out o' yer hole, you old badger, or I'll pen you up so you can't get out.

POSTMASTER: (*Opening the window.*) Didn't I tell you to come at eight o'clock?

BETSEY: And didn't I tell you to get my letter now? You don't sleep another wink till you give me my letter.

POSTMASTER: (*Tartly.*) How do you know you have one?

BETSEY: Wal, I don't, but I ought to have one. Look and see.

POSTMASTER: Where on earth do you come from?

BETSEY: Didn't I come all the way from Pike county, across the Plains? Didn't my Uncle Joe get sick on the Desert, and didn't I drive the team in? Didn't I stand guard agin the Indians? Didn't I—Do you see this pretty plaything? (*Suddenly draws a pistol and presents it.*) Shall I take a lock of yer hair off your figure-head, like I did the scalp lock from a digger on the Humboldt? Say, will you give me my letter—yes or no?

POSTMASTER: I'll do anything to get rid of you. What's your name?

BETSEY: Caroline Elizabeth Martin, commonly know as High Betty Martin, in the Settlements. You'll see it on the letter if you can read hand write. Will you look?

POSTMASTER: Yes, yes—I'll look. (*Disappears.*)

BETSEY: Thar, Sluice, do you see that? Ef you *will* do a thing you will if you only will. You see that some things can be done as well as others, and there's no use to cry for being a fool oncst in a while.

SLUICE: You have taught me a lesson I shan't forget. I'll go to the Mines and be a man again.

POSTMASTER: (*Opens the window and hands out a letter.*) Here, Bedlam. (*Retires.*)

BETSEY: I know'd it! I know'd it! Jess is true as a percussion—a snap and a boo! bang! Thar, Sluice, read it to me. I don't know much about dictionary larnin; we hoed corn and pulled flax, in the Settlements—we did.

SLUICE: (*Opens the letter and reads.*) "Dear Carolina Betsey:—I take my pick in hand—I mean my pen—and hope you ar enjoying the same blessing. My stake is stuck at Stringtown, on Feather River. Beef is four bits a pound, and scarce at that. Hard bread and hard work is plenty sometimes, but difficult to get. I drive three mules and a jackass, and slapjacks and molasses is our common doins; but corn dodgers and hoe cake and possom fat can't be got no how. Take the trail to Stringtown and don't stop at Humbug, for the diggers is poor thar. 'My pen is poor, my ink is pale, / One of my mules has lost his tail.'—Bit off by a grizzly. Respectfully yours, Jessy Jenkins, known here as Pike County Jess."

BETSEY: Wal, I declar! Jess always was a scholard—he licked the schoolmaster oncst—and then he writes so sentimental like, so poetetic—Stringtown, Feather River—three mules and a jackass—thar's whar I'm gwine. Come along, Sluice. Who haw! Gee up, Berry! (*Exeunt.*)

SCENE IV: *Stringtown Hill.—Wild and romantic high mountains around, and in the distance, with deep ravines. A tent is discovered, closed.—Pike is seen lying outside, in his blankets.*

PIKE: (*Rousing up from sleep.*) Cock-a-doodle-doo-oo-oo! (*Crowing.*) The lizards are crawlin out, and it's time for me to crawl out too. The gal and her man seem to sleep—I'll let 'em snooze till I get my mules up.

(*Enter Mary, from the tent.*)

PIKE: Eh, what! rolled out so airly? Did you stand guard all night, gal?

MARY: Good morning, Pike. No, I slept soundly; the ground seemed as soft as a bed of down, and oh! such sweet dreams!

PIKE: All in use, all in use, gal—only get used to it. Feather beds are only a vexation—in fact, they're only modern inventions to make people lazy—and I'll marry no gal who sleeps on one; she'd want me to git up and get breakfast for her. Eh! here's another prairie dog crawling out of his hole—(*Enter John.*) I'll warrant the red ants drove him from his nest.

JOHN: No, I never slept better, and I begin to like mountain life. I turned out to help you pack the mules.

PIKE: No, no, you tried that yesterday, and what work you made of it. Pack turned, your gal rolled down hill, mule rolled after her; pots, pans, and crockery smashed up, and if you hadn't moved your boots, pretty freely you'd have been smashed too.

MARY: For heaven's sake, John, don't pack my mule again, if you have any regard for me. I think something of my own bones yet.

PIKE: The fact ar thar's about as much riggin about a mule to secure a cargo as there is about a clipper.[18] You don't know how to trim your load, and ef you don't trim right and tighten right, your cargo will be turning somersets,[19] as your gal did yesterday, worse nor a circus rider. No greenhorn knows the quirks and flumadiddles of an aparaho.[20]

JOHN: Ha! ha! I hope you don't consider me a greenhorn by this time.

MARY: *I* do, John, of the greenest kind.

PIKE: Thar! the gal git my sentiments exactly. All you are fit for is to hippah mula.[21] Whar did your wife go to comin over Bidwell ridge? humph! took lodgings in a clump of mansinieto[22] bushes. You followed like a ten-pin ball, and Short-Tail came within an ace of making a ten-strike after you, and the rattling of frying-pans and coffee-pots was worse than the gongs of a Chinese theatre.[23]

MARY: It was a Providential escape, however.

PIKE: I don't think Providence had anything to do with it. It was all owing to John's miserable packin. Short-Tail is a varmint that never tempts Providence, nohow; I've driv him a year, and never knew the animal to stampede, lay down, or dodge in the bushes before, and I think it was all because a greenhorn packed him, and a live woman rid him.

JOHN: It is possible, but I won't be a greenhorn long, ha! ha! Well, where are we, Pike?

PIKE: On the pinnacle of Stringtown Hill. That gulch that daylight doesn't shine into is whar the South Fork of Feather flows. To get to it, you've got to roll and tumble about a mile down into the bowels of the airth, and when you get to the bottom, you can hear the tinkers at work on the other side. If it wasn't for the ravines and side gulches, the quickest way to get down would be to roll, but as it is, you'd be squashed into a jelly by going it on the perpendicular over the crags; so we have to go it zigzag, like a water snake, till we fetch up on the first bench for a breathin spell.

MARY: How in the world are we to get to the bottom of such a gulf?

PIKE: Thar's only one way that I knows of.

MARY: How is that?

PIKE: Lend me your petticoat.

MARY: My petticoat? gracious!

JOHN: A petticoat, Pike—you're jesting.

PIKE: A petticoat—I want to borrow a petticoat—I do.

MARY: To get me down the hill?

PIKE: Sartain.

JOHN: Explain.

PIKE: Why, a public officer must always have his vouchers, and I, being commissary and wagon-master, must have mine. I can't get a live woman, three mules, and a jackass into camp at oncst—no human could do it down sich a hill. The boys in the cabin must be short of feed, and they shan't go hungry; so the mules must go with the provisions fust, and you must wait till the next load. Now, if I go into camp and tell the boys I've got a live female woman as part cargo, they'll think I'm drunk or crazy and won't believe a word—but if I show the papers, with a clear bill of health, they'll acknowledge the corn, and tote you in.

MARY: Ha! ha! Well, if I can't reach the diggins without a passport, you shall have it. (*Goes into the tent and brings out a petticoat.*) Here it is, and I hope they'll believe the book.

PIKE: All O.K. Now make yourselves comfortable till I bring up pay dirt. (*Goes out, and is heard driving his mules.*) Get up, Mula! ah, Short-Tail! huppah! Mula—arriva! arrea, Jacky. Huppah! you devils! huppah! (*Exeunt, left.*)

SCENE V: *The Hill, lower down. Jones discovered clinging to a tree.*

JONES: (*Solo.*) Here I am, brought up all standing, with a round turn at that. If this isn't the cussedest hill in all Californy! I don't know which end up I came down. If it hadn't been for this pine, the Lord only knows where I should have went to. I'll hold on to the roots and take an observation. (*Sits down.*) I wonder where this trail leads to—wonder if there is anything to eat at the bottom of the gulch—wonder if I shall live to get there? O, my stomach! um! (*Groans.*) What would I give to see a water cart coming down the hill, loaded with bread, bacon, and brandy cocktails, and smash up against this tree! O, Jones, you won't be Jones much longer. O, my stomach! (*Groans.*)

PIKE: (*Outside.*) Stop that mule! stop that mule! d——n[24] her! don't you see Short-Tail going over the rocks? (*Rushes in.*) Why the d——l didn't you stop that infarnel varmint?

JONES: (*Lugubriously.*) Humph! It was all I could do to stop myself, and if it hadn't been for this tree, my carcass wouldn't have stopped rolling for the next generation. (*Groans.*)

PIKE: It's the first time I ever know'd Short-Tail to stampede; and it's all owin to bein rid by a woman. I believe, in my soul, that woman will make a stampede among all the mules and asses in the diggins.

JONES: Stranger, you haven't got such a thing as a biscuit about ye, have ye? I'm so hungry that I could eat a young digger,[25] and wash it down with about a gallon of brandy, and three of the biggest dams on the Yuba.

PIKE: Why, who ar you—what ar you prospecting here for?

JONES: My name is Jones, and I've stuck my stake here because I can't stick it anywhere else.

PIKE: Jones—I've heard that name before. Any relation of Sam Jones, the fisherman, who fished for clams off Sandy Hook?

JONES: No, I don't belong to that family, though I've been going it hook and line for the last three years.

PIKE: Maybe you're John Jones, stranger?

JONES: Nary time—he was hung, in company with John Brown and John Smith, at Nevada.

PIKE: Wal, who the d——l ar you, anyhow?

JONES: My name's Bill Jones called for short William E. Jones, Esq., type-setter by profession and roller by practice, for I rolled from the top of this hill till I brought up against this tree.

PIKE: O! a printer man, ar ye? Goin to establish a paper in the diggins?

JONES: Well, I've had a press for the last forty-eight hours. My *form* is about *locked up*, and my leader, I think will be an obituary, with an epitaph on the death of the late editor, William E. Jones, Esq. Humph! I'm about knocked into pie—I wish a pie was knocked into me. (*Groans.*)

PIKE: I'm glad to see you, old fellow. Thar's a good opening for a paper at String-town, and I always patronize a paper. What will it be—the Stringtown Gazette?

JONES: Yes, and I shall gazette my own death and burial in the maus of the Cayotes,[26] I reckon. Haven't you got the least slice of pork, a handful of dried beans about you? I havn't ate a mouthful for three days, and I'm as hungry as a printer's devil.

PIKE: What! haven't ate for three days? Why, you are famishing. Hold on till I overhaul[27] "Short-Tail." Why, I'll divide the last biscuit with you, and give you the biggest half. (*Runs out and brings in a pack.*) Here, here, old fellow, here's liquor; here's bacon, here's bread—pitch in, pitch in—thar's beans, thar's cold slapjacks,[28] thar's—thar's—pitch in—no surface diggins, lay hold, and go to the bed rock.

JONES: (*Laughs deliriously.*) Ha! ha! ha! The water cart's come. I say, waiter, a broiled chicken, with butter gravy—don't be particular—cook the whole of her, coop, feathers and all. (*Seizes a bottle.*) Gentlemen, your health—ha! ha! ha! (*Drinks and eats.*) Do you know what I think?

PIKE: Poh! how should I?

JONES: Well, I think that Noah never had a sweeter piece of bacon in the ark than this. Hogs are delicious animals, ain't they?

PIKE: Judging by some speciments I've seen, I think they're rather voracious. All right, all right—a streak of luck for you, Bill Jones. Now tell me how you got in close quarters.

JONES: Why, you see—(*drinks*)—your health—I like good manners next to good fare. I had a claim in Jackass Gulch, but it got so d——d poor, it didn't pay but an ounce a day, and I couldn't stand that, and I determined to find better diggins. I heard they were taking out fifty dollars to a man on Humbug Flat, so Jim Simmons, from Whiskey Bar, and Sam Slope, from Shirt Tail Canyon, come along, and we agreed to go prospecting together. We loaded a mule with provisions, and struck across the South Fork of Yuba in search of Humbug, and I've found it to a dead certainty.

PIKE: Wal?

JONES: Towards evening of the second day, we halted on a little branch. The boys were gathering wood to build a fire, and I was about unpacking the mule, when an almighty grizzly, with two cubs, rushed out of the chapparel,²⁹ and made at us with a mouth open seventeen miles wide. It was devil take the hindmost with us; the boys broke for the tall timber; I climbed a tree, while our mule took a stampede as if seven devils was on her trail.

PIKE: Wal, that was funny. Ha! ha! ha! How did you go it on a swinging limb?

JONES: Why, old griz seemed to think my flesh was the sweetest and tried to climb after me, to get a taste of my toe nails, but the tree was too small, she couldn't get up.

PIKE: Ha! ha! Why didn't you come down?

JONES: Why, I thought if she would let me alone, I would her, and more particularly as the boys had run off with the rifles, and my pistol had no cap on. Well, we sat and grinned at each other for about an hour, and I out-grinned her—she got ashamed of herself and concluded to go somewhere else for a supper.

PIKE: What became of the boys?

JONES: D——d if I know. As soon as I thought it would answer, I slid down and hunted about for the mule and shouted for the boys; but they were gone, hook and line, so I wandered about till midnight, when I turned in all alone, without a blanket or a biscuit—but it wasn't long before I found myself in a settlement.

PIKE: What, when you was all alone?

JONES: Yes, for I found that in the dark I had laid down on a nest of red ants, and in ten minutes I wished myself in the mouth of the old bear, just for a change.

PIKE: Why, yes, that was murder by inches, without benefit of a rope.

JONES: When daylight came, I found I wasn't anywhere, with all the world before me. I was teetotally lost, and all I could do, I couldn't find myself; so I kept going on for three days, when I struck this trail, and I knew it would bring me out somewhere, if I could only hold on—and sure enough, it brought me up with a side-winder against this tree, and if you hadn't come along I should have gone to *quad*, and my *composing stick* filled with *dead lines* and a *dash*.³⁰

PIKE: Wal, Bill Jones, you're on the right trail, now; a few more rolls will bring you to our cabin right side up.

JONES: I'm fond of rolls, but I like 'em hot and well buttered, best.

PIKE: The boys will be glad to see you. We'll set you up and all take your paper. Plenty of contributors in the diggins, too—in fact, you needn't write any thing yourself. Thar's Old Swamp great on sarmons—can go it like a cart-horse. The Judge is a tall coon on law; Stokes is a ra'al wiggler on polotics and can bray a speech like a jackass, and I'm a riproarer on poetry.

JONES: You a poet?

PIKE: You may lay your life on that! Never read my poem on true love, did you?

JONES: No.

PIKE: I reckon not—the printer man at Sacramento wouldn't print it—didn't 'preciate genius, but you shall print it, and we'll sell it at two bits a copy and divide the profits, old fel. O, it's capital. (*Reciting.*)
  "O, Carolina Betsy's yaller hair
  Has laid my heart and innards bare."

JONES: There, there—take a drink, and let the rest go till we get to the bottom of the hill. There is genuine poetry in your heart, if there is not in your poem, and I'll set *you* up in capitals, if I don't your *rhymes.*

PIKE: Well, help me straighten up Short-Tail, who's lodged in the mansinietos, and we'll straighten the pome when your press gets to grinding.

JONES: Go ahead. For once in my life I'm in luck. (*Exeunt.*)

SCENE VI: *Inside of a miner's cabin; a group of miners variously engaged—some mending clothes, some cooking, some washing clothes at the wash-tub, some lying in bunks; Old Swamp is trying to bake slapjacks in a frying-pan.*

JOE: (*Trying to mend boot with fork.*) I say, Old Swamp, I'm savage as a meat-ax—ain't breakfast most ready. The lizards have been licking their chops the last hour.

OLD SWAMP: (*Trying to turn a cake in the pan.*) Swallow a piece of your boot, Joe, to keep your stomach. This is the last we've got, any how, and unless Pike gets back pretty soon, you'll have a chance to girt up, Indian fashion, unless you're good at catching rats.

JOE: Traps are all broke—powder gone—and rats shy and half starved, Old Swamp. Have to go it on fried boots.

OLD SWAMP: Leetle too much cold water in this batter—the cakes don't get done brown, and don't turn easy.

JOE: Put a little whisky in 'em, Old Swamp—they'll soon turn over on their own hook.

OLD SWAMP: Pshaw! the Judge and Stokes drank up the last drop—not enough left te wet your eye. No matter—the cakes will go further half cooked.

STOKES: (*At the wash tub.*) Judge, I see you are on the bench—what case is on the docket for to-day?

JUDGE: (*Mending a very ragged pair of pants.*) Action for rents—an old suit—parties trying to compromise.

STOKES: What's the prospect, Judge?

JUDGE: (*Holds up the pants.*) Doubtful whether the parties agree. I can see through the *hole,* but the parties may trick anon for a new trial—they're trying to patch it up somehow.

STOKES: How is the evidence?

JUDGE: Strong on one side—and a good deal of re-button testimony will be required to uphold the suit. Old Swamp, I want to examine you.

OLD SWAMP: Want me to swear, Judge?

JUDGE: No, no—you swear wickedly enough every day to answer any court in the mines.

OLD SWAMP: Then you won't take me up for contempt?

JUDGE: Not if you go according to Bacon.

OLD SWAMP: I've been on bacon the last fifteen minutes, and it's the last piece in the cabin; there isn't grease enough in the bone to fry itself—but it will go further half cooked.

JUDGE: Stand aside—such testimony won't pay my fees—you'll starve judge, jury, and all the parties out.

OLD SWAMP: Have to stay proceedings for want of grease to grease the griddle. It's a fact—we can't go on much longer.

STOKES: (*Who is washing a shirt—sleeves rolled up.*) The question of ways and means is before the house.

JOE: "Hark! from the tombs a doleful sound."

STOKES: Mr. Speaker—I call the gentleman to order. A thorough renovation is necessary to our larder, gentlemen; our stores have been consumed; the relentless rats—

JOE: Two-legged rats, Mr. Speaker.

STOKES: I call the gentleman to order. The bill which I am about to offer to the house will have a soaporific effect upon the shirt bosoms of my constituents.

JOE: Hope I shan't have to pay the gentleman's bill, Mr. Speaker; too much liquor in it for a temperance man.

STOKES: I say, Mr. Speaker, my bill will have a soaporific effect.

JUDGE: On the bowels, man—on the bowels. Hang your law and legislation for spare diet; empty stomachs require strong tonics and stimulants.

OLD SWAMP: Not pork enough left to stimulate the stomach of a horned toad—only a mouthful left.

JOE: Enough for a taste all round. Tie a string to it—swallow it and pull it back again—and so let it go around; you'll all have a taste, and a grand operation will be produced.

JUDGE: I object to such practice in my court; some knave of a lawyer will bite the string off, and the bacon will be teetotally incarcerated.

STOKES: Mr. Speaker—the gentleman's plan is ingenious, but will not apply to all cases. Some of my constituents have throats that no string can fathom, if I may judge by the streams of fluid running down.

JOE: Dam them up, then, by tying a string tight outside.

OLD SWAMP: Don't be afraid, boys—if worse comes to worst, we'll mend the traps and go it on rats; I'm great on trappin.

JOE: O, for a friccaseed rat. Here, Old Swamp, fry that—(*throws his boot out*)—don't cook it quite done, it will go further; it has already gone several miles. (*Sings.*)

O, Susannah, don't you cry for me—
I'm eating up my boots in Californi*ee*.

JUDGE: Hark! there's a noise at the door.

JOE: Some poor devil coming to beg a breakfast—I shall have to divide my boot with him. Old Swamp, don't cook it done—'twill go further.

OLD SWAMP: Boys, it's Pike; I know the tramp—it's Pike and the jackass. Plenty to eat now.

(*Enter Pike and Jones.*)

ALL: Huzzah! for Pike—huzza! for Short-Tail, slapjacks and molasses! Pork and beans now, and no mistake.

PIKE: I'm glad to see you, boys. Thar's no place like home arter[31] all, with plenty of hog and hominy—hoe cake and possum fat.

OLD SWAMP: Two days over time, Pike. We concluded the diggers were on your trail, and that you had fell into the stomach of a digger squaw like a roasted caterpillar.

PIKE: Never fell into a woman's bosom as deep as that in all my life. Devil to pay with Short-Tail; got rid by a witch; took the stampede; rolled down hill, and finally, Short-Tail and I got into the editor business, and picked up a printer man, who was mighty near struck off; hadn't ate a mouthful in a month, and the way he pitched into the bacon and brandy was like a greenhorn on his first day's work. Here he is, boys—let him dig for himself now.

JONES: I'm like a licked politician, gentlemen—nothing to say but keep up a devil of a thinking. My long primer was about run out, and if Pike hadn't come along, I shouldn't have had an index by this time.

OLD SWAMP: A miner's latch string is always out—pull, and the door of his heart, as well as his cabin, will open to distress. We'll divide our last biscuit with you.

JUDGE: We will share such as we have with you.

STOKES: I vote aye to that.

JOE: Old Swamp, cook t'other boot now—well done and plenty of gravy.

JONES: No abbreviations of periods to my thanks, gentlemen—I am an exclamation—not a single leaded column in my heart.

PIKE: Thar, Bill Jones, didn't I tell you so? Depend upon it, ef thar's a mean streak in a man so long (*measures the tip of his finger*), it's bound to come out of him in California, and ef he has got a good streak he can't keep it in, no how you can fix it.[32] Boys, do you know what this is? (*Holds up the petticoat.*)

OLD SWAMP: You've been stealing a white shirt, Pike.

STOKES: It's a long petition on parchment, for the relief of widows—grass widows, Mr. Speaker.

JOE: No, no, it's a table-cloth to eat fried boots on. (*Pike gets into it.*)

JUDGE: It's a petticoat, by heavens! O Blackstone, what revolution is at hand?

MINERS: A petticoat! A petticoat! Huzza! huzza!

OLD SWAMP: What female woman have you murdered to get that skin?

PIKE: Do you s'pose I'd kill a woman to get her petticoat? I'd rather destroy a dozen petticoats to get one live woman, you varmints—and you know it, you do. I hope I may never strike a lead[33] if the animal didn't give it to me with her own hands.

STOKES: You've robbed some washerwoman's clothes line in Sacramento.

PIKE: Nary time, old fellow. Haven't been near a clothes line since my mother walloped me with one for drowning kittens in the wash tub. The fact ar, the animal who owns this skin is at the top of the hill, and sends this by Short-Tail, with her compliments, and hopes you'll help her down.

OLD SWAMP: A real live woman comin to the Mines—unpossible!

PIKE: As true as yer born, boys. Short-Tail and I fetched her ourselves—she put the devil into the mule tho'.

JOE: The millenium has come!

PIKE: No, it's only a woman.

JOE: Let's eat breakfast in a hurry and go and tote her into town.

JUDGE: D——n the breakfast, boys—let us go and get a sight of her before the dew carries her off.

STOKES: Slapjacks and molasses would be worse than emetics now. Let's hear from you, old minister—what do you say?

OLD SWAMP: (*Slowly and with emphasis.*) Joe, take down that fiddle and rosin the bow.

JOE: (*Jumps after it.*) It's in tune, and if it ain't it's no matter.

OLD SWAMP: Now, boys, remember you had mothers oncst—don't make fools of yourselves, but make a carcle. (*They circle around Pike.*) Now Joe, give us Hail Columby, Star Spangled, Yankee Doodle, and Rory O'More all at oncst! and, boys, let your legs go prospecting as if the richest kind of a lead was before you. Try your boots, boys—try your boots. (*Plays a lively air; miners dance merrily around Pike in a grotesque manner.*)

PIKE: (*Unable to contain himself, dances inside the ring, crowing.*) Cock-a-doodle-doo-oo-oo!

(*Joe becomes too much excited to play and capers about without music.*)

STOKES: Hello! We've danced the fiddle into the negative. Old Swamp, take it up where Joe left off.

OLD SWAMP: (*Sings.*)
    A petticoat flag is the miner's delight—
    It awakens sweet thoughts of our mothers at home;
    Our sweethearts and wives to dear memory bright:
    All the girls we will welcome whenever they come.

Now, boys, get your rifles and pistols—Joe, hand me the whisky bottle. Form line, boys—form line; go it in millintary order. Joe, give us General Washington's most particular grand march. (*Joe plays.*) Shoulder arms! forard march.

MINERS: Huzza! huzza for a "live woman in the mines." (*Exeunt.*)

SCENE VII: *The top of the hill. Miners enter before the tent—give a cheer and fire a salute; Mary screams inside, and John rushes out alarmed.*

JOHN: Good heavens, gentlemen! what is the matter?

MINERS: Old Swamp! Old Swamp!

OLD SWAMP: (*Gets up on a rock.*) Stranger, we were white men oncst; it seems like a very long time ago—but we have a tradition that some of us wore white shirts and short beards, but it is so long, I don't vouch for it. It has been handed down to us, by various letters through the post-office, that we war born into the world, and that our mothers were live female women. It is so long since we have seen a woman, that we don't exactly know what they are, but the doctor here says a woman is a female man of the human *specie*. Pike County Jess showed us a skin of a strange animal and swears it belongs to a female woman of the human specie; he says, too, that you have caught the animal and had her alive on exhibition. Now, stranger, we want to take a look at the thing, and I pledge you my honor we won't stampede her.

JOHN: Ha! ha! ha! gentlemen—well, this is a droll specimen of the mines—yes, I have caught such an animal—rather rabid, but if you will risk the consequences, I'll show her up.

OLD SWAMP: We'll take the chances—trot her out—trot her out.

(*Exit John into the tent. Enter John and Mary.*)

MINERS: Huzza for "a live woman in the mines!" Huzza for our mothers, our wives, and sweethearts at home!

PIKE: Huzza for Carolina Elizabeth Martin!—commonly known as High Betty Martin—that's my gal, it is.

MINERS: Huzza! Huzza!

MARY: Gentlemen, I thank you for your kind reception—may I be able to make you some return?

OLD SWAMP: Hi! gal! won't you sew the buttons on our pants? won't you make light bread and bunkum hoe-cake? won't you make good gruel for a sick miner? won't you make us wear white shirts of a Sunday, and help Pike make poetry and me sarmons?

MARY: Indeed, I'll do all I can for you, I'm sure. O, John, when we were starving in Sacramento, we little thought of finding such warm hearted friends in the mines!

OLD SWAMP: Friends, gal? why we'd all be fathers and mothers and brothers and sisters to you. Boys, a drink all round! here, gal—beauty before age. (*Hands her the bottle; she drinks from it.*[34]) Now, boys, strike the tent. (*Tent is taken down.*) Make a chair for the gal, two o' ye. (*They make a chair by clasping hands.*) Three cheers for the first "live woman in the mines." (*Cheers.*)

JOE: Three cheers for the first white man who brought his wife to the mines.

PIKE: And three cheers for High Betty Martin, who's coming to the mines.

(*The Miners seat Mary between them; others shoulder John; Joe strikes up a march; Pike raises the petticoat for a flag as they march out. Curtain on picture.*)

END OF ACT I

ACT II

SCENE I: *A deep gulf.—Hillsides rocky and steep, and covered with undergrowth. An emigrant wagon a little in the background.*

(*Enter Betsey and Sluice.*)

BETSEY: Sluice, whar are we?

SLUICE: According to the best of my judgment, we are here.

BETSEY: Lord, Sluice! any fool knows that. But whar's our wharabouts?

SLUICE: In a devilish deep gulch, in my opinion.

BETSEY: How are we to get out of it?

SLUICE: I don't know, unless we wait till the world gets upside-down and fall out.

BETSEY: Ain't thar no cend[35] to it?

SLUICE: Yes, one end has a perpendicular fall over the rocks a hundred feet—the other end hasn't any beginning, so far as I can see.

BETSEY: What on airth did we come down for?

SLUICE: I don't know any other reason than by the force of gravitation, and woman's will. I told you we had better head the gulch, and go around it, but no, down you would come, over rocks and bushes, and now you are like a rat in a trap—can't neither back out nor go further. Now you see where woman's will has brought you to.

BETSEY: I don't care a snap, Bill Sluice. I wasn't going six miles around to make half a mile—I go it on short cuts, I do.

SLUICE: Well, we shall go it on short cuts now, for it won't take long to starve to death here.

BETSEY: Who talks of starving to death? If you are so easily discouraged, you'd better go back to Sacramento and practice in the Round Tent.

SLUICE: I had rather starve to death with you.

BETSEY: Good. If worse comes to worse, we'll pack the cattle, leave the wagon, and work our way to Stringtown.

SLUICE: And leave Uncle Joe sick to be eaten up by the wolves.

BETSEY: No, no, no—that won't do—no, never. You shall go to Stringtown, hunt up Jess, bring him here, and then we'll take our wagon to pieces,[36] carry it up the hill wheel at a time, shoulder Uncle Joe, drive the cattle up, put the wagon together, and—whoa! haw! Berry, who's afraid?

SLUICE: A woman's wit, a woman's wit forever! It's a pity you wasn't a man.

BETSEY: Why, Sluice?

SLUICE: You'd make a capital general. You would have fought your way through Mexico as well as General Taylor,[37] without men, money or provisions.

BETSEY: I should need better soldiers than you, then.

SLUICE: Can't I shoot—can't I fight—can't I dig?

BETSEY: Yes, and you can lay in the gutter like a loafer.

SLUICE: Um! (Groans.) That's ungenerous.

BETSEY: Pshaw! you draw a close sight, but you can't stand grief—you're like a faithful dog—can fight well, but want somebody to set you on. You'd make a good soldier, but a poor general.

SLUICE: I give it up—there is no use in disputing with a woman. Let her have her own way, and its all sunshine—contradict her, and a thunder storm raises directly. Well, general, what is to be done?

BETSEY: Put a piece of bread and bacon in your pocket, shoulder your rifle, and go out on scout, and see if thar's any place to get our wagon out. I'll stand guard over the cattle and Uncle Joe, and mind, don't you come back without finding a trail—d'ye hear?

SLUICE: (Going.) I'm gone.

BETSEY: Stop!

SLUICE: I'm stopped.

BETSEY: Whar's your rifle?

SLUICE: In the wagon.

BETSEY: Get it. Never stir from your camp in a wild country without your arms. Suppose you meet an Indian, or a grizzly—what show would you have for your own skin?

SLUICE: Right again, general. The fact is, if California is ever invaded by an enemy, with a regiment of Pike County women we can defy the devil. (Gets his rifle, and exits.)

BETSEY: (Sitting down on a rock.) O, dear, what trouble I have in hunting up a man—come two-thousand miles and havn't found him yet; ef it had been any body else but Jess, I'd seen all the men hung first, afore I'd wore out so much shoe-leather in running arter 'em! Ef it hadn't been for him, I'd have been hoein corn and pulling flax on the plantation now, instead of climbing these hills. These pesky men do bother our heads so orfully when they do get in; thar's no getting along without one—and after all thar isn't one in a hundred that's worth the trouble they give us. Then, like a flea, thar's no sartinty of catching one—for just as yer get yer finger on him, like as any way he's hoppin off arter somebody else. Let me catch Jess hoppin arter somebody else. Giminy! wouldn't I give him jessie?—wouldn't I crack him? O, Jess, Jess—you run arter somebody else! O, murder! O, ef he should? O! O! (Weeps.) I'm a poor, lone, lorn woman—Uncle

Joe sick—lost in the mountains—and Jess, my Jess, to serve me so! My courage is gone—my boots worn out—wagon tire getting loose—my best har comb broke—all trying to find a man, and him to use me so. (*Weeps.*) It will break my heart! O! O! O! (*A gun shot is heard.*) Ha! (*Springs up and listens.*) Sluice in trouble? (*Forgets her lamentation instantly; runs to the wagon and seizes a rifle.*) Keep still, Uncle Joe—ef thar's danger, I'm ready for it.

(*Enter Sluice, running.*)

BETSEY: What is it, Sluice—what is it?

SLUICE: O, nothing in particular—no harm done yet—can't say what may come.

BETSEY: Let it come, Sluice; only give us a fair chance for a skrimmage.

SLUICE: I was picking my way through the chapparel, when I discovered fresh digger tracks, and I thought some of the Indians were lurking about to stampede our cattle. Directly I got a glimpse of one of the rascals, and I thought I'd give him leave to quit, so I just put a ball through the top of his hair, and such an almighty yell you never heard, and such a scratching of gravel you never saw, for the black devil ran as if a young earthquake was at his heels—I didn't hurt him though; only gave him a hint to move his boots.

BETSEY: That's right; never take a human life except in self-defense. Ef *they'll* let *us* alone, we will let *them.*[38] Glad it's no worse. Did you find a chance to get the wagon out?

SLUICE: Yes, I found a side ravine, and by taking the point, I think we can get the wagon up—it's a tight squeeze though, for it's a little less than a perpendicular.

BETSEY: We'll go it on the perpendicular then, and go it clar. As for staying here, I shan't do it, so thar. (*To herself.*) And ef I do find Jess in cahoot with any live woman, won't I wake snakes and peel his skin. (*Exit and is heard behind the scenes.*) Whoa—haw Buck! Gee up, Berry!

SCENE II: *Exterior of log cabin. Enter John and Mary. Mary with a broom.*

MARY: Well, Mr. Storekeeper, how do you sell beans to-day?

JOHN: By the pound, generally, Mrs. Express Man.

MARY: Ha! ha! I didn't know but you sold them by the yard—are you sure that you know beans?

JOHN: I profess an acquaintance with them when they are well baked—think I can tell a bean from a broomstick, madam.

MARY: (*Raising her broom, threatening good-naturedly.*) Perhaps I had better test your knowledge.

JOHN: No, no—not now; try me on beans first.

MARY: Well, weigh me out five pounds, then, for dinner.

JOHN: Got the dust to pay for them? No credit here—pay as you go.

MARY: (*Raising her broom.*) I'll raise a dust for you if you don't get the beans—no beans, no dinner!

JOHN: How sharp you are—you shall have the beans.

MARY: And you'll be sharp enough, too, when the beans are cooked.

JOHN: I'll try to get my pay, anyhow.

MARY: No fear of that, for you already have a miner's appetite.

JOHN: Nothing better than our pure mountain air for that.

MARY: O, John, we are so happy, now! Everybody is so kind to us—all are so good natured. Why, I never was happier in my life—and it is so much better here than starving in the city!

JOHN: I never knew I was good for anything till I came here.

MARY: Nor I, either; now I know I am worth beans. Ha! ha!

JOHN: Circumstances make men—aye, and women, too—and if we are only willing to help ourselves, why, in due time—in miner's language—we may strike a lead.

MARY: True—and we have struck the lead—let us follow it. The kind-hearted boys have set us up in business, and scarcely ever seem satisfied unless when they are doing something to help us on.

JOHN: God bless them! Any package for me in your department, madam Express Man?

MARY: Yes, an empty pail and an ax; I want the charges paid.

JOHN: Pail and ax—charges! What are the charges?

MARY: Fill the pail at the spring—cut an armful of wood—and get five pounds of beans.

JOHN: Charges outrageous! I'll forfeit the packages!

MARY: If you do, you'll forfeit your dinner—take your choice—can't cook beans without water and fire.

JOHN: And I can't eat beans without being cooked; I'll take the pail and pay the charges. No getting ahead of a woman, I see.

MARY: And be quick, John dear, for the express will be in soon, and you know what a throng we shall have around us. By the way, I found two letters in the box, this morning, addressed to me.

JOHN: Two letters? Somebody making love to you, I suppose, already.

MARY: Yes, indeed—is that any business of yours? (*Playfully.*)

JOHN: I suppose not, in California, where women do business on their own account, independent of their husbands. Still, I might be just the least bit in the world jealous.

MARY: And with some reason, John—for if they are not love letters, they are loves of letters.

JOHN: I'm all curiosity—besides, I want to know who I've got to shoot.

MARY: No doubt! Well, here they are—read them. (*Handing him the letters.*)

JOHN: They look as if they had been written with a pick or shovel, rather than a pen. (*Reads.*) "For and in consideration of mending pants, sewing on buttons and patching shirts, and trying to make an old man happy by sundry kindnesses—know all men and female women by these here presents: I hereby sell and make over to Mary Wilson, my half interest in claim No. 10—situate, lying and being on Whisky Bar, Feather River diggins, State of Californy, United States of Ameriky—for her whole soul's benefit and behoof, and her husband hasn't anything to do with it." (The deuce he hasn't—setting up for yourself without advertising, are you?) "And I agree to prospect her said claim with pick, shovel and pump, clear to the bed rock, free gratis for nothing, from date."[39] Ambrose Swamp. Shan't shoot old Swamp for that. (*Opens the other.*)

Poetry, eh? this must be a love letter in earnest. (*Reads.*)
"I, Jessie Jenkins by name,
Give Mary Wilson my half claim—
Know'd as number ten
By all the mining men—
Which I, in cahoot
With that ar old brute
Call'd Swamp, on Whisky ba
Hopin she may clar
Ten thousand dollars on sight.
To which I subscribe my hand write
With a pen like a pole—
And may the Lord have mercy on your soul."

Jess Jenkins,
Known as Pike County Jess.—Amen.

Ha! ha! ha! Shan't shoot Pike for that—God bless him! Ah! Mary, Mary, if you havn't fallen in love with the boys, I have; they are doing so much for us, I—I can't—(*Affected. Post horn is heard.*)

MARY: Ah! here is the express rider; hurry, John—hurry. (*He takes the pail and ax and goes out.*)

(*Enter Express Rider with his bags.*)

EXPRESS RIDER: Up to time and a leetle ahead, madam. Run the gauntlet between a pack of cayotes, three grizzlies, and a whole tribe of Digger Indians—killed two horses and jumped a ledge a hundred feet—hung myself by the heels in the bushes—turned forty somersets down a canyon—slept three nights on a snow bank—froze three legs stiff, had 'em amputated and climbed the hill next morning on crutches, and have brought lots of letters for the boys, and newspapers for the old ones. Please take the bags, and give me a glass of brandy and water without any water in it.

MARY: Ha! ha! ha! Merry as an express man yet, I see. Well, come in, come in—we have always something for you. (*Mary goes to the express counter.*)

(*Enter Miners, hastily, as if running from their work. Half a dozen voices at once.*)

MINERS: Any letters for me? Have I got a letter?
MARY: Wheugh! wheugh! One at a time—one at a time—can't look for all at once!
OLD SWAMP: Form a line, boys—form a line; give the gal a chance.
1ST MINER: I'll give five dollars for a letter!
2ND MINER: I'll give ten—only give me a letter!
OLD SWAMP: Form line, boys, or you'll never get a letter. (*They range in line.*) Now, gal, look for me.
MARY: (*Looking over the letters, calls out.*) Ambrose Swamp. (*Hands him a letter.*)
OLD SWAMP: Glory! Here's five dollars. (*Takes the letter and is going off.*)
MARY: It's only a dollar—here's the change.
OLD SWAMP: O, d——n the change—keep it, gal—the letter's from Betsey and the

children.

1ST MINER: Jonathan Sims!

MARY: No letter for Jonathan Sims.

1ST MINER: (*Passing on.*) Go to thunder with your express—I won't strike a blow to-day—I'll get drunk.

2ND MINER: Roswell Rattail.

MARY: No letter for Roswell Rattail.

STOKES: William Stokes.

MARY: Letter for William Stokes. (*Hands it.*)

STOKES: Petitioner's prayer has been granted, and bill passed, Mr. Speaker. (*Throwing his purse on the counter.*) Take out an ounce, madam, never mind details. (*Turns off to read his letter, leaving the purse.*)

JUDGE: Edward Smaile.

MARY: Letter for Edward Smaile.

JUDGE: (*Sings and dances.*) Fol lol de riddle lol rol lol lol. (*Throws down money.*) D——n the change. Boys, what'll you drink? I'll treat the whole crowd.

PIKE: Jessie Jenkins, commonly known as Pike County Jess.

MARY: Sorry to say no letter for Pike.

PIKE: No letter! I'll give that gal, High Betty Martin, the sack, by all the weasles that wear a skin, I will. No letter! I'll go and whip Short-Tail out of spite, I will.

JOE: Joseph Nudge.

MARY: No letter for Joseph Nudge.

JOE: No letter? Havn't heard from home in a year. Don't believe I've got any friends in America. D——n the luck—I'll emigrate to the North Pole and fish for grizzlies through the ice.

(*Others are passing in dumb show—some receiving letters, some none—some getting newspapers, and ranging themselves around—some sitting on the floor, some leaning against the wall, reading their letters and papers. Old Swamp is in the foreground, leaning against the wall, reading his letter and wiping his eyes.*)

MARY: Package for Old Swamp.

OLD SWAMP: (*Still absorbed with his letter.*) Anan!

MARY: Pass it over to him. (*Pike takes it and puts it in his hand.*)

PIKE: Here, old fellow. Why—why, Old Swamp, you're cryin—bad news from home?

OLD SWAMP: (*Struggling with emotion.*) N—no; all well, thank God. What's this? (*Holding up the package.*)

PIKE: Don't know—reckon it's a dogeretype;[40] peel the skin off and see.

OLD SWAMP: (*Tears off the paper, and opens it.*) It's my Betsey, and Jennie, and Bill! (*Looks at it a moment—kisses it, much affected.*) My wife! My children! O, if I could fly, wouldn't I be with you. O, the misery of separation! My wife, my children, my home! (*Bursts into tears. Miners gather round respectfully—Mary comes and takes his hand kindly.*)

MARY: My father, there are better days coming—joy shall yet lighten your path, and home and happiness shall be yours again. Courage, my good father. You labor here to make them independent at home, and your love for them and your present self-denial surely will be rewarded. You will yet be happy together.

OLD SWAMP: (*Still affected.*) God bless you, gal. (*Struggling with his feelings.*) I'm an old fool. Somehow, women always get on the soft side of me. (*With fervor.*) I've got the best wife, the best children—thar—thar—read—read it aloud. (*Hands Mary the letter.*)

MARY: (*Reads.*) "My dear husband:—I received your draft for one-thousand dollars safe. I didn't know exactly what to do to get the money, so I took it up to Squire Gibbs. If you had seen him when he looked at the draft—I never saw a politer man—he actually sot a chair for me. 'Did your old man send all this to you? Why, I'll take it, and give you the cash.' I tell you I felt proud of my old man that blessed minute, and I wish I could put my arms about his neck, and if you will come home, I will, and Bill and Jennie will—but you had better not come, for you will be kissed to death. Didn't I feel rich with all that money—I was afraid I should lose it before I got home, but I didn't. I went right off and paid up the mortgage on our place; then I paid the store debt, then the shoemaker, and everybody else, and I had nigh a hundred dollars left, and we didn't owe a dime in the world, and I felt so happy that I sat down and cried—I don't care, I cried like a child. The children thought we were so rich that we needn't take in washing any more, but I told them father might have bad luck, so we must keep at work and save all we could. Bill said he'd bring water, and Jennie said she'd pound the clothes, but I told the darlings they should go to school, for my heart was light enough to do all the work. Bill says he'll never owe nothing to nobody, and he will work for father and mother when they get old and they needn't work at all. We all talk about you every night, and want to see you right bad. Dear husband, let the Californy chunks go, and come home to your chunks here. We send a thousand kisses."

OLD SWAMP: Ain't sich a wife and children worth workin for, boys?

MINERS: Three cheers for Old Swamp and his wife at home!

PIKE: Three cheers for High Betty—no, nary cheer, the gal didn't write me a letter to-day. (*Exeunt.*)

SCENE III: *Front wood glen. Enter Cash and Dice.*

DICE: A pretty mess, we've made of it, Cash. Do you know where we are?

CASH: I know we have got clear of the harpies of the law, and that is all I care for till the thing is blown over a little.

DICE: We've had a lucky escape—but what made you shoot that fellow?

CASH: Shoot him? Who wouldn't have shot him rather than lost the money? Everything was going right till the fellow saw me turn up the wrong card. The fact was, the wax on my fingers had worn smooth, and my thumb slipped, and he saw the trick. He accused me of cheating and grabbed the money. Of course I wouldn't stand that, so I put a bullet through him, grabbed the money, and put out through the back door before the police could arrest me.

DICE: You hadn't much time to spare, for a hornet's nest was raised in less than ten minutes.

CASH: That ten minutes saved me, for I ran to the slough, and, as luck would have it, I found a boat, and in two minutes I was in the chapparel on the other side, made my way to the American,[41] swam that, and was safe in our rendezvous till you came.

DICE: Well, it will blow over in a month, so we can go back again.

CASH: Yes, no trouble about that, for who cares about a miner? They're only fair game for gamblers and lawyers to pluck. The only difference is, we win their money honorably, while the lawyers steal it by law.

DICE: And if there is any fuss, why, we can buy up law, lawyers, judges, witnesses, and jurymen. The only trouble is, it may cost something to prove an alibi, or buy up straw bail.[42]

CASH: Exactly, and if they put us in jail, for form's sake, why, it is not much trouble to break out by getting on the right side of the jailor.

DICE: We'll have a little play-spell now by going on to some of the Bars[43] and prospecting in the pockets of miners at home. They work and we win.

CASH: Right, old fellow. I had rather have a dozen lucky miners at my table than a whole plantation of niggers—I'll make more out of them, and if, now and then, one gets rapped over the head for being too lucky, who cares—whose business is it?

DICE: Good. Well, push ahead—we'll see where this trail leads to. (*Exeunt.*)

SCENE IV: *Stringtown. Pike and Swamp digging on Mary's claim, in the foreground—Miners at work in the distance.*

OLD SWAMP: Thar, Pike, we're comin to gravel, and the dirt looks right. (*Examines.*)

PIKE: Mary's claim may turn out a good egg, arter all. Old Swamp, I love that gal.

OLD SWAMP: It's lucky High Betty Martin don't hear you say that—she'd be in your hair worse nor a steel trap into a hairy coon.

PIKE: Geet out, you old varmint. My gal knows I'm true as steel to her. She knows that every gal I love is for her sake, and you know too that I don't want to stampede Mary Wilson.

OLD SWAMP: Humph! I'd trust you about as far as I would a fox with a goose, and your gal wouldn't trust you at all.

PIKE: Pooh! make it up in a minute—Californy gals mighty forgiving. A leetle soft sodder, a trifle of honey, and fair promises, and they'll pull the wool over their own eyes, kiss, and forgive.

OLD SWAMP: But they don't forget, eh? I'd like to know, Pike, how on airth sich an ungainly varmint as you are made out to catch any gal.

PIKE: Ha! ha! ha! Ain't I a beauty—ain't I a roarer, a perfect wild bull on the prairie? Why, the gal don't live on air and hoe-cake that kin stand the glance of my eye. We were at a huskin[44] frolic. When it come to the hoe dig, I pulled High Betty Martin on to the floor for a double shuffle breakdown. O, I'm death on the toe and heel. Well, Bill Sampson steps up, and swore he'd dance with my gal fust, and he gin me a push. He mought as well have tried to upset a steamboat. "Hold on," says I, Bet sees fair play, and I pitched into the varmint, worse nor a gang of niggers into a cotton field. "Go your death, boys," shouted Betty—"I don't care which whips—but, Jess Jenkins, if you don't lick him, I'll lick you." In just two minutes by the watch, Bill Sampson was the worst-licked man in the

Settlement, and he owned up that he thought a young airthquake had hold on him. I popped the question to the gal that very night, and she caved like a young possom—said I was the boy for her beauty. Cock-a-doodle-doo!

OLD SWAMP: What made you fall in love with her?

PIKE: I seed her lift a barrel of whisky plump and square out of the cart on to the ground. I thought the gal what could do that could manage niggers as well as make gingerbread, and I didn't sleep a wink for three nights for thinking of her. (*Enter Jones.*) Here comes the printer man. Well, old fellow, got your press a-going?

JONES: No; hain't dug enough to set up a *form*, nor made money enough to buy the types to set it up with. Have to start for Humbug again.

PIKE: Can't you rig out a printing machine on a sluice box, and make it go on the undershot principle? I'm great on machine poetry—can't you be great on machine printing?

JONES: O yes; no trouble about that; the printing machine would be about equal to your poetry, but then there would be the devil to pay.

PIKE: The devil? what's he got to do with your machine, or my poetry?

JONES: A good deal—every printer has his devil.

PIKE: Well, I know they're as saucy as the devil, but I didn't know they always kept one on hand.

JONES: Always, Pike—and they've got stomachs to fill—you've heard of a man being as hungry as the devil—that means the printer's devil.

PIKE: Yes, I saw you in the same fix oncst, and didn't you pitch in?

JONES: Pretty much as I did into a turkey dinner once.

OLD SWAMP: How's that?

JONES: Bought a splendid turkey once, to give the devil, and all the other office imps a grand dinner. Fed him four times a day for six weeks, and when the old sinner got so fat he couldn't stand, I cut his head off, pulled out his feathers, stuffed him with gingerbread and oysters, and hung him outside the house to freeze him tender. Went out the next morning to bring him in to roast, and found he had given me the slip, leaving a card that read "A bird in the hand is worth two in the bush."[45]

PIKE: What! a dead turkey run away? Must have been of the Shanghai[46] breed, and crowed his legs off the nail.

JONES: Some hungry devil stole the turkey and left nothing but the joke for us.

OLD SWAMP: And your guests?

JONES: O, made it up on bacon and eggs, only there wasn't any eggs, and the bacon was boiled codfish.

(*Enter Chinaman, left, much alarmed.*)

CHINAMAN: Me help! Me help! shooty me! bang me shooty! one, tree, five-hundred Indian! O! O! O!

PIKE: Shoot you, bang you, two or three hundred Indians? What the devil do you want with so many Indians?

CHINAMAN: No, no, no! Pop! bang! bullet shooty me!

OLD SWAMP: Indians shoot you?

CHINAMAN: Gold prospect, me hill over. Par one dollar—one dollar, two bit—one dollar half. Indian come! me bang! bang! bullet! pop me! two, three, five hundred!

PIKE: Hey! Indians coming to the Settlement? We must look to it.

OLD SWAMP: That ar a fact. Rally the boys; call all hands; we must drive them back.

PIKE: (Shouts.) Indians, boys, Indians! Hurrah for a fight! Fun, boys, fun—drop your tools, and run, boys, run.

(Miners rush in, with their arms.)

OLD SWAMP: The diggers are upon us, boys—let's meet them on the hill and surprise them.

PIKE: And lick them before they have a chance to scalp Short-Tail. (All rush out except Chinaman, with a "Huzzah!")

CHINAMAN: Chinaman no fight; Chinaman skin good skin; keep him so. Mellican man big devil—no hurty bullet him.

SCENE V: Top of the Hill. Enter Betsey, with boots in her hand, and Sluice.

SLUICE: Here's a trail that leads somewhere, and by the lay of the land, Feather River must be at the bottom of the gulch.

BETSEY: I'm glad on't. I've worn out one pair of good boots in hunting up a man, (holds up boots) I wouldn't give another pair for the best man alive, except Jess.

SLUICE: Well, let us go a little higher on the Ridge to ascertain our position. Stringtown cannot be very far off. (They walk up the stage.)

(Enter Pike, Swamp, and party.)

PIKE: The varmints can't be far off, boys. Stay here—tracks—boots, too. They've killed somebody and stole their clothes—squat, boys, squat! lay low till I take a peep. (All lay or squat down.)

OLD SWAMP: Hold, Pike—there's two of 'em. (Pointing to Sluice and Betsey.) Squat, boys, squat! (Betsey and Sluice advance slowly.)

PIKE: Cock your pieces, boys—don't fire till I give the word. Swamp and I will take them two—as fast as you fire drop down and load. Old Swamp, I'll take that tall squaw—you take the buck. (Pike and Swamp crouch down behind a tree, as Betsey and Sluice advance.) Are you ready, Swamp? Say the word. (Taking aim.)

OLD SWAMP: Stay, Pike! That's a white woman.

PIKE: No; it's a d——d squaw.

OLD SWAMP: I swear it's a woman.

PIKE: (Looking close.) Boys, it's a fact—they are humans from the settlements—get up, and three cheers for another live woman in the mines. (Miners rise and cheer.)

BETSEY: (Drawing a knife and pistol, in alarm, rushes towards Pike, as if to shoot him.) You varmints! Do you mean to harm a woman?

PIKE: Snakes and alligators! That's Betsey—whoo-ra! whoo-ra!

BETSEY: Jess—Jess—my Jess, it it you? (*They rush into each other's arms.*)

PIKE: Boys, it's my own blessed High Betty Martin herself, it is.

MINERS: (*Shout.*) Hurrah for High Betty Martin and Pike County Jess—Short-Tail and all!

PIKE: Why, Betty, I hope I may be shot if I didn't take you for a Digger squaw; I was going to shoot you.

BETSEY: May I never pull another acre of flax ef I didn't take you for a robber; I was going to knife you.

OLD SWAMP: Ha! ha! One looks like a squaw, and the other like a robber, sure enough, but so long as the heart is in the right place, it's no matter.

PIKE: Well, boys, we'll let the diggers go—the Chinaman was more scared than hurt. (*To Betsey.*) Somebody shot at one of the Johns,[47] and he thought a tribe of Indians was on his trail.

BETSEY: Ha! ha! ha! It was Sluice, thar. He thought he saw an Indian through the bushes, and fired his rifle to scare him off. It's done no harm, and only brought us together sooner.

OLD SWAMP: It's the first time I ever knowed gunpowder to act as a messenger of love.

BETSEY: Well, Sluice—bring up the wagon—I've found the man, and let the boots be hanged. (*Exit all, laughing and cheering.*)

SCENE VI: *Inside of a miner's store—miners lounging around. Cash and Dice seated at a table with a Monte Box.*

DICE: Come, boys, here's a chance for a fortune. Never say die with the money in hand. Come down, boys, come down. (*Miners gather around the table—some throw money on the table.*) Down, boys—any more? all down? (*Draws the cards.*) King—ace—knave in the door. Bank wins. (*Cash scrapes it up.*)

(*Enter Old Swamp as Dice is speaking.*)

OLD SWAMP: Knave in the door? A knave is always in the door of a gambler's bank. Boys, you are fools. Doesn't your money come hard enough, that you must throw it away?

CASH: Come down, gentlemen. Fortune to the brave—don't be backward in coming forward—down—down—all down?

OLD SWAMP: Boys, don't fool away your money. Remember your wives and children at home; save your money for them; don't rob them.

DICE: Bank wins. (*Scrapes it up.*) Come down, boys—no preaching here, old man —plenty of luck and good liquor. Landlord, six juleps, four brandy smashes, at my expense—all down?

OLD SWAMP: The varmints! I've a mind to break their heads, bank and all, the fools.

JONES: (*Who is reading a paper.*) Old Swamp, read this article in the Sacramento paper. (*Hands the paper, pointing to the article.*)

OLD SWAMP: (*Puts on his spectacles and reads.*) It is as true as I am a living man.

JONES: No mistake, they are the very men.

OLD SWAMP: Boys, I want to read you a leetle news—rayther important.

CASH: Come down, come down—don't mind the old fool.

JOE: What is it Old Swamp?

MINERS: Yes, let's hear it.

OLD SWAMP: Boys, keep your eyes skinned while I read—let no one leave the room. (*Reads.*) "Proclamation—One-thousand dollars reward will be paid for the apprehension of a gambler, named Jacob Cash, who committed a brutal murder by shooting a miner named George Doan, on the 17th inst., in Sacramento. Said Cash is about five-feet nine or ten inches in height, sandy hair, grey eyes, dark complexion, with a bold address. The murderer was accompanied in his flight by a confederate named Richard Dice, a man about—"

CASH: The devil! Boys, the game is up for to-day. (*Gathers up the money. To Dice.*) I want to speak with you.

OLD SWAMP: Yes, villains, your game is up. Seize them, boys—they are the rascals. (*Miners make demonstrations of taking them. Cash and Dice rise and draw their pistols.*)

DICE: The first that moves is a dead man. Gentlemen, it is all a mistake—that is not the man—he is as innocent as I am.

OLD SWAMP: Very likely. Birds of a feather flock together.

(*Enter Pike and Betsey.*)

PIKE: What's the row, boys—any chance for me to take a hand?

OLD SWAMP: A murder has been committed in Sacramento—thar stands the murderer. Here's the Governor's proclamation, in black and white, offering a reward of one-thousand dollars for his apprehension.

PIKE: As sure as I'm a Christian, them's the very varmints who tried to stampede Mary Wilson. Boys, I know the dogs—let's pin 'em.

CASH AND DICE: (*Presenting their pistols.*) The first man that stirs gets a bullet in him.

BETSEY: (*Leveling her gun.*) Mister, two can play at that game.

PIKE: High Betty Martin forever; (*Presents his rifle.*) Shall we shoot first, or will you?

(*Enter John and Mary.*)

JOHN: What is this, my friends?—I hope no difficulty among yourselves.

MARY: John, John! there stand the villains who sought to entrap us in Sacramento.

JOHN: The very men. Good heavens! What a strange chance!

DICE: (*To Cash.*) By heavens! The very woman.

PIKE: You've got just one minute to surrender. Ef you don't cave at oncst, we'll make riddles of your carcasses, and send you to the Devil's Monte Bank.

DICE: It's no use—(*To Cash.*)—they're too many. Will you give us the benefit of the law?

PIKE: Law? No—we'll hang you like dogs by miner's law.

OLD SWAMP: No, boys—'bide the law. If the law will do its duty, 'bide the law.

It's time enough to take the law in hand when the authorities become scoundrels—till then, 'bide the law. We'll send them to Sacramento.

PIKE: With one condition, I agree to that. Give them the law of Moses first, so that they will not forget Stringtown—"forty lashes save one."

MINERS: Agreed! Agreed!

DICE: We surrender. Cash, we'll get off easy enough when we get a chance of the law. (*They surrender—and, as they are led out—*)

PIKE: Make them dance to their own music, boys—a fiddle with one string, and a bow in a strong hand. (*A shout is heard without.*)

(*Enter miners, tumultuously—one holding a prospecting pan.*)

MINERS: Mary Wilson! Mary Wilson! Huzza for the "live woman in the Mines!"

JOHN: What is it, boys? I hope you are not going to hang my wife.

STOKES: You be hanged, yourself. Mary Wilson has struck a lead rich—rich as Croesus! Look—look! piles of gold!

MARY: Mine—is it true? O, heavens!

OLD SWAMP: Yes, gal—No. 10 is a ten-strike—it's yours, and no mistake. You are rich, gal, but don't get proud.

MARY: O, I am proud—I am proud of your friendship, I am proud of the miners, my friends, I am proud of everything—everybody in the Mines.

PIKE: We're all proud of you, and—John Wilson, I shall kiss your wife.

BETSEY: (*Good humoredly.*) Jess, if you kiss that man's wife, I'll kiss that woman's husband. (*Throws her arms about John, and kisses him heartily.*)

PIKE: I'm so happy, I could kiss Short-Tail himself, ef it wasn't for stampeding him.

MARY: O, John, are we not well paid for all our trials and misfortunes? How can I ever repay you for your many, many kindnesses? (*To miners.*)

OLD SWAMP: Pshaw! by sewing on our buttons, nursing poor, sick miners, giving kind words to all, and making us think of and love still better our wives and sweethearts at home, as you have done.

PIKE: And by being bridesmaid to my Carolina Betsey, commonly known as High Betty Martin, who is to be spliced to Pike County Jess, by the Judge, this blessed night. (*Advancing to the front of the stage.*) And ef thar's any more female women in these diggins who wants to strike a lead, and go in cahoots with an A No. 1 miner for a husband, she is welcome to Short-Tail to ride on a prospecting tour, to become "A LIVE WOMAN IN THE MINES."

END

FOOTNOTES

[1]*"Old Block"*: pen-name of Alonzo Delano, humorist and playwright.

[2]*Pike County Jess*: his name indicates his origin: Pike County, Missouri; as portrayed by Delano, he's a cousin to the stage-frontiersman, Nimrod Wildfire, in *The Lion of the West*, but he also typifies Pike County men, lacking in polish, but forthright in manner and full of

vitality.

[3]*Modern and Mining*: Delano's "modern" costumes are those of 1857, which now makes them period; mining-garb is depicted in Currier and Ives prints and in the paintings of Christian Nahl and others who captured the Far West on paper and canvas.

[4]*Panama fever*: malaria, Yellow Fever; since many gold-seekers took ship from the East to Panama through the Caribbean, crossing the Isthmus of Panama overland, to take ship again on the Pacific Coast, bound for San Francisco, exposure to the disease was a frequent hazard.

[5]*Thy God my God*: thus spoke Ruth to Naomi, amid the alien corn, in the *Book of Ruth*, 1:16.

[6]*Backed water*: steam-boating term; held back, hesitated.

[7]*Sluice Forks'*: shortly after, Sluice is referred to by Dice as Sluice Box; both are contemptuous. Forks probably is a reference to a fork of a river in the goldfields; a sluice-box was a wooden device, mounted on rockers so it could agitate the gold-bearing sand or dirt—liberally washed over with water, or sluiced—to permit the gold flakes and nuggets to settle in the sluice-box, while the lighter, worthless materials flowed away.

[8]*Round Tent*: a notorious gambling "hell" in Sacramento in the early days of the Gold Rush.

[9]*Diggins*: miners prospected for gold, and when they found it, they staked a "claim," since the land was regarded as previously belonging to no one, even though in some cases gold-strikes were on land owned by Captain John Sutter or Mexican landowners, who had land grants from Spanish or Mexican officials. Seizing another's claim was called "jumping." In the Gold Rush of 1849, the gold sought was in flakes ("colors") and nuggets found in the sand of river and creekbeds or in the earth from which it had to be dug—hence, "diggins"—and washed free of impurities. The process was known as Placer Mining: literally, pleasure mining, from its supposed ease of operation. Later, with the discovery of veins of gold in quartz, "Hard-rock" mining largely replaced the placer process.

[10]*Vamos*: later altered to "vamoose": literally, "let's go," but here used in the sense of "get out."

[11]*Stringtown*: a gold-mining center in Butte County.

[12]*An original*: an eccentric, an original type.

[13]*Carolina Betsey*: she comes from Pike County; is Delano, in choosing this name, thinking of the folk-song "Sweet Betsey from Pike"?

[14]*Dirking*: stabbing.

[15]*Hangtown*: the Gold Rush colloquial name for Placerville; the name also refers to the speedy and popular method of local justice.

[16]*Rocker*: the sluice-box, on rockers.

[17]*On the left*: this is Delano's own footnote: "The post-office was there in 1850."

[18]*Clipper*: clipper-ship.

[19]*Somersets*: somersaults.

[20]*Aparaho*: a Mexican pack-saddle.

[21]*Hippah mula*: Get up, mule!

[22]*Mansinieto*: Manzanita, a Far Western shrub with gnarled branches; literally, "Little Apple."

[23]*Chinese theatre*: Chinese immigrants, flocking to the goldfields and the cities of Sacramento and San Francisco, brought this and othe aspects of their traditional culture with them, so Jess could very well have seen such a performance.

[24]*D--n her*: considering the care British and American dramatists usually took to protect the ears of family audiences in the theatre from strong oaths, Delano was apparently more interested in suggesting some of the actual force and quality of a miner's speech.

[25]*Digger*: a California Indian, living in the Sierra foothills.

[26]*Maus of the Cayotes*: maws of the coyotes, referring to the wolf-like Far Western predator.

[27]*Overhaul*: catch, catch up with.

[28]*Slapjacks*: flapjacks, pancakes.

[29]*Chapparel*: chaparral: scrub-oaks; low, often dense brush, from which horsemen were to protect themselves with "chaps" (shaps).

[30]*Dead lines and a dash*: printer's terms, used here to indicate violent death.

[31]*Arter*: after.

[32]*Fix it*: Delano's own footnote: "The actual expression of a young Pike County man to the author."

[33]*Strike a lead*: hit a vein of gold.

[34]*She drinks from it*: considering the refinement required of melodrama heroines on the Eastern Seaboard, Mary's alacrity in drinking from a communal bottle of what is surely potent "fire-water" suggests a rapid adaptation to Western ways—and possibly a somewhat more realistic portrait of a woman on stage than was the rule. So much for Temperance!

[35]*Cend*: ascend, way of ascent.

[36]*Wagon to pieces*: descending and ascending the steep, rocky mountains and chasms of the Sierras, the emigrants occasionally had to dismantle their wagons and lower (or hoist) them, themselves, and their livestock on ropes secured around trees at the tops of such slopes. Emigrant Gap, in the High Sierras near Lake Tahoe and not far from Grass Valley, of which Delano was a founder, was just such a precipitous challenge to the gold-seekers.

[37]*General Taylor*: Zachary Taylor, a hero of the Mexican War, known popularly as "Old Rough-and-Ready," a name also used, in his honor, to designate a mining center near Grass Valley, memorialized by Bret Harte in *A Millionaire of Rough and Ready*. (The editor of these plays grew up on a ranch outside Rough and Ready.)

[38]*We will let them*: so much for the Indians' birthright to the land before the Forty-Niners arrived!

[39]*Free gratis for nothing, from date*: although this may seem improbable, so lonely were these men without women for the sight of one of the "fair creatures," that similar acts of

generosity were recorded; not to mention the largesse of nuggets and gold-dust that miners are said to have showered on such performers as the almost legendary Lola Montez and little Lotta Crabtree, "The Darling of the Forty-Niners."

[40]*Dogeretype*: Daguerreotype, a pioneer form of photograph, developed by Louis Daguerre, in which a silvered copper-plate, sensitized to light, recorded an image; the process became immensely popular in America, after its 1839 introduction from France.

[41]*American*: the American River; a slough is a swampy inlet.

[42]*Straw bail*: cheap bail intended to be forfeited by flight.

[43]*Bars*: although this suggests fleecing miners in whiskey-bars, it actually refers to mining settlements which took their names from this geological feature, a large sandbar in a river.

[44]*Huskin*: this refers to the popular rural custom of combining communal work—husking corn—with social pleasures; a husking-bee.

[45]*Two in the bush*: as Delano has indicated in his introduction to *A Live Woman in the Mines*, this story was told him by an actual printer—the model for Jones in this play—who assured him the tale was true.

[46]*Shanghai*: this is a reference to the practice of kidnapping men for service on ships bound for the Orient: "Shanghai-ing."

[47]*Johns*: short for the colloquial term for Chinese immigrants: "Chinamen John."

TWO MEN OF SANDY BAR

BY

BRET HARTE

DRAMATIS PERSONA

Sandy, son of Alexander Morton, Sr.
John Oakhurst, his former partner, personating the prodigal son, Sandy
Col. Starbottle, Alexander Morton, Sr.'s legal adviser
Old Morton, Alexander Morton, Sr.
Don José, father of Jovita Castro
Capper, a detective
Concho, major-domo of Don José's rancho
York, an old friend of Oakhurst
Pritchard, an Australian convict
Soapy & Silky, his pals.
Jackson, confidential clerk of Alexander Morton, Jr. and confederate of Pritchard
Hop Sing, a Chinese laundryman
Servant of Alexander Morton, Sr.—Policeman
Miss Marry Morris, the schoolmistress of Red Gulch, in love with Sandy, and cousin of Alexander Morton, Sr.
Dona Jovita Castro, in love with John Oakhurst and daughter of Don Jose
The Duchess, wife of Pritchard, illegally married to Sandy, and former "dame" of John Oakhurst
Manuela, servant of Castro, and maid to Dona Jovita

ACT I: The Rancho of the Blessed Innocents, and House of Don José Castro

ACT II: Red Gulch

ACT III: The Banking-house of Morton & Son, San Francisco

ACT IV: The Villa of Alexander Morton, Sr., San Francisco

COSTUMES

Alexander Morton ("Sandy")—First dress: Mexican vaquero:[1] black velvet trousers, open from knee, over white trousers; laced black velvet jacket, and broad white sombrero; large silver spurs. Second dress: miner's white duck jumper, and white duck trousers; (sailor's) straw hat. Third dress: fashionable morning costume. Fourth dress: full evening dress.

John Oakhurst—First dress: riding dress, black, elegantly fitting. Second and third dress: fashionable. Fourth dress: full evening dress.

Col. Starbottle—First dress: blue double-breasted frock, and white "strapped" trousers; white hat. Second dress: same coat, blue trousers, and black broad-brimmed felt hat; cane, *semper*,[2] ruffles. Third dress: the same. Fourth dress: the same, with pumps.

York—Fashionable morning dress.

Jackson—Business suit.

Concho—First dress: vaquero's dress. Second dress: citizen's dress.

Hop Sing—Dress of Chinese coolie: dark-blue blouse, and dark-blue drawers gathered at ankles; straw conical hat, and wooden sabots.

Don Jose—First dress: serape, black, with gold embroidery. Second dress: fashion-able suit, with broad-brimmed black stiff sombrero.

Old Morton—First, second, third, and fourth dress: black, stiff, with white cravat.

Capper—Ordinary dress of period.

Miss Mary—First dress: tasteful calico morning dress. Second dress and third dress: lady's walking-costume—fashionable. Fourth dress: full dress.

Dona Jovita—First dress: handsome Spanish dress, with manta.[3] Second dress: more elaborate, same quality.

The Duchess—First dress: elaborate but extravagant fashionable costume. Second dress: travelling dress.

Manuela—The *saya y manta*:[4] white waist, and white or black skirt, with flowers.

ACT I

SCENE I: *Courtyard and Corridors of the Rancho.*

MANUELA: (*Arranging supper-table in corridor, solus.*[5]) There! Tortillas, chocolate, olives, and—the whiskey of the Americans! And supper's ready. But why
Don Jose chooses tonight, of all nights, with this heretic fog lying over the Mission Hills like a wet serape,[6] to take his supper out here, the saints only know.
Perhaps it's some distrust of his madcap daughter, the Dona Jovita; perhaps to
watch her—who knows? And now to find Diego. Ah, here he comes. So! The
old story. He is getting Dona Jovita's horse ready for another madcap journey.
Ah! (*Retires to table.*)

(*Enter cautiously from corridor, Sandy Morton, carrying lady's saddle and blanket; starts on observing Manuela, and hastily hides saddle and blanket in recess.*)

SANDY: (*Aside.*) She's alone. I reckon the old man's at his siesta yet. Ef he'll only
hang on to that snooze ten minutes longer, I'll manage to let that gal Jovita slip
out to that yer fandango, and no questions asked.
MANUELA: (*Calling Sandy.*) Diego!
SANDY: (*Aside, without heeding her.*) That's a sweet voice for a serenade. Round,
full, high-shouldered, and calkilated to fetch a man every time. Only thar ain't,
to my sartain knowledge, one o' them chaps within a mile of the rancho.
(*Laughs.*)
MANUELA: Diego!
SANDY: (*Aside.*) Oh, go on! That's the style o' them Greasers.[7] They'll stand rooted
in their tracks, and yell for a chap without knowin' whether he's in sight or
sound.
MANUELA: (*Approaching Sandy impatiently.*) Diego!

SANDY: (*Starting, aside.*) The devil! Why, that's *me* she's after. (*Laughs.*) I clean disremembered that when I kem yer I tole those chaps my name was James—James Smith (*laughs*), and thet they might call me "Jim." And De-a-go's their lingo for Jim. (*Aloud.*) Well, my beauty, De-a-go it is. Now, wot's up?

MANUELA: Eh? no sabe![8]

SANDY: Wot's your little game? (*Embraces her.*)

MANUELA: (*Aside, and recoiling coquettishly.*) Mother of God! He must be drunk again. These Americans have no time for love when they are sober. (*Aloud and coquettishly.*) Let me go, Diego. Don Jose is coming. He has sent for you. He takes his supper tonight on the corridor. Listen, Diego. He must not see you thus. You have been drinking again. I will keep you from him. I will say you are not well.

SANDY: Couldn't you, my darling, keep him from *me*? Couldn't you make him think *he* was sick? Couldn't you say he's exposin' his precious health by sittin' out thar tonight; thet ther's chills and fever in every breath? (*Aside.*) Ef the old Don plants himself in that chair, that gal's chances for goin' out tonight is gone up.

MANUELA: Never. He would suspect at once. Listen, Diego. If Don Jose does not know that his daughter steals away with you to meet some caballero,[9] some lover—you understand, Diego—it is because he does not know, or would not *seem* to know, what every one else in the rancho knows. Have a care, foolish Diego! If Don Jose is old and blind, look you, friend, we are *not*. You understand?

SANDY: (*Aside.*) What the devil does she expect?—money? No! (*Aloud.*) Look yer, Manuela, you ain't goin' to blow on that young gal! (*Putting his arm around her waist.*) Allowin' that she hez a lover, thar ain't nothin' onnateral in thet, bein' a purty sort o' gal. Why, suppose somebody should see you and me together like this, and should just let on to the old man.

MANUELA: Hush! (*Disengaging herself.*) Hush! He is coming. Let me go, Diego! It is Don Jose!

(*Enter Don Jose, who walks gravely to the table, and seats himself. Manuela retires to table.*)

SANDY: (*Aside.*) I wonder if he saw us. I hope he did: it would shut that Manuela's mouth for a month of Sundays. (*Laughs.*) God forgive me for it! I've done a heap of things for that young gal, Dona Jovita, but this yer gettin' soft on the Greaser maid-servant to help out the missus is a little more than Sandy Morton bargained fur.

DON JOSE: (*To Manuela.*) You can retire. Diego will attend me. (*Looks at Diego attentively. Exit Manuela.*)

SANDY: (*Aside.*) Diego will attend him! Why, blast his yeller skin, does he allow that Sandy Morton hired out as a purty waiter-gal? Because I calkilated to feed his horses, it ain't no reason thet my dooty to animals don't stop there. Pass his hash![10] (*Turns to follow Manuela, but stops.*) Hello, Sandy! wot are ye doin', eh? You ain't going back on Miss Jovita, and jest spile that gal's chances to git out to-night, on'y to teach that God-forsaken old gov'ment mule manners? No! I'll humor the old man, and keep one eye out for the gal. (*Comes to table, and leans familiarly over the back of Don Jose's chair.*)

DON JOSE: (*Aside.*) He seems insulted and annoyed. His manner strengthens my worst suspicions. He has not expected this. (*Aloud.*) Chocolate, Diego.

SANDY: (*Leaning over table carelessly.*) Yes, I reckon it's somewhar thar.

DON JOSE: (*Aside.*) He is unused to menial labor. If I should be right in my suspicions! If he really were Dona Jovita's secret lover! This gallantry with the servants is only a deceit! Bueno! I will watch him. (*Aloud.*) Chocolate, Diego!

SANDY: (*Aside.*) I wonder if the old fool reckons I'll pour it out. Well, seein' he's the oldest—(*Pours chocolate awkwardly, and spills it on the table and Don Jose.*)

DON JOSE: (*Aside.*) He *is* embarassed. I am right. (*Aloud.*) Diego!

SANDY: (*Leaning confidentially over Don Jose's chair.*) Well, old man!

DON JOSE: Three months ago my daughter the Dona Jovita picked you up, a wandering vagabond, in the streets of the Mission. (*Aside.*) He does not seem ashamed. (*Aloud.*) She—she—ahem! The aguardiente, Diego.

SANDY: (*Aside.*) That means the whiskey. It's wonderful how quick a man learns Spanish. (*Passes the bottle, fills Don Jose's glass, and then his own. Don Jose recoils in astonishment.*) I looks toward ye,[11] ole man. (*Tosses off liquor.*)

DON JOSE: (*Aside.*) This familiarity! He *is* a gentleman. Bueno! (*Aloud.*) She was thrown from her horse; her skirt caught in the stirrup; she was dragged; you saved her life. You—

SANDY: (*Interrupting, confidentially drawing a chair to the table, and seating himself.*) Look yer! I'll tell you all about it. It wasn't that gal's fault, ole man. The hoss shied at me, lying drunk in a ditch, you see; the hoss backed, the surcle[12] broke; it warn't in human nature for her to keep her seat, and that gal rides like an angel; but the mustang throwed her. Well, I sorter got in the way o' thet hoss, and it stopped. Hevin' bin the cause o' the hoss shyin', for I reckon I didn't look much like an angel lyin' in that ditch, it was bout the only square thing for me to waltz in and help the gal. Thar, thet's about the way the thing pints. Now, don't you go and hold that agin her!

DON JOSE: Well, well! She was grateful. She has a strange fondness for you Americans, and at her solicitation I gave you—*you*, an unknown vagrant—employment here as groom. You comprehend, Diego. I, Don Jose Castro, proprietor of this rancho, with a hundred idle vaqueros on my hands—I made a place for you.

SANDY: (*Meditatively.*) Umph.

DON JOSE: You said you would reform. How have you kept your word? You were drunk last Wednesday.

SANDY: Thet's so.

DON JOSE: And again last Saturday.

SANDY: (*Slowly.*) Look yer, ole man, don't ye be too hard on me: that was the same old drunk.

DON JOSE: I am in no mood for trifling. Hark ye, friend Diego. You have seen, perhaps—who has not?—that I am a fond, an indulgent father. But even my consideration for my daughter's strange tastes and follies has its limit. Your conduct is a disgrace to the rancho. You must go.

SANDY: (*Meditatively.*) Well, I reckon, perhaps I'd better.

DON JOSE: (*Aside.*) His coolness is suspicious. Can it be that he expects the girl will follow him? Mother of God! perhaps it has already been planned between them. Good! Thank Heaven I can end it here. (*Aloud.*) Diego!

SANDY: Old man.

DON JOSE: For my daughter's sake, you understand—for her sake—I am willing to try you once more. Hark ye! My daughter is young, foolish and romantic. I have reason to believe, from her conduct lately, that she has contracted an intimacy with some Americano, and that in her ignorance, her foolishness, she has allowed that man to believe that he might aspire to her hand. Good! Now listen to me. You shall stay in her service. You shall find out—you are in her confidence—you shall find out this American, this adventurer, this lover if you please, of the Dona Jovita my daughter, and you will tell him this—you will tell him that a union with him is impossible, forbidden; that the hour she attempts it, without my consent, she is *penniless*; that this estate, this rancho, passes into the hands of the Holy Church, where even your laws cannot reach it.

SANDY: (*Leaning familiarly over the table.*) But suppose that he sees that little bluff, and calls ye.

DON JOSE: (*Coldly.*) I do not comprehend you.

SANDY: Suppose he loves that gal, and will take her as she stands, without a cent, or hide or hair of yer old cattle.

DON JOSE: (*Scornfully.*) Suppose—a miracle! Hark ye, Diego! It is now five years since I have known your countrymen, these smart Americanos. I have yet to know when love, sentiment, friendship, was worth any more than a money value in your market.

SANDY: (*Truculently and drunkenly.*) You hev, hev ye? Well, look yar, old man. Suppose I *refuse*. Suppose I'd rather go than act as a spy on that young gal, your darter! Suppose that—hic—allowin' she's my friend, I'd rather starve in the gutters of the Mission than stand between her and the man she fancies. Hey? Suppose I would—damn me! Suppose I'd see you and your derned old rancho in—t'other place—hic—damn me. You hear me, ole man! That's the kind o' man I am—damn me.

DON JOSE: (*Aside, rising contemptuously.*) It is as I suspected. Traitor—Ingrate! Satisfied that his scheme has failed, he is ready to abandon her. And this—*this* is the man for whom she has been ready to sacrifice everything—her home, her father. (*Aloud, coldly.*) Be it so, Diego; you shall go.

SANDY: (*Soberly and seriously, after a pause.*) Well, I reckon I had better. (*Rising.*) I've a few duds, old man, to put up. It won't take me long. (*Goes to exit and pauses.*)

DON JOSE: (*Aside.*) Ah! he hesitates! He is changing his mind. (*Sandy returns slowly to table, pours out glass of liquor, nods to Don Jose and drinks.*)

SANDY: I looks towards ye, ole man. Adios! (*Exit Sandy.*)

DON JOSE: His coolness is perfect. If these Americans are cayotes[13] in their advances, they are lions in retreat! Bueno! I begin to respect him. But it will be just as well to set Concho to track him to the Mission, and I will see that he leaves the rancho alone. (*Exit Jose.*)

(*Enter hurriedly Jovita Castro in riding habit, with whip.*)

JOVITA: So! Chiquita not yet saddled, and that spy Concho haunting the plains for the last half-hour. What an air of mystery! Something awful, something deliciously dreadful has happened! Either my amiable drunkard has forgotten to dispatch Concho on his usual fool's errand, or he is himself lying helpless in some ditch. Was there ever a girl so persecuted? With a father wrapped in mystery, a lover nameless and shrouded in the obscurity of some Olympian height, and her only confidant and messenger a Bacchus instead of a Mercury! Heigh ho! And in another hour Don Juan—he told me I might call him John—will be waiting for me outside the convent wall! What if Diego fails me? To go there alone would be madness! Who else would be as charmingly unconscious and inattentive as this American vagabond! (*Crosses.*) Ah, my saddle and blanket hidden! He *has* been interrupted. Someone has been watching. This freak of my father's means something. And tonight, of all nights, the night that Oakhurst was to disclose himself and tell me all! What is to be done? Hark! (*Diego, without, singing:* "*Oh, here's your aguardiente, drink it down!*") It is Diego; and Mother of God! drunk again!

(*Enter Sandy, carrying pack, intoxicated; staggers to center, and, observing Jovita, takes off his hat respectfully.*)

JOVITA: (*Shaking him by the shoulders passionately.*) Diego! How dare you! And at such a time!

SANDY: (*With drunken solemnity.*) Miss Jovita, did ye ever know me to be drunk afore at such a time?

JOVITA: No.

SANDY: Zachy so. It's abnormal. And it means—the game's up.

JOVITA: I do not understand. For the love of God, Diego, be plain!

SANDY: (*Solemnly and drunkenly.*) When I say your game's up, I mean the old man knows it all. You're blowed upon.[14] Hearken, miss! (*Seriously and soberly.*) Your father knows all that I know, but, as it wasn't my business to interfere with, I hev sorter helped along. He knows that you meet a stranger, an American, in these rides with me.

JOVITA: (*Passionately.*) Ingrate! You have not dared to tell him! (*Seizing him by the collar and threatening him with the horsewhip.*)

SANDY: (*Rising with half-drunken, half-sober solemnity.*) One minit, miss! one minit! Don't ye! don't ye do that! Ef ye forget (and I don't blame ye for it), ef ye forget that I'm a man, don't ye, don't ye forget that you're a woman! Sit ye down, sit ye down, so! Now, ef ye'll kindly remember, miss, I never saw this yer man, yer lover. Ef ye'll recollect, miss whenever you met him, I allers hung back and waited round in the mission, or in the fields beyond for ye, and allowed ye to hev your own way, it bein' no business o' mine. Thar isn't a man on the ranch who, ef he'd had a mind to watch ye, wouldn't hev known more about yer lover than I do.

JOVITA: (*Aside.*) He speaks truly. He always kept in the background. Even Don Juan never knew that I had an attendant until I told him. (*Aloud.*) I made a mistake, Diego. I was hasty. What am I to do? He is waiting for me even now.

SANDY: (*With drunken gravity.*) Well, ef ye can't go to him, I reckon it's the square thing for him to come to ye.

JOVITA: Recollect yourself, Diego. Be a man!

SANDY: Thash jus wot I say. Let him be a man, and come to ye here. Let him ride up to this ranch like a man, and call out to yer father that he'll take ye jist as ye are, without the land. And if the old man allows, rather than hev ye marry that stranger, he'll give this yer place to the church, why, let him do it, and be damned.

JOVITA: (*Recoiling, aside.*) So! That is their plan. Don Jose has worked on the fears or the cupidity of this drunken ingrate.

SANDY: (*With drunken submission.*) Ye was speaking to me, miss. Ef ye'll take my advice—a drunken man's advice, miss—ye'll say to that lover of yours, ef he's afeard to come for ye here, to take ye as ye stand, he ain't no man for ye. And ontil he does, ye'll do as the ole man says. Fur ef I do say it, miss—and thar ain't no love lost between us—he's a good father to ye. It ain't every day that a gal kin afford to swap a father like that, as she *does know*, fur the husband that she *don't*! He's a proud old fool, miss, but to ye, to ye, he's clar grit all through.

JOVITA: (*Passionately, aside.*) Tricked, fooled, like a child! and through the means of this treacherous, drunken fool. (*Stamping her foot.*) Ah! we shall see! You are wise, you are wise, Don Jose, but your daughter is not a novice, nor a helpless creature of the Holy Church. (*Passionately.*) I'll—I'll become a Protestant tomorrow!

SANDY: (*Unheeding her passion, and becoming more earnest and self-possessed.*) Ef ye hed a father, miss, ez instead o' harkinin' to your slightest wish, and surroundin' ye with luxury, hed made your infancy a struggle for life among strangers, and your childhood a disgrace and a temptation; ef he had left ye with no company but want, with no companions but guilt, with no mother but suffering; ef he had made your home, this home, so unhappy, so terrible, so awful, that the crowded streets and gutters of a great city was something to fly to for relief; ef he had made his presence, his very name—your name, miss, allowin' it was your father—ef he had made that presence so hateful, that name so infamous, that exile, that flyin' to furrin' parts, that wanderin' among strange folks didn't know ye, was the only way to make life endurable; and ef he'd given ye—I mean this good old man Don Jose, miss—ef he'd given ye as part of yer heritage a taint, a weakness in yer very blood, a fondness for a poison, a poison that soothed ye like a vampire bat and sucked yer lifeblood (*seizing her arm*) ez it soothed ye; ef this curse that hung over ye dragged ye down day by day, till hating him, loathing him, ye saw yerself day by day becoming more and more like him, till ye knew that his fate was yours, and yours his—why then, Miss Jovita (*rising with an hysterical drunken laugh*), why then, I'd run away with ye myself—I would, damn me!

JOVITA: (*Who has been withdrawing from him scornfully.*) Well acted, Diego. Don Jose should have seen his pupil. Trust me, my father will reward you. (*Aside.*) And yet there were tears in his drunken eyes. Bah! it is the liquor: he is no longer sane. And, either hypocrite or imbecile, he is to be trusted no longer. But where and why is he going? (*Aloud.*) You are leaving us, Diego.

SANDY: (*Quietly.*) Well, the old man and me don't get on together.

JOVITA: (*Scornfully.*) Bueno! I see. Then you abandon me?

SANDY: (*Quickly.*) To the old man, miss—not the young one. (*Walks to the table and begins to pour out liquor.*)

JOVITA: (*Angrily.*) You would not dare to talk to me thus, if John Oakhurst—ah!

(*Checking herself.*)

SANDY: (*Drops glass on table, hurries to center and seizes Dona Jovita.*) Eh! Wot! Wot name did you say? (*Looks at her amazed and bewildered.*)

JOVITA: (*Terrified, aside.*) Mother of God! What have I done? Broken my sacred pledge to keep his name secret. No! No! Diego did not hear me! Surely this wretched drunkard does not know him. (*Aloud.*) Nothing. I said nothing: I mentioned no name.

SANDY: (*Still amazed, frightened, and bewildered, passing his hand over his forehead slowly.*) Ye mentioned no name? Surely. I am wild, crazed. Tell me, miss—ye didn't—I know ye didn't, but I thought it sounded like it—ye didn't mention the name of—of—of—John Oakhurst?

JOVITA: (*Hurriedly.*) No, of course not! You terrify me, Diego. You are wild.

SANDY: (*Dropping her hand with a sigh of relief.*) No, no! In course ye didn't. I was wild, miss, wild; this drink has confused me yer. (*Pointing to his head.*) There are times when I hear that name, miss—times when I see his face. (*Sadly.*) But it's when I've took too much—too much. I'll drink no more—no more!—tonight—tonight! (*Drops his head slowly in his hands.*)

JOVITA: (*Looking at Diego—aside.*) Really, I'm feeling very uncomfortable. I'd like to ask a question of this maniac. But nonsense! Don Juan gave me to understand Oakhurst wasn't his real name; that is, he intimated there was something dreadful and mysterious about it that mustn't be told—something that would frighten people. *Holy Virgin!* it has! Why, this reckless vagabond here is pale and agitated. Don Juan shall explain this mystery tonight. But then, how shall I see him? Ah, I have it. The night of the last fiesta, when I could not leave the rancho, he begged me to show a light from the flat roof of the upper corridor, that he might know I was thinking of him—dear felllow! He will linger tonight at the Mission; he will see the light; he will know that I have not forgotten. He will approach the rancho; I shall manage to slip away at midnight to the ruined Mission. I shall—ah, it is my father! Holy Virgin, befriend me now with self-possession. (*Stands quietly, looking toward Sandy, who still remains buried in thought, as—*)

(*Enter Don Jose; regards his daughter and Diego with a sarcastic smile.*)

DON JOSE: (*Aside.*) Bueno! It is as I expected—an explanation, an explosion, a lover's quarrel, an end to romance. From his looks I should say she has been teaching the adventurer a lesson. Good! I could embrace her! (*Crosses to Sandy—aloud.*) You still here!

SANDY: (*Rising with a start.*) Yes! I—a—I was only taking leave of Miss Jovita that hez been kind to me. She's a good gal, ole man, and won't be any the worse when I'm gone—Good-bye, Miss Jovita (*extending his hand*), I wish ye luck.

JOVITA: (*Coldly.*) Adios, friend Diego. (*Aside, hurriedly.*) You will not expose my secret?

SANDY: (*Aside.*) It ain't in me, miss. (*To Don Jose, going.*) Adios, ole man. (*Shouldering his pack.*)

DON JOSE: Adios, friend Diego. (*Formally.*) May good luck attend you! (*Aside.*)

You understand, on your word as—as—as—*a gentleman!*—you have no further communication with this rancho, or aught that it contains.

SANDY: (*Gravely.*) I hear ye, ole man. Adios. (*Goes to gateway, but pauses at table, and begins to fill a glass of aguardiente.*)

DON JOSE: (*Aside, looking at his daughter.*) I could embrace her now. She is truly a Castro. (*Aloud to Jovita.*) Hark ye, little one! I have news that will please you, and—who knows?—perhaps break up the monotony of the dull life of the rancho. Tonight come to me two famous caballeros, Americanos, you understand: they will be here soon, even now. Retire, and make ready to receive them. (*Exit Jovita.*)

DON JOSE: (*Aside, looking at Sandy.*) He lingers. I shall not be satisfied until Concho has seen him safely beyond the Mission wall.

(*Enter Concho.*)

CONCHO: Two caballeros have dismounted in the corral and seek the honor of Don Jose's presence.

DON JOSE: Bueno! (*Aside.*) Follow that fellow beyond the Mission. (*Aloud.*) Admit the strangers. Did they give their names?

CONCHO: They did, Don Jose—Colonel Culpepper Starbottle and the Don Alexandro Morton.

SANDY: (*Dropping glass of aguardiente, and staggering stupidly to the center, confronting Don Jose and Concho, sitll holding bottle.*) Eh! Wot? Wot name did you say? (*Looks stupidly and amazedly at Concho and Don Jose, and then slowly passes his hand over his forehead. Then slowly and apologetically.*) I axes your pardon, Don Jose, and yours, sir (*to Concho*), but I thought ye called me. No!—that ez—I mean—I mean—I'm a little off color here (*pointing to his head*). I don't follow suit—I—eh—eh! Oh!—ye'll pardon me, sir, but thar's names—perhaps yer darter will remember that I was took a bit ago on a name—thar's names sorter hangin' round me yer (*pointing to his head*), that I thinks I hear—but bein' drunk—I hopes ye'll excoos me. Adios. (*Staggers to gateway, Concho following.*)

CONCHO: (*Aside.*) There is something more in this than Don Jose would have known. I'll watch Diego, and keep an eye on Miss Jovita too.

(*Exit, following Sandy, who, in exit, jostles against Colonel Starbottle entering, who stops and leans exhaustedly at the wall to get his breath; following him closely, and oblivious of Sandy Morton, Alexander Morton, Sr. Enter Col. Starbottle and Alexander Morton, Sr.*)

SCENE 2: *The Same.*

COL. STARBOTTLE: (*Entering, to Don Jose.*) Overlooking the insult of —er—er[15] —inebriated individual, whose menial position in this—er—er—houshold precludes a demand for personal satisfaction, sir, I believe I have the honor of addressing Don Jose Castro. Very good, sir. Permit me, sir, to introduce myself as Colonel Culpepper Starbottle—damn me! the legal adviser of Mr. Alexander Morton, Sr., and I may add, sir, the friend of that gentleman, and as such, sir—er—er—personally—personally responsible.

ALEXANDER MORTON: (*Puritanically and lugubriously.*) As a God-fearing and forgiving Christian, Mr. Castro, I trust you will overlook the habitual profanity of the erring but well-meaning man, who, by the necessities of my situation, accompanies me. I am the person—a helpless sinner—mentioned in the letters which I believe have preceded me. As a professing member of the Cumberland Presbyterian Church, I have ventured, in the interest of works rather than faith, to overlook the plain doctrines of the church in claiming sympathy of a superstitious papist.

STARBOTTLE: (*Interrupting, aside to Alexander Morton.*) Ahem! ahem! (*Aloud to Don Jose.*) My friend's manner, sir, reminds me of—er—er—Ram Bootgum Sing, first secretary of Turkish legation at Washington in '45; most remarkable man—damn me—most remarkable—and warm personal friend. Challenged Tod Robinson for putting him next to Hebrew banker at dinner, with remark—damn me—that they were both believers in the profit! he, he! Amusing, perhaps; irreverent, certainly. Fought with scimitars. Second pass, Ram divided Tod in two pieces—fact, sir—just here (*pointing*)—in—er—er—region of moral emotions. Upper half called to me—said to me warningly—last words—never forget it—"Star,"—always called me Star—"respect man's religious convictions." Legs dead; emotion confined to upper part of body—pathetic picture. Ged, sir, something to be remembered!

DON JOSE: (*With grave Spanish courtesy.*) You are welcome, gentlemen, to the rancho of the Blessed Fisherman. Your letters, with honorable report, are here. Believe me, senores, in your modesty you have forgotten to mention your strongest claim to the hospitality of my house—the royal right of strangers.

MORTON: Angels before this have been entertained as strangers, says the Good Book, and that, I take it, is your authority for this ceremoniousness which else were but lip-service and papist airs. But I am here in the performance of a duty, Mr. Castro—the duty of a Christian father. I am seeking a prodigal son. I am seeking him in his winehusks and among his harl—

STARBOTTLE: (*Interrupting.*) A single moment. (*To Don Jose.*) Permit me to—er—explain. As my friend Mr. Morton states, we are, in fact, at present engaged in—er—er—quest—er—pilgrimage that possibly to some, unless deterred by considerations of responsibility—personal responsibility, sir—Ged, sir, might be looked upon as visionary, enthusiastic, sentimental, fanatical. We are seeking a son, or, as my friend tersely and scripturally expresses it—er—er—prodigal son. I say scripturally, sir, and tersely, but not, you understand it, literally, nor I may add, sir, legally. Ged, sir, as a precedent, I admit we are wrong. To the best of my knowledge, sir, the—er—Prodigal Son sought his own father. To be frank, sir—and Ged, sir, if Culpepper Starbottle has a fault, it is frankness, sir . . . As Nelse Buckthorne said to me in Nashville, in '47, "You would infer, Colonel Starbottle, that I equivocate." I replied, "I do, sir, and permit me to add that equivocation has all the guilt of a lie, with cowardice superadded." The next morning at nine o'clock, Ged, sir, he gasped to me—he was lying on the ground, hole through his left lung just here (*illustrating with Don Jose's coat*)—he gasped, "If you have a merit, Star, above others, it is frankness!" his last words, sir—damn me . . . To be frank, sir, years ago, in the wild exuberance of youth, the son of this gentleman left his—er—er—er—boyhood's home, owing to an innocent but natural misunderstanding with the legal protector of his youth—

MORTON: (*Interrupting gravely and demurely.*) Driven from home by my own sinful and unregenerate hand—

STARBOTTLE: (*Quickly.*) One moment, a simple moment. We will not weary you with—er—er—history, or the vagaries of youth. He—er—came to California in '49. A year ago, touched by—er—er—parental emotion and solicitude, my friend resolved to seek him here. Believing that the—er—er—lawlessness of—er—er—untrammeled youth and boyish inexperience might have led him into some trifling indiscretion, we have sought him successively in hospitals, alms-houses, reformatories, State's prisons, lunatic and inebriate asylums, and—er—er—even on the monumental inscriptions of the—er—er—country churchyards. We have thus far, I grieve to say, although acquiring much and valuable information of a varied character and interest, as far as the direct matter of our search—we have been, I think I may say, unsuccessful. Our search has been attended with the—er—disbursement of some capital under my—er—er—direction, which, though large, represents quite inadequately the—er—er—earnestness of our endeavors.

(*Enter Manuela.*)

MANUELA: (*To Don Jose.*) The Dona Jovita is waiting to receive you.

DON JOSE: (*To Morton.*) You shall tell me further of your interesting pilgrimage hereafter. At present my daughter awaits us to place this humble roof at your disposal. I am a widower, Don Alexandro, like yourself. When I say that, like you, I have an only child, and that I love her, you will understand how earnest is my sympathy. This way, gentlemen. (*Leading to door in corridor, and awaiting them.*)

STARBOTTLE: (*Aside.*) Umph! an interview with lovely woman means—er—intoxication, but—er—er—no liquor. It's evident that the Don doesn't drink. Eh! (*Catches sight of table in corridor, and bottle.*) Oh, he does, but some absurd Spanish formality prevents his doing the polite thing before dinner. (*Aloud, to Don Jose.*) One moment sir, one moment. If you will—er—er—pardon the—er—seeming discourtesy, for which I am, I admit—er—personally responsible, I will for a few moments enjoy the—er—er—delicious air of the courtyard, and the beauties of Nature as displayed in the—er—sunset. I will—er—rejoin you and the—er—er—ladies a moment later.

DON JOSE: The house is your own, senor: do as you will. This way, Don Alexandro. (*Exit Don Jose and Morton, Sr.*)

STARBOTTLE: "Do as you will." Well, I don't understand Spanish ceremony, but that's certainly good English. (*Going to table.*) Eh! (*Smelling decanter.*) Robinson County whiskey! Umph! I have observed that the spirit of American institutions, sir, are already penetrating the—er—er—superstitions of—er—foreign and effete civilizations. (*Pours out glass of whiskey and drinks; pours again, and observes Manuela watching him respectfully.*) What the devil is that girl looking at? Eh! (*Puts down glass.*)

MANUELA: (*Aside.*) He is fierce and warlike. Mother of God! But he is not so awful as that gray-haired caballero, who looks like a fasting St. Anthony. And he loves aguardiente: he will pity Diego the more. (*Aloud.*) Ahem! Senor. (*Courtesies coquettishly.*)

STARBOTTLE: (*Aside.*) Oh, I see. Ged! not a bad-looking girl—a trifle dark, but Southern, and—er—tropical. Ged, Star, Star, this won't do, sir; no, sir. The filial affections of Aeneas are not to be sacrificed through the blandishments of—er—Dodo—I mean a Dido.

MANUELA: Ah senor, you are kind, you are good! You are an Americano, one of a great nation. You will feel sympathy for a poor young man—a mere muchaco[16]—one of your own race, who was a vaquero here, senor. He has been sent away from us here disgraced, alone, hungry, perhaps penniless. (*Wipes her eyes.*)

STARBOTTLE: The devil! Another prodigal. (*Aloud.*) My dear, the case you have just stated would appear to be the—er—er—normal condition of the—er—youth of America. But why was he discharged? (*Pouring out liquor.*)

MANUELA: (*Demurely glancing at the colonel.*) He was drunk, senor.

STARBOTTLE: (*Potently.*) Drunkenness, my child, which is—er—weakness in the—er—er—gentleman, in the subordinate is a crime. What—er—excites the social impulse and exhilarates the fancy of the—er—master of the house, in the performance of his duty, renders the servant unfit for his. Legally it is a breach of contract. I should give it as my opinion—for which I am personally responsible—that your friend Diego could not recover. Ged! (*Aside.*) I wonder if this scapegoat could be our black sheep.

MANUELA: But that was not all, senor. It was an excuse only. He was sent away for helping our young lady to a cavalier. He was discharged because he would not be a traitor to her. He was sent away because he was too good, too honorable—too—(*Bursts out crying.*)

STARBOTTLE: (*Aside.*) Oh, the devil! *this* is no Sandy Morton. (*Coming forward gravely.*) I have never yet analyzed the—er—er—character of the young gentleman I have the honor to assist in restoring to his family and society, but judging—er—calmly—er—dispassionately, my knowledge of his own father—from what the old gentleman must have been in his unregenerate state, and knowing what he is now in his present reformed Christian condition, I should say clamly and deliberately that the son must be the most infernal and accomplished villain unhung. Ged, I have a thought, an inspiration. (*To Manuela, tapping her under the chin.*) I see, my dear; a lover, ha, ha! Ah, you rogue! Well, well, we will talk of this again. I will—er—er—interest myself in this Diego. (*Exit Manuela.*)

STARBOTTLE: (*Solus.*) How would it do to get up a prodigal? Umph! Something must be done soon: the old man grows languid in his search. My position as a sinecure is—er—in peril. A prodigal ready-made! But could I get a scoundrel bad enough to satisfy the old man? Ged, that's serious. Let me see: he admits that he is unable to recognize his own son in face, features, manner or speech.

Good! If I could pick up some rascal whose—er—irregularities didn't quite fill the bill, and could say—Ged!—that he was reforming. Reforming! Ged, Star! That very defect would show the hereditary taint, demn me! I must think of this seriously. Ged, Star! the idea is—an inspiration of humanity and virtue. Who knows? it might be the saving of the vagabond—a crown of glory to the old man's age. Inspiration, did I say? Ged, Star, it's a *duty*—a sacred, solemn duty, for which you are responsible—personally responsible.

(Lights down half. Enter from corridor Morton, Don Jose, Dona Jovita, and Manuela.)

JOVITA: *(Stepping forward with exaggerated Spanish courtesy.)* A thousand graces await your Excellency, Commander Don—Don—

STARBOTTLE: *(Bowing to the ground with equal delight and exaggerated courtesy.)* Er—Coolpepero!

JOVITA: Don Culpepero! If we throw ourselves unasked at your excellency's feet *(courtesy)*, if we appear unsought before the light of your excellency's eyes *(courtesy)*, if we err in maidenly decorum in thus seeking unbidden your excellency's presence *(courtesy)*, believe us, it is the fear of some greater, some graver indecorum in our conduct that has withdrawn your excellency's person from us since you have graced our roof with your company. We know, Senor Commander, how superior are the charms of the American ladies. It is in no spirit of rivalry with them, but to show—Mother of God!—that we are not absolutely ugly, that we intrude upon your excellency's solitude. *(Aside.)* I shall need the old fool, and shall use him.

STARBOTTLE: *(Who has been bowing and saluting with equal extravagance, during this speech—aside.)* Ged! she is beautiful! *(Aloud.)* Permit me—er—Dona Jovita, to correct—Ged, I must say it, correct erroneous statements. The man who should—er—utter in my presence remarks, disparaging those—er—charms it is my privilege to behold, I should hold responsible—Ged! personally responsible. You—er—remind me of—er—incident, trifling perhaps, but pleasing, Charleston in '52—a reception at John C. Calhoun's. A lady, one of the demnedest beautiful women you ever saw, said to me, "Star!"—she always called me Star—"you avoided me, you have, Star! I fear you are no longer my friend."—"Your friend, madam," I said. "No, I've avoided you because I am your lover." Ged, Miss Jovita, a fact—demn me. Sensation. Husband heard garbled report. He was old friend, but jealous, rash, indiscreet. Fell at first fire—umph—January 5th. Lady—beautiful woman—never forgave: went into convent. Sad affair. And all a mistake—demn me—all a mistake, though perhaps extravagant gallantry and compliment. I lingered here, oblivious perhaps of—er—beauty, in the enjoyment of Nature.

JOVITA: Is there enough for your excellency to share with me, since it must be my rival? See, the fog is clearing away: we shall have moonlight. *(Don Jose and Morton seat themselves at table.)* Shall we not let these venerable caballeros enjoy their confidences and experiences together? *(Aside.)* Don Jose watches me like a fox, does not intend to lose sight of me. How shall I show the light three times from the courtyard roof? I have it! (*Takes Starbottle's arm.*) It is too pleasant to withdraw. There is a view from the courtyard wall your excellency shall see. Will you accompany me? The ascent is easy.

STARBOTTLE: (*Bowing.*) I will ascend, although, permit me to say, Dona Jovita, it would be—er—impossible for me to be nearer—er—heaven, than—er—at present.

JOVITA: Flatterer! Come, you shall tell me about this sad lady who died. Ah, Don Culpepero, let me hope all your experiences will not be so fatal to us! (*Exit Dona Jovita and Starbottle.*)

MORTON: (*Aside.*) A forward daughter of Baal, and, if I mistake not, even now concocting mischief for this foolish, indulgent, stiff-necked father. (*Aloud.*) Your only daughter, I presume.

DON JOSE: My darling, Don Alexandro. Motherless from her infancy. A little wild and inclined to gaiety, but I hope not seeking for more than these walls afford. I have checked her but seldom, Don Alexandro, and then I did not let her see my hand on the rein that held her back. I do not ask her confidence always: I only want to know that when the time comes it can be given to me without fear.

MORTON: Umph!

DON JOSE: (*Leaning forward confidentially.*) To show that you have not intrusted your confidence regarding your wayward son—whom may the saints return to you!—to unsympathetic or inexperienced ears, I will impart a secret. A few weeks ago I detected an innocent intimacy between this foolish girl and a vagabond vaquero in my employ. You understand, it was on her part romantic, visionary; on his, calculating, shrewd, self-interested, for he expected to become my heir. I did not lock her up. I did not tax her with it. I humored it. Today I satisfied the lover that his investment was not profitable, that a marriage without my consent entailed the loss of the property and then left them together. They parted in tears, think you, Don Alexandro? No, but mutually hating each other. The romance was over. An American would have opposed the girl, have driven her to secrecy, to an elopement, perhaps. Eh?

MORTON: (*Scornfully.*) And you believe that they have abandoned their plans?

DON JOSE: I am sure—hush! she is here!

(*Enter on roof of corridor, Starbottle and Jovita.*)

STARBOTTLE: Really, a superb landscape! An admirable view of the—er—fog—rolling over the Mission Hills, the plains below, and the—er—er—single figure of—er—motionless horseman—

JOVITA: (*Quickly.*) Some belated vaquero. Do you smoke, Senor Commander?

STARBOTTLE: At times.

JOVITA: With me. I will light a cigarette for you: it is the custom. (*Starbottle draws match from his pocket, and is about to light, but is stopped by Dona Jovita.*) Pardon, your excellency, but we cannot endure your American matches. There is a taper in the passage. (*Starbottle brings taper; Dona Jovita turns to light cigarette but manages to blow out candle.*) I must try your gallantry again. That is once I have failed. (*Significantly. Starbottle relights candle, business, same results.*) I am stupid and nervous tonight. I have failed *twice.*

(With emphasis. Starbottle repeats business with candle. Dona Jovita lights cigarette, hands it to the colonel.) Thrice, and I have succeeded. (*Blows out candle.*)

STARBOTTLE: A thousand thanks! There is a—er—er—light on the plain.

JOVITA: (*Hastily.*) It is the vaqueros returning. My father gives a festa to peons in honor of your arrival. There will be a dance. You have been patient, Senor Commander: you shall have my hand for a waltz.

(*Enter vaqueros, their wives and daughters. A dance, during which the "sembi canca*[17]" *is danced by Col. Starbottle and Dona Jovita. Business, during which the bell of Mission Church, faintly illuminated beyond the wall, strikes twelve. Dancers withdraw hurriedly, leaving alone Manuela, Dona Jovita, Starbottle, Don Jose, and Concho. Concho formally hands keys to Don Jose.*)

DON JOSE: (*Delivering keys to Morton with stately impressiveness.*) Take them, Don Alexandro Morton, and with them all that they unlock for bliss or bale. Take them, noble guest, and with them the homage of this family—tonight, Don Alexandro, your humble servants. Good night, gentlemen. May a thousand angels attend you, O Don Alexandro, and Don Culpepero!

JOVITA: Good night, Don Alexandro. May your dreams tonight see all your wishes fulfilled! Good night, O Senor Commander. May she you dream of be as happy as you!

MANUELA AND CONCHO: (*Together.*) Good night, O senores and illustrious gentlemen! May the Blessed Fisherman watch over you! (*Both parties retreat into opposite corridors, bowing.*)

SCENE 3: *The same. Stage darkened. Fog passing beyond wall outside, and occasionally obscuring moonlit landscape beyond. Enter Jovita softly, from corridor. Her face is partly hidden by Spanish mantilla.*

JOVITA: All quiet at last; and, thanks to much aguardiente, my warlike admirer snores peacefully above. Yet I could swear I heard the old Puritan's door creak as I descended. Pshaw! What matters! (*Goes to gateway, and tries gate.*) Locked! Carramba! I see it now. Under the pretext of reviving the old ceremony, Don Jose has locked the gates, and placed me in the custody of his guest. Stay! There is a door leading to the corral from the passage by Concho's room. Bueno! Don Jose shall see! (*Exit.*)

(*Enter cautiously Old Morton.*)

MORTON: I was not mistaken! It was the skirt of that Jezebel daughter that whisked past my door a moment ago, and her figure that flitted down that corridor. So! The lover driven out of the house at four p.m., and at twelve o'clock at night the young lady trying the gate secretly. This may be Spanish resignation and filial submission, but it looks very like Yankee disobedience and forwardness. Perhaps it's well that the keys are in my pocket. This fond confiding papist may find the heretic American father of some service. (*Conceals himself behind pillar of corridor.*)

(*After a pause the head of John Oakhurst appears over the wall of corridor: he climbs up to roof of corridor, and descends very quietly and deliberately to stage.*)

OAKHURST: (*Dusting his clothing with his handkerchief.*) I never knew before why these Spaniards covered their adobe walls with whitewash. (*Leans against pillar in shadow.*)

(*Re-enter Jovita, hastily.*)

JOVITA: All is lost; the corral door is locked; the key is outside, and Concho is gone —gone where? Madre di Dios! to discover, perhaps to kill him.
OAKHURST: (*Approaching her.*) No.
JOVITA: Juan! (*Embracing him.*) But how did you get here? This is madness!
OAKHURST: As you did not come to the Mission, I came to the rancho. I found the gate locked—by the way, is not that a novelty here?—I climbed the wall. But you, Miss Castro, you are trembling! Your little hands are cold!
JOVITA: (*Glancing around.*) Nothing, nothing! But you are running a terrible risk. At any moment we may be discovered.
OAKHURST: I understand you: it would be bad for the discoverer. Never fear, I will be patient.
JOVITA: But I feared that you might meet Concho.
OAKHURST: Concho—Concho—(*meditatively*). Let me see—tall, dark, long in the arm, weighs about one hundred and eighty, and active.
JOVITA: Yes; tell me! You have met him?
OAKHURST: Possibly, possibly. Was he a friend of yours?
JOVITA: No!
OAKHURST: That's better. Are his pursuits here sedentary or active?
JOVITA: He is my father's major-domo.
OAKHURST: I see: a sinecure. (*Aside.*) Well, if he has to lay up for a week or two, the rancho won't suffer.
JOVITA: Well?
OAKHURST: Well!
JOVITA: (*Passionately.*) There, having scaled the wall, at the risk of being discovered—this is all you have to say! (*Turning away.*)
OAKHURST: (*Quietly.*) Perhaps, Jovita. (*Taking her hand with grave earnestness.*) To a clandestine intimacy like ours there is but one end. It is not merely elopement, not merely marriage, it is exposure! Sooner or later you and I must face the eyes we now shun. What matters if tonight or later?
JOVITA: (*Quickly.*) I am ready. It was you who—
OAKHURST: It was I who first demanded secrecy, but it was I who told you when we last met that I would tell you why tonight.
JOVITA: I am ready; but hear me, Juan, nothing can change my faith in you.
OAKHURST: (*Sadly.*) You know not what you say. Listen, my child. I am a gambler. Not the man who lavishes his fortune at the gaming-table for excitement's

sake; not the fanatic who stakes his own earnings—perhaps the confided earnings of others—on a single coup. No, he is the man who loses—whom the world deplores, pities, and forgives. I am the man who wins—whom the world hates and despises.

JOVITA: I do not understand you, Juan.

OAKHURST: So much the better, perhaps. But you must hear me. I make a profession—an occupation more exacting, more wearying, more laborious, than that of your meanest herdsmen—of that which others make a dissipation of the senses. And yet, Jovita, there is not the meanest vaquero in this ranch who, playing against me, winning or losing, is not held to be my superior. I have no friends—only confederates. Even the woman who dares to pity me must do it in secret.

JOVITA: But you will abandon this dreadful trade. As the son of the rich Don Jose, no one dare scorn you. My father will relent. I am his heiress.

OAKHURST: No more, Jovita, no more. If I were the man who could purchase the world's respect though a woman's weakness for him, I should not be here to-night. I am not here to sue your father's daughter with hopes of forgiveness, promises of reformation. Reformation, in a man like me, means cowardice or self-interest. (*Old Morton, becoming excited, leans slowly out from the shadow of the pillar, listening intently.*) I am here to take, by force if necessary, a gambler's wife—the woman who will share my fortunes, my disgrace, my losses, who is willing to leave her old life of indulgence, of luxury, of respectability, for mine. You are frightened, little dove: compose yourself. (*Soothing her tenderly and sadly.*) You are frightened at the cruel hawk who has chosen you for a mate.

MORTON: (*Aside.*) God in heaven! This is like *him*! like me!—before the blessed Lord lifted me into regeneration. If it should be! (*Leans forward anxiously from pillar.*)

OAKHURST: (*Aside.*) Still silent! Poor dove, I can hear her foolish heart flutter against mine. Another moment decides our fate. Another moment: John Oakhurst and freedom, or Red Gulch and—she is moving. (*To Jovita.*) I am harsh, little one, and cold. Perhaps I have had much to make me so. (*With feeling.*) But when I first met you; when, lifting my eyes to the church porch, I saw your beautiful face; when, in sheer recklessness and bravado, I raised my hat to you; when you—you, Jovita—lifted your brave eyes to mine, and there, there in the sanctuary, returned my salute—the salutation of the gambler, the outcast, the reprobate—then, then I swore that you should be mine, if I tore you from the sanctuary. Speak now, Jovita: if it was coquetry, speak now; I forgive you: if it was sheer wantonness, speak now; I shall spare you: but if—

JOVITA: (*Throwing herself in his arms.*) Love, Juan! I am yours, now and forever. (*Pause.*) But you have not told me all. I will go with you tonight—now. I leave behind me all—my home, my father, my—(*pause*) my name. You have forgotten, Juan, you have not told me what I change *that* for: you have not told me *yours*.

(*Old Morton, in eager excitement, leans beyond shadow of pillar.*)

OAKHURST: (*Embracing her tenderly, with a smile.*) If I have not told you who I am, it was because, darling, it was more important that you should know what I am. Now that you know that—why—(*embarrassedly*) I have nothing more to tell. I did not wish you to repeat the name of Oakhurst—because—(*aside*) how the devil shall I tell her that Oakhurst was my real name, after all, and that I only feared she might divulge it?—(*aloud*) because—because—(*determinedly*) I doubted your ability to keep a secret. My real name is—(*looks up and sees Morton leaning beyond pillar*) is a secret. (*Pause, in which Oakhurst slowly recovers his coolness.*) It will be given to the good priest who tonight joins our fate forever, Jovita—forever, in spite of calumny, opposition, or spies! the padre whom we shall reach, if enough life remains in your pulse and mine to clasp these hands together. (*After a pause.*) Are you content?

JOVITA: I am.

OAKHURST: Then there is not a moment to lose. Retire, and prepare yourself for a journey. I will wait here.

JOVITA: I am ready now.

OAKHURST: (*Looking toward pillar.*) Pardon, my darling: there was a bracelet—a mere trifle—I once gave you. It is not on your wrist. I am a trifle superstitious, perhaps: it was my first gift. Bring it with you. I will wait. Go! (*Exit Jovita.*)

(*Oakhurst watches her exit, lounges indifferently toward gate; when opposite pillar suddenly seizes Morton by the throat, and drags him noiselessly to center.*)

OAKHURST: (*Hurriedly.*) One outcry—one single word—and it is your last. I care not who *you* may be!—who I am—you have heard enough to know, at least, that you are in the grip of a desperate man. (*Keys fall from Morton's hand. Oakhurst seizes them.*) Silence! on your life.

MORTON: (*Struggling.*) You would not dare! I command you—

OAKHURST: (*Dragging him to gateway.*) Out you must go.

MORTON: Stop, I command you! *I* never turned *my* father out of doors!

OAKHURST: (*Gazing at Morton.*) It is an *old* man! I release you. Do as you will, only remember that that girl is mine forever, that there is no power on earth will keep me from her.

MORTON: On conditions.

OAKHURST: Who are you that make conditions? You are not—her father?

MORTON: No, but I am *yours!* Alexander Morton, I charge you to hear me.

OAKHURST: (*Starting in astonishment; aside.*) Sandy Morton, my lost partner's father! This is fate.

MORTON: You are astonished: but I thought so. Ay, you will hear me now! I am your father, Alexander Morton, who drove you, a helpless boy, into disgrace and misery. I know your shameless life: for twenty years it was mine, and worse, until, by the grace of God, I reformed, as you shall. I have stopped you in a disgraceful act. Your mother—God forgive me!—left *her* house for *my* arms, as wickedly, as wantonly, as shamelessly—

OAKHURST: Stop, old man! Stop! Another word, (*seizing him*) and I may forget your years.

MORTON: But not your blood. No, Alexander Morton, I have come thousands of miles for one sacred purpose—to save you; and I shall, with God's will, do it now. Be it so, one one condition. You shall have this girl; but lawfully, openly, with the sanction of Heaven and your parents.

OAKHURST: (*Aside.*) I see a ray of hope. This is Sandy's father; the cold, insensate brute, who drove him into exile, the one bitter memory of his life. Sandy disappeared, irreclaimable, or living alone, hating irrevocably the author of his misery: why should not I—

MORTON: (*Continuing.*) On one condition. Hear me, Alexander Morton. If within one year, you, abandoning your evil practices, your wayward life, seek to reform beneath my roof, I will make this proud Spanish Don glad to accept you as the more than equal of his daughter.

OAKHURST: (*Aside.*) It would be an easy deception. Sandy has given me the details of his early life. At least, before the imposition was discovered I shall be—(*Aloud.*) I—I—(*Aside.*) Perdition! *she* is coming! There is a light moving in the upper chamber. Don Jose is awakened. (*Aloud.*) I—I—accept.

MORTON: It is well. Take these keys, open yonder gate, and fly! (*As Oakhurst hesitates.*) Obey me. I will meet your sweetheart, and explain all. You will come here at daylight in the morning, and claim admittance, not as a vagabond, a housebreaker, but as my son. You hesitate. Alexander Morton, I, your father, command you. Go!

(*Oakhurst goes to the gate, opens it, as the sound of Diego's voice, singing in the fog, comes faintly in.*)

Oh, yer's your Sandy Morton,
   Drink him down!
Oh, yer's your Sandy Morton,
   Drink him down!
Oh, yer's your Sandy Morton,
For he's drunk, and goin' a-courtin',
Oh, yer's your Sandy Morton,
   Drink him down!

(*Oakhurst recoils against gate, Morton hesitates as window in corridor opens, and Don Jose calls from upper corridor.*)

DON JOSE: Concho! (*Pause.*) 'Tis that vagabond Diego, lost his way in the fog. Strange that Concho should have overlooked him. I will descend.

MORTON: (*To Oakhurst.*) Do you hear?

(*Exit Oakhurst through gateway. Morton closes gate, and returns to center. Enter Jovita hurriedly.*)

JOVITA: I have it here. Quick! There is a light in Don Jose's chamber; my father is coming down. (*Sees Morton and screams.*)

MORTON: (*Seizing her.*) Hush! for your own sake; for *his*; control yourself. He is gone, but he will return. (*To Jovita, still struggling.*) Hush, I beg, Miss Jovita. I beg, I command you, my daughter. Hush!

JOVITA: (*Whispering.*) His voice has changed. What does this mean? (*Aloud.*) Where has he gone? And why are *you* here?

MORTON: (*Slowly and seriously.*) He has left me here to answer the unanswered question you asked him. (*Enter Don Jose and Col. Starbottle.*) I am here to tell you that I am his father, and that he is Alexander Morton.

(*Tableaux. Curtain.*)

END OF ACT I

ACT II

SCENE I: *Red Gulch. Canon of river, and distant view of Sierras, snow-ravined. Schoolhouse of logs in right middle distance. Ledge of rocks in center. On steps of schoolhouse, two large bunches of flowers. Enter Starbottle, slowly climbing rocks, panting and exhausted. Seats himself on rock, foreground, and wipes his face with his pocket-handkerchief.*

STARBOTTLE: This is evidently the er—locality. Here are the—er—groves of Academus—the heights of er—Ida! I should say that the unwillingness which the—er—divine Shakespeare points out in the—er—"whining schoolboy" is intensified in—er—climbing this height, and the—er—alacrity of his departure must be in exact ratio to his gravitation. Good idea. Ged! say it to school-ma'am. Wonder what she's like? Humph! the usual thin, weazened, hatchet-faced Yankee spinster, with an indecent familiarity with Webster's Dictionary! And this is the woman, Star, you're expected to discover and bring back to affluence and plenty. This is the new fanaticism of Mr. Alexander Morton, Sr. Ged! not satisfied with dragging his prodigal son out of merited obscurity, this miserable old lunatic commissions *me* to hunt up another of his abused relatives; some forty-fifth cousin, whose mother he had frozen, beaten, or starved to death! And all this to please his prodigal! Ged! if that prodigal hadn't presented himself that morning, I'd have picked up—er—some—er—reduced gentleman—Ged, that knew how to spend the old man's money to better advantage. (*Musing.*) If this school mistress were barely good-looking, Star—and she's sure to have fifty thousand from the old man—Ged, you might get even with Alexander Sr., for betrothing his prodigal to Dona Jovita, in spite of the—er—evident preference that the girl showed for you. Capital idea! If she's not positively hideous, I'll do it! Ged! I'll reconnoitre first! (*Musing.*) I could stand one eye; yes—er—single eye wouldn't be positively objectionable in the—er—present experiments of science toward the—er—the substitution of glass.[18] Red hair, Star, is—er—Venetian—the beauty of Giorgione. (*Goes up to schoolhouse window, and looks in.*) Too early! Seven empty benches; seven desks splashed with ink. The—er—rostrum of the awful Minerva empty, but—er—adorned with flowers, nosegays—demn me! And here, here on the—er—very threshold (*looking down*), floral tributes. The—er—conceit of these New England schoolma'ams, and their—er—evident Jesuitical influence over the young, is fraught, sir, fraught with—er—darkly political significance. Eh, Ged! there's a caricature on the blackboard. (*Laughing.*) Ha, ha! Absurd chalk outline of ridiculous fat person. Evidently the schoolma'am's admirer. Ged! immensely funny! Ah! boys will be boys. Like you, Star, just like you—always up to tricks like that. A sentence scrawled below the figure seems to be—er—explanation. Hem! (*Takes out eyeglass.*) Let's see. (*Reading.*) "This is old"—old—er—old—demme, sir—"Starbottle!" This is infamous. I haven't been forty-eight hours in the place, and to my certain knowledge haven't spoken to a child. Ged, sir, it's the—er—posting of a libel! The woman, the—er—female, who permits this kind of thing, should be made responsible—er—personally responsible. Eh, hush! What have we here? (*Retires to ledge of rocks.*)

(*Enter Miss Mary, reading letter.*)

MISS MARY: Strange! Is it all a dream? No! here are the familiar rocks, the distant snow-peaks, the schoolhouse, the spring below. An hour ago I was the poor schoolmistress of Red Gulch, with no ambition nor hope beyond this mountain wall, and now—oh, it must be a dream! But here is the letter. Certainly this is no delusion: it is too plain, formal, business-like. (*Reads.*)

My Dear Cousin—I address the only surviving child of my cousin Mary and her husband John Morris, both deceased. It is my duty as a Christian relative to provide you with a home—to share with you that wealth and those blessings that Providence has vouchsafed me. I am aware that my conduct to your father and mother, while in my sinful and unregenerate state, is no warrantee for my present promises, but my legal adviser, Colonel Starbottle, who is empowered to treat with you, will assure you of the sincerity of my intention, and my legal ability to perform it. He will conduct you to my house; you will share its roof with me and my prodigal son Alexander, now by the grace of God restored, and mindful of the error of his ways. I enclose a draft for one-thousand dollars; if you require more, draw upon me for the same.

Your cousin,
Alexander Morton, Sr.

My mother's cousin—so! Cousin Alexander! a rich man, and reunited to the son he drove into shameful exile. Well! we will see this confidential lawyer, and until then—until then—why, we are the schoolmistress of Red Gulch and responsible for its youthful prodigals! (*Going to the schoolhouse door. Stopping to examine flowers.*) Poor, poor Sandy! Another offering, and, as he fondly believes, unknown and anonymous! As if he were not visible in every petal and leaf! The mariposa blossom of the plain. The snow-flower I longed for, from those cool snow-drifts beyond the ridge. And I really believe he was sober when he arranged them. Poor fellow! I begin to think that the dissipated portion of this community are the most interesting. Ah! some one behind the rock—Sandy, I'll wager. No! a stranger!

STARBOTTLE: (*Aside, and advancing.*) If I could make her think I left those flowers! (*Aloud.*) When I state that—er—I am perhaps—er—stranger—

MISS MARY: (*Interrupting him coldly.*) You explain, sir, your appearance on a spot which the rude courtesy of even this rough miner's camp has preserved from intrusion.

STARBOTTLE: (*Slightly abashed, but recovering himself.*) Yes—Ged!—that is, I—er—saw you admiring—er—tribute—er—humble tribute of flowers. I am myself passionately devoted to flowers. Ged! I've spent hours—in—er—bending over the—er—graceful sunflower, in—er—plucking the timid violet from the overhanging but reluctant bough, in collecting the—er—*fauna*—I mean the—er—*flora*—of this—er—district.

MISS MARY: (*Who has been regarding him intently.*) Permit me to leave you in uninterrupted admiration of them. (*Handing him flowers.*) You will have ample time in your journey down the gulch to indulge your *curiosity!*

(*Hands Starbottle flowers, enters schoolhouse, and quietly closes door on Starbottle, as Sandy Morton enters cautiously and sheepishly. Sandy stops in astonishment on observing Starbottle and remains by wing.*)

STARBOTTLE: (*Smelling flowers, and not noticing Miss Mary's absence.*) Beautiful—er—exquisite. (*Looking up at closed door.*) Ged! Most extraordinary disappearance! (*Looks around and discovers Sandy; examines him for a moment through his eyeglass, and then, after a pause, inflates his chest, turns his back on Sandy, and advances to schoolhouse door. Sandy comes quickly, and, as Starbottle raises his cane to rap on door, seizes his arm. Both men, regarding each other fixedly, holding each other, retreat slowly and cautiously to center. Then Starbottle disengages his arm.*)

SANDY: (*Embarrassedly but determinedly.*) Look yer, stranger. By the rules of this camp, this place is sacred to the schoolma'am and her children.

STARBOTTLE: (*With lofty severity.*) It is! Then—er—permit to me to ask, sir, what *you* are doing here.

SANDY: (*Embarrassed, dropping his head in confusion.*) I was—passing. There is no school today.

STARBOTTLE: Then, sir, Ged! permit me to—er—*demand—demand*, sir—an apology. You have laid, sir, your hand upon my person—demn me! Not the first time, sir, either; for, if I am not mistaken, you are the—er—inebriated menial, sir, who two months ago jostled me, sir—demn me—as I entered the rancho of my friend Don Jose Castro.

SANDY: (*Starting, aside.*) Don Jose! (*Aloud.*) Hush, hush! She will hear you. No—that is—(*Stops, confused and embarrassed. Aside.*) She will hear of my disgrace. He will tell her the whole story.

STARBOTTLE: I shall await your apology one hour. At the end of that time, if it is not forthcoming, I shall—er—er—waive your menial antecedents, and expect the—er—satisfaction of a gentleman. Good morning, sir. (*Turns to schoolhouse.*)

SANDY: No, no; you shall not go!

STARBOTTLE: Who will prevent me?

SANDY: (*Grappling him.*) I will. (*Appealingly.*) Look yer, stranger, don't provoke me, I, a desperate man, desperate and crazed with drink—don't ye, don't ye do it! For God's sake, take your hands off me! Ye don't know what ye do. Ah! (*Wildly, holding Starbottle firmly, and forcing him backward to precipice beyond ledge of rocks.*) Hear me. Three years ago, in a moment like this, I dragged a man—my friend—to this precipice. I—I—no! no!—don't anger me now! (*Sandy's grip on Starbottle relaxes slightly and his head droops.*)

STARBOTTLE: (*Coldly.*) Permit me to remark, sir, that any reminiscence of your—er—friend—or any other man is—er—at this moment, irrelevant and impertinent. Permit me to point out the—er—fact, sir, that your hand is pressing heavily, demned heavily, on my shoulder.

SANDY: (*Fiercely.*) You shall not go!

STARBOTTLE: (*Fiercely.*) Shall not?

(*Struggle. Starbottle draws derringer from his breastpocket, and Sandy seizes his arm. In this positon, both parties struggle to ledge of rocks, and Col. Starbottle is forced partly over.*)

MISS MARY: (*Opening schoolhouse door.*) I thought I heard voices. (*Looking toward ledge of rocks, where Col. Starbottle and Sandy are partly hidden by trees. Both men relax grasp of each other at Miss Mary's voice.*)

STARBOTTLE: (*Aloud and with voice slightly raised, to Sandy.*) By—er—leaning over this way a moment, a single moment, you will—er—perceive the trail I speak of. It follows the canyon to the right. It will bring you to—er—the settlement in an hour. (*To Miss Mary, as if observing her for the first time.*) I believe I am—er—right, but, being—er—more familiar with the locality, you can direct the gentleman better.

(*Sandy slowly sinks on his knees beside rock, with his face averted from schoolhouse, as Col. Starbottle disengages himself and advances jauntily and gallantly to schoolhouse.*)

STARBOTTLE: In—er—er—showing the stranger the—er—way, I perhaps interrupted our interview. The—er—observances of—er—civility and humanity must not be foregone, even for—er—the ladies. I—er—believe I address Miss Mary Morris. When I—er—state that my name is Colonel Starbottle, charged on mission of—er—delicate nature, I believe I—er—explain *my* intrusion.

(*Miss Mary bows, and motions to schoolhouse door; Col. Starbottle, bowing deeply, enters, but Miss Mary remains standing by door, looking toward trees that hide Sandy.*)

MISS MARY: (*Aside.*) I am sure it was Sandy's voice! But why does he conceal himself?

SANDY: (*Aside, rising slowly to his feet, with his back to schoolhouse door.*) Even this conceited bully overcomes me and shames me with his readiness and tact. He was quick to spare her—a stranger—the spectacle of two angry men. I—I—must needs wrangle before her very door! Well, well! better out of her sight forever, than an object of pity or terror. (*Exit slowly and with downcast eyes.*)

MISS MARY: (*Watching the trail.*) It *was* Sandy! And this concealment means something more than bashfulness. Perhaps the stranger can explain. (*Enters schoolhouse, and closes door.*)

SCENE 2: *The same. Enter Concho, lame, cautiously. Pauses, and then beckons to Hop Sing, who follows.*

CONCHO: (*Impatiently.*) Well! you saw him?

HOP SING: Me see him.

CONCHO: And you recognized him?

HOP SING: No shabe likoquize.[19]

CONCHO: (*Furiously.*) You knew him, eh? Carramba! You *knew* him.

HOP SING: (*Slowly and sententiously.*) Me shabe man you callee Diego. Me shabbee Led Gulchee call Sandy. Me shabbee man Poker Flat callee Alexandlee Molton. Allee same, John![20] Allee same!

CONCHO: (*Rubbing his hands.*) Bueno! Good John! good John! And you knew he was called Alexander Morton? And go on—good John—go on!

HOP SING: Me plentee washee shirtee—Melican man Poker Flat. Me plentee washee shirt Alexandlee Molton. Always litee, litee on shirt allee time. (*Pointing to tail of his blouse, and imitating writing with finger.*) Alexandlee Molton. Melican man tellee me—shirt say Alexandlee Molton—shabbee?[21]

CONCHO: Bueno! Excellent John. Good John. His linen marked Alexander Morton. The proofs are gathering! (*Crosses.*)—the letter I found in his pack, addressed to Alexander Morton, Poker Flat, which first put me on his track; the story of his wife's infidelity, and her flight with his partner to Red Gulch, the quarrel and fight that separated them, his flight to San Jose, his wanderings to the mission of San Carmel, to the rancho of the Holy Fisherman. The record is complete!

HOP SING: Alexandlee Molton—

CONCHO: (*Hurriedly, returning to Hop Sing.*) Yes! good John; yes, good John—go on. Alexander Morton—

HOP SING: Alexandlee Molton. Me washee shirt, Alexandlee Molton; he no pay washee. Me washee flowty dozen hep—four bittie dozen—twenty dollar hep. Alexandlee Molton no payee. He say, "Go to hellee!" You pay me (*extending his hand.*)

CONCHO: Car—! (*Checking himself.*) *Poco tiempo,*[22] John! In good time, John. Forty dollar—yes. Fifty dollar! Tomorrow, John!

HOP SING: Me no likee "tomollow!" Me no likee "nex time, John!" Allee time Melican man say, "Chalkee up, John," "No smallee change, John,"—umph. Plenty foolee me!

CONCHO: You shall have your money, John, but go now—you comprehend. Carramba! go! (*Pushes Hop Sing to wing.*)

HOP SING: (*Expostulating.*) Flowty dozen, hep, John! twenty dollar, John. Sabe. Flowty—twenty—(*gesticulating with fingers.*)

(*Exit Hop Sing, pushed off by Concho.*)

CONCHO: The pagan dolt! But he is important. Ah! If he were wiser, I should not rid myself of him so quickly! And now for the schoolmistress—the sweetheart of Sandy. If these men have not lied, he is in love with her, and, if he is, he has told her his secret before now, and she will be swift to urge him to his rights. If he has not told her—umph! (*Laughing.*) It will not be a *day*—an *hour*—before she will find out if her lover is Alexander Morton, the rich man's son, or "Sandy," the unknown vagabond. Eh, friend Sandy! It was a woman that locked up your secret; it shall be a woman, Madre di Dios![23] who shall unlock it. Ha! (*Goes to door of schoolhouse as door opens, and appears Col. Starbottle.*)

CONCHO: (*Aside.*) A thousand devils! the lawyer of the old man Morton. (*Aloud.*) Pardon, pardon! I am a stranger. I have lost my way on the mountain. I am seeking a trail. Senor, pardon!

STARBOTTLE: (*Aside.*) Another man seeking the road! Ged, I believe he's lying too. (*Aloud.*) It is before you, sir, *down*—down the mountain!

CONCHO: A thousand thanks, senor. (*Aside.*) Perdition catch him! (*Aloud.*) Thanks, senor. (*Exit.*)

STARBOTTLE: Ged, I've seen that face before. Ged, it's Castro's major-domo. Demn me, but I believe all his domestics have fallen in love with the pretty schoolma'am.

(*Enter Miss Mary from schoolhouse.*)

MISS MARY: (*Slowly refolding letter.*) You are aware, then, of the contents of this note, and you are the friend of Alexander Morton, Sr.?

STARBOTTLE: Permit me a moment, a single moment, to—er—er—explain. I am Mr. Morton's legal adviser. There is—er—sense of—er—responsibility—er—personal responbility, about the term "friend," that at the—er—er—present moment I am not—er—prepared to assume. The substance of the letter is before you. I am here to—er—express its spirit. I am here (*with great gallantry*) to express the—er—yearnings of cousinly affection. I am aware—er—that *our* conduct—if I may use the—er—the plural of advocacy—I am aware that—er—*our* conduct has not in the past years been of—er—er—exemplary character. I am aware that the—er—death of our lamented cousin, your sainted mother, was—er—hastened—I may—er—say precip—itated—by our—er—indiscretion. But we are here to—er—confess judgment—with—er—er—costs.

MISS MARY: (*Interrupting.*) In other words, your client my cousin, having ruined my father, having turned his own widowed relation out of doors, and sent me, her daughter, among strangers to earn her bread; having seen my mother sink and die in her struggle to keep her family from want—this man now seeks to condone his offenses—pardon me, sir, if I use your own legal phraseology—by offering me a home; by giving me part of his ill-gotten wealth, the association of his own hypocritical self, and the company of his shameless, profligate son—

STARBOTTLE: (*Interrupting.*) A moment, Miss Morris—a single moment! The epithets you have used, the—er—vigorous characterization of our—er—conduct, is—er—within the—er—strict rules of legal advocacy, correct. We are—er—rascals! we are—er—scoundrels! we are—er—well, I am not—er—prepared to say that we are not—er—demn me—hypocrites! But the young man you speak of—our son, whose past life (speaking as Colonel Starbottle) no one more sincerely deprecates than myself—that young man has reformed; has been for the past few months a miracle of sobriety, decorum, and industry; has taken, thanks to the example of—er—friends, a position of integrity in his father's business, of filial obedience in his father's household; is, in short, a paragon and, demn me, I doubt if he's his father's son.

MISS MARY: Enough, sir! You are waiting for my answer. There is no reason why it should not be as precise, as brief, and as formal as your message. Go to my cousin; say that you saw the person he claims as his relation; say that you found her, a poor schoolmistress, in a rude mining-camp, dependent for her bread on the scant earnings of already impoverished men, dependent for her honor on the rude chivalry of outcasts and vagabonds; and say that then and there she repudiated your kinship and respectfully declined your invitation.

STARBOTTLE: (*Aside.*) Ged! Star! this is the—er—female of your species! This is the woman—the—er—one woman—for whom you are responsible, sir!—personally responsible!

MISS MARY: (*Coldly.*) You have my answer, sir.

STARBOTTLE: Permit me—er—single moment—a single moment! Between the—er—present moment, and that of my departure—there is an—er—interval of twelve hours. May I, at the close of that interval—again present myself—without prejudice, for your final answer?

MISS MARY: (*Indifferently.*) As you will, sir. I shall be here.

STARBOTTLE: Permit me. (*Takes her hand gallantly.*) Your conduct and manner, Miss Morris, remind me—er—singularly—of—er—beautiful creature—one of the—er—first families. (*Observing Miss Mary regarding him amusedly, becomes embarrassed.*) That is—er—I mean—er—er—good morning, Miss Morris! (*Passes by the schoolhouse door, retreating and bowing, and picks up flowers from doorstep.*) Good morning!

MISS MARY: Excuse me, Colonel Starbottle (*with winning politeness*), but I fear I must rob you of those flowers. I recognize them now as the offering of one of my pupils. I fear I must revoke my gift (*taking flowers from astonished colonel's hand*), all except a single one for your buttonhole. Have you any choice, or shall I (*archly*) choose for you? Then it shall be this. (*Begins to place flowers in buttonhole, Col. Starbottle exhibiting extravagant gratitude in dumb show. Business prolonged through Miss Mary's speech.*) If I am not wrong, colonel, the gentleman to whom you so kindly pointed out the road this morning was not a stranger to you. Ah! I am right. There,—one moment,—a sprig of green, a single leaf, would set off the pink nicely. Here he is known only as "Sandy;" you know the absurd habits of this camp. Of course he has another name. There! (*Releasing the colonel.*) It is much prettier now.

STARBOTTLE: Ged, madam! The rarest exotic—the Victoria Regina—is not as—er—graceful—er—tribute!

MISS MARY: And yet you refuse to satisfy my curiosity?

STARBOTTLE: (*With great embarrassment, which at last resolves itself into increased dignity of manner.*) What you ask is—er—er—impossible! You are right: the—er—gentleman you allude to is known to me under—er—er—another name. But honor—Miss Morris, honor!—seals the lips of Colonel Starbottle. (*Aside.*) If she should know he was a menial! No. The position of the man you have challenged, Star, must be equal to your own. (*Aloud.*) Anything, Miss Morris, but—er—that!

MISS MARY: (*Smiling.*) Be it so. Adios, Colonel Starbottle.

STARBOTTLE: (*Gallantly.*) Au revoir, Miss Morris. (*Exit, impressively.*)

MISS MARY: So! Sandy conceals another name, which he withholds from Red Gulch. Well! Pshaw! What is that to me? The camp is made up of refugees, —men who perhaps have good reason to hide a name that may be infamous, the name that would publish a crime. Nonsense! Crime and Sandy! No, shame and guilt do not hide themselves in those honest but occasionally somewhat blood-shot eyes. Besides, goodness knows! the poor fellow's weakness is palpable enough. No, that is not the reason. It is no guilt that keeps his name hidden, —at least, not his. (*Seating herself, and arranging flowers in her lap.*) Poor Sandy! he must have climbed the eastern summit to get this. See, the rosy sunrise still lingers in its very petals; the dew is fresh upon it. Dear little mountain baby! I really believe that fellow got up before daylight, to climb that giddy height and secure its virgin freshness. And to think, in a moment of spite, I'd have given it to that bombastic warrior! (*Pause.*) That was a fine offer you refused just now, Miss Mary. Think of it: a home of luxury, a position of assured respect and homage; the life I once led, with all its difficulties smoothed away, its uncertainty dispelled,—think of it! My poor mother's dream fulfilled,—I, her daughter, the mistress of affluence, the queen of social power! What a temptation! Ah, Miss Mary, *was* it a temptation? Was there nothing in your free life here that stiffened your courage, that steeled the adamant of your refusal? Or was it only the memory of your mother's wrongs? Luxury and wealth! Could you command a dwelling more charming than this? Position and respect! Is not the awful admiration of these lawless men more fascinating than the perilous flattery of gentlemen like Colonel Starbottle? Is not the devotion of these outcasts more complimentary than the lip-service of perfumed gallantry? (*Pause.*) It's very odd he doesn't come. I wonder if that conceited old fool said anything to him. (*Rises, and then seats herself smiling.*) He *has* come. He is dodging in and out of the manzanita[24] bushes below the spring. I suppose he imagines my visitor still here. The bashful fool! If anybody should see him, it would be enough to make a petty scandal! I'll give him a talking-to. (*Pause.*) I wonder if the ridiculous fool has gone to sleep in those bushes. (*Rises.*) Well, let him; it will help him to recover his senses from last night's dissipation; and you, Miss Mary, it is high time you were preparing the lessons for tomorrow. (*Goes to schoolhouse, *enters door, and slams it behind her; after a moment reappears with empty bucket.*) Of course there's no water, and I am dying of thirst. (*Goes slowly to left and pauses embarrassedly and bashfully, presently laughs,—then suddenly frowns and assumes an appearance of indignation.*) Miss Mary Morris, have you become such an egregious fool that you dare not satisfy the ordinary cravings of human nature, just because an idle, dissipated, bashful blockhead— nonsense! (*Exit, brandishing pail.*)

SCENE 3: *The Same.*

(*A pause. Sandy's voice, without.*) This way, miss: the trail is easier.
(*Miss Mary's voice, without.*) Never mind me, look after the bucket.

(*Enter Sandy, carrying bucket with water, followed by Miss Mary. Sandy sets bucket down.*)

MISS MARY: There, you've spilt half of it. If it had been whiskey, you'd have been more careful.

SANDY: (*Submissively.*) Yes, miss.

MISS MARY: (*Aside.*) "Yes, miss!" The man will drive me crazy with his saccharine imbecility. (*Aloud.*) I believe you would assent to anything, even if I said you were—an impostor!

SANDY: (*Amazedly.*) An impostor, Miss Mary?

MISS MARY: Well, I don't know what other term you use in Red Gulch to express a man who conceals his real name under another.

SANDY: (*Embarrassed, but facing Miss Mary.*) Has anybody been tellin' ye I was an imposter, miss? Has that derned old fool that I saw ye with—

MISS MARY: "That old fool," as you call him, was too honorable a gentleman to disclose your secret, and too loyal a friend to traduce you by an epithet. Fear nothing, Mr. "Sandy"; if you have limited your confidence to *one* friend, it has not been misplaced. But, dear me, don't think I wish to penetrate your secret. No. The little I learned was accidental. Besides, his business was with me; perhaps, as his friend, you already know it.

SANDY: (*Meekly.*) Perhaps, miss, he was too honorable a gentleman to disclose *your* secret. His business was with me.

MISS MARY: (*Aside.*) He has taken a leaf out of my book! He is not so stupid after all. (*Aloud.*) I have no secret. Colonel Starbottle came here to make me an offer.

SANDY: (*Recoiling.*) An offer!

MISS MARY: Of a home and independence. (*Aside.*) Poor fellow! how pale he looks! (*Aloud.*) Well, you see, I am more trustful than you. I will tell you *my* secret, and you shall aid me with your counsel. (*They sit on ledge of rocks.*) Listen! My mother had a cousin once,—a cousin cruel, cowardly, selfish, and dissolute. She loved him, as women are apt to love such men,—loved him so that she beguiled her own husband to trust his fortunes in the hands of this wretched profligate. The husband was ruined, disgraced. The wife sought her cousin for help for her necessities. He met her with insult and proposed that she should fly with him.

SANDY: One moment, miss: it wasn't his pardner,—his pardner's wife—eh?

MISS MARY: (*Impatiently.*) It was the helpless wife of his own blood, I tell you. The husband died broken-hearted. The wife, my mother, struggled in poverty, under the shadow of a proud name, to give me an education, and died while I was still a girl. Today this cousin—this more than murderer of my parents—old, rich, self-satisfied, *reformed*, invites me, by virtue of that kinship he violated and despised, to his home, his wealth, his—his family rooftree! The man you saw was his agent.

SANDY: And you—

MISS MARY: Refused.

SANDY: (*Passing his hand over his forehead.*) You did wrong, Miss Mary.

MISS MARY: Wrong, sir? (*Rising.*)

SANDY: (*Humbly, but firmly.*) Sit ye down, Miss Mary. It aint for ye to throw your bright young life away yer in this place. It ain't for such as ye to soil your fair young hands by raking in the ashes to stir up the dead embers of a family wrong. It ain't for ye—ye'll pardon me, Miss Mary, for sayin' it—it ain't for ye to allow when it's *too late* fur a man to reform, or to go back of his reformation. Don't ye do it, miss, fur God's sake,—don't ye do it! Harkin, Miss Mary. If ye'll take my advice—a fool's advice, maybe—ye'll go. And when I tell ye that that advice, if ye take it, will take the sunshine out of these hills, the color off them trees, the freshness outer them flowers, the heart's blood outer me,—ye'll know that I ain't thinkin' o' myself, but of ye. And I wouldn't say this much to ye, Miss Mary, but you're goin' away. There's a flower, miss, you're wearin' in your bosom,—a flower I picked at daybreak this morning, five miles away in the snow. The wind was blowing chill around it, so that my hands that dug for it were stiff and cold, but the roots were warm. Miss Mary, as they are now in your bosom. Ye'll keep that flower, Miss Mary, in remembrance of my love for ye, that kept warm and blossomed through the snow. And, don't start, Miss Mary,—for ye'll leave behind ye, as I did, the snow and rocks through which it bloomed. I axes your parding, miss: I'm hurtin' yer feelin's, sure.

MISS MARY: (*Rising with agitation.*) Nothing,—nothing, but climbing these stupid rocks has made me giddy; that's all. Your arm. (*To Sandy impatiently.*) Can't you give me your arm? (*Sandy supports Miss Mary awkwardly toward shoolhouse. At door Miss Mary pauses.*) But if this reformation is so easy, so acceptable, why have you not profited by it? Why have you not reformed? Why have I found you here, a disgraced, dissipated, anonymous outcast, whom an honest girl dare not know? Why do you presume to preach to me? Have you a father?

SANDY: Hush, Miss Mary, hush! I had a father. Harkin. All that you have suffered from a kinship even so far removed, I have known from the hands of one who should have protected me. *My* father was—but no matter. You, Miss Mary, came out of your trials like gold from the washing. I was only the dirt and gravel to be thrown away. It is too late, Miss Mary, too late. My father has never sought me, would turn me from his doors had I sought him. Perhaps he is only right.

MISS MARY: But why should he be so different from others? Listen. This very cousin whose offer I refused had a son,—wild, wayward, by all report the most degraded of men. It was part of my cousin's reformation to save this son, and, if it were possible, snatch him from that terrible fate which seemed to be his only inheritance—

SANDY: (*Eagerly.*) Yes, miss.

MISS MARY: To restore him to a regenerated home. With this idea he followed his prodigal to California. I, you understand, was only an afterthought, consequent upon his success. He came to California upon this pilgrimage two years ago. He had no recollection, so they tell me, by which he could recognize this erring son and at first his search was wild, profitless, and almost hopeless. But by degrees, and with a persistency that seemed to increase with his hopelessness, he was rewarded by finding some clue to him at—at—at—

SANDY: (*Excitedly.*) At Poker Flat?

MISS MARY: Ah, perhaps you know the story—at Poker Flat. He traced him to the Mission of San Carmel.

SANDY: Yes, miss: go on.

MISS MARY: He was more successful than he deserved, perhaps. He found him. I see you know the story.

SANDY: Found him! Found him! Miss, did you say found him?

MISS MARY: Yes, found him. And today Alexander Morton, the reclaimed prodigal is part of the household I am invited to join. So you see, Mr. Sandy, there is still hope. What has happened to him is only a promise to you. Eh! Mr. Sandy—what is the matter? Are you ill? Your exertion this morning, perhaps. Speak to me! Gracious heavens, he is going mad! No! No! Yes—it cannot be—it is—he *had* broken his promise: he is drunk again.

SANDY: (*Rising, excited and confused.*) Excuse me, miss, I am a little onsartain *here* (*pointing to his head.*) I can't—I disremember—what you said jus' now; ye mentioned the name o' that prodigal that was found.

MISS MARY: Certainly: compose yourself,—my cousin's son, Alexander Morton. Listen, Sandy; you promised *me*, you know; you said for *my* sake you would not touch a drop. (*Enter cautiously toward schoolhouse the Duchess, stops on observing Sandy, and hides behind rock.*)

SANDY: (*Still bewildered and incoherent.*) I reckon. Harkin, miss, is that thar thing (*Pointing towards rock where Duchess is concealed.*)—is that a tree, or—or—a woman? Is it sorter movin' this way?

MISS MARY: (*Laying her hand on Sandy's.*) Recover your senses, for Heaven's sake, Sandy,—for *my* sake! It is only a tree.

SANDY: (*Rising.*) Then, miss, I've broke my word with ye: I'm drunk. P'r'aps I'd better be a-goin' (*Looking round confusedly.*) till I'm sober. (*Going toward L.*)

MISS MARY: (*Seizing his hand.*) But you'll see me again, Sandy, you'll come here—before—before I go?

SANDY: Yes, miss,—before ye go. (*Staggers stupidly toward L. Aside.*) Found him! Found Alexander Morton! It's a third time, Sandy, the third time: it means—it means—you're mad! (*Laughs wildly, and exits.*)

MISS MARY: (*Springing to her feet.*) There is a mystery behind all this, Mary Morris, that you—you—must discover. That man was *not* drunk; he *had not* broken his promise to me. What does it all mean? I have it. I will accept the offer of this Alexander Morton. I will tell him the story of this helpless man, this poor, poor, reckless Sandy. With the story of his own son before his eyes, he cannot but interest himself in his fate. He is rich; he will aid me in my search for Sandy's father, for Sandy's secret. At the worst, I can only follow the advice of this wretched man—an advice so generous, so kind, so self-sacrificing. Ah—

SCENE 4. *The same. Enter the Duchess, showily and extravagantly dressed. Her manner at first is a mixture of alternate shyness and bravado.*

THE DUCHESS: I heerd tell that you was goin' down to 'Frisco[25] tomorrow, for your vacation and I couldn't let ye go till I came to thank ye for your kindness to my boy—little Tommy.

MISS MARY: (*Aside, rising abstractedly, and recalling herself with an effort.*) I see —a poor outcast, the mother of my anonymous pupil. (*Aloud.*) Tommy! a good boy—a dear, good little boy.

DUCHESS: Thankee, miss, thankee. If[26] I am his mother, thar ain't a sweeter, dearer, better boy lives than him. And if I ain't much as says it, thar ain't a sweeter, dearer, angeler teacher than he's got. It ain't for you to be complimented by me, miss; it ain't for such as me to be comin' here in broad day to do it, neither, but I come to ask a favor,—not for me, miss, but for the darling boy.

MISS MARY: (*Aside—abstractedly.*) This poor, degraded creature will kill me with her wearying gratitude. Sandy will not return, of course, while she is here. (*Aloud.*) Go on. If I can help you or yours, be assured I will.

DUCHESS: Thankee, miss. You see, thar's no one the boy has any claim on but me, and I ain't the proper person to bring him up. I did allow to send him to 'Frisco, last year, but when I heerd talk that a schoolma'am was comin' up, and you did, and he sorter tuk to ye natril[27] from the first, I guess I did well to keep him yer. For, oh, miss, he loves ye so much, and if you could hear him talk in his purty way, ye wouldn't refuse him anything.

MISS MARY: (*With fatigued politeness and increasing impatience.*) I see. I see; pray go on.

DUCHESS: (*With quiet persistency.*) It's natril he should take to ye miss; for his father, when I first knowed him, miss, was a gentleman like yourself, and the boy must forget me sooner or later—and I ain't goin' to cry about *that*.

MISS MARY: (*Impatiently.*) Pray tell me how I can serve you.

DUCHESS: Yes, miss; you see, I came to ask you to take my Tommy—God bless him for the sweetest, bestest boy that lives!—to take him with you. I've money plenty, and it's all ours and his. Put him in some good school whar ye kin go and see and sorter help him to—forget—his mother. Do with him what you like. The worst you can do will be kindness to what he would learn with me. You will; I know you will, won't you? You will make him as pure and as good as yourself, and when he has grown up and is a gentleman, you will tell him his father's name—the name that hasn't passed my lips for years—the name of Alexander Morton.

MISS MARY: (*Aside.*) Alexander Morton! The prodigal! Ah, I see—the ungathered husks of his idle harvest.

DUCHESS: You hesitate, Miss Mary. (*Seizing her.*) Do not take your hand away. You are smiling. God bless you! I know you will take my boy. Speak to me, Miss

Mary.

MISS MARY: (*Aloud.*) I will take your child. More than that, I will take him to his father.

DUCHESS: No, no! for God's sake, no, Miss Mary! He has never seen him from his birth; he does not know him. He will disown him. He will curse him—will curse me!

MISS MARY: Why should he? Surely his crime is worse than yours.

DUCHESS: Hear me, Miss Mary. (*Aside.*) How can I tell her? (*Aloud.*) One moment miss. I was once—ye may not believe it, miss—as good, as pure, as you. I had a husband, the father of this child. He was kind, good, easy, forgiving—too good for me, miss, too simple and unsuspecting. He was what the world calls a fool, miss: he loved me too well—the kind o' crime, miss,—beggin your pardon, and all precepts to the contrary—the one thing that women like me never forgives. He had a pardner, miss, that governed him as *he* never governed me; that held him with the stronger will, and maybe *me* too. I was young, miss—no older than yourself then, and I ran away with him; left all and ran away with my husband's pardner. My husband—nat'rally—took to drink. I axes your pardin', miss, but ye'll see now, allowin' your larnin', that Alexander Morton ain't the man as will take my child.

MISS MARY: Nonsense. You are wrong. He has reformed; he has been restored to his home—your child's home, your home if you will claim it. Do not fear: I will make that right.

(*Enter Sandy slowly and sheepishly; stops on observing the Duchess and stands amazed and motionless.*)

MISS MARY: (*Observing Sandy—aside.*) He *has* returned. Poor fellow! How shall I get rid of this woman? (*Aloud.*) Enough. If you are sincere, I will take your child, and, God help me! bring him to his home and yours. Are you satisfied?

DUCHESS: Thank ye! Thank ye, miss, but—but thar's a mistake somewhar. In course—it's natural—ye don't know the father of that child, my boy Tommy, under the name o' Alexander Morton. Yur's thinking, like as not, of another man. The man I mean lives yer, in this camp; they calls him Sandy, miss,—*Sandy*!

MISS MARY: (*After a pause, coming forward, passionately.*) Hush! I have given you my answer, be it Alexander Morton or Sandy. Go now: bring me the child this evening at my house. I will meet you there. (*Leads the Duchess to wing. The Duchess endeavors to fall at her feet.*)

DUCHESS: God bless you miss!

MISS MARY: (*Hurriedly embracing her.*) No more, no more—but go! (*Exit Duchess. Miss Mary returns hurriedly to center, confronting Sandy.*)

MISS MARY: (*To Sandy, hurriedly and excitedly.*) You have heard what that woman said. I do not ask you under what *alias* you are known here; I only ask a single question[28]—Is *she* your wife? Are you the father of her child?

SANDY: (*Sinking upon his knees before her, and covering his face with his hands.*) I am!

MISS MARY: Enough! (*Taking flower from her bosom.*) Here, I give you back the flower you gave me this morning. It has faded and died here upon my breast. But I shall replace it with your foundling—the child of that woman, born like that flower in the snow! And I go now, Sandy, and leave behind me, as you said this morning, the snow and rocks in which it bloomed. Good-by! Farewell, farewell—forever! (*Goes toward schoolhouse as—*)

(*Enter Col. Starbottle.*)

MISS MARY: You are here in season, sir. You must have come for an answer to your question. You must first give me one to mine. Who is this man (*Pointing to Sandy.*), the man you met upon the rocks this morning?

STARBOTTLE: Ahem! I am—er—now fully prepared and responsible, I may say, miss—er—personally responsible, to answer that question. When you asked it this morning, the ordinary courtesy of the—er—code of honor threw a—er—cloak around the—er—antecedents of the—er—man whom I—er—elected by a demand from personal satisfaction, to the equality of myself, an—er—gentleman! That—er—cloak is now removed. I have waited six hours for an apology or a—er—reply to my demand. I am now free to confess that the—er—person you allude to was first known by me, three months ago, as an inebriated menial,—a groom in the houshold of my friend Don Jose Castro,—by the—er—simple name of "Diego."

MISS MARY: (*Slowly.*) I am satisfied. I accept my cousin's invitation. (*Exit slowly, supported by Col. Starbottle.*)

(*As Starbottle and Miss Mary exeunt, Concho and Hop Sing enter cautiously. Sandy slowly rises to his feet, passes his hand across his forehead, looks around toward exit of Starbottle and Miss Mary.*)

SANDY: (*Slowly, but with more calmness of demeanor.*) Gone, gone—forever! No: I am not mad, nor crazed with drink. My hands no longer tremble. There is no confusion here. (*Feeling his forehead.*) I heard them all. It was no dream. I heard her every word. Alexander Morton, yes, they spoke of Alexander Morton. She is going to him, to my father. She is going—she, Mary, my cousin—she is going to my father. He has been seeking me—has found—ah! (*Groans.*) No, no, Sandy! Be patient, be calm; you are not crazy—no, no, good Sandy, good old boy! Be patient, be patient; it is coming, it is coming. Yes, I see; some one has leaped into my place; some one has leaped into the old man's arms. Some one will creep into *her* heart! No! by God. No! I am Alexander Morton. Yes, yes! But how, how shall I prove it?—how? Who (*Concho steps cautiously forward towards Sandy unobserved.*) will believe the vagabond, the outcast—my God!—the crazy drunkard?

CONCHO: (*Advancing and laying his hand on Sandy.*) I will!

SANDY: (*Staggering back amazedly.*) You!

CONCHO: Yes—I, I,—Concho! You know me, Diego, you know me—Concho, the major-domo of the Blessed Innocents. Ha! You know me now. Yes, I have come to save you. I have come to make you strong. So—I have come to help you strip the Judas that has stepped into your place—the sham prodigal that has had the fatted calf and the ring—ah! ah!

SANDY: You? You do not know me!

CONCHO: Ah! you think, you think, eh? Listen: since you left, I have tracked *him—the impostor*, this Judas, this coyote—step by step, until his tracks crossed yours, and then I sought you out. I know all. I found a letter you had dropped; that brought me to Poker Flat. Ah, you start! I have seen those who knew you as Alexander Morton. You see! Ah, I am wise.

SANDY: (*Aside.*) It is true. (*Aloud.*) But (*Suspiciously.*) Why have you done this? You, Concho?—you were not my friend.

CONCHO: No, but *he* is my enemy. Ah, you start! Look at me, Alexander Morton, Sandy, Diego! You knew a man, strong, active, like yourself. Eh! Look at me now! Look at me, a cripple! Eh! lame and crushed here (*Pointing to his leg.*), broken and crushed here (*Pointing to his heart.*), by him,—the impostor! Listen, Diego. The night I was sent to track you from the rancho, he—this man—struck me from the wall, dashed me to the earth, and made *my body*, broken and bruised, a stepping-stone to leap the wall into your place, Diego—into your father's heart—into my master's home. They found me dead, they thought—no, not dead, Diego! It was sad, they said—unfortunate. They nursed me; they talked of money—eh, Diego!—money! They would have pensioned me to hush scandal—eh! I was a dog, a foreigner, a Greaser! Eh! That is why I am here. No! I love you not, Diego; you are of his race; but I hate—Mother of God!—I *hate* him!

SANDY: (*Rising to his feet, aside.*) Good! I begin to feel my courage return; my nerves are stronger. Courage, Sandy! (*Aloud.*) Be it so, Concho; there is my hand! We will help each other,—you to my birthright; I to your revenge! Hark ye! (*Sandy's manner becomes more calm and serious.*) This impostor is *no* craven, *no* coyote. Whoever he is, he must be strong. He has most plausible evidences. We must have rigid proofs. I will go with you to Poker Flat. There is one man, if he be living, knows me better than any man who lives. He has done me wrong—a great wrong, Concho—but I will forgive him. I will do more— I will ask his forgiveness. He will be a witness no man dare gainsay—my partner—God help him and forgive him as I do!—John Oakhurst.

CONCHO: Oakhurst your parnter!

SANDY: (*Angrily.*) Yes. Look ye, Concho, he has wronged me in a private way: that is *my* business, not *yours*, but he was *my* partner; no one shall abuse him before me.

CONCHO: Be it so. Then sink here! Rot here! Go back to your husks, O prodigal! Wallow in the ditches of this camp, and see your birthright sold for a dram of aguadiente! Lie here, dog and coyote that you are, with your mistress under the protection of your destroyer! For I tell you—I, Concho, the cripple—that the man who struck me down, the man who stepped into your birthright, the man who tomorrow welcomes your sweetheart in his arms, who holds the custody of your child, is your partner—John Oakhurst!

SANDY: (*Who has been sinking under Concho's words, rising convulsively to his feet.*) God be merciful to me a sinner! (*Faints.*)

CONCHO: (*Standing over his prostrate body exultingly.*) I am right. You are wise, Concho, you are wise! You have found Alexander Morton.

HOP SING: (*Advancing slowly to Sandy's side, and extending open palm.*) Me washee shirt flo you, flowty dozen hab. You no payee me. Me wantee twenty dollar hep. Sabe!

(*Curtain.*)

END OF ACT II

ACT III

SCENE 1: *The bank parlor of Morton & Son, San Francisco. Room richly furnished; two square library desks, left and right. At right, safe in wall; at left, same with practicable doors. Folding-door in flat, leading to counting-room. Door in left to private room of Alexander Morton, Sr.; door in right to private room of Morton, Jr. Alexander Morton, Sr., discovered at desk, right, opening and reading letters.*

MORTON, SR.: (*Laying down letter.*) Well, well, the usual story; letters from all sorts of people, who have done or intend to do all sorts of things for my reclaimed prodigal. (*Reads.*) "Dear Sir: Five years ago I loaned some money to a stranger who answers the description of your recovered son. He will remember Jim Parker—Limping Jim, of Poker Flat. Being at present short of funds, please send twenty dollars, amount loaned, by return mail. If not convenient, five dollars will do as installment." Pshaw! (*Throws letter aside, and takes up another.*) "Dear Sir: I invite your attention to inclosed circular for a proposed Home for Dissipated and Anonymous Gold-Miners. Your well-known reputation for liberality, and your late valuable experience in the reformation of your son, will naturally enlist your broadest sympathies. We inclose a draft for five-thousand dollars, for your signature." We shall see! Another: "Dear Sir: The Society for the Formation of Bible Classes in the Upper Stanislaus[29] acknowledge your recent munificent gift of five-hundred dollars to the cause. Last Sabbath Brother Hawkins, of Poker Flat, related with touching effect the story of your prodigal to an assemblage of over two hundred miners. Owing to unusual expenses, we regret to be compelled to draw upon you for five-hundred dollars more." So! (*Putting down letter.*) If we were given to pride and vainglory, we might well be puffed up with the fame of our works and the contagion of our example: yet I fear that, with the worldly-minded, this praise of charity to others is only the prayerful expectation of some personal application to the praiser. (*Rings handbell.*)

(*Enter Jackson*)

(*To Jackson*) File these letters (*Handing letters.*) with the others. There is no answer. Has young Mr. Alexander come in yet?

JACKSON: He only left here an hour ago. It was steamerday yesterday: he was up all night, sir.

OLD MORTON: (*Aside.*) True. And the night before he traveled all night, riding two hours ahead of one of our defaulting agents, and saved the bank a hundred-thousand dollars. Certainly his devotion to business is unremitting. (*Aloud.*) Any news from Colonel Starbottle?

JACKSON: He left this note, sir, early this morning.

OLD MORTON: (*Takes it, and reads.*) "I think I may say on my own personal responsibility, that the mission is successful. Miss Morris will arrive tonight with a female attendant and child." (*To Jackson.*) That is all, sir. Stop! Has any one been smoking here?

JACKSON: Not to my knowledge, sir.

OLD MORTON: There was a flavor of stale tobacco smoke in the room this morning when I entered, and ashes on the carpet. I *know* that young Mr. Alexander has abandoned the pernicious habit. See that it does not occur again.

JACKSON: Yes, sir. (*Aside.*) I must warn Mr. Alexander that his friends must be more careful, and yet those ashes were good for a deposit of fifty-thousand.

OLD MORTON: Is any one waiting?

JACKSON: Yes, sir,—Don Jose Castro and Mr. Capper.

OLD MORTON: Show in the Don; the policeman can wait.

JACKSON: Yes, sir. (*Exit.*)

OLD MORTON: (*Taking up Starbottle's note.*) "Miss Morris will arrive tonight." And yet he saw her only yesterday. This is not like her mother: no. She would never have forgiven and forgotten so quickly. Perhaps she knew not my sin and her mother's wrongs; perhaps she has—has—*Christian* forgiveness (*Sarcastically.*); perhaps, like my prodigal, she will be immaculately perfect. Well, well, at least her presence will make my home less lonely. "An attendant and child." A child! Ah, if *he*, my boy, my Alexander, were still a child, I might warm this cold, cold heart in his sunshine! Strange that I cannot reconstruct from this dutiful, submissive, obedient, industrious Alexander—this redeemed outcast, this son who shares my life, my fortunes, my heart—the foolish, willful, thoughtless, idle boy that once defied me. I remember (*musing, with a smile*) how the little rascal, ha, ha! once struck me,—*struck me!*—when I corrected him: ha, ha! (*Rubbing his hands with amusement, and then suddenly becoming grave and lugubrious.*) No, no. These are the whisperings of the flesh. Why should I find fault with him for being all that a righteous conversion demands,—all that I asked and prayed for? No, Alexander Morton: it is you, *you*, who are not yet regenerate. It is *you* who are ungrateful to Him who blessed you, to Him whose guiding hand led you to—

(*Enter Jackson.*)

JACKSON: Don Jose Castro.

(Enter Don Jose.)

DON JOSE: A thousand pardons, senor, for interrupting you in the hours of business; but it is—it is of business I would speak. *(Looking around.)*

OLD MORTON: *(To Jackson.)* You can retire. *(Exit Jackson.)* Be seated, Mr. Castro; I am at your service.

DON JOSE: It is of your—your son—

OLD MORTON: Our firm is Morton & Son; in business we are one, Mr. Castro.

DON JOSE: Bueno! Then to you as to him I will speak. Here is a letter I received yesterday. It has significance, importance perhaps. But whatever it is, it is something for you, not me, to know. If I am wronged much, Don Alexandro, *you*, you are wronged still more. Shall I read it? Good. *(Reads.)* "The man to whom you have affianced your daughter is not the son of Alexander Morton. Have a care. If I do not prove him an impostor at the end of six days, believe me one, and not your true friend and servant, Concho." In six days, Don Alexandro, the year of probation is over, and I have promised my daughter's hand to your son. *(Hands letter to Morton.)*

OLD MORTON: *(Ringing bell.)* Is that all, Mr. Castro?

DON JOSE: All, Mr. Castro? Carramba! is it not enough?

(Enter Jackson.)

OLD MORTON: *(To Jackson.)* You have kept a record of this business during the last eighteen months. Look at this letter. *(Handing letter.)* Is the handwriting familiar?

JACKSON: *(Taking letter.)* Can't say, sir. The form is the old one.

OLD MORTON: How many such letters have you received?

JACKSON: Four-hundred-and-forty-one, sir. This is the four-hundred-and-forty-second application for your son's position, sir.

DON JOSE: Pardon. This is not an application; it is only information or caution.

OLD MORTON: *(To Jackson.)* How many letters of information or caution have we received?

JACKSON: This makes seven-hundred-and-eighty-one, sir.

OLD MORTON: How, sir! *(Quickly.)* There were but seven-hundred-and-seventy-nine last night.

JACKSON: Beg pardon, sir! The gentleman who carried Mr. Alexander's valise from the boat was the seven-hundred-and-eightieth.

OLD MORTON: Explain yourself, sir.

JACKSON: He imparted to me, while receiving his stipend, the fact that he did not believe young Mr. Alexander was your son. An hour later, sir, he also imparted to me confidentially that he believed you were his father, and requested the loan of five dollars, to be repaid by you, to enable him to purchase a clean shirt and appear before you in respectable conditions. He waited for you an hour and expressed some indignation that he had not an equal show with others, to throw himself into your arms.

DON JOSE: *(Rising, aside, and uplifting his hands.)* Carramba! These Americans are of the Devil! *(Aloud.)* Enough, Don Alexandro! Then you think this letter is only worth—

OLD MORTON: One moment. I can perhaps tell you exactly its market value. (*To Jackson.*) Go on, sir.

JACKSON: At half-past ten, sir, then being slightly under the influence of liquor, he accepted the price of a deck passage to Stockton.

OLD MORTON: How much was that?

JACKSON: Fifty cent.

OLD MORTON: Exactly so! There you have, sir (*To Don Jose.*), the market value of the information you have received. I would advise you, as a business matter, not to pay more. As a business matter, you can at any time draw upon us for the amount. (*To Jackson.*) Admit Mr. Capper. (*Exit Jackson.*)

DON JOSE: (*Rising with dignity.*) This is an insult, Don Alexandro.

OLD MORTON: You are wrong, Mr. Castro; it is *business*; sought, I believe, by yourself. Now that it is transacted, I beg you to dine with me tomorrow to meet my niece. No offense, sir, no offense. Come, come! Business, you know, business.

DON JOSE: (*Relaxing.*) Be it so! I will come. (*Aside.*) These Americanos, these Americanos, are of the Devil! (*Aloud.*) Adios. (*Going.*) I hear, by report, that you have met with the misfortune of a serious loss by robbery?

OLD MORTON: (*Aside.*) So our mishap is known everywhere! (*Aloud.*) No serious misfortune, Mr. Castro, even if we do not recover the money. Adios.

(*Exit Don Jose.*)

OLD MORTON: The stiff-necked Papist! That he should dare, for the sake of his black-browed, froward daughter, to question the faith on which I have pinned my future! Well, with God's blessing, I gave him some wholesome discipline. If it were not for my covenant with Alexander—and nobly he has fulfilled his part—I should forbid his alliance with the blood of this spying Jesuit.

(*Enter Mr. Jackson, leading in Capper.*)

JACKSON: Policeman, sir.

CAPPER: (*Turning sharply.*) Who's that man?

OLD MORTON: Jackson, clerk.

CAPPER: Umph! Been here long?

OLD MORTON: A year. He was appointed by my son.

CAPPER: Know anything of his previous life?

OLD MORTON: (*Stiffly.*) I have already told you he is an appointee of my son's.

CAPPER: Yes! (*Aside.*) "Like master, like man." (*Aloud.*) Well, to business. We have worked up the robbery. We have reached two conclusions—one, that the work was not done by professionals; the other, consequent upon this, that you can't recover the money.

OLD MORTON: Excuse me, sir, but I do not see the last conclusion.

CAPPER: Then listen. The professional thief has only one or two ways of disposing of his plunder, and these ways are always well known to us. Good! Your stolen coin has not been disposed of in the regular way, through the usual hands which we could at any time seize. Of this we are satisfied.

OLD MORTON: How do you know it?

CAPPER: In this way. The only clue we have to the identification of the missing money were two boxes of Mexican doubloons.

OLD MORTON: (*Aside.*) Mr. Castro's special deposit! He may have reason for his interest. (*Aloud.*) Go on.

CAPPER: It is a coin rare in circulation in the interior. The night after the robbery the dealer of a monte-table in Sacramento paid out five-thousand dollars in doubloons. He declared it was taken in at the table and could not identify the players. Of course, *of course!* So far, you see, you are helpless. We have only established one fact, that the robber is—is—(*Significantly.*) a gambler.

OLD MORTON: (*Quietly.*) The regular trade of the thief seems to me to be of little importance, if you cannot identify him or recover my money. But go on, sir, go on; or is this all?

CAPPER: (*Aside.*) The old fool is blind. That is natural. (*Aloud.*) It is not all. The crime will doubtless be repeated. The man who has access to your vaults, who has taken only thrity-thousand dollars, when he could have secured half a million—this man, who has already gambled that thirty-thousand away—will not stop there. He will in a day or two, perhaps today, try to retrieve his losses out of *your* capital. *I* am here to prevent it.

OLD MORTON: (*Becoming interested.*) How?

CAPPER: Give me, for forty-eight hours, free access to this building. Let me conceal myself somewhere, anywhere, within these walls. Let it be without the knowledge of your clerks, even of *your son!*

OLD MORTON: (*Proudly.*) Mr. Alexander Morton is absent today. There is no other reason why he should not be here to consent to the acts of his partner and father.

CAPPER: (*Quickly.*) Very good. It is only to insure absolute secrecy.

OLD MORTON: (*Aside.*) Another robbery might excite a suspicion, worse for our credit than our actual loss. There is a significant earnestness about this man that awakens my fears. If Alexander were only here. (*Aloud.*) I accept. (*Capper has been trying doors.*)

CAPPER: What room is this?

OLD MORTON: My son's; I would prefer—

CAPPER: And this?

OLD MORTON: Mine, sir; if you choose—

CAPPER: (*Locking door and putting key in his pocket.*) This will do. Oblige me by making the necessary arrangements in your counting-room.

OLD MORTON: (*Hesitating and aside.*) He is right; perhaps it is only prudence, and I am saving Alexander additional care and annoyance. (*Exit*)

(*Enter Mr. Shadow cautiously.*)

SHADOW: (*In a lisping whisper to Capper.*) I've got the litht of the clerkth complete.

CAPPER: (*Triumphantly.*) Put it in your pocket, Shadow. We don't care for the lackeys now; we are after the master.

SHADOW: Eh! the mathther?

CAPPER: Yes: the master—the young master, the reclaimed son, the reformed prodigal! ha, ha!—the young man who compensates himself for all this austere devotion to business and principle by dipping into the old man's vaults when he wants a *pasear*:[30] eh, Shadow? That's the man we're after. Look here! *I* never took any stock in that young man's reformation. Ye don't teach old sports like him new tricks. They're a bad lot, father and son,—eh, Shadow?—and he's a chip of the old block. I spotted him before this robbery, before we were ever called in here professionally. I've had my eye on Alexander Morton, alias John Oakhurst, and, when I found the old man's doubloons raked over a monte-table at Sacramento, I knew where to look for the thief. Eh, Shadow?

SHADOW: (*Aside.*) He ith enormouth, thith Mithter Capper.

(*Enter Old Morton.*)

OLD MORTON: I have arranged everything. You will not be disturbed or suspected here in my private office. Eh! (*Looking at Shadow.*) Who slipped in here?

CAPPER: Only my Shadow, Mr. Morton, but I can rid myself even of that. (*Crosses to Shadow.*) Take this card to the office and wait for further orders. Vanish, Shadow! (*Exit Shadow.*)

(*Enter Jackson.*)

JACKSON: Mr. Alexander has come in, sir. (*Old Morton and Capper start.*)

OLD MORTON: Where is he?

JACKSON: In his private room, sir.

MORTON: Enough; you can go. (*Exit Jackson.*)

CAPPER: (*Crossing to Morton.*) Remember, you have given your pledge of secrecy. Beware! Your honor, your property, the credit and reputation of your bank are at stake.

OLD MORTON: (*After a pause of hesitation, with dignity.*) I gave you my word, sir, while my son was not present. I shall save myself from breaking my word with you, or concealing anything from him, by withdrawing myself. For the next twenty-four hours, this room (*Pointing to private room.*) is yours.

(*Each regards the other. Exit Old Morton as Capper exits in private room. After a pause, door of other room opens, and Harry York appears, slightly intoxicated, followed by John Oakhurst.*)

HARRY YORK: (*Looking around.*) By Jove! Morton, but you've got things in style here. And this yer's the gov'nor's desk, and here old Praise God Barebones sits opposite ye. Look yer, old boy (*Throwing himself in chair.*), I kin allow how it comes easy for ye to run this bank, for it's about as exciting, these times, as faro was to ye in '49, when I first knew ye as Jack Oakhurst, but how the devil you can sit opposite that stiff embodiment of all the Ten Commandments, day by day, damn it! That's wot *gets* me! Why, the first day I came here on business, the old man froze me so that I couldn't thaw a deposit out of my pocket. It chills me to think of it.

OAKHURST: (Hastily.) I suppose I am accustomed to him. But come, Harry: let me warm you. (Opens door of safe, and discovers cupboard, decanter, and glasses.)

YORK: (Laughing.) By Jove! under the old man's very nose. Jack, this is like you. (Takes a drink.) Well, old boy, this is like old times. But you don't drink?

OAKHURST: No, nor smoke. The fact is, Harry, I've taken a year's pledge. I've six days still to run: after that (Gloomily.), why (With a reckless laugh.), I shall be Jack Oakhurst again.

YORK: Lord! to think of your turning out to be anybody's son, Jack!—lest of all, his! (Pointing to chair.)

OAKHURST: (Laughing recklessly.) Not more strange than that I should find Harry York, the spendthrift of Poker Flat, the rich and respected Mr. York, produce-merchant of San Francisco.

YORK: Yes, but, my boy, you see I didn't strike it—in a rich father. I gave up gambling, married and settled down, saved my money, invested a little here and there, and—worked for it, Jack, damn me—worked for it like a damned horse!

OAKHURST: (Aside.) True, this is not work.

YORK: But that ain't my business with ye now, old boy: it's this. You've had some trials and troubles in the bank lately—a defalcation of agents one day, a robbery next. It's luck, my boy, luck! But ye know people will talk. You don't mind my sayin' that there's rumors round. The old man's mighty unpopular because he's a saint, and folks don't entirely fancy you because you used to be the reverse. Well, Jack, it amounts to 'bout this: I've withdrawn my account from Parkinson's, in Sacramento, and I've got a pretty heavy balance on hand—nigh on two-hundred-thousand—in bonds and certificates here, and if it will help you over the rough places, old boy, as a deposit, yer it is. (Drawing pocket-book.)

OAKHURST: (Greatly affected, but endeavoring to conceal it.) Thank you, Harry old fellow—but—

YORK: (Quickly.) I know: I'll take the risk, a business risk. You'll stand by me all you can, old boy; you'll make it pay all you can, and if you lose it—why—all right!

OAKHURST: (Embarrassed.) As a deposit with Morton & Son, drawing two per cent monthly interest—

YORK: Damn Morton & Son! I'll back it with Jack Oakhurst, the man I know.

OAKHURST: (Advancing slowly.) I'll take it, Harry.

YORK: (Extending his hand.) It's a square game, Jack!

OAKHURST: (Seizing his hand with repressed emotion.) It's a square game, Harry York, if I live.

YORK: Then I'll travel. Goodnight, old boy. I'll send my clerk around in the morning to put things right. Goodnight. (Going.)

OAKHURST: (Grasping York's hand.) One moment—no—nothing! Goodnight. (Exit York.)

(Oakhurst follows him to door, and then returns to desk, throwing himself in chair, and burying his face in his hands.)

OAKHURST: (*With a deep feeling.*) It needed but this to fill the measure of my degradation. I have borne the suspicions of the old man's enemies, the half-pitying, half-contemptuous sympathy of his friends, even his own cold, heartless, fanatical fulfillment of his sense of duty, but *this*—this confidence from one who had most reason to scorn me, this trust from one who knew me as I *was*—this is the hardest burden. And he, too, in time will know me to be an impostor. He too—a reformed man, but he has honorably retraced his steps and won the position I hold by a trick, an imposture. And what is all my labor beside his honest sincerity? I have fought against the chances that might discover my deception, against the enemies who would overthrow me, against the fate that put me here, and I have been successful—yes, a successful impostor! I have even fought against the human instinct that told this fierce, foolish old man that *I* was an alien to his house, to his blood; I have even felt him scan my face eagerly for some reflection of his long-lost boy, for some realization of his dream, and I have seen him turn away, cold, heartsick, and despairing. What matters that I have been to him devoted, untiring, submissive, ay, a better son to him than his own weak flesh and blood would have been? He would tomorrow cast me forth to welcome the outcast, Sandy Morton. Well, what matters? (*Recklessly.*) Nothing. In six days it will be over; in six days the year of my probation will have passed; in six days I will disclose to him the deceit I have practiced and will face the world again as Jack Oakhurst the gambler, who staked and lost *all* on a single cast. And Jovita! Well, well!—the game is made: it is too late to draw out now. (*Rings bell. Enter Jackson.*) Who has been here?

JACKSON: Only Don Jose, and Mr. Capper the detective.

OAKHURST: The detective? What for?

JACKSON: To work up the robbery, sir.

OAKHURST: True! Capper, Capper, yes! A man of wild and ridiculous theories, but well meaning, brave, and honest. (*Aside.*) This is the old man's idea. He does not know that I was on the trail of the thieves an hour before the police were notified. (*Aloud.*) Well, sir?

JACKSON: He told your father he thought the recovery of the money hopeless, but he came to caution us against a second attempt.

OAKHURST: (*Aside, starting.*) True! I had not thought of that. (*Excitedly.*) The success of their first attempt will incite them to another; the money they have stolen is gone by this time. (*Aloud.*) Jackson, I will stay here tonight and tomorrow night, and relieve your regular watchman. You will, of course, say nothing of my intention.

JACKSON: Yes, sir. (*Lingering.*)

OAKHURST: (*After a pause.*) That is all, Mr. Jackson.

JACKSON: Beg your pardon, Mr. Morton, but Colonel Starbottle, with two ladies, was here half an hour ago, and said they would come again when you were alone.

OAKHURST: Very well; admit them.

JACKSON: Beg pardon, sir, but they seemed to avoid seeing your father until they had seen you. It looked mysterious, and I thought I would tell you first.

OAKHURST: (*Laughing.*) Admit them, Mr. Jackson. (*Exit Jackson.*) This poor fellow's devotion is increasing. He, too, believes that his old associate in dissipation, John Oakhurst, *is* the son of Alexander Morton. He, too, will have to share in the disgrace of the impostor. Ladies! umph! (*Looking down at his clothes.*) I'm afraid the reform of Alexander Morton hasn't improved the usual neatness of John Oakhurst. I haven't slept, nor changed my clothes, for three days. (*Goes to door of Morton, Sr.'s room.*) Locked, and the key on the inside! That's strange. Nonsense! the old man has locked his door and gone out through the private entrance. Well, I'll find means of making my toilet here. (*Exit into private room.*)

(*Enter Jackson, leading in Col. Starbottle, Miss Mary, the Duchess, and child of three years.*[31])

JACKSON: Mr. Alexander Morton, Jr., is in his private room. He will be here in a moment. (*Exit Jackson.*)

STARBOTTLE: One moment, a single moment, Miss Mary. Permit me to—er—if I may so express myself, to—er—group the party, to—er—place the—er—present company into position I have—er—observed as part of my—er—legal experience, that in cases of moral illustration a great, I may say—er—tremendous, effect on the—er—jury, I mean the—er—guilty party, has been produced by the attitude of the—er—victim and martyr. You, madam, as the—er—injured wife (*Placing her.*), as Moral Retribution, leaning toward and slightly appealing to me, the image of—er—er—Inflexible Justice! (*Inflates his chest, puts his hand in his bosom, and strikes an attitude.*)

(*Door of young Morton's room opens and discloses Mr. Oakhurst gazing at the group. He starts slightly on observing the Duchess, but instantly recovers himself, and faces the company coldly. The Duchess starts on observing Oakhurst and struggles in confusion towards the door, dragging with her the child and Miss Mary, who endeavors to reassure her. Col. Starbottle looks in astonishment from one to the other and advances to front.*)

STARBOTTLE: (*Aside.*) The—er—tableau, although striking in moral forces, is apparently—er—deficient in moral stamina.

MISS MARY: (*Angrily to the Duchess.*) I'm ashamed of you! (*To Oakhurst, advancing.*) I don't ask pardon for my intrusion. If you are Alexander Morton, you are my kinsman, and you will know that I cannot introduce myself better than as the protector of an injured woman. Come here! (*To the Duchess, dragging her towards Oakhurst.*) (*To Oakhurst.*) Look upon this woman: she claims to be—

STARBOTTLE: (*Stepping between Miss Mary and the Duchess.*) A moment, Miss Mary, a single moment! Permit me to—er—explain. The whole thing, the—er—situation reminds me, demn me, of most amusing incident at Sacramento in '52. Large party at Hank Suedecois'; know Hank? Confirmed old bach of sixty. Dinner for forty. Everything in style, first families, Ged,—Judge Beeswinger, Mat Boompointer, and Maje Blodgett of Alabam'; know old Maje Blodgett? Well, Maje was there. Ged, sir, delay—everybody waiting. I went to Hank. "Hank," I says, "What's matter? Why delay?"—"Star," he says,—always called me Star,—"Star,—it's cook!"—"Demn cook," I says, "discharge cook—only a black mulatto anyway!" "Can't, Star," he says, "impossible!"—"Can't?" says I.

"No," says he. "Listen, Star," he says, "family secret! Honor—Can't discharge cook, because cook—demn it—'s *my wife!*" Fact sir, fact—showed marriage certificate—married privately seven years! Fact, sir—

DUCHESS: (*To Miss Mary.*) Some other time, miss. Let us go now. There's a mistake, miss, I can't explain. Some other time, miss! See, miss, how cold and stern he looks! Another time, miss! (*Struggling.*) For God's sake, miss, let me go!

MISS MARY: No! This mystery must be cleared up now, before I enter *his* house—before I accept the charge of this—

STARBOTTLE: (*Interrupting and crossing before Miss Mary.*) A moment—a single moment, miss. (*To Oakhurst.*) Mr. Morton, you will pardon the exuberance, and perhaps, under the circumstances, somewhat natural impulsiveness, of the—er—sex, for which I am perhaps responsible; I may say—er—personally, sir—personally responsible—

OAKHURST: (*Coldly.*) Go on, sir.

STARBOTTLE: The lady on my right is—er—the niece of your father,—your cousin. The lady on my left, engaged in soothing the—er—bashful timidity of infancy, is—er—that is—er—claims to be, the mother of the child of Alexander Morton.

OAKHURST: (*Calmly.*) She is right.

MISS MARY: (*Rushing forward.*) Then you are—

OAKHURST: (*Gently restraining her.*) You have another question to ask; let me ask it. (*Crossing to the Duchess.*) You have heard my answer. Madam, are you the legal wife of Alexander Morton?

DUCHESS: (*Sinking upon her knees, and dropping her face in her hands.*) No!

OAKHURST: Enough: I will take the child. Pardon me, Miss Morris, but you have heard enought to know that your mission is accomplished, but that what else passes between this woman and myself becomes no stranger to hear. (*Motions toward room.*)

MISS MARY: (*Aside.*) It is *his* son. I am satisfied. (*Going.*) Come, colonel. (*Exeunt into room Starbottle and Miss Mary.*)

DUCHESS: (*Crossing to Oakhurst and falling at his feet.*) Forgive me, Jack, forgive me! It was no fault of mine. I did not know that you were here. I did not know that you had taken his name!

OAKHURST: Hush—on your life!

DUCHESS: Hear me, Jack! I was anxious only for a home for my child. I came to *her*—the schoolmistress of Red Gulch—for aid. I told her the name of my boy's father. She—she brought me here. Oh, forgive me, Jack! I have offended you!

OAKHURST: How can I believe you? You have deceived *him*—you have deceived me. Listen! When I said, a moment ago, you were not the wife of Alexander Morton, it was because I knew that your first husband—the Australian convict Pritchard—was still living; that you had deceived Sandy Morton as you had deceived me. That was why I left you. Tell me, have you deceived me also about him, as you did about the other? Is *he* living, and with you, or dead, as you declared?

DUCHESS: (*Aside.*) He will kill me if I tell him. (*Aloud.*) No, no. He is gone—is dead these three years.

OAKHURST: You swear!

DUCHESS: (*Hesitates, gasps, and looks around for her child; then seizing it and drawing it toward her.*) I—swear.

OAKHURST: Enough. Seek not to know why *I* am here and under his name. Enough for you that it has saved your child's future and secured him his heritage past all revocation. Yet remember! a word from you within the next few days destroys it all. After that, I care not what you say.

DUCHESS: Jack! One word, Jack, before I go. I never thought to bring my shame to you!—to *him*!

OAKHURST: It was no trick, then, no contivance that brought her here. No; it was fate. And at least I shall save this child.

(*Re-enter Starbottle, Miss Mary, and Duchess.*)

STARBOTTLE: (*Impressively.*) Permit me, Mr. Alexander Morton, as the friend of my—er—principal, to declare that we have received—honorable—honorable—satisfaction. Allow me, sir, to grasp the hand, the—er—cherished hand of a gentleman who, demn me! has fulfilled all his duties to—er—society and gentlemen. And allow me to add, sir, should any invidious criticism of the present—er—settlement be uttered in my presence, I shall hold that critic responsible, sir—er—personally responsible!

MISS MARY: (*Sweeping truculently and aggressively up to John Oakhurst.*) And permit *me* to add, sir, that if you can see your way clearly out of this wretched muddle, it's more than I can. This arangement may be according to the California code of morality, but it doesn't accord with my Eastern ideas of right and wrong. If this foolish, wretched creature chooses to abandon all claim upon you, chooses to run away from you—why, I suppose, as a *gentleman*, according to your laws of honor, you are absolved. Goodnight, Mr. Alexander Morton. (*Goes to door, and exit, pushing out Starbottle, the Duchess, and child. Mr. Oakhurst sinks into chair at desk, burying his face in his hand. Re-enter slowly and embarrassedly, Miss Mary; looks toward Oakhurst and comes slowly down stage.*)

MISS MARY: (*Aside.*) I was too hard on him. I was not so hard on Sandy, when I thought that he—he—was the father of her child. And he's my own flesh and blood, too, and—he's crying. (*Aloud.*) Mr. Morton.

OAKHURST: (*Slowly lifting his head.*) Yes, Miss Mary.

MISS MARY: I spoke hastily just then. I—I—thought—you see—I—(*Angrily and passionately.*) I mean this. I'm a stranger. I don't understand your Californian ways, and I don't want to. But I believe you've done what you thought was right, according to a *man's* idea of right; and—there's my hand. Take it, take it; for it's a novelty, Mr. Morton: it's the hand of an honest girl!

OAKHURST: (*Hesitates, then rises, sinks on one knee, and raises Miss Mary's fingers to his lips.*) God bless you, miss! God bless you!

MISS MARY: (*Retreating to center door.*) Goodnight, goodnight (*Slowly.*)—cousin —Alexander. (*Exit. Dark stage.*)

OAKHURST: (*Rising swiftly.*) No, no; it is false! Ah! She's gone. Another moment, and I would have told her all. Pshaw! courage, man! It is only six days more, and you are free, and this year's shame and agony forever ended.

(*Enter Jackson.*)

JACKSON: As you ordered, sir, the night watchman has been relieved and has just gone.

OAKHURST: Very good, sir; and you?

JACKSON: I relieved the porter, sir, and I shall bunk on two chairs in the counting-room. You'll find me handy, if you want me, sir. Goodnight, sir. (*Exit.*)

OAKHURST: I fear these rascals will not dare to make their second attempt tonight. A quiet scrimmage with them—enough to keep me awake or from thinking—would be a good fortune. No, no! no such luck for you tonight, John Oakhurst! You are playing a losing game. . . . Yet the robbery was a bold one. At eleven o'clock, while the bank was yet lighted, and Mr. Jackson and another clerk were at work here, three well-dressed men pick the lock of the counting-house door, enter, and turn the key on the clerks in this parlor, and carry away a box of doubloons, not yet placed in the vaults by the porter, and all this done so cautiously that the clerks within knew nothing of it, until notified of the open street door by the private watchman, and so boldly that the watchman, seeing them here, believed them clerks of the bank, and let them go unmolested. No: this was the coincidence of good luck, not of bold premeditation. There will be no second sttempt. (*Yawns.*) If they don't come soon, I shall fall asleep. Four nights without rest will tell on a man, unless he has some excitement to back him. (*Nods.*) Hallo! What was that? Oh! Jackson in the counting-room getting to bed. I'll look at that front-door myself. (*Takes revolver from desk and goes to door, tries lock, comes down stage with revolver, examines it, and lays it down.*) (*Slowly and quietly.*) The door is locked on the outside: that may have been an accident. The caps are taken from my pistol: *that* was not! Well, here is the vault, and here is John Oakhurst: to reach the one, they must pass the other. (*Takes off his coat, seizes poker from grate, and approaches safe.*) Ha! some one is moving in the old man's room. (*Approaches door of room as . . .*)

(*Enter noiselessly and cautiously from room Pritchard, Silky, and Soapy. Pritchard and his confederates approach Oakhurst from behind, carrying lariat, or slip-noose.*)

OAKHURST: (*Listening at door.*) Good. At least I know from what quarter to expect the attack. Ah!

PRITCHARD: (*Throws slip-noose over Oakhurst from behind; Oakhurst puts his hand in his breast as the slip-noose is drawn across his bosom, pinioning one arm over his breast, and the other at his side. Silky and Soapy, directed by Pritchard, drag Oakhurst to chair facing front, and pinion his legs. Pritchard regarding him.*)

OAKHURST: (*Very coolly.*) You have left me my voice, I suppose, because it is useless.

PRITCHARD: That's so, pard. 'Twon't be no help to ye.

OAKHURST: Then you have killed Jackson.

PRITCHARD: Lord love ye, no! That ain't like us, pard! Jackson's tendin' door for us, and kinder lookin' out gin'rally for the boys. Thar's nothin' mean about Jackson.

SOAPY: No! Jackson's a squar man. Eh, Silky?

SILKY: Ez white a man[32] ez they is, pard!

OAKHURST: (*Aside.*) The traitor! (*Aloud.*) Well!

PRITCHARD: Well, you want ter know our business. Call upon a business man in business hours. Our little game is this, Mr. Jack Morton Alexander Oakhurst. When we was here the other night, we was wantin' a key to that theer lock (*pointing to vault*), and we sorter dropped in in passin' to get it.

OAKHURST: And suppose I refuse to give it up?

PRITCHARD: We were kalkilatin' on yer bein' even that impolite, wasn't we, boys?

SILKY AND SOAPY: We was that.

PRITCHARD: And so we got Mr. Jackson to take an impression of it in wax. Oh, he's a squar man—is Mr. Jackson!

SILKY: Jackson is a white man, Soapy!

SOAPY: They don't make no better men nor Jackson, Silky.

PRITCHARD: And we've got a duplicate key here. But we don't want any differences, pard: we only want a squar game. It seemed to us—some of your old pards as knew ye, Jack—that ye had a rather soft thing here, reformin' and we thought ye was kinder throwin' off the boys, not givin' 'em any hand in the game. But thar ain't anythin' mean about us. Eh, boys?

SOAPY: We is allers ready to chip in ekal[33] in the game. Eh, Silky?

SILKY: That's me, Soapy.

PRITCHARD: Ye see, the boys is free and open handed, Jack. And so the proposition we wanter make to ye, Jack, is this. It's reg'lar on the squar. We reckon, takin' Mr. Jackson's word—and thar ain't no man's word ez is better nor Jackson's—that there's nigh on to two-millions in that vault, not to speak of a little speshil de-posit o' York's, ez we learn from that accommodatin' friend, Mr. Jackson. We propose to share it with ye, on ekal terms—us five—countin' Jackson, a squar man. In course, we takes the risk o' packin' it away tonight comfortable. Ez your friends, Jack, we allow tis yer little arrangement to be a deuced sight easier for you than playin' Sandy Morton on a riglar salary, with the chance o' the real Sandy poppin' in upon ye any night.

OAKHURST: It's a lie. Sandy is dead.

PRITCHARD: In course, in course! That is your little game! But we kalkilated, Jack, even on that, on yer bein' rambunktious and contrary, and so we went ter Red Gulch, and found Sandy. Ye know I take a kind o' interest in Sandy; he's the second husband of my wife, the woman you run away with, pard. But thar's nothin' mean about me! eh, boys?

SILKY: No! he's the forgivingest kind of a man, is Pritchard.

SOAPY: That's so, Silky.

PRITCHARD: And thinkin' ye might be dubious, we filled Sandy about full o' rye whiskey, and brought him along, and one of our pards is preambulatin' the streets with him, ready to bring him on call.

OAKHURST: It's a lie, Pritchard—a cowardly lie!

PRITCHARD: Is it? Hush!

SANDY: (*Without singing.*)—

Oh, yer's yer Sandy Morton,
Drink him down!
Oh, yer's yer Sandy Morton,
Drink him down!
Oh, yer's yer Sandy Morton,
All alive and just a-snortin'!
Oh, yer's yer Sandy Morton,
Drink him down!

PRITCHARD: We don't propose to run him in yer, 'cept we're took, or yer unaccommodatin' to the boys.

OAKHURST: And if I refuse?

PRITCHARD: Why, we'll take what we can get, and we'll leave Sandy Morton with you yer, to sorter alleviate the old man's feelin's over the loss of his money. There's nothin' mean about us; no! eh, boys? (*Going toward safe.*)

OAKHURST: Hear me a moment, Henry Pritchard. (*Pritchard stops abreast of Oakhurst.*) Four years ago you were assaulted in the Arcade Saloon in Sacramento. You would have been killed, but your assailant suddenly fell dead by a pistol-shot fired from some unknown hand. I stood twenty feet from you with folded arms, but that shot was fired by me—me, Henry Pritchard—through my clothes, from a derringer hidden in my waistcoat! Understand me, I do not ask your gratitude now. But that pistol is in my right hand and now covers you. Make a single motion—of a muscle—and it is your last.

PRITCHARD: (*Motionless, but excitedly.*) You dare not fire! No, dare not! A shot here will bring my pal and Sandy Morton to confront you. You will have killed me to save exposure, have added murder to imposture! You have no witness to this attempt!

CAPPER: (*Opening door of room at the same moment that two policemen appear at door center, and two at other room.*) You are wrong: he has five (*Crossing to Silky and Soapy and laying his hands on their shoulders.*), and, if I mistake not, he has two more in these gentlemen, whom I know, and who will be quite as willing to furnish the necessary State's evidence of the robbery as of the fact that they never knew any other Alexander Morton than the gentleman who sits in that chair.

SOAPY: That's so, Silky.

SILKY: That's so, Soapy.

CAPPER: (*To policemen.*) Take them away.

(*Exit policemen with Pritchard, Soapy, and Silky.*)

(*Capper unbinds Oakhurst.*)

OAKHURST: Then I have to thank you, Mr. C.

CAPPER: Yes! "A man of ridiculous theories, but well meaning, brave, and honest." No, sir; don't apologize: you were right, Mr. Oakhurst. It is I who owe *you* an apology. I came here, believing *you* were the robber, having no faith in you or your reformation, expecting,—yes, sir,—hoping, to detect you in the act. Hear me! From the hour you first entered the bank, I have shadowed your every movement; I have been the silent witness of all that has passed in this room. You have played a desperate game, Mr. Oakhurst, but I'll see you through it. If you are true to your resolve, for the next six days, I will hold these wretches silent. I will protect your imposture with the strong arm of the law. I don't like *your* theories, sir, but I believe you to be well-meaning, and I know you to be brave and honest.

OAKHURST: (*Grasping his hand.*) I shall not forget this. But Sandy—

CAPPER: I will put my men on his track and have him brought quietly here. I can give you no aid beyond that. As an honorable man, I need not tell you your duty. Settle it with *him* as best you can.

OAKHURST: You are right; I *will* see him! (*Aside.*) Unless he has changed, he will listen to me; he will obey me.

CAPPER: Hush! (*Blows out candle.*) Stand here!

(*Capper and Oakhurst retreat to wing, as enter Morton, Sr., from his room.*)

MORTON: The private door open, the room dark, and Capper gone. I don't like this. The more I think of the mystery of that man's manner this morning, the more it seems to hide some terrible secret I must fathom! There are watches here. (*Strikes a light, as Capper draws Oakhurst, struggling, back into shadow.*) What's this? (*Picking up key.*) The key of the vault. A chair overturned. (*Touches bell.*) No answer! Jackson gone! My God! A terrible suspicion haunts me! No. Hush! (*Retreats to private room as other door opens and—*)

(*Enter Sandy.*)

SANDY: (*Drunkenly.*) Shoo! Shoo! boys, whar are ye, boys, eh? Pritchard, Silky, Soapy! Whar are ye, boys?

MORTON: (*Aside.*) A crime has been committed, and here is one of the gang. God has delivered him into my hands. (*Draws revolver and fires, as Oakhurst breaks from Capper, and strikes Morton's pistol. Capper at same moment seizes Sandy and drags him in room. Morton and Oakhurst struggle to center.*)

MORTON: (*Relaxing hold of Oakhurst.*) Alexander! Good God! Why are you here? Why have you stepped between me and retribution? You hesitate. God in heaven! Speak, Alexander, my son, speak for God's sake! Tell me—tell me that this detective's suspicions are not true. Tell me that you are not—not—no, I cannot say it. Speak, Alexander Morton, I command you! Who is this man you have saved? Is it—is it—your accomplice?

OAKHURST: (*Sinking at his feet.*) Don't ask me! You know not what you ask. I implore you—

CAPPER: (*Appearing quietly from room and locking door behind him.*) Your son has acted under *my* orders. The man he has saved, as he has saved you, was a *decoy*—one of my policemen.

(*Tableau: Capper, Morton, Oakhurst. Curtain.*)

END OF ACT III

ACT IV

SCENE 1: *Mr. Morton's villa, Russian Hill. Night. Oakhurst's bedroom. Sofa in alcove center, door in flat, left. Sandy Morton discovered, unconscious, lying on sofa; Oakhurst standing at his head, two policemen at his feet. Candles on table, left.*

OAKHURST: That will do. You are sure he was unconscious as you brought him in?

1ST POLICEMAN: Sure, sir? He hasn't known anything since we picked him up on the sidewalk outside the bank.

OAKHURST: Good! You have fulfilled your orders well, and your chief shall know it. Go now. Be as cautious in going out as you were on entering. Here is the private staircase. (*Opens door.*) (*Exit policemen.*)

OAKHURST: (*Listening.*) Gone! and without disturbing any one. So far, luck has befriended me. He will sleep tonight beneath his father's roof. His father! umph! would the old man recognize him here? Would he take to his heart this drunken outcast, picked from the gutters of the street and brought here by the strong arm of the law? Hush! (*A knock without.*) Ah, it is the colonel; he is prompt to the hour. (*Opens door cautiously, and admits Col. Starbottle.*)

STARBOTTLE: (*Looking around, and overlooking Sandy.*) I presume the other—er—principal is not yet on the ground?

OAKHURST: (*Motioning to sofa.*) He is!

STARBOTTLE: (*Starting as he looks toward sofa.*) Ged, you don't mean to say it's all *over*, without witnesses, without my—er—presence?

OAKHURST: Pardon me, Colonel Starbottle, but if you look again, you will perceive that the gentleman is only a drunk.

STARBOTTLE: Eh? Ged, not uncommon, sir, not uncommon! I remember singular incident at—er—Louisville in '47. Old Judge Tollim—know old Judge Tolly?— Ged! he came to ground drunk, sir; couldn't stand! Demn me, sir, had to put him into position with kitchen poker down his back, and two sections of lightning-rod in his—er—trousers, demn me! Firm, sir, firm, you understand, here (*Striking his breast.*), but—here (*Striking his legs.*)—er—er—wobbly! No, sir! Intoxication of principal not a bar, sir, to personal satisfaction! (*Goes toward sofa with eyeglass.*) Good Ged! why it's Diego! (*Returning stiffly, to Oakhurst.*) Excuse me, sir, but this is a case in which I cannot act. Cannot, sir—impossible! absurd! pre—post—er—ous! I recognize in the—er—inebriated menial on yonder sofa, a person, sir, who, having already declined my personal challenge, is—er—excluded from the consideration of gentlemen. The person who lies there, sir, is Diego—a menial of Don Jose Castro,—alias "Sandy," the vagabond of Red Gulch.

OAKHURST: You have omitted one title, his true one. He is Alexander Morton, son of the master of this house.

STARBOTTLE: (*Starting in bewilderment.*) Alexander Morton! (*Aside.*) Ged! my first suspicions were correct. Star, you have lost the opportunity of making your fortune as a scoundrel, but you have, at a pecuniary sacrifice, preserved your honor.

OAKHURST: Yes. Hear me, Colonel Starbottle. I have summoned you here tonight, as I have already intimated, on an affair of honor. I have sought you as my father's legal counsel, as a disinterested witness, as a gentleman of honor. The man who lies before you was once my friend and partner. I have wronged him doubly. As his partner, I ran away with the woman he believed, and still believes, to be his wife; as his friend, I have for a twelvemonth kept him from the enjoyment of his home, his patrimony, by a shameful deception. I have summoned you tonight to witness my confession; as a lawyer, to arrange those details necessary to restore to him his property; as a man of honor, to receive from me whatever retribution he demands. You will be a witness to our interview. Whatever befalls me here, you will explain to Mr. Morton—to Jovita—that I accepted it as a man and did not avoid here or elsewhere the penalty of my crime. (*Folding his arms.*)

STARBOTTLE: Umph! The case is, as you say, a delicate one, but not—not—peculiar. No, sir, Ged! sir, I remember Tom Marshall—know Tom Marshall of Kentucky?—said to me, "Star!"—always calls me Star—"how in blank, sir, can you remember the *real* names of your clients?"—"Why," says I, "Tom"—always called him Tom—"yesterday I was called to make a will—most distinguished family of Virginia—as lawyer and gentleman, you understand; can't mention name. Waited for signature—most distinguished name; Ged, sir, man signed Bloggins,—Peter Bloggins. Fact, demme! 'Mistake,' I said,—'excitement; exaltation of fever. *Non compos.* Compose yourself, Bob.'—'Star,' he said,—always called me Star—'for forty-seven years I have been an impostor!' —his very words, sir. 'I am not—' you understand, 'I *am* Peter Bloggins!' "

OAKHURST: But, my dear colonel, I—

STARBOTTLE: (*Loftily.*) Say no more, sir! I accept the —er—position. Let us see! The gentleman will, on recognition, probably make a personal attack. You are armed. Ah, no? Umph! On reflection I would not permit him to strike a single blow; I would anticipate it. It would provoke the challenge from him, leaving *you*, sir, the—er—choice of weapons.

OAKHURST: Hush! he is moving! Take your stand here, in this alcove. Remember, as a gentleman and a man of honor, Colonel Starbottle, I trust you not to interfere between the injured man and—justice! (*Pushes Col. Starbottle into alcove behind couch and approaches Sandy.*)

SANDY: (*Waking slowly—and incoherently.*) Hush, Silky! Hush! Eh? Oh, hush yourself! (*Sings.*)

Oh, yer's yer Sandy Morton,
   Drink him down!

Eh! Oh! (*Half sits up on couch.*) Where the devil am I?

OAKHURST: (*Advancing and leaning over Sandy's couch.*) In the house of your father, Alexander Morton.

SANDY: (*Recoiling in astonishment.*) His voice, John Oakhurst! What—ah! (*Rises, and rushes towards Oakhurst with uplifted hand.*)

STARBOTTLE: (*Gesticulating in whisper.*) A blow! a single blow would be sufficient.

SANDY: (*Looking at Oakhurst, who regards him calmly.*) I—eh! I—eh! Ha, ha! I'm glad to see—old pard! I'm glad to see ye! (*Col. Starbottle lifts his hand in amazement.*)

OAKHURST: (*Declining his hand.*) Do you understand me, Sandy Morton? Listen. I am John Oakhurst—the man who has deceived your father, who has deceived you.

SANDY: (*Without heeding his words, but regarding him affectionately.*) To think of it—Jack Oakhurst! It's like him, like Jack. He was allers onsartin, the darned little cuss! Jack! Look at him, will ye, boys? look at him! Growed too, and dressed to kill, and sittin' in this yer house as natril as a jay-bird! (*Looking around.*) Nasty, ain't it, Jack? And this yer's your house—the old man's house—eh? Why, this is—this is where she came. Jack! Jack! (*Eagerly.*) Tell me, pard—where is she?

STARBOTTLE: (*Aside, rubbing his hands.*) We shall have it now!

OAKHURST: She has gone—gone! But hear me! She had deceived you as she has me. She has gone—gone with her first husband, Henry Pritchard.

SANDY: (*Stupefied.*) Gone! Her first husband! Pritchard!

OAKHURST: Ay, your wife!

SANDY: Oh, damn my wife! I'm talking of Mary—Miss Mary—the little school-ma'am, Jack; the little rose of Poker Flat. Oh! I see—ye didn't know her, Jack—the pertiest, sweetest little—

OAKHURST: (*Turnign away coldly.*) Ay, ay! She is here!

SANDY: (*Looking after him affectionately.*) Look at him, boys! Allers the same—high-toned, cold, even to his pardner! That's him—Jack Oakhurst! But Jack, Jack, you're goin' to shake hands, ain't ye? (*Extends his hand after a pause. Oakhurst takes it gloomily.*)

STARBOTTLE: (*Who has been regarding interview with visible scorn and disgust, advancing to Oakhurst.*) You will—er—pardon me if, under the—er—circumstances, I withdraw from this—er—disgraceful proceeding. The condonation, by that man, of two of the most tremendous offenses to society and to the code, without apology or satisfaction, Ged, sir, is—er—er—of itself an insult to the spectator. I go, sir—

OAKHURST: But, Colonel Starbottle—

STARBOTTLE: Permit me to say, sir, that I hold myself for this, sir, responsible, sir —personally responsible. (*Exit Starbottle, glancing furiously at Sandy, who sinks on sofa laughing.*)

OAKHURST: (*Aside.*) He will change his mind in half an hour. But, in the meantime, time is precious. (*Aloud.*) Sandy, come!

SANDY: (*Rising with alacrity.*) Yes, Jack, I'm ready.

OAKHURST: We are going (*Slowly and solemnly.*)—we are going to see your father.

SANDY: (*Dropping back with bashful embarrassment and struggling to release his arm from Oakhurst.*) No, Jack! Not just yet, Jack; in a little while, ol' boy! In about six months, or mebbe—a year, Jack. Not now, not now! I ain't feelin' exactly well, Jack—I ain't.

OAKHURST: Nonsense, Sandy! Consider your duty and my honor.

SANDY: (*Regaining his seat.*) That's all very well, Jack, but ye see, pard, you've known the old man for night on a year, and it's twenty-five since I met him. No, Jack; you don't play any ol' man on to me tonight, Jack. No, you and me'll just drop out for a *pasear*—Jack, eh? (*Taking Oakhurst's arm.*) Come!

OAKHURST: Impossible! Hush! (*Listening.*) It is *he* passing through the corridor. (*Goes to wing and listens.*)

SANDY: (*Crowding hastily behind Oakhurst in alarm.*) But, I say, Jack! he won't come in here? He's goin' to bed, you know. Eh? It ain't right for a man o' his years—and he must be goin' on ninety, Jack—to be up like this. It ain't healthy.

OAKHURST: You know him not. He seems to need no rest. (*Sadly.*) Night after night, long after the servants are abed, and the house is still, I hear that step slowly pacing the corridor. It is the last sound as I close my eyes, the first challenge of the morning.

SANDY: The ol' scound— (*Checking himself.*)—I mean, Jack, the ol' man has suthin' on his mind. But, Jack (*In great alarm.*), he don't waltz in upon ye, Jack? He don't p'int them feet in yer, Jack? Ye ain't got to put up with that, Jack, along o' yer other trials?

OAKHURST: He often seeks me here. Ah—yes—he is coming this way now.

SANDY: (*In ludicrous terror.*) Jack, pard, quick! hide me somewhere, Jack!

OAKHURST: (*Opening door.*) In there, quick! Not a sound, as you value your future! (*Exit Sandy hurriedly.*)

SCENE 2: *The same. Enter Old Morton, in dressing-gown with candle.*

OLD MORTON: Not abed yet, Alexander? Well, well, I don't blame you, my son; it has been for you a trying, trying night. Yes, I see: like me, you are a little nervous and wakeful. (*Slowly takes chair and comfortably composes himself.*)

OAKHURST: (*Aside.*) He is in for a midnight gossip. How shall I dispose of Sandy?

OLD MORTON: Ay. I heard voices, and saw a light in your window. I came to tell you, Alexander, Capper has explained all about—about the decoy! More; he has told me of your courage and your invaluable assistance. For a moment, sir—I don't mind telling you now in confidence—I doubted *you*—

OAKHURST: (*In feigned deprecation.*) Oh, sir!

OLD MORTON: Only for a moment. You will find, Alexander, that even that doubt shall have full apology when the year of your probation has expired. Besides, sir, I know all.

OAKHURST: (*Starting.*) All!

OLD MORTON: Yes, the story about the Duchess and your child. You are surprised. Colonel Starbottle told me all. I forgive you, Alexander, for the sake of your boy.

OAKHURST: My boy, sir!

OLD MORTON: Yes, your boy. And let me tell you, sir, he's a fine young fellow. Looks like you—looks as you did when *you* were a boy. He's a Morton too, every inch of him, there's no denying that. No, sir. *You* may have changed, but he—he—is the living image of my little Alexander. He took to me, too—lifted his little arms—and—and—(*Becomes affected and leans his head in his hands.*)

OAKHURST: (*Rising.*) You are not well, sir. Let me lead you to your room.

OLD MORTON: No! It is nothing: a glass of water, Alexander.

OAKHURST: (*Aside.*) He is very pale. The agitation of the night has overcome him. (*Goes to table.*) A little spirits will revive him. (*Pours from decanter in glass and returns to Morton.*)

OLD MORTON: (*After drinking.*) There was spirits in that water, Alexander. Five years ago, I vowed at your mother's grave to abandon the use of intoxicating liquors.

OAKHURST: Believe me, sir, my mother will forgive you.

OLD MORTON: Doubtless. It has revived me. I am getting to be an old man, Aleck. (*Holds out his glass half unconciously and Oakhurst replenishes it from decanter.*) Yes, an old man, Aleck, but the boy—ah, I live again in him. The little rascal! He asked me, Aleck, for a "chaw tobacker"[34] and wanted to know if I was the "ol' duffer." Ha, ha! He did. Ha, ha! Come, come, don't be despondent. I was like you once, damn it—ahem—it's all for the best, my boy, all for the best. I'll take the young rascal—(*Aside.*) damn it, he's already taken me—(*Aloud.*) on equal terms. There, Aleck, what do you say?

OAKHURST: Really, sir, this forbearance—this kindness—(*Aside.*) I see a ray of light.

OLD MORTON: Nonsense! I'll take the boy, I tell you, and do well for him—the little rascal!—as if he were the legal heir. But, I say, Aleck (*Laughing.*), ha, ha!—what about—ha, ha!—what about Dona Jovita, eh? And what about Don Jose Castro, eh? (*Poking Oakhurst in the ribs.*) What will the Don say to the family succession? Ha, ha!

OAKHURST: (*Proudly.*) Really, sir, I care but little.

OLD MORTON: (*Aside.*) Oh, ho! I'll sound him. (*Aloud.*) Look ye, Alexander, I have given my word to you and Don Jose Castro, and I'll keep it. But if you can do any better, eh—if—eh?—the schoolma'am's a mightly pretty girl and a bright one, eh, Aleck? And it's all in the family—eh? And she thinks well of you, and I will say, for a girl brought up as she's been, and knowin' your relations with the Duchess and the boy, to say a kind word for ye, Aleck, is a good sign—you follow me, Aleck—if you think—why, old Don Jose might whistle for a son-in-law, eh?

OAKHURST: (*Interrupting indignantly.*) Sir! (*Aside.*) Stop! (*Aloud.*) Do you mean to say, sir, that if I should consent to this—suggestion—that, if the lady were willing, *you* would offer no impediment?

OLD MORTON: Impediment, my dear boy! you should have my blessing.

OAKHURST: Pardon me a moment. You have in the last year, sir, taught me the importance of business formality in all the relations of life. Following that idea, the conditions of my engagement with Jovita Castro were drawn up with your hand. Are you willing to make this recantation as formal, this new contract as business-like and valid?

OLD MORTON: (*Eagerly.*) I am.

OAKHURST: Then sit here and write at my dictation. (*Pointing to table. Old Morton takes seat at table.*) "In view of the evident preferences of my son Alexander Morton, and of certain family interests, I hereby revoke my consent to his marriage with the Dona Jovita Castro, and accord him full permission to woo and win his cousin, Miss Mary Morris, promising him the same aid and assistance previously offered in his suit with Miss Castro."

OLD MORTON: (*Signing.*) Alexander Morton, Sr. There, Aleck! You have forgotten one legal formality. We have no witness. Ha, ha!

OAKHURST: (*Significantly.*) *I* will be a sufficient witness.

OLD MORTON: Ha, ha! (*Fills glass from decanter, after which Oakhurst quietly removes decanter beyond his reach.*) Very good! Aleck, I've been thinking of a plan—I've been thinking of retiring from the bank. I'm getting old, and my ways are not the popular ways of business here. I've been thinking of you, you dog—of leaving the bank to you—to you, sir—eh—the day you marry the schoolma'am—eh. I'll stay home and take care of the boy—eh—hic! The little rascal!—lifted his arms to me—did, Aleck! by God! (*Incoherently.*) Eh!

OAKHURST: Hush! (*Aside.*) Sandy will overhear him, and appear.

OLD MORTON: (*Greatly affected by liquor.*) Hush! eh!—of course—shoo! shoo! (*The actor will here endeavor to reproduce in Old Morton's drunken behavior, without exactly imitating him, the general characteristics of his son's intoxication.*) Eh—I say, Aleck, old boy! what will the Don say? Eh? Ha, ha, ha! And Jovita, that firebrand, how will she—hic—like it, eh? (*Laughs immoderately.*)

OAKHURST: Hush! We will be overheard! The servants, sir!

OLD MORTON: Damn the servants! Don't I—hic—pay them wages—eh?

OAKHURST: Let me lead you to your own room. You are nervously excited. A little rest, sir, will do you good. (*Taking his arm.*)

OLD MORTON: No, shir, no shir, 'm nerrer goin' to bed any more. Bed's bad habit! —hic—drunken habit. Lesh stay up all ni', Aleck! You and me! Lesh nev'r—go—bed any more! Whar's whiskey—eh? (*Staggers to the table for decanter, as Oakhurst seizes him, struggles up stage, and then Old Morton, in struggle, falls helplessly on sofa, in same attitude as Sandy was discovered.*)

(*Enter Sandy cautiously.*)

SANDY: (*To Oakhurst.*) Jack! Eh, Jack—

OAKHURST: Hush! Go! I will follow you in a moment! (*Pushes him back to door.*)

SANDY: (*Catching sight of Old Morton.*) Hallo! What's up?

OAKHURST: Nothing. He was overtaken with a sudden faintness. He will revive presently: go!

SANDY: (*Hesitating.*) I say, Jack, he wasn't taken sick along o'me, eh, Jack?

OAKHURST: No! No! But go. (*Pushing him toward door.*)

SANDY: Hold on: I'm going. But, Jack, I've got a kind of faintness yer, too. (*Goes to side-table and takes up decanter.*) And thar's nothing reaches that faintness like whiskey. (*Fills glass.*)

OLD MORTON: (*Drunkenly and half consciously from couch.*) Whiskey—who shed —whiskey—eh? Eh—O—gim'me some, Aleck—Aleck, my son,—my son!— my old prodigal—Old Proddy, my boy—gim'me—whiskey—(*Sings:*)

Oh, yer's yer good old whiskey,
　　Drink it down!

Eh? I com—mand you—pass the whiskey!

(*Sandy, at first panic-stricken, and them remorsefully conscious, throws glass down, with gesture of fear and loathing. Oakhurst advances to his side hurriedly.*)

OAKHURST: (*In hurried whisper.*) Give him the whiskey, quick! It will keep him quiet. (*Is about to take decanter, when Sandy seizes it; struggle with Oakhurst.*)

SANDY: (*With feeling.*) No, no, Jack, no! (*Suddenly, with great strength and deter-mination, breaks from him, and throws decanter from window.*) No, never!

OLD MORTON: (*Struggling drunkenly to his feet.*) Eh—who shed never? (*Oakhurst shoves Sandy in room and follows him, closing door.*) Eh, Aleck? (*Groping.*) Eh, where'sh light? All gone. (*Lapses on sofa again, after an ineffectual struggle to get up, and then resumes his old attitude.*)

(*Changes scene quickly.*)

SCENE 3. *Ante-room in Mr. Morton's villa. Front scene. Enter Don Jose Castro and Concho, preceded by servant.*

SERVANT: This way, gentlemen.

DON JOSE: Carry this card to Alexander Morton, Sr.

SERVANT: Beg pardon, sir, but there's only one name here, sir. (*Looking at Con-cho.*)

DON JOSE: (*Proudly.*) That is my servant, sir. (*Exit servant.*)

DON JOSE: (*Aside.*) I don't half like this business. But my money locked up in his bank, and my daughter's hand bound to his son, demand it. (*Aloud.*) This is no child's play, Concho, you understand.

CONCHO: Ah! I am wise. Believe me, if I have not proofs which shall blanch the cheek of this old man, I am a fool Don Jose!

(*Re-enter Servant.*)

SERVANT: Mr. Morton, Sr. passed a bad night and has left word not to be disturbed this morning. But Mr. Morton, Jr. will attend you, sir.

CONCHO: (*Aside.*) So the impostor will face it out. Well, let him come.

DON JOSE: (*To Servant.*) I await his pleasure. (*Exit Servant.*)

DON JOSE: You hear, Concho? You shall face this man. I shall repeat to him all you have told me. If you fail to make good your charge, on your head rests the consequences.

CONCHO: He will of course deny. He is a desperate man; he will perhaps attack me. Eh! Ah! (*Drawing revolver.*)

DON JOSE: Put up your foolish weapon. The sight of the father he has deceived will be more terrible to him than the pistol of the spy.

(*Enter Col. Starbottle.*)

STARBOTTLE: Mr. Alexander Morton, Jr., will be with you in a moment. (*Takes attitude by door, puts his hand in his breast, and inflates himself.*)

CONCHO: (*To Don Jose, aside.*) It is the bullying lawyer. They will try to outface us, my patron, but we shall triumph. (*Aloud.*) He comes, eh!—Mr. Alexander Morton, gentlemen. I will show you a cheat, an impostor!

(*Enter, in correct, precise morning dress, Sandy Morton. There is in his make-up and manner a suggestion of the father.*)

CONCHO: (*Recoiling, aside.*) Diego! The real son! (*Aloud, furiously.*) It is a trick to defeat justice,—eh!—a miserable trick! But it shall fail!

STARBOTTLE: Permit me, a moment,—a single moment. (*To Concho.*) You have —er—er—characterized my introduction of this—er—gentleman as a "cheat" and an "imposture." Are you prepared to deny that this is Alexander Morton?

DON JOSE: (*Astonished, aside.*) These Americanos are of the Devil! (*Aloud and sternly.*) Answer him, Concho, I command you.

CONCHO: (*In half-insane rage.*) It is Alexander Morton, but it is a trick,—a cowardly trick! Where is the other impostor, this Mr. John Oakhurst?

SANDY: (*Advancing with dignity and something of his father's cold manner.*) He will answer for himself when called for. (*To Don Jose.*) You have asked for me, sir; may I inquire your business?

CONCHO: Eh! It is a trick,—a trick!

DON JOSE: (*To Concho.*) Silence, sir! (*To Sandy, with dignity.*) I know not the meaning of this masquerade. I only know that your are *not* the gentleman hitherto known to me as the son of Alexander Morton. I am here, sir, to demand my rights as a man of property and a father. I have received this morning a check from the house of Morton & Son, for the amount of my deposit with them. So far—in view of this complication—it is well. Who knows? Bueno! But the signature of Morton & Son to the check is not in the handwriting I have known. Look at it, sir. (*To Sandy, handing check.*)

SANDY: (*Examining check.*) It is my handwriting, sir, and was signed this morning. Has it been refused?

DON JOSE: Pardon me, sir. It has not been presented. With this doubt in my mind, I preferred to submit it first to you.

STARBOTTLE: A moment, a single moment, sir. While as a—er—gentleman and a man of honor, I—er—appreciate your motives, permit me to say, sir, as a lawyer, that your visit is premature. On the testimony of your own witness, the identification of Mr. Alexander Morton, Jr., is—er—complete; he has admitted the signature as his own; you have not yet presented the check to the bank.

DON JOSE: Pardon me, Colonel Starbottle. It is not all. (*To Sandy.*) By a written agreement with Alexander Morton, Sr., the hand of my daughter is promised to his son, who now stands before me, as my former servant, dismissed from my service for drunkenness.

SANDY: That agreement is revoked.

DON JOSE: Revoked!

SANDY: (*Handing paper.*) Cast your eyes over that paper. At least you will recognize *that* signature.

DON JOSE: (*Reads.*) "In view of the evident preferences of my son Alexander Morton, and of certain family interests, I hereby revoke my consent to his marriage with the Dona Jovita Castro, and accord him full permission to woo and win his cousin, Miss Mary Morris; promising him the same aid and assistance previously offered in his suit with Miss Castro.—Alexander Morton, Sr."

CONCHO: Ah! Carramba! Do you not see the trick—eh, the conspiracy? It was this man, as Diego, your daughter's groom, helped his friend Mr. Oakhurst to the heiress. Ah, you comprehend! It was an old trick! You shall see, you shall see! Ah! I am wise, I am wise.

DON JOSE: (*Aside.*) Could I have been deceived? But no! This paper that releases *him* gives the impostor no claim.

SANDY: (*Resuming his old easy manner, dropping his formality, and placing his hand on Don Jose's shoulder.*) Look yar, ole man; I didn't allow to ever see ye agin, and this yer ain't none o' *my* seekin'. But since ye're here, I don't mind tellin' ye that but for me that gal of yours would have run away a year ago and married an unknown lover. And I don't mind adding, that hed I known that unknown lover was my friend John Oakhurst, I'd have helped her do it. (*Going.*) Good morning, Don Jose.

DON JOSE: Insolent! I shall expect an account for this from your—father, sir.

SANDY: Adios, Don Jose. (*Exit.*)

CONCHO: It is a trick—I told you. Ah, I am wise. (*Going to Don Jose.*)

DON JOSE: (*Throwing him off.*) Fool! (*Exit Don Jose.*)

CONCHO: (*Infuriated.*) Eh! Fool yourself—dotard! No matter: I will expose all— ah! I will see Jovita—I will revenge myself on this impostor! (*Is about to follow, when Col. Starbottle leaves his position by the door and touches Concho on the shoulder.*)

STARBOTTLE: Excuse me.

CONCHO: Eh?

STARBOTTLE: You have forgotten something.

CONCHO: Something?

STARBOTTLE: An apology, sir. You were good enough to express—er—incredulity —when I presented Mr. Morton; you were kind enough to characterize the conduct of my—er—principal by—an epithet. You have alluded to me, sir,—ME—

CONCHO: (*Wrathfully.*) Bully! (*Aside.*) I have heard that this pomposo, this braggart, is a Yankee trick too; that he has the front of a lion, the liver of a chicken. (*Aloud.*) Yes, I have said, you hear I have said, I, Concho (*striking his breast*), have said you are a—bully!

STARBOTTLE: (*Coolly.*) Then you are prepared to give me satisfaction, sir,— personal satisfaction.

CONCHO: (*Raging.*) Yes, sir, now—you understand, now (*taking out pistol*), any- where, here! Yes, here. Ah! you start,—yes, here and now! Face to face, you understand, without seconds,—face to face. So! (*Presenting pistol.*)

STARBOTTLE: (*Quietly.*) Permit me to—er—apologize.

CONCHO: Ah! It is too late!

STARBOTTLE: (*Interrupting.*) Excuse me, but I feared you would not honor me so completely and satisfactorily. Ged, sir, I begin to respect you! I accede to all your propositions of time and position. The pistol you hold in your hand is a der- ringer, I presume, loaded. Ah—er—I am right. The one I now produce (*show- ing pistol*) is—er—as you will perceive the same size and pattern, and—er— unloaded. We will place them both, so, under the cloth of this table. You shall draw one pistol, I will take the other. I will put that clock at ten minutes to nine, when we will take our positions across this table; as you—er—happily ex- press it, "face to face." As the clock strikes the hour, we will fire on the second stroke.

CONCHO: (*Aside.*) It is a trick, a Yankee trick! (*Aloud.*) I am ready. Now—at once!

STARBOTTLE: (*Gravely.*) Permit me, sir, to thank you. Your conduct, sir, reminds me of singular incident—

CONCHO: (*Angrily interrupting.*) Come, come! It is no child's play. We have much of this talk, eh! It is action, eh, you comprehend—action.

(*Starbottle places pistol under the cloth, and sets clock. Concho draws pistol from cloth; Starbottle takes remaining pistol. Both men assume position, presenting their weapons; Starbottle pompously but seriously, Concho angrily and nervously.*)

STARBOTTLE: (*After a pause.*) One moment, a single moment—

CONCHO: Ah, a trick! Coward! you cannot destroy my aim.

STARBOTTLE: I overlook the—er—epithet. I wished only to ask, if you should be—er—unfortunate, if there was anything I could say to your—er—friends.

CONCHO: You cannot make the fool of me, coward. No!

STARBOTTLE: My object was only precautionary. Owing to the position in which you—er—persist in holding your weapon, in a line with my right eye, I perceive that a ray of light enters the nipple, and—er—illuminates the barrel. I judge from this, that you have been unfortunate enough to draw the—er—er—un- loaded pistol.

CONCHO: (*Tremulously lowering weapon.*) Eh! Ah! This is murder! (*Drops pis- tol.*) Murder!—eh—help (*retreating*), help! (*Exit hurriedly door center, as clock strikes. Col. Starbottle lowers his pistol, and moves with great pomposity to the other side of the table, taking up pistol.*)

STARBOTTLE: (*Examining pistol.*) Ah! (*Lifts it, and discharges it.*) It seems that I am mistaken. (*Going.*) The pistol *was*—er—loaded! (*Exit.*)

SCENE 4: *Front scene. Room in villa. Enter Miss Mary and Jovita.*

MISS MARY: I tell you, you are wrong. You are not only misunderstanding your lover, which is a woman's privilege, but you are abusing my cousin, which, as his relative, I won't put up with.

JOVITA: (*Passionately.*) But hear me, Miss Mary. It is a year since we were betrothed; and such a betrothal! Why, I was signed, sealed, and delivered to him, on conditions, as if I were part of the rancho; and the very night, too, I had engaged to run away with him! And during that year, I have seen the gentleman twice,—yes, twice!

MISS MARY: But he has written?

JOVITA: Mother of God! Yes,—letters delivered by my father, sent to *his care*, read by him first, of course; letters hoping that I was well and obeying my father's commands; letters assuring me of his unaltered devotion; letters that, compared with the ones he used to hide in the confessional of the ruined mission church, were as ice to fire, were as that snow-flower you value so much, Mary, to this mariposa blossom I wear in my hair. And then to think that this man—this John Oakhurst, as I knew him; this man who used to ride twenty miles for a smile from me on the church porch; this Don Juan, who leaped that garden wall (fifteen feet, Mary, if it is an inch), and made old Concho his stepping-stone; this man, who daily periled death for my sake—is changed into this formal, methodical man of business—is—is—I tell you there's a *woman* at the bottom of it! I know it sure!

MISS MARY: (*Aside.*) How can I tell her about the Duchess? I won't! (*Aloud.*) But listen, my dear Jovita. You know he is under probation for you, Jovita. All this is for you. His father is cold, methodical, unsympathetic. *He* looks only to his bond with this son—this son that he treats, even in matters of the heart, as a *business* partner. Remember, on his complete reformation, and subjection to his father's will, depends your hand. Remember the agreement!

JOVITA: The agreement; yes! It is the agreement, always the agreement. May the Devil fly away with the agreement! Look you, Miss Mary, I, Dona Jovita, didn't fall in love with an agreement: it was with a man! Why, I might have married a dozen agreements—yes, of a shorter limitation than this! (*Crossing.*)

MISS MARY: Yes. But what if your lover had failed to keep those promises by which he was to gain your hand? What if he were a man incapable of self-control? What if he were—a—a—drunkard!

JOVITA: (*Musing.*) A drunkard! (*Aside.*) There was Diego; he was a drunkard, but he was faithless. (*Aloud.*) You mean a weak, faithless drunkard?

MISS MARY: No! (*Sadly.*) Faithless only to himself, but devoted—yes, devoted to *you.*

JOVITA: Miss Mary, I have found that one big vice in a man is apt to keep out a great many smaller ones.

MISS MARY: Yes, but if he were a slave to liquor?

JOVITA: My dear, I should try to change his mistress. Oh, give me a man that is capable of a devotion to anything, rather than a cold, calculating average of all the virtues!

MISS MARY: (*Aside.*) I, who aspire to be her teacher, am only her pupil. (*Aloud.*)

But what if, in this very drunkenness, this recklessness, he had once loved and worshipped another woman? What if you discovered all this after—after—he had won your heart?

JOVITA: I should adore him! Ah, Miss Mary! Love differs from all the other contagious diseases: the last time a man is exposed to it, he takes it most readily, and has it the worst! But you, *you,* you cannot sympathize with me. You have some lover, the ideal of the virtues; some man as correct, as well regulated, as calm as—yourself; someone who addresses you in the fixed morality and severe penmanship of the copy-books. He will never precipitate himself over a garden wall or through a window. Your Jacob will wait for you through seven years and receive you from the hands of your cousin and guardian—as a reward of merit! No, you could not love a vagabond.

MISS MARY: (*Very slowly and quietly.*) No?

JOVITA: No! (*Passionately.*) No, it is impossible. Forgive me, Miss Mary: you are good; a better girl than I am. But think of me! A year ago my lover leaped a wall at midnight to fly with me; today, the day that gives me to him, he writes a few cold lines, saying that he has business, *business*—you understand—business, and that he shall not see me until we meet in the presence of—of—of—our fathers.

MISS MARY: Yes, but you will see him at least, perhaps alone. Listen: it is no formal meeting, but one of festivity. My guardian has told me, in his quaint scriptural way, it is the killing of the fatted calf, over his long lost prodigal. Have patience, little one. Ah! Jovita, we are of a different race, but we are of one sex, and as a woman I know how to accept another woman's abuse of her lover. Come, come! (*Exeunt Miss Mary and Jovita.*)

SCENE 5: *The drawing-room of Mr. Morton's villa. Large open arch in center, leading to veranda, looking on distant view of San Francisco; richly furnished— sofas, armchairs, and tete-a-tetes. Enter Col. Starbottle carrying bouquet, preceded by Servant, bowing.*

STARBOTTLE: Take my kyard to Miss Morris. (*Exit Servant.*) Star! This is the momentous epoch of your life! It is a moment for which you—are—I may say alone responsible—personally responsible! She will be naturally gratified by the—er—flowers. She will at once recognize this bouquet as a delicate souvenir of Red Gulch and will appreciate your recollection. And the fact, the crushing fact, that you have overlooked the—er—ungentlemanly conduct of her *own* cousin Sandy, the real Alexander Morton, that you have—er—assisted to restore the ex-vaquero to his rights, will—er—er—at once open the door to—er—mutual confidence and—er—a continuance of that—er—prepossession I have already noticed. Ahem! here she is.

(*Enter Miss Mary in full dress.*)

MISS MARY: You are early, Colonel Starbottle. This promptitude does honor to our poor occasion.

STARBOTTLE: Ged, Miss Mary, promptness with a lady and an adversary is the first duty of—er—gentlemen. I wished that—er—the morning dew might still be—er—fresh in these flowers. I gathered them myself (*presenting bouquet*) at er—er—flower stand in the—er—California market.

MISS MARY: (*Aside.*) Flowers! I needed no such reminder of poor Sandy. (*Aloud.*) I thank you, colonel.

STARBOTTLE: Ged, ma'am, I am repaid doubly. Your conduct, Miss Mary, reminds me of little incident that occurred at Richmond, in '53. Dinner party—came early—but obliged to go—as now—on important business, before dessert—before dessert. Lady sat next to me—beautiful woman—excuse me if I don't mention names—said to me, "Star,"—always called me Star,—"Star, you remind me of the month of May."—Ged, madam,"—I said, "delighted, proud, but why?"—"Because," she said, "you come in with the—er—oysters"— No! Ged, pardon me—ridiculous mistake! I mean—er—"you come in with the —er—flowers, and go before the—er—fruits."

MISS MARY: Ah, colonel! I appreciate her disappointment. Let us hope, however, that some day you may find that happy woman who will be able to keep you through the whole dinner and the whole season, until December and the ices!

STARBOTTLE: Ged! excellent! Capital! (*Seriously.*) Miss Mary! (*Suddenly inflating his chest, striking attitude, and gazing on Miss Mary with languishing eyes.*) There is—er—such a woman!

MISS MARY: (*Aside.*) What can he mean?

STARBOTTLE: (*Taking seat beside her.*) Allow me, Miss Mary, a few moments of confidential—er—confidential disclosure. Today is, as you are aware—the day on which, according to—er—agreement between parties, my friend and client Mr. Morton, Sr., formally accepts his prodigal son. It is my—er—duty to state that—er—the gentleman who has for the past year occupied that position has behaved with great discretion, and—er—fulfilled his part of the—er—agreement. But it would—er—appear that there has been a—er—slight delusion regarding the identity of that prodigal—a delusion shared by all the parties except, perhaps, myself. I have to prepare you for a shock. The gentleman whom you have recently known as Alexander Morton, Jr., is not the prodigal son; is not your—er—cousin; is, in fact, no relation to you. Prepare yourself, Miss Mary, for a little disappointment—for—er—degradation. The genuine son has been—er—discovered in the person of—er—low menial—er—vagabond— "Sandy," the—er—outcast of Red Gulch!

MISS MARY: (*Rising in astonishment.*) Sandy! Then he was right. (*Aside.*) The child is his, and that woman—

STARBOTTLE: Compose yourself, Miss Mary. I know the—er—effect of—er— revelation like this upon—er—proud and aristocratic nature. Ged! My own, I assure you, beats in—er—responsive indignation. You can never consent to remain beneath this roof, and—er—receive a—er—vagabond and—er—menial on equal terms. The—er—necessities of my—er—profession may—er—compel me, but you—er—never! Holding myself—er—er—responsible for having introduced you here, it is my—er—duty to provide you with—another home! It is my—er—duty to protect—

MISS MARY: (*Aside.*) Sandy here and beneath this roof! Why has he not sought me? Ah, I know too well: he dare not face me with his child!

STARBOTTLE: (*Aside.*) She turns away! It is maiden coyness. (*Aloud.*) If, Miss

Mary, the—er—devotion of a lifetime; if the—er—chivalrous and respectful adoration of a man—er—whose record is—er—not unknown in the Court of Honor (*dropping on one knee with excessive gallantry*); if the—er—measure—

MISS MARY: (*Oblivious of Col. Starbottle.*) I *will*—I *must* see him! Ah! (*looking left*) he is coming!

(*Enter Sandy.*)

STARBOTTLE: (*Rising with great readiness and tact.*) I have found it. (*Presenting flower.*) It had fallen beneath the sofa.

SANDY: (*To Miss Mary, stopping short in embarrassment.*) I did not know you—I —I thought there was no one here.

MISS MARY: (*To Starbottle.*) May I ask you to excuse me for a moment? I have a few words to say to—to my *cousin!*

(*Starbottle bows gallantly to Miss Mary, and stiffly to Sandy, and exits. A long pause; Miss Mary remains seated, pulling flowers; Sandy remains standing by wing, foolish and embarrassed. Business.*)

MISS MARY: (*Impatiently.*) Well?

SANDY: (*Slowly.*) I axes your pardon, miss, but you have told *that* gentleman you had a few words—to say to me.

MISS MARY: (*Passionately, aside.*) Fool! (*Aloud.*) I had, but I am waiting to first answer your inquiries about your—your—child. I have fulfilled my trust, sir.

SANDY: You have, Miss Mary, and I thank you.

MISS MARY: I might perhaps have expected that this revelation of our kinship would have come from other lips than a stranger's, but—no matter! I wish you joy, sir, of your heritage. (*Going.*) You have found a home, sir, at last, for yourself and—and—your child. Good-day, sir.

SANDY: Miss Mary!

MISS MARY: I must make ready to receive your father's guests. It is his orders; I am only his poor relation. Good-by, sir. (*Exit.*)

SANDY: (*Watching her.*) She is gone!—gone! No! She has dropped on the sofa in the ante-room and is crying. Crying! I promised Jack I wouldn't speak until the time came. I'll go back. (*Hesitating and looking toward left.*) Poor girl! How she must hate me! I might just say a word, one word to thank her for her kindness to Johnny—only one word, and then go away. I—I—can keep from liquor. I swore I would to Jack, that night I saw the old man—drunk,—and I have. But—I can't keep—from—her! No—damn it! (*Going toward left.*) No!—I'll go! (*Exit.*)

(*Enter hurriedly and excitedly Jovita, followed by Manuela.*)

JOVITA: Where is she? Where is *he?*—the traitor!

MANUELA: (*Entreatingly.*) Compose yourself, Dona Jovita, for the love of God! This is madness; believe me, there is some mistake. It is some trick of an enemy

—of that ingrate, that coyote, Concho, who hates the Don Alexandro.

JOVITA: A trick! Call you this a trick? Look at this paper, put into my hands by my father a moment ago. Read it. Ah! listen. (*Reads.*) "In view of the *evident preferences* of my son Alexander Morton, I hereby revoke my consent to his marriage with the Dona Jovita Castro, and accord him full permission to woo and win his cousin, Miss Mary Morris!" Call you this a trick, eh? No, it is their perfidy! This is why *she* was brought here on the eve of my betrothal. This accounts for his silence, his absence. Oh, I shall go mad!

MANUELA: Compose yourself, miss. If I am not deceived, there is one here who will aid us—who will expose this deceit. Listen: an hour ago, as I passed through the hall, I saw Diego, our old Diego—your friend and confidant, Diego.

JOVITA: The drunkard—the faithless Diego!

MANUELA: Never, Miss Jovita; not drunken! For as he passed before me, he was straight, as upright, as fine as your lover. Come, miss, we will seek him.

JOVITA: Never! He, too, is a traitor.

MANUELA: Believe me, no! Come, Miss Jovita. (*Looking toward left.*) See, he is there. Someone is with him.

JOVITA: (*Looking.*) You are right, and it is *she—she*, Miss Mary! What? he is kissing her hand! And she—*she*, the double traitress—drops her head upon his shoulder! Oh, this is infamy!

MANUELA: Hush! Someone is coming. The guests are arriving. They must not see you thus. This way, Miss Jovita—this way. After a little, a little, the mystery will be explained. (*Taking Jovita's hand, and leading her right.*)

JOVITA: (*Going.*) And this was the correct schoolmistress, the preceptress and example of all the virtues! ha! (*laughing hysterically*) ha! (*Exeunt Jovita and Manuela.*)

SCENE 6: *The same. Enter Servant; opens folding doors, revealing veranda, and view of distant city beyond. Stage, fog*[35] *effect from without. Enter Starbottle and Oakhurst in full evening dress.*

STARBOTTLE: (*Walking towards veranda.*) A foggy evening for our anniversary.

OAKHURST: Yes. (*Aside.*) It was such a night as this I first stepped into Sandy's place; I first met the old man. Well, it will be soon over. (*Aloud.*) You have the papers and transfers all ready?

STARBOTTLE: In my—er—pocket. Mr. Morton, Sr., should be here to receive his guests.

OAKHURST: He will be here presently; until then the duty devolves on me. He has secluded himself even from me! (*Aside.*) Perhaps it is in very shame for his recent weakness.

(*Enter Servant.*)

SERVANT: Don Jose Castro, Miss Castro, and Miss Morris.

(*Enter Don Jose with Jovita and Miss Mary on either arm. All formally salute Mr.*

Oakhurst, except Miss Jovita, who turns coldly away, taking seat remotely on sofa. Col. Starbottle gallantly approaches Miss Mary and takes seat beside her.)

OAKHURST: (*Aside.*) They are here to see my punishment. There is no sympathy even in her eyes.

(*Enter Servant.*)

SERVANT: Mr. Concepcion Garcia and Mr. Capper.
CONCHO: (*Approaching Oakhurst, rubbing his hands.*) I wish you joy, Mr. Alexander Morton!
OAKHURST: (*Excitedly, aside.*) Shall I throw him from the window! The dog!—even he!
CAPPER: (*Approaching Mr. Oakhurst.*) You have done well. Be bold. *I* will see you through. As for *that* man (*pointing to Concho*), leave him to *me*! (*Lays his hand on Concho's shoulder, and leads him to sofa. Oakhurst takes seat in chair, as Sandy enters quietly from door and stands leaning upon his chair.*)
STARBOTTLE: (*Rising.*) Ladies and gentlemen, we are waiting only for the presence of Mr. Alexander Morton, Sr. I regret to say that for the last twenty-four hours—he has been—er—exceedingly preoccupied with the momentous cares of the—er—occasion. You who know the austere habits of my friend and—er—client will probably understand that he may be at this very moment engaged in prayerful and Christian meditation, invoking the Throne of Grace, previous to the solemn duties of—er—er—tonight.

(*Enter Servant.*)

SERVANT: Mr. Alexander Morton, Sr.

(*Enter Old Morton, drunk, in evening costume, cravat awry, coat half buttoned up, and half surly, half idiotic manner. All rise in astonishment. Sandy starts forward. Oakhurst pulls him back.*)

MORTON: (*Thickly.*) Don't rishe! Don't rishe! We'll all sit down! How do you do, sir? I wish ye well, miss. (*Goes around and laboriously shakes hands with everybody.*) Now lesh all take a drink! lesh you take a drink, and you take a drink, and you take a drink!
STARBOTTLE: Permit me, ladies and gentlemen, to—er—explain: our friend is—er—evidently laboring under—er—er—accident of hospitality! In a moment he will be himself.
MORTON: Hush up! Dry up—yourself—old turkey-cock! Eh!
SANDY: (*Despairingly.*) He will not understand us! (*To Starbottle.*) He will not know me! What is to be done?
MORTON: Give me some whishkey. Lesh all take a drink! (*Enter Servant with decanter and glasses. Morton starting forward.*) Lesh all take a drink!
SANDY: Stop!
MORTON: (*Recovering himself slightly.*) Who says stop? Who dares countermand

my ordersh?

CONCHO: (*Coming forward.*) Who? I will tell you: eh! eh! Diego—dismissed from the rancho of Don Jose for drunkenness! Sandy—the vagabond of Red Gulch!

SANDY: (*Passionately seizing Old Morton's arm.*) Yes, Diego—Sandy—the outcast —but, God help me! no longer the drunkard. I forbid you to touch that glass!— I, your son, Alexander Morton! Yes, look at me, father: I, with drunkenness in my blood, planted by you, fostered by you—I whom you sought to save—I—I, stand here to save you! Go! (*To Servant.*) Go! While he is thus, I—*I,* am master here!

MORTON: (*Cowed and frightened.*) That voice! (*Passing his hand over his forehead.*) Am I dreaming? Aleck, where are you? Alexander, speak, I command you: is this the truth?[36]

OAKHURST: (*Slowly.*) It is!

STARBOTTLE: One moment—a single moment: permit me to—er—er—explain. The gentleman who has just—er—dismissed the refreshment is, to the best of my legal knowledge, your son. The gentleman who for the past year has so admirably filled the functions of that office is—er—prepared to admit this. The proofs are—er—conclusive. It is with the—er—intention of offering them, and —er—returning your lawful heir, that we—er—are here tonight.

MORTON: (*Rising to his feet.*) And I renounce you both! Out of my house, out of my sight, out of my heart, forever! Go! liars, swindlers, confederates! Drunk—

OAKHURST: (*Retiring slowly with Sandy.*) We are going, sir!

MORTON: Go! open the doors there *wide,* wide enough for such a breadth of infamy! Do you hear me? *I* am master here!

(*Stands erect, as Oakhurst and Sandy, hand in hand, slowly retreat backward to center,—then suddenly utters a cry, and falls back heavily on sofa. Both pause: Oakhurst remains quiet and motionless; Sandy, after a moment's hesitation, rushes forward, and falls at his feet.*)

SANDY: Father, forgive me!

MORTON: (*Putting his hand round Sandy's neck, and motioning him to door.*) Go! both of you, both of you! (*Resisting Sandy's attempt to rise.*) Did you hear me? Go!

STARBOTTLE: Permit me to—explain. Your conduct, Mr. Morton, remind me of sing'lar incident in '47—

MORTON: Silence!

OAKHURST: One word, Mr. Morton! Shamed and disgraced as I am, I leave this roof more gladly than I entered it. How I came here, you best know. How I yielded madly to the temptation, the promise of a better life; how I fell, through the hope of reformation,—no one should know better than you, sir, the reformer. I do not ask your pardon. You know that I did my duty to you as your presumed son. Your real son will bear witness that, from the hour I knew of his existence, I did my duty equally to him. Colonel Starbottle has all the legal transfers and papers necessary to make the restoration of your son—the integrity of your business name—complete. I take nothing out of this life that I did not bring in it,—except my self-respect! I go—as I came—alone!

JOVITA: (*Rushing towards him.*) No! no! You shall take *me*! I have wronged you, Jack, cruelly; I have doubted you, but you shall not go alone. I care not for this contract! You are more to me, by your own right, Jack, than by any kinship with such as these!

OAKHURST: (*Raising her gently.*) I thank you, darling. But it is too late now. To be more worthy of you, to win *you*, I waived the title I had to you in my own manhood, to borrow another's more legal claim. I, who would not win you as a gambler, cannot make you now the wife of a convicted impostor. No! Hear me, darling! do not make my disgrace greater than it is. In the years to come, Jovita, think of me as one who loved you well enough to go through shame to win you, but too well to ask you to share with him that shame. Farewell, darling, farewell! (*Releases himself from Jovita's arms, who falls beside him.*)

CONCHO: (*Rubbing his hands, and standing before him.*) Oho! Mr. John Oakhurst—eh—was it for this, eh—you leaped the garden wall, eh? Was it for this you struck me down, eh? You are not wise, eh? You should have run away with the Dona when you could—ah, ah, impostor!

SANDY: (*Leaping to his feet.*) Jack, you shall not go! I will go with you!

OAKHURST: No! Your place is there. (*Pointing to Old Morton, whose head has sunk drunkenly on his breast.*) Heed not this man; his tongue carries only the borrowed lash of his master.

CONCHO: Eh! you are bold now—bold, but I said I would have revenge—ah, revenge!

SANDY: (*Rushing towards him.*) Coward!

DON JOSE: Hold your hand, sir! Hold! I allow no one to correct my menials but myself. Concho, order my carriage!

CONCHO: It is ready, sir.

DON JOSE: Then lead the way to it, for my daughter and her husband, John Oakhurst.—Goodnight, Mr. Morton. I can sympathize with you, for we have both found a son. I am willing to exchange my dismissed servant for your dismissed *partner*.

STARBOTTLE: (*Advancing.*) Ged, sir, I respect you! Ged, sir, permit me, sir, to grasp that honorable hand!

MORTON: (*Excitedly.*) He is right, my partner. What have I done! The house of Morton & Son dissolved. The man known as my partner—a fugitive! No, Alexander!

STARBOTTLE: One moment—a single momet! As a lawyer, permit me to say, sir, that the whole complication may be settled, sir, by the—er—addition of—er—single letter! The house of Morton & Son shall hereafter read Morton & Sons. The papers for the legal adoption of Mr. Oakhurst are—er—in my pocket.

MORTON: (*More soberly.*) Have it your own way, sir! Morton & Sons be it. Hark ye, Don Jose! We are equal at last. But—hark ye, Aleck! How about the boy, eh?—my grandson, eh? Is this one of the sons by adoption?

SANDY: (*Embarrassedly.*) It is my own, sir.

CAPPER: (*Advancing.*) He can with safety claim it, for the mother is on her way to Australia with her husband.

MORTON: And the schoolma'am, eh?

MISS MARY: She will claim the usual year of probation for your prodigal, and
then—

SANDY: God bless ye, Miss Mary!

MORTON: I am in a dream! But the world—my friends—my patrons—how can I
explain?

STARBOTTLE: I will—er—explain. (*Advancing slowly to front—to audience.*)
One moment—er—a single moment! If anything that has—er—transpired this
evening—might seem to you, ladies and gentlemen—er—morally or—er—
legally—or honorably to require—er—apology or—er—explanation!—permit
me to say—that I—Colonel Culpepper Starbottle, hold myself responsible—er
—personally responsible.

(*Curtain.*)

END

FOOTNOTES

[1]*Vaquero*: horseman or cowboy.

[2]*Semper*: always.

[3]*Manta*: shawl.

[4]*Saya y manta*: skirt and shawl.

[5]*Solus*: alone.

[6]*Serape*: blanket, cloak, poncho; worn over the shoulder or shoulders.

[7]*Greasers*: American slang for Mexicans, suggested by the supposedly more oily complex-
ions of the Hispanics, compared with the dry-skinned Yankees.

[8]*No sabe*: I don't know.

[9]*Caballero*: gentleman, swain, horseman.

[10]*Pass his hash!*: leave it alone; forget it!

[11]*I looks toward ye*: Here's looking at you; your health; a toast.

[12]*Surcle*: colloquial for cinch, the strap which holds the saddle on the mount.

[13]*Cayotes*: coyotes; an insult.

[14]*You're blowed upon*: you're given away; your secret is known; your cover is blown.

[15]*Er—er*: Harte's method of indicating that Col. Starbottle stammers, intended as a comic
effect.

[16]*Muchacho*: boy.

[17]*Sembi Canca*: a dance of the period; related to the Can Can.

[18]*Glass*: a glass-eye, regarded as comical—and undesirable in a prospective mate; red hair was also thought unattractive and was long worn by comic characters.

[19]*No shabe likoquize*: stage-dialect Chinese for: *No sabe* recognize; *no sabe* meaning "I don't know."

[20]*Alle same, John*: They're all the same man, to John; here, Hop Sing uses an American slang designation for Chinese: "Chinaman John."

[21]*Shabbee*: dialect for *sabe*; colloquial: savvy; meaning, "Do you understand?"

[22]*Poco tiempo*: In a little while.

[23]*Madre de Dios*: Mother of God!

[24]*Manzanita*: literally "little apple," a Western shrub with gnarled branches and tiny blossoms from which bees make aromatic honey.

[25]*'Frisco*: slang for San Francisco; San Francisco newspaper columnist Herb Caen has insisted: "Don't call it 'Frisco."

[26]*If*: the meaning is "Even if . . ."

[27]*Natril*: dialect for natural.

[28]*A single question*: from what follows, it's clear that there are *two* questions; an oversight by playwright Harte.

[29]*Upper Stanislaus*: the Stanislaus River, which had some prosperous placer mines on or near it.

[30]*Pasear*: a walk, a promenade, but here in the sense of having a night out.

[31]*Three years*: since Sandy's son, Tommy, has earlier been described as a pupil of Miss Mary's at the Red Gulch School, this sudden reduction in the boy's age appears a device to elicit audience sympathy; it may have been an awkward expedient in the stage-production, but Bret Harte permitted it to remain in all printings of his *Collected Works*. Tots of three didn't go to school, though they might begin as early as five years.

[32]*Ez white a man ez they is*: "He's as white a man as there is"; a colloquial compliment similar to the 19th century British and American: "You've behaved like a white man!" and "That's mighty white of you!"

[33]*Ekal*: equal.

[34]*Chaw tobacker*: a chew of tobacco; chewing-tobacco.

[35]*Fog*: a distinctive attribute of San Francisco's climate, then as now.

[36]*Is this the truth*: considering the slovenly drunk-scene obviously intended for comic effect immediately preceding, this rapid recovery of self-possession and speech clarity to facilitate the denouement seems improbable.

A BRIEF CHRONOLOGY OF CALIFORNIA HISTORY

1542 — Spanish expedition under Cabrillo.

1579 — Sir Francis Drake explores the California Coast.

1768 — Spanish colonization of California—for fear of British and Russian en-croachments—through the efforts of Padre Junipero Serra in founding the Missions; Franciscan fathers converted native Indians and taught them to work on the Mission lands and build the Mission-churches and compexes; the Spanish also established *presidios*—military stations—and *pueblos*—civilian towns. Early *pueblos* in California were those of Nuestra Senora de Los Angeles and Yerba Buena (San Francisco), among others.

1812 — Russians establish Fort Ross on the California coast above San Francisco Bay; they are engaged in the fur trade.

1822 — Spanish domination of Mexico ends; Mexican self-rule begins, including what will one day be the State of California.

1826 — Jedediah Smith and a group of trappers make the first overland entry by white men into California; whaling-men and sea-born fur traders from the Eastern United States are also becoming familiar with the area; some begin to settle.

1833 — Mexico secularizes the Mission lands, making generous land-grants from them and other areas occupied only by Indians; some grants give title to as many as 50,000 acres.

1841 — The first overland settlers arrive from the East.

1842-45 — Exploratory expeditions by U.S. General John C. Fremont.

1846 — (14 June) "Bear Flag Revolt" in Sonoma; William Ide and other feisty American settlers—alleging a Mexican threat to drive them from their homes and ranches—capture the astonished local Mexican authorities and declare a California

Republic, with the distinctive bear emblem that is later to become the state flag. The U.S. Navy is conveniently close in Monterey.

1848 — (24 January) At Sutter's Mill in Coloma, on the South Fork of the American River, James Marshall discovers the first important gold nugget, triggering the great Gold Rush to California.

1848 — (2 February) Under the Treaty of Guadelupe Hidalgo, the Mexican government, defeated in a war with the United States, cedes California and other valuable western territories, including what will become the State of Nevada; in 1859, the fabulous Comstock Lode in Virginia City begins to produce $300 million in gold and silver in just two decades.

1849 — The year of the great Gold Rush; Monterey is the California capital.

1850 — (9 September) California becomes the 31st state in the union; it's admitted as a "free state," in the controversy between North and South regarding slavery. The Nevada lands are made part of the Utah Territory; only in 1861, as a result of Comstock wealth, will they become the Nevada Territory, with statehood in 1864, through Civil War pressures.

1851 — San Francisco has its first Vigilance Committee, in which irate citizens, angered at crime and corruption, take the law into their own hands.

1853 — Gold-bearing quartz ore is discovered in Grass Valley, California, giving new life to the northern goldfields, seemingly exhausted by placer mining; this signals the era of "hard-rock" mining, with experienced miners brought from Cornwall ("Cousin Jacks") and from Wales.

1854 — Sacramento becomes the new state capital.

1856 — San Francisco has a new group of vigilantes, who lynch their prey, Cora and Casey, among other extra-legal activities.

1857 — The Butterfield Overland Mail is inaugurated.

1858 — With the amazing number of quartz-gold strikes being made, there are now some 280 quartz-mills in California, used for crushing the ore so that gold particles can be separated from it.

1860 — The Pony Express begins its services.

1861 — The transcontinental telegraph is completed.

1869 — With the driving of the Golden Spike at Promontory, Utah, the transcontinental railroad is finished, linking California with the East—and promoting even more theatrical trouping from the East than before had been possible by sea and overland.

1882 — Concerned by the presence of so many Chinese immigrants in California, brought first by the lure of gold and work, and later imported as cheap labor to build the railroads, Western lawmakers succeed in getting the Senate and the House of Representatives to pass the (Oriental) Exclusion Act.

BIBLIOGRAPHY
Selected Works

Ashley, Celeste. *Gold Rush Theatre in Nevada City, California*. Unpublished M.A. Thesis, Stanford University, 1957.

Delano, Alonzo ("Old Block"). *A Live Woman in the Mines; or, Pike County Ahead!*. New York: Samuel French, 1857.

Foster, Lois M. *Annals of the San Francisco Stage—1850-1880*. Unpublished Federal Theatre/WPA Project Manuscript, San Francisco, 1937.

Gaer, Joseph. *The Theatre of the Gold Rush Decade in San Francisco*. New York: Burt Franklin, 1970.

Gagey, Edmond M. *The San Francisco Stage*. New York: Columbia University Press, 1950.

Goldberg, Isaac. *Queen of Hearts: the Passionate Pilgrimage of Lola Montez*. New York: The John Day Co., 1936.

Harte, Bret. *Two Men of Sandy Bar*. Boston: J. R. Osgood, 1876. Also in Harte's *Collected Works*.

Howe, Charles E. B. *Joaquin Murieta de Castillo, the Celebrated California Bandit*. San Francisco: Commercial Book and Job Steam Printing Establishment, 1858.

Hyde, Stuart Wallace. *The Representation of the West in American Drama from 1849 to 1917*. Unpublished Ph.D. Dissertation, Stanford University, 1954.

Leman, Walter. *Memories of an Old Actor*. San Francisco: A. Roman & Co., 1886.

MacMinn, George R. *The Theatre in the Golden Era in California*. Caldwell, Idaho: Caxton Printers, 1941.

McElhaney, John. *The Professional Theatre in San Francisco, 1880-1889*. Unpublished Ph.D. Dissertation, Stanford University, 1972.

Phillips, Levi Damon. *Arthur McKee Rankin's Touring Production of Joaquin Miller's "The Danites."* Unpublished Ph.D. Dissertation, University of California at Davis, 1981.

Robinson, Dr. D. G. *Comic Songs; Or, Hits at San Francisco.* San Francisco: Commercial Book and Job Office, 1853.

Rourke, Constance. *Troupers of the Gold Coast; or, The Rise of Lotta Crabtree.* New York: Harcourt, Brace & Co., 1928.

San Francisco Theatre Research. 1st Series, edited by Lawrence Estavan. San Francisco: Mimeographed monographs, prepared for the Federal Theatre under WPA Project 8386, 1938.

TO YOUR HEALTH

TO YOUR HEALTH
The Pleasures, Problems,
and Politics of Alcohol

RICHARD S. SHORE, M.D.
JOHN M. LUCE, M.D.

A Continuum Book
THE SEABURY PRESS, NEW YORK

To our wives, Diana and Judith

1976

The Seabury Press
815 Second Avenue
New York, New York 10017

Printed in the United States of America

Library of Congress Cataloging in Publication Data

Shore, Richard S.   1937–
  To your health.

  (A Continuum book)
  Includes bibliographical references and index.
  1. Alcoholism. 2. Alcoholism—Prevention.
3. Alcoholism—Treatment. I. Luce, John M., joint
author. II. Title.
HV5035.S56   613.8′1   76–16050
ISBN 0-8164-9298-0

CONTENTS

Preface: Our Ambivalence About Alcohol   vii

1. The Triumph of Dionysus   1

2. A Noble Experiment That Failed   18

3. American Drinking Practices and Problems   38

4. To Dream But Not to Sleep   61

5. Forgetfulness of Things Past   82

6. The Disease Concept of Alcoholism   109

7. Beyond the Disease Concept   146

8. Dealing With Problem Drinking   180

Notes   213

Index   222

PREFACE: OUR AMBIVALENCE
ABOUT ALCOHOL

Alcohol is an ungrateful subject. Most people who are interested in the subject are already partisans on one side or the other, and nobody of impartial opinion exists who is ready to be guided by scientific inquiry. The majority of those who would give any attention to original work on the subject would do so less to gain knowledge than to find answers and argument to support their preconceived opinion.

LORD O'ABERNON, *Alcohol: Its Action on the Human Organism* (1918)

Alcohol is known as the neutral spirit, but as the above quotation from Lord O'Abernon suggests, few people are neutral about alcohol. In fact, most books on the subject are so biased that they offer personal testimonials in place of scientific facts or use medical data to buttress essentially moral arguments. Some of these books stress the benefits of alcohol and overlook the drug's detrimental effects. Others dwell only on the detriment, creating the impression that alcohol is a noxious agent and nothing more.

An agent is a person authorized by another to act in his behalf, yet the word also embraces the idea of perpetrator, assistant, and instrument, as well as a substance that participates in a chemical reaction. All these definitions apply to alcohol, but for centuries it has been seen as something apart from man: a gift from the gods or the devil incarnate. Only recently, and not yet entirely, have we begun to accept the fact that, although it is a naturally occurring substance, alcohol also is manufactured by men and women for their own pleasure or problems. A weak acid, alcohol is not chemically neutral. But in the human sphere, alcohol is what mankind makes of it, and in this respect it can claim neutrality.

Because alcohol is a cultural artifact, it also is a political issue. By this we do not mean that the drug is connected with a political party, although this may be the case, but that it pertains to almost every aspect of public affairs. Such an association may have been more obvious during Prohibition, but it has existed throughout history and exists today in our country. As people who have participated in politics and government, we know how difficult it is to be objective about alcohol.

Other experiences have reinforced this opinion. In the first place, we enjoy drinking, occasionally to excess, and we belong to a society in which such drinking is accepted, if not esteemed. Secondly, as physicians, we know more than most people, problem drinkers excluded, about the medical and social difficulties associated with alcohol. And third, our thoughts have been shaped by our professional training and our clinical exposure. Thus, perhaps inevitably, we are ambivalent in our position regarding the drug. We find its history illuminating, its pharmacology fascinating, its benefits significant, and its ravages deplorable.

Naturally, we want to help lessen such ravages. But we do not think that this can be done through preaching or prohibition, any more than we consider total abstinence the appropriate treatment for all alcohol abusers. Although we try to emphasize facts in this book, we feel that since true objectivity is a myth, it is less imperative to seek the truth than to develop a spirit of tolerance and understanding. We also believe that a major difference between pleasure and problem drinkers is that the former wish to expand awareness and the latter wish to confine it. Thus, our primary purpose in writing this book is to increase society's awareness of and respect for this ungrateful subject, alcohol.

Many people have helped in the preparation of this book. In addition to those mentioned in the text, we want especially to thank the staff members of the Bureau of Alcoholism of San Francisco's Community Mental Health Services, who have shared their ideas and experience with us. Charles Becker and Don Cahalan have read our manuscript and contributed their suggestions, and we are grateful to them. We also wish to thank Cheryl Wilson for typing our manuscript.

TO YOUR HEALTH

1. THE TRIUMPH OF DIONYSUS

Far beyond me lie
Those golden rivered lands, Lydia and Phrygia,
Where my journey began. Overland I went,
Across the steppes of Persia where the sun strikes
   hotly
Down, through Bactrian fastness and the grim waste
And so, along all Asia's swarming littoral
Of towering cities where Greeks and foreign nations,
Mingling, live, my progress made. There I taught
my dances to the feet of living men,
Establishing my mysteries and rites
That I might be revered on earth for what I am:
A God.

EURIPIDES, *The Bacchae* (circa B.C. 408)

The word alcohol is derived from the Arabic *al kuhul*. According to Berton Roueché, this term originally referred to an eye cosmetic made of powdered antimony, but eventually was associated with any finely divided substance, distillate, or spirit, including the spirit of wine.[1] Today we may think of alcohol and alcoholic spirits as being synonymous. Yet to a chemist, an alcohol is any of an entire class of compounds. The first member of this class, methyl alcohol or methanol, is used commercially as a solvent and as a component in canned heat. Isopropyl alcohol, also known as rubbing alcohol, serves as a drying agent and disinfectant. Ethyl alcohol or ethanol shares these functions but differs from other alcohols in also being suitable as a beverage ingredient and intoxicant. It is therefore the only member of this chemical class that we call simply, if imprecisely, alcohol.

Ethanol also differs from other alcohols in being a palatable source of energy as well as euphoria. When completely metabolized by the body, each gram of pure alcohol yields seven calories, compared with nine calories per gram of fat and four of carbohydrate and protein. There are approximately 15 grams of ethanol in 15 milliliters or one-half ounce of 100 percent alcohol, so each half ounce provides 105 calories. The same number of calories is available from 30 milliliters or a one-ounce shot of 100-proof distilled spirits, the proof of an alcoholic beverage being twice its ethanol content.

This one-ounce shot, which is 50 percent alcohol, contains approximately as much ethanol as a four-ounce glass of wine, which is 12 percent alcohol, or a 12-ounce can of beer, which is 4 percent. Most people can metabolize 15 grams or 15 milliliters of pure alcohol per hour for a total of 2,520 calories per 24 hours. If we use 2,500 calories each day at an average metabolic rate, we can obtain all of our caloric requirements from distilled spirits. And since undistilled preparations may provide additional calories from starch and sugar retained in their manufacture, wine and beer can meet more than our daily caloric needs.

Unfortunately, these are empty calories, for distillation and modern production techniques strip alcoholic beverages of vitamins, minerals, and other essential food substances. The nonalcoholic calories also are being eliminated today from many beers in deference to weight-conscious customers. Furthermore, ethanol cannot be stored by the body and thus is burned to the exclusion of fat and other substances, making it more of a fuel than a foodstuff. As a result of these factors, people who attempt to subsist on alcohol alone may meet their energy requirements only to experience nutritional deficiencies and metabolic abnormalities, in addition to problems caused by the direct toxic properties of ethanol. Pre-industrial man was subject to the same toxicity, yet he obtained valuable nutrients from the raw materials conserved in more unsophisticated beverages. Because of this, throughout history such beverages have been regarded as important foods.

They have also been revered, more than any other substances, as mystical and medicinal agents. In recent years we have stripped away much of the mystery surrounding alcohol and now recognize it as a drug with distinct pharmacological effects which will be discussed at length in later chapters. But our knowledge, incomplete as it is, rests on a heritage of myth and speculation summoned to explain alcohol's mood and mind-altering properties, properties that ancient peoples believed enabled them to communicate with their gods. Subsequently, healers saw ethanol as the elixir of life, applied it to almost every illness, and elevated it to the status of the world's first panacea. Since contemporary religion and medicine evolved out of these traditions, it is hardly surprising that, consciously or not, we still endow alcohol with uncanny qualities.

This magical chemical is produced by the simple process of fermentation, through which plant sugars are converted by the enzymes of a ferment into ethyl alcohol, carbon dioxide, and a variety of incidental compounds, including other alcohols, aldehydes, and acids, which are called congeners. The most common ferment is yeast, a minute one-celled fungus used to leaven bread as well as to induce fermentation. Since yeasts are ubiquitous in nature, it is likely that man first discovered the effects of alcohol by sampling a mash of fruit or berries acted upon by airborne yeasts in his environment. Presumably, he then began collecting crops with which to make fermented beverages.

These beverages were mild by today's standards, containing at most 14 percent ethanol. This is because fermentative yeasts cannot survive in stronger solutions, and because the yield of alcohol in a given preparation is limited by the amount of available sugar and the time required for fermentation. Honey was the most concentrated natural source of sugar available to primitive man, and Berton Roueché believes that the first commonly produced alcoholic beverage was mead, or fermented honey. In fact, he notes, the roots of the word mead in Sanskrit and Greek mean not only honey, but also the concepts of intoxicating drink and drunkeness.[2] The nectar of the Greek deities, mead was used throughout the classical world and survived as a favorite drink among the tribes of Northern Europe long after other beverages had surpassed it in popularity elsewhere.

The drink that first rivaled mead was beer. This beverage is made from barley and other cereal grains which after harvesting are allowed either to germinate at their own pace or are encouraged by dampening. This germination is aborted by heat, which converts the grain into malt. The malt then is crushed and heated with water and other cereals, such as corn and rice, to dissolve the solids and permit the malt enzymes to turn the cereal starch into sugar. Next the liquid mash, which is called malt syrup, wort, or wash, is drained into vats and boiled with various flavorful substances. Of these substances, the historical favorite is the hop, an herbaceous perennial of the mulberry family which is native to Europe. The ripened female flowers of the hop plant contain eupalin, a yellow powder that imparts a bitter taste to beer and aids in its preservation.

Once it is mixed with hops or similar substances, the malt extract is exposed to yeasts and fermented. In ancient times this exposure was probably fortuitous, with the yeasts causing fermentation as they settled on the top layer of brewing vats. Yet once brewers suspected the role played by the fungi, they began to grow their own supplies of yeast. They also developed different yeast strains, so that today beers can be made by both top and bottom fermentation by yeasts which are grown in pure culture. Airtight storage, refrigeration, and most recently, pasteurization have been used to limit the fermenting process and to prevent the decomposition of ethyl alcohol by the enzymes of bacterial microorganisms into acetaldehyde and acetic acid, the principal component of vinegar. Yet these techniques were unavailable to primitive peoples, who brewed their beer in open vats and drank the beverage as soon as possible.

No one has identified the first beer drinkers, and mythology makes little reference to the beverage's origins. But historians believe that beer originated in the Middle East, where barley grew wild thousands of years ago, and eventually was grown under human supervision. In addition to the rich Tigris and Euphrates Valley, barley was also cultivated in Egypt, where the first known brewery was constructed in 3700 B.C. The Egyptians are also credited with first adding spices and herbs to beer to counteract the sweet taste of malt. They introduced beer and brewing to the Greeks, who passed their knowledge on to the Romans. The Romans, in turn, introduced the beverage to England and the rest of Europe.

Beer achieved its greatest popularity in these areas for two major reasons. One is the fact that England and the continent had ample quantities of barley, which flourishes from the tropics to the Arctic Circle and is the easiest cereal to grow. The second reason is that since beer ferments at temperatures as low as 40° Fahrenheit, it can be brewed in relatively cold climates. English and European brewing was originally the province of bakers because of their familiarity with grains and yeast. Their products were often sold directly from the breweries and then through small shops or taverns. Yet as the secrets of brewing were disseminated, home brewing assumed greater social and economic significance, just as barley and other cereal sources of alcohol became important agricultural commodities.

Although beer making was introduced to England by the Romans, it became widespread only after the Danes invaded the isle. Actually, neither the Danes nor the English drank beer as we know it, but rather thick and strong ales, including porter and stout, which were brewed without hops until 1800. The first hopped, top fermented malt beverages were brought to England by the fifteenth-century Dutch. Eventually consumed throughout Europe, these beers were rivaled only by those of Germany, which were top fermented and were called "lagers" after the places in which they were stored.

Beer has remained the favorite alcoholic drink in the northern countries, but its popularity was supplanted in the Mediterranean area by wine. According to Persian mythology, wine was first discovered by a concubine of King Jamshid, who stored his grapes in jars. On one occasion the king found that his grapes were no longer sweet, that is, that they had become fermented, and imagining that the liquor in his jars was poisonous, he labeled the containers accordingly. His concubine, seeking death as a relief from persistent illness, drank some of the poison, fainted, and awoke to find her symptoms gone. She then reported her experience to the king, who distributed the new drink among his subjects.

Historical records do not exist to corroborate this myth. Yet the Persian account does coincide temporally and geographically with the estimates of André Simon, who places the origin of viticulture and wine making somewhere between the Caspian and Black Seas during the period from 8000 to 6000 B.C.[3] The account also fits with our knowledge of the Eurasian vine, *Vitis vinifera,* which requires a great amount of heat and sunlight to ripen properly and cannot survive, as barley can, where winter temperatures drop below freezing for more than a few days at a time.

Vitis vinifera grows today in two weather zones: the Mediterranean, with a two-season climate characterized by mild, rainy winters and hot, dry summers, and the European, where four seasons provide scattered rainfall and highly variable temperatures during the growing season. Combined with the mineral-rich soil in much of Europe, this climatic variability produces acidic grapes which are considered essential for the very best vintages. Yet the same variability which accounts for a fine wine one year may kill an entire crop the next. Thus, the Mediterranean climate is safer from a survival standpoint, and *Vitis vinifera* probably gained its first ecological foothold there.

This occurrence was aided by the unique genetic history of the Eurasian vine. In their wild state, grapevines exist as separate male and female plants which reproduce by cross-pollination. But according to Philip Wagner, wild mutants of the species *Vitis vinifera* appeared around 8000 B.C. near the Caspian Sea. With flowers containing both male and female parts, these plants were capable of self-fertilization. They also could propagate vegetatively, so that a cutting of a vine could strike roots and become a parent plant. As a result of such propagation, any vine hybrid or mutant could be multiplied uniformly and indefinitely.[4]

Another advantage of this hermaphrodism was that it could be introduced by cross-pollination into the genetic make-up of wild vines that lacked the trait but possessed rich fruit and other desirable qualities.[5] Thus, entirely by accident, the early inhabitants of Persia inherited a vine ripe for cultivation. At first they probably sat back and allowed superior plants to be produced by natural selection. They then cultivated their preferred vines, evolving from grape gatherers into growers in the process. That the Persians next became vinters is indicated by the ancient grape presses and fermenting tanks that have been discovered near the Black Sea. Apparently, they taught their trade to the Egyptians as well, for comparable equipment is pictured in the tomb of Phtah-Hotep, who lived near Memphis in northern Egypt around 4000 B.C.

The art of wine making first practiced by the Persians and Egyptians involves three stages. These include the crushing of the grapes to obtain their juice, the fermenting of the juice to obtain wine, and the maturing of the wine to prepare it for consumption. Crushing is a simple mechanical process which produces a mash called grape must, containing pips, skin, flesh, and juice. The flesh of most grapes is white, and red skins will impart their color unless they are separated from the must. As described by André Simon, the juice itself is composed of water, grape sugar (which is mostly glucose and dextrose), cellulose, and tartaric acid, the source of a white crystalline salt known as cream of tartar.[6]

Tartaric acid and cellulose remain as the grape juice becomes wine, but under the influence of yeast enzymes most of the sugar is transformed into ethyl alcohol and carbon dioxide. The fermenting process is stopped prematurely in the manufacture of sweet wines, and extra sugar is often added to insure sweetness. However, in dry wines some 95 percent of the sugar is fermented. Most of the remainder is consumed by the yeasts or converted into congeners, including other alcohols and aldehydes in addition to the esters and volatile acids which give wine its distinctive aroma and taste.

As with beer, steps must be taken to prevent the decomposition of wine to acetaldehyde and acetic acid. Proper storage helps forestall spoilage, and certain containers can impart flavors, such as the tannins found in wood, and thereby contribute to the taste of a given wine while allowing for its gradual maturation. Today great emphasis is placed on this aging process, and certain wines are considered valuable primarily because of their mature character. Yet primitive man had neither the desire nor the technology required for wine maturation. Early wine was fermented in open vats and drunk within a year of its manufacture, just as beer and bread produced from the grain of one harvest were consumed before the next.

Although crude, these beverages were esteemed by early socities. The Persians in particular were impressed with wine's supernatural powers and equated the juice of the grape with human blood. The Persians also believed that their vines grew best in areas where their rivals had fallen in combat. They therefore used wine primarily as a libation, assuming that both they and their gods would profit from imbibing the essence of their enemies. The Egyptians subscribed to this blood belief and employed wine as a god-given medicine useful in treating all diseases. Alcoholic beverages were used for comparable purposes in China and by the Indians, who drank *soma,* a wine fashioned from the leafless vine, *Asclepius acide,* a member of the milkweed family. And wine was incorporated into the medical practices and the religious rituals of the early Jews.

Although the Jews today are known as a temperate people, the ancient tribes of Israel and Judah engaged in heavy drinking, especially when celebrating their many gods. This practice probably reflected the social uncohesiveness of the Jews and may have contributed to the Babylonian capture of Palestine and the subsequent Hebrew diaspora. Thus when the Jews returned from exile and captivity, they became a monotheistic people and modified their drinking behavior. As part of the modification, they condemned group intoxication and sanctioned fermented beverages for use primarily as medicines and as sacraments in their rites of passage and religious holidays.

This shift from heavy to moderate drinking is seen in the evolution of the Passover holiday. Passover originated with the polytheistic Jews as a celebration of the coming of spring which was characterized by drunkenness and sacrifice. But according to Kurt Schlesinger, the Passover ceremony was changed after the diaspora to commemorate the exodus from Egypt. Actual sacrifice became symbolic, while group intoxication gave way to ritual drinking. Because the ancient holiday celebrating the vernal equinox antedated the shift toward moderation in Jewish culture, the amount of drinking allowed during Passover was greater than on other occasions. However, it stopped short of drunkenness and was strictly proscribed.[7]

After Palestine fell to the Romans and the Jews were forced into European ghettos, drunkenness became identified with outsiders. This identification is reflected in the Yiddish phrase, "shikker is a goy," through which the Jews elevate their own status at the expense of their adversaries, and in the saying, "a yid a shikker, zull gehrget veren," meaning, "A Jew who's a drunkard, may he get killed." On one level, the latter expression stresses that an intoxicated person is conspicuous and therefore vulnerable to persecution. On another, it suggests that inebriates deserve their fate because they have forsworn the Hebrew virtue of sobriety.

At the same time, the expression conveys a deep-seated Jewish fear of drunkenness. This fear is implicit in the ceremonial benediction over a cup of wine which is part of the Kiddush ceremony. According to Mark Keller, the Kiddush originally began with young Jews exhibiting the wine crop to their elders and saying "salve maranan, ha-yayin mishtaker," that is, "attention, my masters, wine causes drunkenness." The elders then responded "le-haiim" or "it's for your health," signifying that the use of wine in moderation met with their approval. Over the centuries, the permissive toast, "le-haiim," has been retained in the Kiddush so that Jews still toast to one another's health. Yet the warning against intoxication has disappeared from the ceremonial benediction, suggesting to Dr. Keller that drunkenness is no longer feared among Jews.[8]

Another interpretation is that the Jews have internalized the ancient prohibition and thus have learned unconsciously how to drink. They have also institutionalized the idea of how not to drink in their constant reference to the hedonism of outsiders. The end result has been the perpetuation of moderate drinking practices, behavior that may have contributed to political cohesion among the Jewish people and also may have helped their culture survive.[9]

Moderation also was an issue to the ancient Greeks, who rejected magic and were suspicious of intoxicating beverages. Homer, the earliest Greek poet of record, portrayed in his works a rational universe ruled by Olympian deities. Ostensibly Zeus chaired the Olympian circle, but Homer's muse was Apollo, who stood for art and order and upon whose shrine at Delphi were inscribed the words, "nothing in excess." Extremism existed in Homer's universe, but, as described by E. R. Dodds, it was hardly a virtue. Instead, it was associated with *ate*, a state of temporary insanity to which the poet attributed unaccountable conduct. Like all insanity, *ate* was ascribed not to physical or psychological causes, but to demonic agencies or spirits, among them the spirit of wine.[10]

The Homeric universe was accepted in Greece until the reign of Pericles. Dissatisfaction then arose with the Olympians and a religious revolt was waged against Apollo and Delphi. Its figurehead was a new god, Dionysus, whom Homer had never admitted to Olympus.[11] In the Eleusinian mysteries, Dionysus was the son of Zeus and Semele, daughter of King Cadmus of Thebes. Angered by her husband's infidelity, Hera, Zeus' immortal wife, disguised herself as Semele's nurse and challenged Semele to make Zeus come to her in his splendors, and thereby prove his identity. Zeus, unable to refuse this request, appeared as thunder and lightning and turned Semele to cinders. Meanwhile, Semele's son was sewed inside Zeus' thigh for safekeeping until Hera ordered the Titans to seize Dionysus and tear him to shreds. He subsequently was reconstituted and raised by nymphs on Mt. Nysa in Libya, where he discovered grapes and the process of extracting their precious juice. But when he grew to manhood, Hera recognized him and drove him mad.

Dionysus then wandered about the world, teaching viticulture and vinification and establishing a worship both drunken and orgiastic. Accompanying him were satyrs, lascivious woodland deities represented as half man and half goat, and maenads, frenzied women often pictured with their heads thrown back in wild abandon. Everywhere the god went, mountain dancing festivals were held in his honor, culminating in the dismembering and devouring of animals. These acts commemorated the destruction of the infant Dionysus and also allowed votaries to incorporate a symbolic piece of the god.[12]

As Robert Graves points out, Dionysus' mythological history actually documents the spread of wine in Hellenic society. Hera's hatred of Dionysus probably reflected conservative opposition not only to orgiastic festivals but also to the ritual use of wine in place of more traditional beverages. Both mead and beer preceded wine in Thebes, for example, and beer revels were performed on Mt. Nysa before grapes were harvested there. Dionysus' triumph, according to Graves, was that wine superseded other intoxicants in the Mediterranean area.[13]

But his real triumph came through cultural assimilation. The Greeks were far too entranced with Apollo to adopt Dionysus without modification. At the same time, they saw the need for reform in their religion and psychological release in their society. Because of this, they did not attempt to prohibit worship of the god but instead accepted him as a liberator who could free man temporarily from himself. This acceptance led to a union of the worships of Apollo and Dionysus. Dionysus was admitted to the Olympian circle and revered as a patron of the arts. His mountain rites were turned into harvest festivals; the maenads became country maidens; and their singing and dancing evolved into dithyrambs, lyrics with exchanges between the leaders and chorus which later became the model for Greek Tragedy.

Wine, Dionysus' gift, also underwent a transformation. Red wine had been customary in previous cultures, until the Greeks created white wines by separating the red grape skins from grape juice. They also developed nonporous amphorae which they shipped around the Mediterranean, introducing wine to Sicily, Spain and southern France. These jars allowed for some aging, but because the Greeks could not completely prevent the decomposition of alcohol they diluted their wine with sea water and spiced it with pine resin to decrease its intoxicating powers and disguise its taste.

In this diluted form, wine was consumed during ordinary meals. It also was drunk at symposia, elaborate dinner parties at which the beverage was used judiciously to facilitate philosophic conversation. The symposia were also highlighted by a ritual in which the Greeks passed out ceremonial wine cups and toasted one another with the phrase, "this to thee." Our holding out the wine glass and saying "to your health" probably is a relic of this ancient custom, as well as the ceremonial benediction of the Jews.

The Greeks also incorporated wine into the first modern system of medicine. It was fathered by Hippocrates of Cos, a contemporary of Pericles, who dissociated therapeutics from religion in rejecting the Egyptian concept that diseases were divine. According to Salvatore Lucia, Hippocrates based his techniques on observations of the responses of patients to treatment, which often included wine. He prescribed the beverage as a wound dressing, a local and general anesthetic, a dietary beverage, a cooling agent, a diuretic, an antidote for misfortune, and a necessary component of the good life.[14] The philosopher Plato had his own ideas on living and preferred that young men forswear wine, poetry, and other emotional catalysts. Yet he agreed with Hippocrates that wine helped lighten the sourness of senility, which began, he believed, at forty years of age.

The Romans incorporated Dionysus into their system of deities under the name of Liber and then as Bacchus, the term by which he is best known today. And they imported the Greek art of viticulture, although *Vitis vinifera* grew wild in their land. According to Pliny the Elder, Roman Italy produced two-thirds of the world's wine by 112 B.C. The first wine drunk in Germany came with Caesar's legions, although the Eurasian vine was there already. The Romans introduced wine drinking to central France, Portugal, Switzerland, and even England, where the historian Tacitus insisted that neither the vine nor the olive would grow.

In addition, Rome furthered the marriage of alcohol and medicine through physicians like Asclepiades, who based his therapeutics on wine drinking, dieting, and outdoor exercise. But the Romans' greatest contributions were the theriacs, medicated wines that were the world's first panaceas. Most famous of these was *mithridatium*, the formula of which was allegedly based on a universal antidote compounded by the King of Pontius to immunize himself against poison. The ingredients of *mithridatium* varied from pharmacist to pharmacist, but, in general, it contained herb and plant extracts, honey, and other substances dissolved in wine and beer. After being propagated through the Roman Empire, the preparation was copied by Asian pharmacists, prescribed as a cure for the plague, and distributed throughout the Christian world.

The early Christians inherited many Roman drinking habits, including the practice of prohibiting women from drinking in public. In addition, the church aided the spread of alcohol in several ways. One way was to sanctify the use of wine in the Eucharist, a sacrament based on the partaking of bread and wine. The church also enshrined alcohol by allowing it to remain at the center of therapeutic practices. These were derived from the teachings of Galen, a second-century Greek who categorized healing beers and wines and delineated their chemical properties. Galen also devised recipes for theriacs in which alcohol was used to suspend a wide range of animal, vegetable, and mineral substances. During the Middle Ages these recipes were used by Christian monks to make panaceas whose active ingredients were called galenicals. The monks departed from the trial and error medical tradition of Hippocrates in believing that their potions, once blessed, were adequate to treat every disease.

The Christian church also increased the availability of alcohol by fostering Roman viticultural practices. It did so by appropriating lands throughout Europe which had fallen, along with Rome, to the barbarians. On these lands were established monasteries which contained hostelries, breweries, wineries, *herbularia* where medicinal plants were tended, and hospitals where theriacs were dispensed. In turn, many of these lands evolved into the great wine-producing districts of Europe, including the Bordeaux and Burgundy regions of France, Italian Tuscany, and Germany's Moselle and Rhineland.

All three countries developed different drinking practices in spite of their common debt to Dionysus. In Germany, for example, wine drinking never gained great popularity outside of the grape-growing regions near the French border. Elsewhere, Bavarian beer was recognized as the preferred drink, while social custom dictated that it be consumed in settings established specifically for that purpose. Thus, the beer hall became an important center of German political and cultural life. At the same time, alcohol became less an accompaniment to food than a catalyst for comradeship and occasional intoxication.

In Italy, by contrast, wine achieved its greatest status as a foodstuff. Residents of agricultural districts began a tradition of using wine for its calories, and Giorgio Lolli and his colleagues have determined that wine has made up more than 10 percent of the caloric intake of the average Italian throughout much of history. Significantly, since the time of the Romans most of this intake has occurred with meals rather than in between them, and although Italians have welcomed conviviality as much as any other people, they long have regarded drunkenness as a social error tantamount to gluttony.[15]

France, more famous for her food than either Italy or Germany, has outstripped both countries in her devotion to wine for centuries. So deep is this devotion that the French have not limited their wine consumption to meals and have made drinking wine with French bread or by itself a popular custom. The wine-producing districts have dominated French economic and political life, just as the monastery lands controlled medieval culture. Furthermore, like the church leaders before them, the French vintners have been responsible for popularizing the belief that wine is indispensable to health and nutrition. As a result, few Frenchmen would argue with Louis Pasteur, who called wine "the most hygienic of beverages."

Given this cultural acceptance, Roland Sadoun and his associates note that for centuries it has been common to encounter rural peasants and other French citizens who consume as many as three liters of wine a day and never appear very intoxicated. At the same time, the French have always maintained a tender indulgence for drunkards and have resisted attempts to arrest or treat them. Young people have been exposed to drinking as a form of sport, just as masculinity has been decided among adults on the basis of drinking contests. And, in contrast to the paucity of terms describing intoxication in the Italian or Jewish vocabularies, there are innumerable synonyms for drunkenness, including "gazé" for "gassed" and "en plein cirage" for "fully waxed," in the French language.[16]

France, until the twentieth century, has been the scene of almost every technological innovation in the preparation of wine. First was the development, 300 years ago in Burgundy, of the glass bottle, the cork, and the corkscrew. In the seventeenth century, a monk named Dom Perignon from the Champagne district of France added sugar to partially fermented white wine and retained the resulting carbon dioxide in specially reinforced and sealed bottles, thereby creating champagne. Burgundy vintners then introduced racking, a process through which wine is rid of cellulose, tartar, and other sediments by being transferred from vats to casks and then to bottles. Filtration was introduced to strain out microorganisms, followed by sulfurization, which inhibited their growth. Then, in the nineteenth century, Louis Pasteur developed a process for the Bordeaux vintners through which heating alternated with cooling could be used to achieve a partial sterilization of bacteria and thereby prevent the spoilage of wine.

Pasteurization and other advances in wine technology were preceded by the exporting of viticulture, vinification, and the European wine. All three were introduced to Southeast Asia by the French and by the Dutch to the Caribbean. The English, whose homeland was too harsh for commercial grape growing, carried the art to colonies in Australia, New Zealand, and South Africa, areas where *Vitis vinifera* thrives today. Similarly, the Portuguese brought their vine stocks to Brazil, as the Spaniards did to Argentina and Mexico. Prior to this, the people of these areas drank *pulque,* a beer made from the juices of the Maguey plant.

In addition to their alcoholic beverages, the drinking practices of many civilizations indigenous to Central and South America differed from those of early Mediterranean and later European society. *Pulque* and similar preparations were rarely used as medicines or libations, for example, but, according to D. G. Mandelbaum, participants at major Incan religious cele-brations had to drink to the point of intoxication lest their gods be displeased. This ritual drunkenness was neither an adjunct to the ceremonies nor a stimulant for aggressive dis-plays and sexual license. Instead, it was sought both as an end in itself and as a means of achieving group solidarity.[17] These drinking practices were not linked to health problems or pro-longed dependence on ethanol. They have passed virtually unchanged through history and are found today among many peoples, including the Bolivian Camba and the Mexican Tarahumara, who occasionally drink to excess but have no terms for drunkenness in their languages.

The Portuguese and Spanish missionaries were unpre-pared for Indian drinking practices, however, and they spoke disparagingly of them in their communications to home. This attitude was responsible for reinforcing the ancient associa-tion between ritual drunkenness and savagery. Yet the indige-nous American civilizations were hardly savage, and although their periodic intoxication was substantial, the Incas and their descendants could not compete with Europeans in their over-all consumption of alcohol. In retrospect, it appears that the missionaries' tirades about native drunkenness were actually part of a campaign against pagan rituals rather than a prohibi-tion of ethanol per se.[18]

In support of this thought, historical records reveal that the missionaries did their best to wean the native peoples from pulque in favor of mission wines. These wines were produced by Indian labor and were employed both as beverages and as sacraments in Christian ceremonies. The missions where these ceremonies were held contained infirmaries and hostel-ries and were smaller versions of the monasteries that had flourished in Europe during the Middle Ages. Several hun-dred missions were established in Mexico by the Spaniards. During the seventeenth century they spread into California where the mission vine took root, nourished by that area's Mediterranean climate and mineral-rich soil.

In contrast, the wet and heavily forested east coast of North America was hostile to *Vitis vinifera*. Lief Erikson had found wild vines when he visited the area, which he named Vinland, but these were probably representatives of *Vitis labrusca* or *Vitis rotundifolia*, species of grapes which are vital today to the viticulture of Ohio and New York. These native grapes were neglected by the original east coast Indians, who preferred beverages made from fermented birch bark and maple syrup. Wines made from *Vitis labrusca* and *Vitis rotundifolia* also proved tasteless to early American colonists, and although these people fermented plums, elderberries, turnips, carrots, and apples in their search for a suitable alcoholic beverage, their favorite until the American Revolution was beer.

This was not surprising, since most of the early colonists from England and Europe carried a preference for ale and lager with them. Unfortunately, however, they brought little grain and no brewmasters, and for years the colonists had to import beer malt or malt syrup from their mother countries. But by 1630, Plymouth had its first barley crops, and in 1634, the first brewery and tavern was opened in the Massachusetts Bay Colony. New Amsterdam had its own brewery a few years later, as did Philadelphia, where a brewery was opened for German settlers by William Penn.

By 1770, the only colony that lacked major brewing facilities was Virginia, where tobacco was grown instead of barley. This situation was deplored by George Washington and Thomas Jefferson, who had to import French wines and New England grain to Mount Vernon and Monticello. But Washington and Jefferson erected Virginia's first breweries on their property, and on the eve of the Revolution, the American colonies could boast of 132 breweries with an annual production of 185,000 barrels. This was hardly a drop in the European-dominated ocean. Yet it did serve as a source of pride to the colonists and as an indication that fermented beverages had become popular throughout the Western world.

2. A NOBLE EXPERIMENT
THAT FAILED

The defense of the Eighteenth Amendment is much more than a mere question of regulating the liquor traffic. It involves a test of strength between social orders, and when that test is concluded, and if, as seems probable, the Amendment breaks down, the fall will bring down with it the dominion of the older civilization. The Eighteenth Amendment is the rock on which the evangelical church militant is founded, and with it are involved a whole way of life and an ancient tradition. The overcoming of the Eighteenth Amendment would mean the emergence of the cities as the dominant force in America, dominant politically and socially as they are already dominant economically.

WALTER LIPPMANN, *Men of Destiny* (1927)

In spite of the spread of fermented beverages, they remained limited in popularity because of their relatively low alcohol content. The problem eventually was overcome by distillation, the process through which the components of a liquid mixture are separated as they boil off at different temperatures and subsequently are recondensed. According to Berton Roueché, distillation was first performed in A.D. 800 by the Arabian chemist Jabir Ibn Hayyán, also known as Geber, who felt that fermented grape juice harbored a healing spirit. Geber and his Moslem colleagues volatilized this spirit but were disappointed when it did not prove to be the elixir of life. And they never used the principle of distillation to make alcoholic beverages because the Prophet had forbidden the non-medical use of alcohol, even in the form of wine.[1]

Thus, the realization of distillation's commercial value was left to a European. He was Arnauld of Villanova, a professor of medicine at the University of Montpellier in the thirteenth century. Early in his career Arnauld wrote *Liber de Vines,* in which he recommended wine in the treatment of jaundice, gout, seasickness, insanity, and intestinal parasites. Later he heated a crucible of wine and collected the distillate, which he called *aqua vitae*, the water of life. Also termed *eau de vie* and then brandy, after the Dutch *brantewijn*, or burned wine, *aqua vitae* contained as much as 40 percent ethanol and quickly replaced weaker fermented beverages as a therapeutic agent. Its success also inspired the distillation of other fruit juices, which were mixed with herbs for their allegedly health-giving properties.

Originally, these brandies and liqueurs were dispensed only by physicians or priests. But as the nobility sampled such nostrums, a demand was created for their wider distribution. In the sixteenth century, vintners of the Cognac region in France assuaged this demand by distilling brandy in copper pot stills containing long tapering necks topped with special condensers called worms. Since these stills volatilized all types of alcohols, the result of an initial distillation, which was called low wine, was full of congeners. A second run through the still was therefore necessary to produce high wine, which the Cognac vintners aged in wooden casks. They also introduced the use of labels to identify their products, which heretofore had been marked by stamps compressed on the waxes used to seal the cask from insects and damp weather.

Although these vintners made enough brandy to supply the wealthy, their enterprise amounted to little more than a cottage industry. Indeed, for years most brandy was not sold as such but was mixed with weaker wines and sugar to create fortified dessert preparations with extra calories and an alcohol content of 18 to 20 percent. Prominent among these were port, which became an English institution after William of Orange forbade the importation of French wines and brandies into Britain but allowed port to be brought in from Portugal. Madeira, also of Portuguese origin, was the only beverage ever to challenge the popularity of port as an after-dinner drink. Marsala, introduced by Sicilian vintners, became an Italian favorite, while Jerez (sherry) was enjoyed as an aperitif by Shakespeare's Falstaff as well as by members of the Spanish upper class.

The emergence of these fortified beverages coincided with

that of the science of pharmacology. Proponents of this new medical discipline rejected the theriacs of the Middle Ages and also sought a renewal of Hippocratic reliance on observation in place of healing by faith. Yet the early pharmacologists clung to ethanol, which remained as basic to their therapeutics as it had to Hippocrates'. Thus, alcohol was listed more often than any other substance in the first national pharmacopeia, the *Codex Medicamentarium of France*. The *Codex* recommended red wine for diarrhea, white wine to increase urination, champagne for nausea, and port, sherry, marsala, madeira, and other fortified wines during convalescence.

Yet for all their fortification, the dessert wines could not compete commercially with more potent distilled preparations. After brandy, the first of these preparations was whiskey, a word derived from *uisge beathe,* the Irish-Gaelic equivalent of *aqua vitae.* Irish and Scotch whiskies were conceived shortly after distillation was introduced to Europe and for centuries were produced, like brandy, by individual distillers. They were made from a mash of malted barley which was dried over peat fires, fermented into a wash, and then boiled in copper pots comparable to those used in Cognac. The high beer resulting from two runs through the stills was then aged in sherry casks which imparted an orange color but maintained the malt's thick consistency and smoky taste.

Even more than the French brandy distillers, the early Irish and Scots used their whiskey as a form of currency. This was especially the case when real money was unavailable. The Irish in particular employed malt and malt liquor for every conceivable medical and nutritional purpose. For example, they drank to keep warm during damp winters, to alleviate the hunger which so often accompanied their crop failures, and to treat gastrointestinal disorders. They also gave alcohol to children as a reward for approved behavior, much as other people give candy today.

In addition, the Irish are thought to be the first people to use alcoholic beverages in the treatment of the hangover. Some scholars contend that the Irish also originated the expression, "the hair of the dog that bit you," which refers to the idea that that which causes a malady is the best source of its relief. Actually, this expression is an allusion to the more ancient notion that the burnt hair of a dog is an antidote for its bite, as stated in the Latin, *simila similibus curantur.* Yet if the Irish did not originate the expression, at least their hangovers are legendary.

The Irish reputation for heavy drinking and its consequences have considerable historical basis. Indeed, for centuries ethanol has occupied a cardinal position in Irish life literally from the cradle to the grave. Its primary social use was to induce conviviality at christenings and wakes, secular events which were conducted after formal religious ceremonies. The Irish wake in particular bore little resemblance to its modern successor, having evolved out of impromptu gatherings held at night in graveyards and characterized both by heavy drinking and by fights between opposing family factions.

According to R. F. Bales, drunkenness at these and other events was looked on as laughable, pleasurable, and the punctuation of dull routine. Intoxication was condemned only when it involved the squandering of money or property. The church tried to temper drinking excesses and threatened to excommunicate participants in secular celebrations. Today, it is following this tradition in campaigning against drinking in Irish parochial schools, giving students who take pledges of abstinence so-called "pioneer pins" to wear.

In spite of these and other measures, the Irish church has not achieved moderation among its members. Instead, it has divorced itself from their drinking practices and has fostered an ambivalence toward drinking. As a result, Irish drinking practices seem to have evolved in a different fashion from those of the Jews. While Jewish ritual drinking tends to educate participants in temperance and reinforce Hebrew moral and spiritual traditions, Irish convivial drinking leads to inebriation, expresses the solidarity of friends and kinship groups, and celebrates the acceptance of the individual not as a member of a faith, but as a man among men.[2]

These qualities, coupled with the harshness of Irish and Scotch whiskey, limited its consumption to Ireland and the Scottish highlands until the nineteenth century, when Aeneas

Coffey invented the patent still. This device consisted of two copper columns, called the analyzer and rectifier, which were 50 feet high, joined at the top, and divided horizontally into compartments. In operating the still, steam was pumped up the analyzer and washed down the rectifier, and as they met at various levels and temperatures, ethanol and other alcohols were driven off. Since grain mash was used in the distillation, the results were called grain neutral spirits. These spirits were bland in comparison with Scotch malt, but when combined in roughly equal proportions by Andrew Usher of Edinburgh in 1860, they made a palatable and increasingly popular blend.

Before this occurred, however, scotch whiskey was over-shadowed throughout Western Europe by gin. This beverage was first distilled in 1672 by a Dutch chemist, Sylvius of Ley-den, who added juniper berries to Scottish grain alcohol. The Dutch called this concoction *junever,* their word for juniper, but the French changed this to *genievre.* British soldiers who drank the beverage while warring in the Low Countries at the close of the seventeenth century then altered its name to gin. The same soldiers brought their taste for gin back to Britain, where William III, who had created a market for port by barring French wines and brandies, helped the gin industry by urging his subjects to distill spirits from home-grown grain.

Other English rulers also encouraged distillation and in so doing contributed to an unprecedented increase in alcohol ingestion. Although public policy was responsible in part for the increase, it also resulted from the concurrent industrial revolution and the restructuring of society on a capitalistic basis.[3] Gin, whose emergence coincided with this reorganization, was cheap, easy to produce, and available to all social classes. It was a perfect drink for England, with its polluted water and urban poverty. By 1700, nearly one million gallons of gin were being distilled each year in England. And in the century before whiskey blending was perfected, most of the grain neutral spirits produced in Ireland and Scotland were channeled into the British gin trade.

As the trade grew in and outside of England, distillation evolved from a cottage into a collective industry. This trend was reinforced by new traditions of standardization, one of which involved the concept of proof. According to Morris Chafetz, proof is the shortened form of gunpowder proof. This term originated with European distillers who gauged the strength of a given beverage by mixing it with gunpowder, igniting the mixture, and comparing its combustion with the slowly burning blue flame given off by an equal mixture of water and absolute alcohol. The equal mixture was called 100 proof, so the proof of an alcoholic beverage always has been twice its ethanol content. Absolute alcohol should be 200 proof by this formula, but it is not readily available in pure form because it dilutes itself with moisture from the air. Therefore, alcohol of 195 to 198 proof is the standard against which alcoholic preparations are compared.[4]

Spirits containing nearly 100 percent ethanol were distilled in England, but for health reasons only diluted beverages were permitted. The English government also tried to regulate distillation and raise revenue by imposing an unprecedented excise tax on scotch whiskey in 1707. This tax supported the monarchy and was resented throughout the highlands, where for years illicit distilling was commonplace because people refused to regard it as a criminal act. Yet eventually the distillers succumbed to tax laws and licensure, as did their counterparts on the continent. As a result, alcohol became more and more the province of large manufacturing units under government control.

Such control was anathema to many early American colonists. But because the colonists did not produce their own fermented beverages or distilled liquors, they were forced to pay taxes on foreign spirits and raw materials. This situation stimulated the planting of barley and the founding of breweries along the Atlantic Coast. Yet the colonists continued to lament the lack of native distilled liquor until they began distilling rum.

Rum is made by collecting and crushing sugar cane and then fermenting and distilling the molasses that results. The beverage was named after rum bullion, which itself was derived from the Latin *saccharum* for sugar and the Dutch *bulliven* for precious metal. Originally distilled by Dutch planters in the West Indies, rum entered Europe through Holland and was first imported to colonial America in 1650 by Dutch settlers on Staten Island. From there the liquor was brought to Boston, where 40 distilleries were operating by the end of the seventeenth century. With the West Indies needing slaves to grow sugar, New England needing molasses for its distillers, and West Africa needing rum to pay black princes for filling its slave pens, rum bullion became entrenched as currency in this triangular trade.

The British, who preferred that colonists drink imported gin and whiskey, attempted to interrupt this trade in the middle of the eighteenth century by taxing West Indian molasses. But rum distillation was already decreasing because colonial tastes were turning to whiskies produced by Scottish and Irish settlers on the western frontier. Of these whiskies, the most popular were rye from Pennsylvania and bourbon from Kentucky. Bourbon is thought to have been developed in 1789 by a Baptist clergyman named Elijah Craig, who distilled rye and corn mash in copper pots and aged his product in charred oak barrels wherein it lost its natural pallor and acquired a pleasant taste. James Crow altered the flavor of his whiskey by combining it with low beer which was collected from the first still run and then scalded. His sour mash was well received, as were other Kentucky bourbons, and America had 2,000 whiskey distillers and her first indigenous distilled spirit by the end of the Revolutionary War.[5]

No sooner was the war over, however, than the distillers were threatened with a new loss of liberty. This occurred when Alexander Hamilton, first secretary of the treasury, proposed that the federal government pay part of the debts contracted by the states during the War of Independence by imposing an excise tax on distilled spirits at the unheard of rate of 11 cents a gallon. This tax had little effect on New England, where rum was falling from favor, and was supported by those in the Mid-Atlantic region, who preferred beer or imported beverages. But in western Pennsylvania and the South, Hamilton's tax was equated with British tyranny. Several counties formed an armed revolt against the government, and Philadelphia was occupied by so-called "whiskey boys" until President Washington quelled the uprising with federal troops. His actions during the Whiskey Rebellion impressed young America with the power of her fledgling government. But it also alienated the Westerners and contributed to the struggle between states' rights and federalism which culminated in the Civil War.

Once spirits were considered taxable items, American distillers began falling into two camps. One was made up of independent and illicit alcohol makers who came to be called moonshiners because they manufactured corn mash whiskey by moonlight. The other camp contained legal and progressively more organized distillers who were accepted into the community in part because they paid their taxes. By 1810, these distillers were annually turning out ten million taxed gallons of whiskey. Ten years later, their whiskey took its place alongside rum, gin, scotch, and fermented beverages in the first *Pharmacopeia of the United States.* In 1825, bourbon replaced rum in soldiers' rations. Whiskey then made its way west, in the form of "Taos Lightning" and other concoctions, where it was used to subjugate the Indians and ease the hardships of the frontier.

This subjugation has been associated with three assumptions. One is that the Indians were victimized because they could not hold their liquor, that it somehow affected them differently than the white man. Another is that the whites exploited this difference and allowed the Indian to emulate the drinking patterns established by rowdy cowboys. The third is that Indian drinking habits served as a retreat, a way of adapting to their social disorganization in the face of an increasingly complex white society. All three assumptions have merit, and the first has been granted some scientific credence through one recent though unconfirmed study, discussed later in the book, which suggests that Indians metabolize ethanol in a unique fashion. However, the Indians had alcohol long before their lands were invaded, albeit they never discovered distillation. And twentieth-century investigators have emphasized that the Indians never constituted a homogeneous culture and, therefore, used ethanol in many different ways.

119107

Ruth Benedict has explained some of these differences in terms of Dionysian and Apollonian value systems. The desire of the Dionysian, she believes, is to achieve an altered state of consciousness through group or individual experience. Like his namesake, he seeks the abandon of drunkenness, the illumination of frenzy. The Apollonian, on the other hand, follows a moderate course in pursuit of social and religious harmony.

According to Dr. Benedict, many American Indians and those of Mexico were passionately Dionysian and sought a personal or collective enlightenment through fasting, torture, dance, hallucinogenic drugs, and ethanol. Members of these tribes, which included the Plains Indians, were easily attracted to alcoholic beverages and often became peyote cultists or stereotyped drunken Indians. The southwestern Pueblo cultures, however, were Apollonian and eschewed altered states of consciousness in favor of social solidarity.[6] Dr. Benedict has been criticized for her reductionist perspective, and later anthropologists have demonstrated that her Apollonian and Dionysian distinctions are oversimplified. Nevertheless, field researchers have demonstrated that Indians have been and are as diverse as whites in their drinking behavior.

As one indication of this diversity among white people, at the very moment "firewater" was helping to win the West, the eastern United States was being won over by patent medicines. Best known of these was the "Vegetable Compound" which Lydia Estes Pinkham began brewing around 1850 in her Massachusetts kitchen. Within a decade the Compound enjoyed considerable success, ostensibly for its ability to "lessen menstrual discomfort, revive the drooping spirit, give elasticity and firmness to the step, restore natural luster to the eye, and plant on the pale cheeks of woman the fresh roses of life's early springtime." This springtime blush was attributed publicly to the life root and black cohosh contained in the Compound. Less publicized, but presumably more important, was the fact that Lydia Pinkham's concoction had an alcohol content of 18 percent.[7]

Although they were used by both sexes, the Vegetable Compound and other panaceas were prepared primarily for women. They were the socially accepted home beverage equivalent of whiskey, which was associated, along with prostitution, gambling, and gunfights, with the male-oriented saloon. Beer had occupied an intermediate position during colonial days, when it was brewed along Dutch and English lines and consumed as often at home as in local taverns. But in the nineteenth century, the United States became a haven for Europeans who preferred drinking German lager in beer halls. As a result, the first American lager brewery and beer hall was opened in Philadelphia in 1840 and operated primarily for persons of German descent. Yet other people came to like lager, prompting Eberhard Anheuser and Adolphus Busch to start a brewery in St. Louis in 1850 with wider appeal.[8]

August Pabst and Joseph Schlitz opened similar establishments in Milwaukee, which soon became the country's brewing capital because of its large German population and the availability of ice for lagering from Lake Michigan. Milwaukee made most of America's beer for decades, but because the beverage could not be shipped far without refrigeration, westerners were supplied by the Adolph Coors brewery in Golden, Colorado, the Olympia brewery in Tumwater, Washington, and several German breweries in San Francisco. Pasteurization was ultimately introduced, and with it, beer that did not require refrigeration. Yet most brewers continued to concentrate on unpasteurized draft beer for saloon drinkers, and instead of shipping their products started to open branches across the country. Near the turn of the century, the United States Breweries Association was organized, with its journal, *The American Brewer.* By 1900, the members of the Association were producing one million barrels of beer each year.

At the same time, immigration and technological improvements also led to the growth of America's wine-making industry. Its start came in the Finger Lakes region of New York and around Cincinnati, where careful selection of native Catawba and Concord grapes resulted in the preparation of wines which were popular for the most part among people of Southern European extraction. Yet the country's major wine-producing area was to be California, where *Vitis vinifera* had been introduced by the Spaniards as the source of mission wines.

California's first private commercial winery was established in 1827 in Los Angeles, and a few years later California's viticulture found its present center in the temperate valleys around San Francisco Bay. There the industry received its greatest support from Agoston Haraszthy, a Hungarian refugee who, after failing to grow grapes in the Midwest, in 1857 planted a vineyard in the Napa and Sonoma Valleys. From this base, Haraszthy helped found the first California Board of Viticulture and urged the state to create an agricultural school within its university system. He also made repeated trips abroad to gather varietals for planting in the West and is credited with introducing the Zinfandel grape to California.

European vintners sneered at these efforts to establish viticulture and vinification, but they soon had to depend on the United States for survival. This occurred in the 1850s, when the vine louse, *Phylloxera vastatrix*, which originated on the East Coast, was brought to Europe on some botanical specimens of *Vitis labrusca*. Although this native American vine had acquired an immunity to the louse, *Vitis vinifera* was vulnerable, as were the wine industries of France, Germany, Italy, and California. Wine production plummeted until vintners began grafting their vines on root stocks of *Vitis labrusca*, which had carried the louse to Europe. Alerted by this experience, the vintners proceeded to intrude for the first time on the genetic process, supplementing natural selection by artificial cross-fertilization to create plants offering new taste and hardiness. Such intrusion might never have occurred without the emigration of *Phylloxera vastatrix*. Thus it was that the New World, which owed so much to the Old, finally gave it something in return.

Its greatest gift, or curse, as some would say, was the cocktail. The origin of the word is obscure, with suggestions including the tail of the cock; the name of an Aztec princess, Zuchitil, who once used strong drink to seduce a hesitant suitor; and *coquetel*, a mixed drink from France. But whatever the cocktail's etymological roots, the habit of drinking distilled liquors diluted with regular or carbonated water or juices before dinner definitely originated in America. So did the cocktail party, an institution at which participants seek to achieve rapid sociability through the use of strong drink. Europeans resisted the cocktail party, which they considered incompatible with gastronomic health. Yet in sophisticated circles the cocktail superseded the aperitif as an obligatory prelude to the dinner meal.

The success of the cocktail was naturally resented by makers of fermented beverages. It also alarmed those American leaders who associated alcohol in concentrated amounts with social problems. As early as 1744, Benjamin Franklin, acting as foreman of a grand jury in Philadelphia, reported that the increase in vagabonds throughout the colonies was due to the consumption of distilled spirits and recommended a restriction on the number of taverns licensed to sell alcohol. He was seconded by Benjamin Rush, professor of medicine at the University of Pennsylvania and physician general of the Middle Department of the Continental Army, who attacked the notion that alcoholic beverages were essential either to the military or to medicine.

In 1785, Dr. Rush published America's first temperance tract, *An Inquiry Into the Effects of Ardent Spirits Upon the Human Mind and Body,* in which he labeled drunkenness a disease that physicians should treat with cold baths and vegetarian diets. Dr. Rush's real purpose, however, was preventive; he wanted his countrymen to eschew distilled liquors in favor of beer, wine, and hard cider. If this were done, he predicted, by 1915 a drunkard could be "as infamous as a liar or a thief, and the use of spirits as uncommon in families as a drink made of arsenic or hemlock."[9]

Although it did not deter drinking, the prediction was taken seriously by members of the American Temperance Society, which was founded in 1825 primarily by Congregationalist and Presbyterian ministers. Yet in spite of its philosophic debt to Dr. Rush, the Temperance Society considered excessive drinking not a disease but a sign of spiritual weakness. At first, the Society stood for moderation, as its name suggested. But in the wake of western expansion, its members began to call themselves teetotalers and to demand total abstinence.

Several theories have been advanced to explain the origin of the word teetotaler. One holds that the appellation originated at a temperance meeting in New York, whose members included those abstaining only from distilled spirits, whose names were marked "OP" for "Old Pledge" in the rolls, and those who also forswore wine and beer, who were identified by the letter, "T", for total. Another theory is that the teetotalers originated at a meeting where one of the stammering congregation came out for a t-total pledge. The *Oxford English Dictionary* attributes the word to an Englishman in 1834 in a speech advocating abstinence.[10]

Whatever their origins, many of the early teetotalers prided themselves on self-control. According to Joseph Gusfield, they practiced a form of moral athleticism in which they seemed obliged to overcome repeated challenges to their restraint.[11] Alcohol was such a challenge because it threatened to flood its users with forbidden impulses. Perhaps because of the strength of these impulses, there was little support among the temperance leaders for Dr. Rush's plea for moderate drinking. Instead, they advanced the therapeutic model of the Washingtonians, an association of reformed drunkards who conducted soul-baring group confessions and believed that complete abstinence was an unqualified prerequisite for sobriety.

Although their name is little known at present, the Washingtonians constituted this country's first self-help alcohol treatment group. The organization was founded in 1840 by six working men who sought mutual support as an antidote to their drunkenness. Successful with one another, the six then reached out for other inebriates, employing their converts as speakers and leaders of public meetings sponsored by the organization. In 1841, 1,000 reformed drunkards marched in the movement's first anniversary parade in Baltimore. Four years later, the Washingtonians claimed a membership of 100,000.

At this point, the organization gave every indication of longevity. Yet its decline proved to be as rapid as was its initial growth. This decline came about in part because the Washingtonians lacked a well-formulated ideology other than abstinence. Its membership was also public, so that when one initiate became intoxicated, the entire organization could be disgraced. Third, and perhaps most important, the Washingtonians became involved politically with the temperance movement. This alienated some prospective members and led to the organization's being assimilated into the movement rather than achieving an individual identity.[12]

In addition to the Washingtonians, the temperance movement was composed of several other groups after the Civil War. One was made up of New Englanders, many of whom feared the country's new immigrants as much as their alcohol consumption. Another included feminists who associated ethanol with prostitution, male prerogatives and family disruption, and who saw the liquor lobby as very anti-suffragette. A third group numbered Southern fundamentalists. There were also populists from across the country who envied the growing political power and liquor profits of the industrial Northeast. Reformers who were opposed to big business and the boss system of city politics joined scientists who were beginning to appreciate the deleterious effects of heavy drinking. Although unable to agree on all issues, these groups were united against alcohol. They helped form the Prohibition Party in 1861 in Chicago. The Women's Christian Temperance Union (WCTU) was organized in 1874 with 10,000 members, while the Anti-Saloon League, the single most important prohibitionist organization, appeared in 1896.

In fact, all three groups were opposed to the saloon, although only the League identified its true target. To the "typical" prohibitionist, who was a rural native American Protestant of Northern European extraction, the saloon was urban, immigrant, Catholic, Southern European, and, like the package liquor store, a visible symbol of the immigrant way of life. In large cities, the saloon served as an immigration office, labor exchange, union hall, political headquarters, social center, and drinking club. In frontier communities like San Francisco, which had one saloon for every 100 inhabitants, it fulfilled many of the functions of a small church. Unfortunately, however, the religious leaders of the Anti-Saloon League never saw this parallel. Nor did they acknowledge that they and the saloon keepers were competing for the attention of the same individuals.[13]

Thus, it was hardly surprising that the prohibitionists attacked their rivals with such fury. Calling itself "the Protestant Church in Action," the Anti-Saloon League set up an office across from the White House and mounted, with the Methodist Board of Morals, one of the most intensive lobbying campaigns in United States history. The Prohibition Party put forth candidates; the WCTU captured the energies of many American women, including those in the feminist movement; and the Anti-Saloon League sponsored public meetings. So eager were the three federations that by 1912 collectively they were printing from 10 to 12 million book pages of literature each day.

Their efforts reached a crescendo during World War I, when conservation policies prohibited the use of foodstuffs in the manufacture of spirits, and organizations like the Congressional Committee on Public Information tried to convert Americans from their traditional isolationism by horrifying the public with the alleged barbarities of the Hun. Although distilled liquors had been considered more dangerous than fermented beverages since the days of Dr. Rush, the Anti-Saloon League and other organizations focused their opposition on beer. They declared that drinking beer made by a Pabst or a Busch was unpatriotic, labeled alcohol a race poison, and linked it and the spread of veneral disease to a conspiracy on the part of the Central Powers.

The American Medical Association (AMA) endorsed this position, and in 1917, shortly after the *Pharmacopeia of the United States* dropped whiskey and brandy from its list of standard drugs, the executive council of the AMA came out for prohibition and against patent medicines. According to Andrew Sinclair, the nation's largest medical organization then passed a resolution stating that "sexual continence is compatible with health and is the best prevention against venereal infection" and also suggested that syphilis could be curbed if drinking were restricted. As a result, the Navy suspended its practice of distributing contraceptives to sailors on shore leave, and Congress passed legislation setting up so-called "dry and decent zones" around military camps.[14]

America's first statewide prohibition was passed in Maine in 1851. By 1917, according to Andrew McLaughlin, 23 other states, including Kentucky, whose economy was based on bourbon, passed prohibitionary legislation. Only 10 of these states actually were "bone dry"; the other 13 all made provisions for the procurement of alcoholic beverages for personal use. This fact has prompted Dr. McLaughlin to question whether the prohibitionists were aiming at the eradication of alcohol or were more interested in eliminating the saloon and restraining the urban immigrants who used it like a second home.[15]

As an indication of this interest, many of the same states also drew up "dram shop" acts designed to regulate both the times and places alcoholic beverages were made available and to whom such beverages could be sold. Congress in turn passed immigration quotas aimed at Southern and Eastern Europeans; and the House of Representatives voted for a Constitutional prohibition amendment. Woodrow Wilson was opposed to national prohibition, believing that the states should decide the issue. Yet in January, 1919, the Eighteenth Amendment, which forbade the manufacture, sale, import, or export of alcoholic beverages, was ratified against the opposition of urban America and the president.

In 1919, Congress, in order to enforce the Eighteenth Amendment, passed the Volstead Act over President Wilson's veto. Although brewers had argued that beverages containing 2.75 percent ethanol would be nonintoxicating, the act prohibited the manufacture of cereal beverages with more than .5 percent alcohol and limited the use of higher concentrations to medical, religious, and industrial purposes. Anticipating that some people might attempt to ingest the tax-free industrial preparations, the Volstead framers ordered that the legal ethanol be adulterated with toxic substances. The manufacturers were then required to advertise the harmful nature of these substances, while the public was informed by the government that the adulterated beverages were unfit to drink.

One such adulterant was isopropyl alcohol, which is approximately twice as toxic as ethanol. Another was methyl alcohol, which causes blindness in amounts as small as 15 milliliters, or one-half fluid ounce, and is fatal in amounts over 100 milliliters. This toxicity is due to the fact that methanol is metabolized by the body first to formaldehyde, a preservative that selectively destroys cells of the optic retina, and then to formic acid, a poison that alters the body's acid-alkali balance, causing central nervous system depression and death.

The Volstead Act also empowered the Treasury Department to investigate and prosecute violations of the Eighteenth Amendment. But although it was granted legal sanctions, the department never received adequate appropriations or public support. Indeed, the country seemed to regret the Prohibition Amendment even before it was operative. During the last six months of 1919, for example, some 15,000 doctors and 57,000 druggists and drug manufacturers applied for licenses to prescribe and sell allegedly medicinal alcohol preparations. Private clubs and fraternal organizations stockpiled liquor, while magazines featured articles on how to make home brew. By Christmas, 1919, America's tastes were already turning to illicit alcohol, and over 100 people died across the nation after drinking adulterated whiskey on New Year's Eve.[16]

Little was left of the legitimate alcoholic beverage industry on January 20, 1920, when Prohibition finally went into effect. Most wine makers had either plowed under their fields or were producing medicinal and religious wines, the latter being made legally available to the Catholic church and to orthodox Jews, who were permitted eight gallons of wine per year for their ceremonies. Wine makers also were turning out table grapes and grape juice which could be mixed with yeast by enterprising home vintners. The big brewers had converted their equipment to making chocolate, ice cream, and malted milk syrup or were turning out dealcoholized "near beer" to which illicit ethanol later could be added. The major distillers, meanwhile, were either selling their alcohol to the government or finding new interests. The economic climate during Prohibition favored such diversification and permitted the survival of large corporate interests at the expense of the small vineyard, brewery, or distillery.

It also insured the fortunes of the bootleg liquor business. America's first bootleggers were independent colonial traders who tucked bottles in their boot tops and then concealed the liquor under their pants legs when they went to do business with the Indians. Their twentieth-century successors also sold to Indians, among others, but they were better organized and had access to much more alcohol. Some of this alcohol came from those Canadian provinces that had not passed prohibitionary legislation. Other ethanol was smuggled by rum runners based in the Caribbean, manufactured by Southern moonshiners, or produced by "alky cookers" organized into tenement networks in urban centers throughout the country. Another important source was industrial alcohol, which either was diverted directly into the human stomach or mixed with glycerin and oil of juniper before being marketed as bathtub gin.

Prohibition wines were largely cheap Catawba and Concord preparations which were thought to resemble Italian chianti and, therefore, were called "dago red." Much Prohibition beer was brewed openly for sale in rural roadhouses or in the speakeasies created to fill the void previously occupied by urban saloons. New York boasted over 30,000 speakeasies by 1925, compared with 15,000 legal drinking places before Prohibition. Chicago had 10,000 speakeasies, each of which purchased an average of six $55 gallons of beer and two $90 cases of distilled spirits per week from Al Capone and other gang leaders protected by Chicago's police. Such corruption was so commonplace across the country that by 1928, when its responsibilities for enforcing the Eighteenth Amendment, other than control of industrial alcohol, were assumed by the Department of Justice, the Treasury Department had dismissed 706 of its agents for larceny.[17]

Other statistics were equally alarming. By 1930, 550,000 Americans had been arrested for drinking offenses, while at least 50,000 had been blinded or killed by adulterated alcohol. Hundreds of thousands had died in traffic accidents, as driving, drunk as well as sober, had increased by over 500 percent. Nearly 2,000 other citizens, mainly gangsters and beer runners, and 500 Prohibition agents had lost their lives as a result of gang warfare, and almost 2 million illegal stills had been seized by the government. During the same period, doctors wrote an average of ten million prescriptions for more than one million gallons of alcohol each year to soothe the public. Tax receipts on non-medical, religious, or industrial alcohol were not available after 1920, so no one could prove what happened to ethanol consumption. But only the most "dry" American could deny that Prohibition had done as little to deter drinking as it had to stop venereal disease.

Aside from its dismal record, Prohibition was finally destroyed by public desire for drink and by economic pressure to reactivate the alcoholic beverage industry. This pressure came from two organizations: the Association Against the Prohibition Amendment, whose board of directors included 200 of the wealthiest men in the country, and the Women's Organization for National Prohibition Reform, which was composed of many of the same men's wives. Collectively, these groups and their followers accused Prohibition of causing unemployment by limiting alcoholic beverage manufacture, worsening the agricultural economy by eliminating potential crop usage, increasing government spending by creating unenforceable legislation, and decreasing federal income by ending the liquor tax. The opposition of the wealthy was understandable, since they and their corporations were being called upon to make up the deficit in federal revenues during the Depression. Yet the poor were even angrier. Their sentiments were summed up best by Will Rogers, who in 1931 asked, "What does Prohibition amount to if your children are not eating? It's food, not drink, that is our problem."[18]

Another point is that Prohibition was identified with the Republican Party and repeal with the Democrats. The presidential election of 1928 pitted Herbert Hoover, a "dry," rural, native American Protestant against Al Smith, who was "wet," an urban Irish immigrant, and a Catholic. The electorate was not willing to overlook Smith's background in the election, particularly because Prohibition was a key issue. Yet, four years later, the Depression had eclipsed Prohibition, and

Franklin Roosevelt, whose background was more acceptable than Smith's, promised economic recovery and the return of alcohol.

Nine days after taking office, President Roosevelt cut back federal support for the Justice Department's Prohibition Bureau and the Department of the Treasury's Bureau of Industrial Alcohol. He then asked Congress to amend the Volstead Act to allow for the manufacture and sale of beverages containing 3.2 percent alcohol. The brewing industry accepted this figure as a compromise between "near beer" and stronger pre-Prohibition beverages, and 200 brewers of de-alcoholized beer volunteered that they could produce beverages containing alcohol soon after Congress acted on the president's recommendation. Congress did so, and the editor of *The American Brewer* estimated that within 24 hours after the Volstead Act was amended thirsty Americans had consumed more than one and a half million barrels of legal beer.

Several months later, in February, 1933, the Senate voted to submit the Twenty-first Amendment, ending Prohibition, to the states. The amendment was ratified that November, and on December 6, President Roosevelt took to the airwaves to announce repeal. Always hopeful, Roosevelt rivaled Benjamin Rush in optimism that night:

> I trust in the good sense of the American people that they will not bring upon themselves the curse of excessive use of intoxicating liquors to the detriment of health, morals and social integrity. And I ask especially that no state shall by law or otherwise authorize the return of the saloon either in its old form or in some modern guise.[19]

3. AMERICAN DRINKING PRACTICES AND PROBLEMS

This is the century in which for the first time the notion of alcohol and its effect on the human mind and body has been scientifically investigated and, to a large extent, illuminated. It is the century in which for the first time an attempt was made by civil authority in Western countries to prohibit the use of alcohol. It is the century in which the nature of chronic drunkenness has been objectively examined, and the drunkard has been accepted as a sick man rather than a sinner. It is the century in which alcohol has emerged from the saloon and the stag party to the cocktail lounge, the parlor, and the family picnic—in which the ladies' entrance of the bar has become the front door. It is the century in which drinking has become a social obligation—in which to decline a drink is to invite suspicion not that one is a teetotaler but an Alcoholic Anonymous. It is the century in which beer has lost much of its alcohol content and most of its flavor, and in which the strength of spirits has generally been reduced from the once standard one hundred proof to eighty-six or eighty or even less. It is the century of the nursery drink—of rum and Coca Cola, of whiskey and 7 Up, of vodka and tomato juice, of gin and consomme. But it is also the century of the eight-to-one martini, and the telltale glitter of the beer can on the highway.

BERTON ROUECHÉ, *Alcohol in Human Culture* (1963)

President Roosevelt's proclamation signaled the end of the "Noble Experiment," but it did not stop federal efforts to solve the alcohol problem. These efforts differed from those during Prohibition, however, in that the government did not say who should or should not consume alcohol, or under what circumstances. Nor did Washington involve itself with issues like chronic intoxication. Instead, in the Federal Alcohol Administration Act of 1936, it maintained only such prerogatives as the imposition of taxes and the setting of manufacturing standards. This left other issues in the hands of the states, counties, and smaller political jurisdictions, where they had existed before the Eighteenth Amendment was passed.

Essential to the Alcohol Administration Act was the first complete classification of legal alcoholic beverages. According to Gerald Carson, this classification was prepared with the approval and assistance of legitimate liquor makers who hoped to reduce competition and improve their products. Both were facilitated because the Act specified strict criteria for beverages intended for public consumption. Spirits called straight bourbon, for example, were required to be whiskies not exceeding 100 proof which were distilled from fermented mash of not less than 51 percent corn and aged in charred oak barrels for two years or more. To earn the appellation "bottled in bond," such whiskies had to be made at a single distillery during a single year, bottled at 100 proof, sealed with government stamps, and barrel-aged in federal warehouses for at least four years.[1]

Just as the Administration Act delineated legal beverages, so did it disallow Prohibition liquor, homemade beer, and patent medicines containing high concentrations of ethanol. This action against panaceas was augmented by those of the Food and Drug Administration curbing advertising excesses. The combination nearly proved fatal to concoctions like Lydia Pinkham's "Vegetable Compound," the formula for which was purchased by a New Jersey firm which planned to market the Compound solely "for the relief of symptoms of painful menstruation and the change of life."[2]

The demise of patent medicines gratified the American Medical Association, which had intensified its campaign against them during Prohibition, even though many of its members were profiting from the prescription of alcohol. Apparently to appease its membership, in 1928 the association rescinded its executive council's earlier endorsement of the Eighteenth Amendment and reaffirmed its faith in ethanol's therapeutic efficacy. As a result, the *Pharmacopeia of the United States* restored whiskey and brandy, but not beer and wine, to their privileged status, where they remained until 1947, presumably with the blessing of the AMA.

The final provisions of the Administration Act spelled out new tax laws and penalties for their violation. The Act also did away with the Justice Department's Federal Prohibition Bureau and returned enforcement authority to the Department of the Treasury through the Federal Alcohol Control Administration, which later was reorganized into the Alcohol,

Tobacco and Firearms Division of the Bureau of Internal Revenue. Al Capone was on Alcatraz by this time, but the division could not contend with other former bootleggers who had used money made during Prohibition to diversify into labor racketeering, gambling, narcotics, and a host of legitimate, that is, tax-paying, businesses. So it turned its attention to moonshiners and still seizures. Such seizures fell from a high of 102,000 in 1932 to 10,000 two years later, the lowest figure since 1919, and an indication, according to the "revenuers," that their efforts were forcing the moonshiners out of business. But gradually the number of seizures rose, indicating increased activity on the part of moonshiners, until 1960 when seizures reached their present average of 20,000 a year.

Not surprisingly, still seizures were highest in those states where statewide prohibition was maintained after the repeal of the Eighteenth Amendment. Those states included Mississippi, which in 1966 became the last state in America to eliminate its law. But although statewide prohibition ended, partial and country-wide prohibition remained popular in places where the Prohibition Party, the WCTU, and especially the Anti-Saloon League, which was renamed the American Council for Alcohol Problems, continued their activities. The three groups even claimed an increased membership shortly after Prohibition, yet in 1935 they and a dozen other organizations were forced to consolidate their declining strength in the National Temperance and Prohibition Council. The Council in turn became identified with opposition to communism, racial integration, and centralized government as well as to alcohol.

As the temperance movement was broadening its base, many areas across the country either continued to enforce "dram shop" acts and other statutes drawn up before Prohibition or drafted new legislation to regulate drinking. Relatively few laws were enacted against possession of ethanol, in contrast to other intoxicants, but most states placed limits on when, how, by whom, and to whom alcoholic beverages could be sold. American Indians were denied access to alcohol in several southwestern states, for example, and all areas prohibited sales to minors, who generally were classified as persons under 21. New York eventually differed from the majority in fixing its drinking age at 18, much to the consternation of neighboring communities whose sons and daughters were involved in accidents while driving home from New York taverns. At the same time, Wisconsin, Colorado, and other states whose economy depended on beer production and consumption allowed individuals 18 years of age and over to drink 3.2 percent beer.

In addition to these measures, the states adopted two basic approaches to regulating the availability of ethanol. The first, which was called the license approach, was used in 30 states and the District of Columbia. This involved regulating the distribution and retail sale of alcoholic beverages by licensing, either on a state or local level, those segments of private industry responsible for performing these functions. The second, or monopoly approach, was used in 18 states where the private sector was excluded from involvement in the wholesaling or retailing of most alcoholic beverages, especially distilled spirits. Sixteen of these monopoly states also regulated wine sales and distribution, and a few exercised comparable control over beer.

These two regulatory approaches were augmented by other ordinances in many places. For example, some states prohibited the sale of alcoholic beverages on Sundays and during elections. Others curbed liquor advertisements. (West Virginia made it illegal to show a man's hand in contact with a glass or bottle, while in seven states pictures of women drinking were forbidden.) Strict hours of operation were imposed on most package liquor stores, whether licensed or part of a state-owned network. Many states, meanwhile, formally refused to regard alcohol as a foodstuff and, like Colorado, permitted no preparations containing more than 3.2 percent ethanol to be stocked by grocery stores.

Grocers may have been hurt by such provisions, but the saloon suffered more. This venerable institution had been stigmatized before and during Prohibition, but after President Roosevelt cautioned against its return in his repeal proclamation, the saloon suffered a series of further blows. Several states prevented use of the word saloon in advertisements or on store fronts, for example, and eventually drinking establishments came to be known as pubs, inns, bars, or taverns. Swinging doors were outlawed in several communities, along with spittoons and other male trappings, and portraits of nude women were prohibited above bars.

In Iowa, the law required not only that tavern doors remain open but also that customers be clearly visible from the street. Ohio declared that since standing patrons seemed to drink more than their seated counterparts, regular patrons at the bar should squat on mid-sized stools. Utah did away with taverns entirely, replacing them with quasi-private clubs to which members brought bottles purchased at state liquor stores. Yet although the immigrant saloon became history, the more modern tavern survived. Ten years after repeal, Americans were spending more time in drinking establishments than in any other buildings other than private residences or places of employment. And by 1970, the nation's taverns had a greater patronage than all other forms of commercial recreation combined.

Anticipating such success, many lawmakers focused on public intoxication. According to Judge Samuel Kirbens, this had first been made a legal offense in 1606 during the reign of James I, when the English Parliament passed An Act for Repressing the Odious and Loathsome Sin of Drunkenness. Such drunkenness was not an offense unless accompanied by public nuisance under earlier English common law, but Parliament's action allowed the ecclesiastical courts to punish drunkards for the first time. France soon had her own laws against intoxicated vagrants who could not be controlled in any other fashion, while in Germany certain persons were subject to criminal sanctions for the misdemeanor of "deterioration."[3]

Such approaches were carried over to the colonies, where stocks and pillories were used to punish drunks. Public intoxication, thereafter, was regarded as a common law offense in this country, as emphasized in an 1888 case in which the Kansas court held that "voluntary drunkenness in a public place is always a misdemeanor at common law, and it is always wrong, morally and legally." In keeping with this common law tradition, after repeal many states enacted laws against public drunkenness, which was interpreted by the courts as intoxication outside of the home. Some states even prohibited inebriation in any and all settings, and areas like Illinois, which did not legislate against public intoxication, could imprison drunkards under statutes prohibiting disorderly conduct or vagrancy.[4]

The final issue dealt with by the states was that of driving under the influence of alcohol. A correlation between ethanol intake and accidents, vehicular and pedestrian, had long been suspected. But it took the increase in driving, drunk and sober, which occurred during Prohibition to escalate public awareness. The growing importance of the automobile in American life was also appreciated, and many professionals argued that research was necessary to determine the full impact of alcohol on car accidents. This led to two types of studies which demonstrated both the magnitude of the impact and its potential meaning.

In the first studies, experiments were done in which ethanol was given to animal and human subjects whose mental functioning and physical performance were then tested. The overwhelming majority of these studies indicated that performance is impaired in almost direct proportion to a rising blood alcohol concentration, or BAC.

As a result, the government today estimates that the relative probability of being responsible for a fatal crash or an automobile accident of any sort is essentially the same for blood alcohol concentrations of less than 50 milligrams percent, the equivalent of two one-ounce highballs, as it is for people who have no ethanol in their blood. At BACs between 50 milligrams percent and 100 milligrams percent, however, the relative probability of accidents begins to increase over the control population. At a BAC of 100 milligrams percent, a driver is seven times more likely to be responsible for an accident than he would be with no alcohol. The relative hazard curve then rises even more steeply, so that at a BAC of 150 milligrams percent, a driver is 25 times more likely to be responsible for an accident. At 180 milligrams percent he is

60 times more likely, and at 200 milligrams percent he is at least 100 times more likely to be responsible for an accident than if he had not been drinking at all.

In addition to this experimental data, epidemiological research has also underscored the association of automobile accidents and ethanol. According to the *First Special Report to the U.S. Congress on Alcohol and Health,* several studies have shown that fatal accidents tend to occur at night, especially between 10 P.M. and 6 A.M., and on weekends, times at which people might be returning home from taverns or from drinking with friends.[5] Other research has revealed that about a third of those drivers who are fatally injured in multiple vehicle accidents have BACs of 100 milligrams percent or higher, and that when drivers fatally injured in single car accidents are considered as a separate subgroup, over a half are found to have high blood alcohol concentrations. These data emphasize the correlation of drinking and automobile accidents. They also suggest that, other things being equal, drinking drivers are probably less likely to take part in multiple vehicle accidents in which innocent, that is, sober drivers are affected than they are to be involved in single vehicle accidents in which they themselves are killed.[6]

This research has been supplemented by studies describing the personal characteristics of drivers who are involved in vehicular and pedestrian accidents while drinking. These studies have tended to implicate men, who drink—and drive —more than women. Single and divorced men have been found to be responsible for more accidents than their married counterparts, and the incidence of involvement in accidents seems to go up in an inverse relationship to one's socioeconomic status. Young people have been shown to get into trouble at lower BACs and to be responsible for a disproportionate number of accidents when compared to older persons, in part due to the fact that since automobiles have become available, the young have driven more in terms of time and distance than their elders. Finally, the studies have identified an extremely high risk group of individuals, many of them young men, who drink heavily and often drive with BACs of 200 milligrams percent or more, that is, while intoxicated.[7]

Mounting accident statistics, coupled with evidence linking such statistics to heavy alcohol use, led several states after Prohibition to pass laws making drunk driving a criminal offense. Originally, driving under the influence of ethanol was defined in behavioral terms. But as the significance of blood alcohol concentrations was realized and their rapid determination was made possible by means of devices like the Breathalyzer, which is discussed in the next chapter, the influence of ethanol was calculated in terms of the BAC. Only Utah and Idaho followed the lead of those European countries which had passed laws punishing drivers with BACs higher than 75 milligrams percent. Instead, most states settled on the range of 100 to 150 milligrams percent, the equivalent of four to six one-ounce highballs, and imposed nominal penalties for drivers with higher blood alcohol levels, in spite of the fact that research had demonstrated that the majority of people are influenced significantly by smaller amounts of ethanol.

As the twentieth century progressed, California and other states added "implied consent" provisions which require licensed drivers to submit to the determination of their blood alcohol concentrations if they are suspected of operating motor vehicles while under the influence of alcohol or to have their licenses revoked if they refuse such determination. Yet in spite of these and other laws to raise revenue and regulate ethanol use, the states did not choose to limit the production of alcoholic beverages. This allowed the country's beverage makers to recover rather quickly after repeal.

The brewers, who had borne the brunt of pre-Prohibition attacks, actually enjoyed the speediest recovery. According to Stanley Baron, this was possible because they were better organized than other beverage makers. Most brewers also stayed in some sort of business during Prohibition, when a demand was created for their de-alcoholized products, and converted to licit manufacture after the government legalized 3.2 percent beer. Of course, this legalization gave them an advantage over other manufacturers. By June, 1933, 31 brewers were back in operation, with 756 predicting full production by the next year.[8]

Although 75 percent of the beer manufactured in 1915 had been unpasteurized draft beer for saloon drinkers, more and more beer after 1933 was destined for package sales. This change was brought about by several means, including increased use of pasteurization among brewers, widespread availability of refrigeration for consumers, and the introduction of canned beer in 1935. But equally important was the fact that people had come to associate speakeasies with distilled liquor during Prohibition, when spirits were more profitable and convenient for bootleggers to manufacture and transport than fermented beverages. After repeal, as the cocktail lounge replaced the saloon, liquor became identified with drinking outside the home, and beer with drinking at home.

So great was this rise in home consumption by both sexes that by 1940 the level of beer production was equal to that before Prohibition. Production fell off somewhat during World War II, but after the armistice the brewing industry entered another period of expansion. This period was characterized by continued diversification, with some breweries creating cattle feed out of hops and malt, and with the opening of more regional plants. Today the nation's largest brewer is the Anheuser-Busch Company of St. Louis, with nine breweries. The largest single brewery is that of the Adolph Coors Company of Golden, Colorado, which makes beer for sale in 11 western states, including California. Employing a nonpasteurized process which requires that its beer be refrigerated, Coors presently produces 12 million barrels of beer annually, 5,000 times as many as when it started in 1873. This is nearly a tenth of America's total beer output, which was 138 million barrels in 1974.

The wine industry has enjoyed comparable success. Prohibition curbed America's growing wine interest, and vineyards in California, New York, and Ohio which were experimenting with varietal grapes before 1920 either were downgraded or allowed to deteriorate over the next 13 years. Furthermore, many states refused to classify wine, like beer, as a foodstuff, and the small family vintners who survived Prohibition were neither organized nor able to import raw materials and start afresh. As a result of these factors, the wine industry required almost two decades to overcome the damage done during the Prohibition years.

Although belated, recovery occurred first in California, which had produced 50 million gallons of wine in 1915 compared with one million in 1934. In the latter year, those vineyards which had survived Prohibition formed the Wine Institute in San Francisco, and with the help of the University of California, Davis, set out to improve the quality and the quantity of California wines. The search for quality took place for the most part in the valleys around San Francisco. Although a few vintners had been experimenting with varietals before Prohibition, their wines were sold either under generic names common to Europe, such as Rhine or Burgundy, or under the general title "made in California." Wine makers rarely printed the year of a particular vintage, because they assumed both that Americans were not interested in such details and that in California's mild climate local wines fluctuated little in quality. But the vintners gave up these assumptions under the influence of university agronomists and an increasingly sophisticated public. As a result, the wine makers began dating their wines, labeling them by valley or region, and manufacturing them with a fixed percentage of grapes from a particular area.

The next move was from regional wines to dated varietals. This was made possible by technological advances and by the importation and selected breeding of European vines. Today the best known of the California varietals are the Cabernet Sauvignon, a descendant of cuttings brought from the Bordeaux region; the Pinot Chardonnay, well known in the Chablis and Champagne vineyards of France; and the Zinfandel, which is now unique to California. Produced by small northern California vintners, many of whom have been absorbed into larger conglomerates, premium table wines made from these grapes have become increasingly popular and now are competitive with European wines. This has led to further planting, and wine makers have expanded as far as the foothills of the Sierra Nevada mountains. There vintners are growing varietals on the root stocks of *Vitis vinifera,* rather than *Vitis labrusca,* having been assured by oenologists that the *Phylloxera* which once devasted the European vine at sea level will not attack it at higher altitudes.

In spite of such innovations, however, California's premium wine makers have never accounted for more than one-quarter of the state's output. The remainder consists of popularly-priced wines which come for the most part from California's Central Valley. In this area, which has warmer weather and a more alkaline soil than the San Francisco Bay region, the emphasis is on mass production. The undisputed leaders, according to *Business Week,* are Ernest and Julio Gallo, who began making low-priced wines in Modesto after World War II and then proceeded to promote their products with heavy advertising, new bottles and labels, and energetic merchandising. Such promotion has paid off for the Gallos, to the extent that their $250 million company now accounts for nearly half of all California wine production. The latter makes up 85 percent of the country's total, which since 1970 has been over 200 million gallons a year.[9]

In recent years a large proportion of the Central Valley crop has gone into dessert wines and fruit-flavored preparations designed for the youth market. These latter beverages are "a natural transition from soda pop," according to a former Gallo marketing executive: "They're really Kool Aid with some alcohol and carbonation."[10] Fruit-flavored drinks seemed destined to sweep the wine industry during the early 1970s, but since then their sales have leveled off, leaving table wine with the largest share of the market. This means that more and more Americans are drinking wine with meals, in the European tradition. Yet even the success of table wines has limits, believes Arpad Haraszthy, son of the godfather of California viticulture. "We have come far," he declared to the Wine Institute, "but the greatest obstacle to our success is that the average American is a whiskey drinking, coffee drinking, tea drinking, and consequently, a dyspepsia-inviting subject, who does not know the value of pure light table wines taken at the right time and in moderate quantities."[11]

Actually beer is wine's biggest competitor, thanks in part to the dominance of English rather than French traditions, including cooking, in America. Yet Haraszthy is correct in noting that Americans favor distilled alcohol. Originating in colonial times, this preference was reinforced by Prohibition and reflected in the fact that distillers were able to return to full production shortly after repeal. By 1940, when federal taxes on distilled liquor were $4 a gallon, the nation's bourbon makers were enjoying greater profits than before Prohibition. These profits declined during the next five years, as the industry was converted to war production, but by 1950, bourbon sales exceeded those of any other domestic or imported preparation. And in 1960, European distillers and vintners afforded bourbon that meets United States government regulations the same international recognition and protection granted French cognac and Scotch whiskey.

This has meant a wider market for bourbon outside this country, but sales of bourbon have stabilized since 1960 in America. This contrasts with the steady increase in sales of scotch, which, according to David Daiches, won public acceptance during World War II. This acceptance resulted both because of closer ties between the United States and Great Britain and because Winston Churchill ordered his food ministry to allocate cereals for distilling while this country was finding other uses for its grain. Today America is the largest single importer of scotch whiskey, annually consuming over 2.5 million gallons. This compares with two million gallons for France, and 1.5 million for West Germany.[12]

Scotch distillers make much of the age of their whiskies, but an even greater sales increase has been recorded by liquors which are hardly aged at all. These include gin, more of which is now made in the United States than is imported; tequila, a drink distilled from maguey plants in Mexico; and vodka, originally a Russian liquor distilled from potatoes. Now made from vast quantities of grain in this country, vodka recently replaced bourbon as America's favorite distilled beverage. Like gin, it has a bland taste and is said to impart less of an alcoholic odor. Actually, both the smell and the flavor of distilled spirits come from their congeners, not their ethanol content. The same congeners have been implicated in some hangovers, so vodka, which is relatively free of impurities after distillation and remains pure because congeners are not acquired through an aging process, is alleged to cause fewer and milder mornings after than other beverages. Perhaps most important, it is cheap, rivaled only by fortified wines in producing the greatest amount of intoxication at the lowest possible price. Thus, it now occupies in this country the position held in post-feudal England by gin.

Led by vodka, 367 million gallons of distilled liquor were manufactured in the United States during 1970, most of which had ethanol concentrations of around 90 proof or 45 percent. According to Joel Fort, in the same year the entire alcoholic beverage industry employed two million people with an annual payroll of $9 billion. Over 500,000 firms were involved in assisting the distilled liquor makers, who purchased $5 billion of goods and services. Retail sales were $12 billion, resulting in $3 billion in tax revenues. Beer alone accounted for sales of $7 billion and tax revenues of $1 billion, compared with sales of $9 billion for prescription drugs and $3 billion for over-the-counter remedies.[13] In terms of consumers, in 1970, each American adult spent an average of $100 on alcoholic beverages, with roughly half that amount allocated for distilled spirits. This compared with $1,500 in food purchases and $350 for health care.

These figures are significant in their own right, but even more striking is the suggestion that alcohol intake is increasing steadily in our society. This suggestion comes from data on the apparent annual consumption of each major beverage class, and of absolute alcohol from each class, in gallons per person over 15 years of age, which is included in the *First Special Report to the U. S. Congress on Alcohol and Health.* Derived from government records on tax-paid beverages, the data make no allowance for illicit liquor and cover products purchased by consumer outlets rather than individual customers. Furthermore, since apparent consumption is arrived at by dividing the amount of paid beverages by census records of an arbitrary drinking age population, the data say nothing about individuals outside this population and cannot indicate whether more people in the population are drinking, or if the same number of people are consuming more alcohol.

Accepting these limitations, the figures are still revealing. In 1850, the first year statistics were compiled, Americans over 15 years old drank a per capita average of 4.17 gallons of distilled spirits, 0.46 gallons of wine, and 2.70 gallons of beer. This came to a total of 2.10 gallons of absolute alcohol, more than three-quarters of which was in the form of distilled spirits. By 1900, this emphasis had shifted, with Americans consuming 2.11 gallons of distilled liquor, 0.71 gallons of wine, and 26.20 gallons of beer, for a total of 2.39 gallons of absolute alcohol.

Data are not available for Prohibition, of course, and the statistics immediately thereafter are artificially low because the relegalized alcohol trade was just beginning to replace the bootleg industry. But by 1970, people 15 years of age and older were drinking as much as 2.56 gallons of distilled liquor, 1.84 gallons of wine, and 26.95 gallons of beer, for a total of 2.61 gallons of absolute alcohol. This represents an increase of one-half gallon per person since 1850. It also reflects a change in drinking preferences in that people today are taking more than half of their alcohol in the form of wine and beer.[14]

In spite of this increase, however, the *First Special Report* ranks this country only seventh among 20 Western nations in its consumption of alcoholic beverages. This ranking again is derived from government tax figures, which are kept in a different fashion from country to country and hence are not entirely reliable. Nevertheless, they are the only available source of such information. France leads the government list, with an average annual consumption of 2.53 gallons of distilled spirits, 43.04 gallons of wine, and 20.10 gallons of beer. This comes to a total of 6.53 gallons of absolute alcohol per person 15 years of age and older, and places France first in wine consumption and second only to the United States in the consumption of distilled liquor.

Second in overall consumption is Italy, with a per capita average of 4.01 gallons of absolute alcohol, almost all of which is wine. Then comes Switzerland, with a total of 3.39 gallons of absolute alcohol per person; West Germany, with a total of 3.26 gallons; Australia, with 2.89 gallons; Belgium with 2.87 gallons; and the United States, with 2.61 gallons. Ireland stands sixteenth on the list, in spite of other high indices of heavy drinking and the high alcohol intake observed among Irish-Americans. Last is Israel, where only 0.82 gallons of absolute alcohol are consumed annually by each drinking age individual.[15]

Such comparisons place American drinking in perspective and help approximate the average per capita intake of alcohol. Yet they do not disclose who does or does not drink in our own or in other populations. Nor do they reveal where, when, how, and with whom people drink, for what results, and with what results. Finally, the comparisons do not indicate what behavior patterns are associated with alcohol. To determine these factors, government statistics are inadequate. In their place, in-depth surveys are required.

One such survey was carried out in 1964 and 1965 by Don Cahalan and his colleagues. Entitled *American Drinking Practices,* this survey was based on 2,746 personal interviews with a random sample of male and female adults, representative of the United States population aged 21 and older, living in households. The sample was drawn in accordance with probability procedures, and interviews were completed with 90 percent of the 3,043 selected eligible persons. After collecting their raw data, Dr. Cahalan and his coworkers performed multivariate analysis to determine how much Americans drink and how various demographic, sociological, economic, and psychological variables affect their drinking attitudes and behavior.[16]

First, the investigators looked at the amount and variability of drinking among people in this survey. They found that 77 percent of the men and 60 percent of the women used alcohol at least once a year, so that a studywide total of only 32 percent could be considered abstainers. Fifteen percent of the total sample were categorized as infrequent drinkers who drank less than once a month but at least once a year; this corresponded to 10 percent of the males and 18 percent of the females. Similarly, 41 percent of the total sample, amounting to 46 percent of the men and 37 percent of the women, were called light to moderate drinkers who drank at least once a month, often several times, but usually with no more than one to five drinks per occasion. Twenty-one percent of the men, 5 percent of the women, and 12 percent of the total were labeled heavy drinkers because they drank nearly every day with five or more drinks per occasion at least once in a while or drank at least weekly with five or more drinks on most occasions.

In terms of beverage choices, 4 out of every 10 respondents said that they drank wine at least once a year, but only 1 percent were heavy wine drinkers. Distilled spirits were consumed by 51 percent at least once a year, while 6 percent had a heavy intake of spirits. Wine tended to be drunk by people, especially women, of upper socioeconomic status residing in the Pacific and Mid-Atlantic States. Beer was the preferred drink for a large proportion of heavy drinkers, men, and younger persons. Distilled beverages were ingested by relatively more of the heavier drinkers and persons in the upper levels of society.

The survey considered a variety of demographic variables in drinking patterns. Regarding the variable of sex, for example, it revealed that men generally drink more often than women and constitute comparatively more heavy drinkers and fewer abstainers, although this disproportion was disappearing at the time of the survey. In terms of age, the investigators found that 40 percent of male drinker aged 45 to 49 qualified as heavy drinkers, while 25 percent of the younger men and only 11 percent of the male drinkers over 65 drank heavily. Among the women there also was a peak of heavy drinking between 45 and 50. Yet as with the men, this incidence of drinking declined with age, and over half of the total sample said they had changed their drinking habits significantly.

The investigators found that the differences in the proportion of men and women drinkers were smaller in the upper socioeconomic levels. The proportion of drinkers was highest among men aged 21 through 34 in the highest socioeconomic level and lowest among men aged 60 and over in the lowest level. The lower levels generally had smaller proportions of light and moderate drinkers, but their proportion of heavy drinkers was higher. A large proportion of members of the higher socioeconomic levels started drinking later in life and continued drinking, albeit at a light or moderate level, until a later age.

Dr. Cahalan and his coworkers believed that the findings by

occupational distribution revealed patterns probably not attributable to the fact that the various occupational groups had different incomes. They found, for example, that the largest proportion of abstainers occurred in the farm owner group, whereas the largest proportion of drinkers was among professional, managerial, and sales persons. Similarly, the highest proportion of abstainers by sex was found among women with only a grammar school education, while those with higher educational backgrounds were more likely to be drinkers. The single, divorced, or separated had a higher proportion of heavy drinkers on the average than did the married or the widowed. Widows and widowers tended to have the lowest incidence of both drinkers and heavy drinkers, in part because of their usually greater age and lower socioeconomic status.

Although they anticipated that the presence of children in the home might affect drinking patterns, the investigators found that differences in this area were not material. They also learned that there was not much difference in the general level of drinking between persons who did or did not live with both parents up to the age of 16, except that the proportion of heavy drinkers was greater in men brought up by only one parent. However, there were considerable regional differences in drinking. The highest proportions of both drinkers and heavy drinkers were in the Mid-Atlantic, Pacific, New England, and Northeast Central areas, all of which are relatively urban in character, while the lowest proportion occurred in the Southeast Central States and other southern areas. This finding was attributed to the fact that the South is less urban, lower in socioeconomic status, and dominated by conservative Protestant denominations. Yet Southerners who moved to other parts of the country increased their consumption, reflecting a tendency to conform to prevailing drinking customs in a given area.

Dr. Cahalan and his coworkers found that white and black men varied little in their rates of drinking. However, black women differed from white women both in their much higher proportion of abstainers and in their higher rate of heavy drinking. The investigators speculated that this difference in abstinence might be due to the greater family and economic responsibility of certain black women, while the difference in heavy drinking might stem from greater social alienation. White or black, most of the survey respondents were born in the United States, and 74 percent said their fathers were also born in this country. Respondents whose fathers were born outside America reported a substantially higher amount of drinking, but both groups were about equal in the proportion of heavy drinkers. Those whose fathers were born in Ireland had the highest proportion of drinkers, 93 percent, as well as the highest proportion of heavy drinkers. Those whose fathers came from Latin America or the Caribbean had the lowest proportion of drinkers, 60 percent, but a relatively large proportion of those who drank did so heavily.

Comparing religious, rather than national, identity, the authors found that Catholics were usually highest in the proportion of drinkers, followed closely by liberal Protestants, with conservative Protestants trailing far behind. This was borne out by an analysis of current religious affiliation, which revealed that Catholics had the highest proportion of both drinkers and heavy drinkers. Jews, by contrast, had the lowest rate of abstainers and a relatively low rate of heavy drinkers. Similarly, there was a negative relationship between the frequency of church attendance and heavy drinking, in that those who said they never went to church had the highest rate of heavy drinkers, while the proportion of abstainers was relatively high among those who attended church most frequently.[17]

Examining possible behavioral correlates of drinking, the researchers found that parental permissiveness about drinking generally was correlated with a greater amount of drinking in young people. Heavy drinking by wives was correlated closely with heavy drinking by their husbands, and vice versa. People of both sexes said they drank most often with friends, next most often with members of their family, and least often by themselves, although heavy drinkers were more likely than others to drink alone.[18]

Dr. Chahalan and his colleagues then examined some psychological aspects of drinking. Asking respondents what sorts of effects they derived from drinking over the previous year, they found that reports of positive and negative experiences were equally divided and that two-thirds of the respondents recalled no specific effect. A much larger proportion of drinkers under 40 reported adverse effects than those over 40. Yet only 9 percent of all drinkers worried about drinking, although three-quarters of all respondents felt that in general drinking did more harm than good. The two leading attributes of alcohol were that it helped people relax and mix socially. The leading negative aspects were that it was injurious to health and family life. Only complete abstainers mentioned moral or religious reasons for not consuming alcohol.

In contrast to their expectations, the investigators found that heavy drinkers voiced only a slightly lower level of satisfaction in meeting life goals than did lighter drinkers or nondrinkers. The lowest proportion considering themselves to be in good health were abstainers, who were more likely than drinkers to be elderly. Among all drinkers there was a high correlation between drinking and smoking. Having a drink was reported to be helpful when depressed or anxious by more people than was taking tranquilizers or sedatives, and much larger proportions of heavy drinkers were likely to use alcohol for escape purposes than the overall sample. Heavy drinkers also mentioned stronger feelings of alienation, which were found among many abstainers as well.[19]

From this and other data, Dr. Cahalan and his coworkers concluded that drinking is commonplace in the United States, while abstinence and heavy drinking, especially to escape from life's problems, are atypical behavior. The people most likely to be drinkers are men and women of high social status; professional and semiprofessional people; college graduates; suburban residents; persons whose fathers are foreign born, especially Italians and Irish; and members of the Jewish or liberal Protestant faiths. By contrast, those most likely to be heavy drinkers are men aged 45 to 50; men of lower socioeconomic status; laborers; persons who did not attend college; single, widowed, divorced, or separated persons; city dwellers; people whose fathers were Latin American, Caribbean, or Irish; and Catholics and those without religious affiliation. Thus, demographic and sociological factors play a large role in determining who drinks and to what extent. Also important are psychological variables, including feelings of alienation and a tendency to use ethanol to relieve anxiety and depression and for escape purposes.[20]

Among its other accomplishments, the *American Drinking Practices* survey helped distinguish between various types of drinking on the basis of consumption and delineated some differences between moderate drinkers, heavy drinkers, and abstainers. Yet its authors did not consider heavy drinking a problem nor did they decide who in this country experienced difficulties with alcohol. Therefore, in 1967, Dr. Cahalan's group reinterveiwed 1,359 of the original 2,746 respondents and published their findings in a book entitled, *Problem Drinkers.* As was the case with the earlier sample, this subsample was made up of adults living in households, not those belonging to self-help organizations or residing in jails, hospitals, or skidrow conditions. The subsample, therefore, constituted a cross-section of the American community.

For the purposes of this second survey, Dr. Cahalan defined problem drinking as "repetitive use of the beverage alcohol causing physical, psychological or social harm to the drinker or to others."[21] He then focused on 11 problem categories, each of which was graded in terms of severity and frequency of occurrence during the previous three years. These categories corresponded to those emphasized by previous writers including E. M. Jellinek and representatives of Alcoholics Anonymous, so that Dr. Cahalan's data could build upon surveys that went before.

The problems selected by Dr. Cahalan included frequent intoxication, a high score for which was obtained by consuming five or more drinks at least once a week, or eight or more drinks on one of the last ten occasions and twice in the last year, or currently getting intoxicated at least once a week; binge drinking, which consisted of being intoxicated for at least several days at a time, or for two days on more than one occasion; symptomatic drinking, a term employed by Dr. Jellinek and described as the exhibition of signs or symptoms attributable to physical dependence on ethanol, such as drinking to ease a hangover or having difficulty in stopping drinking; psychological dependence on ethanol, manifested by drinking to alleviate anxiety or depression or to escape from the pressures of living; problems with spouses or relatives related to one's drinking, such as the spouse leaving or threatening to leave; problems with one's friends or neighbors, including the report that such individuals had urged the drinker to cut down his or her consumption; problems concerned with one's work, including losing one's job; problems with police, or accidents in which someone was hurt or property damage occurred; health problems, based in part on reports that drinking had been harmful to one's health or that one had been urged to cut down by a physician; financial problems; and finally, belligerence or fighting.[22]

After interviewing the subsample of the *American Drinking Practices* population and grading the various problem areas, Dr. Cahalan concluded that 43 percent of the male subjects and 21 percent of the women, for an overall total of 31 percent, had experienced one or more of the 11 problems during the previous three years. Fourteen percent of the men and 2 percent of the women reported frequent intoxication, for example, and 3 percent of the men and less than .5 percent of the women manifested signs or symptoms of physical dependence, while an equal percentage was psychologically dependent. Eight percent of the men and 1 percent of the women also evidenced problems with their spouses or relatives; 2 percent of the men and .5 percent of the women had problems with friends or neighbors; 3 percent of the men and 1 percent of the women had job problems; 1 percent of the men and 1 percent of the women had problems with police or accidents; 6 percent of the men and 4 percent of the women had health problems; 3 percent of the men and 1 percent of the women had financial problems; and 4 percent of the men and 3 percent of the women reported belligerence or fighting. When the problems were added on a per person basis and differentiated according to their presumed severity, 15 percent of the men and 4 percent of the women qualified as problem drinkers by Dr. Cahalan's criteria.[23]

After determining the incidence of problem drinking among the subsample, Dr. Cahalan investigated the relationship between such drinking and six sociological and psychological and four demographic variables derived from both surveys. The psychological and sociological variables included respondents' attitudes toward drinking, environmental support for heavy drinking, impulsivity and nonconformity among drinkers, alienation and maladjustment, unfavorable life expectations, and looseness of social controls against drinking. The four demographic variables were sex, age, socioeconomic status, and degree of urbanization. After the ten variables were collected, they were correlated with the problem drinking scores.

Dr. Cahalan found that all ten variables bore some relationship to problem drinking and that the most closely correlated were two sociological variables: attitudes toward drinking and environmental support of heavy drinking. The psychological variables of alienation and maladjustment as well as impulsivity and nonconformity were associated with problem drinking, although less strongly. When the six sociological and psychological variables and the four demographic variables were combined to make a risk score, it appeared that those who stood the greatest chance of being problem drinkers were urban men of lower socioeconomic status who viewed drinking to the point of intoxication as appropriate behavior and were reinforced in this belief by their peers. These same men reported greater feelings of alienation and poorer impulse control.[24]

When he combined the findings of his first and second surveys, Dr. Cahalan decided that demographic variables determine in large part whether or not a person drinks at all. Sociological and psychological variables are most important in the amount of drinking and the creation of drinking problems, with sociological factors determining whether one is permitted or encouraged by one's environment. When he set aside the major variable of attitude toward drinking, Dr. Cahalan found that for men environmental factors played a more conspicuous role among the correlates of problem drinking, while for women alienation and maladjustment seemed most important. This, he decided, was probably due to the greater social disapprobation of heavy drinking on the part of women, which might account for the finding that women with drinking problems generally have higher scores on psychological maladjustment than do men with the same problem. Yet this fact is changing, as is the fact that more and more American women are reporting increased alcohol consumption and a growing number of drinking problems.[25]

Perhaps the most important conclusion from both surveys is that change is the hallmark of drinking practices and problems. *American Drinking Practices* revealed a high turnover in the drinking and nondrinking status of many respondents, in addition to a tendency for older persons to drop out of drinking. *Problem Drinkers* showed that the highest frequency of drinking problems in the United States occurs among persons, especially men, who are under 25 years of age and not among older individuals who are hospitalized for health problems related to prolonged heavy drinking. Furthermore, fully one-third of the people who reported to Dr. Cahalan that they had drinking problems at a certain point in their lives were either problem-free three years later or were able to decrease their ethanol intake for reasons of health, finances, increased maturity, and other factors. Thus, although drinking problems, like drinking itself, are commonplace, they and their escalation may not be so inevitable as some believe.

4. TO DREAM BUT NOT TO SLEEP

He thought of the sandwich he had started to buy a day or so ago (when was it?) and wondered what had prevented him. No food in all that time. But he couldn't think of it or wonder about it, because now a new thought possessed him: interminable and agonizing though the long day would be, it was bound to end, sometime, somehow, and darkness would finally fall. What did that not mean? Delirium was a disease of the night, yes; but also—oh, worse!—delirium never came while you were drinking. Only after you had stopped. And there was no way of starting again. Unable to go out and get liquor, trapped here the whole day without it, what would tonight be like? It was a prospect so terrifying that at once he tried to busy himself, occupy his mind, with something to do.

CHARLES JACKSON, *The Lost Weekend* (1944)

Although it is not verified by the research of Don Cahalan and others, the idea that drinking problems inexorably progress is supported by the fact that ethanol is a drug with appealing pharmacological properties. This appeal gives alcohol a high potential for abuse, which Jerome Jaffe describes as "the self-administration of substances which deviates from approved medical or social patterns."[1] Dr. Jaffe's description places drug abuse in a proper cultural context, yet it overemphasizes deviance and thus cannot be applied to chemicals like ethanol which are both subject to abuse and socially acceptable. Because of this, we consider drug abuse comparable to Dr. Cahalan's concept of problem drinking and define it as a style of behavior in which the single or repetitive administration of pharmacological substances leads to physical, psychological, or social harm. This behavior is adaptive. It represents the expression of biological forces, intrapsychic processes, and cultural phenomena.

This wider definition encompasses the injudicious intake of nonprescription vitamins and analgesics in addition to the taking of psychoactive compounds that cause changes in mood and mental status. Since these changes generally are enjoyable, most psychoactive drugs can produce psychological dependence or habituation, which occurs when people prefer the altered consciousness or the conditions associated with the taking of a given chemical to their normal state. Although such habituation may motivate behavior, substances which cause psychological dependence can be given up without changes other than anxiety and depression. Physical dependence, by contrast, refers to an altered condition which results from repeated drug taking and is so pronounced that continued administration of the drug is necessary to prevent a withdrawal or abstinence syndrome. Closely associated with physical dependence is tolerance, a situation that prevails when, after repeated administration of a drug, a given dosage produces a decreasing effect or, conversely, increasingly larger doses are required to achieve the drug's initial effects.[2]

Many substances are associated with psychological dependence. But true physical dependence and tolerance are seen primarily with two classes of drugs, both of which depress the central and the autonomic nervous systems. The central nervous system is an assemblage of many billion nerve cells which include the cerebral hemispheres, cerebellum, brain stem, and spinal cord. The central nervous system governs consciousness, voluntary motion, sensation, coordination, perception, memory, thought, and judgment as well as regulation of autonomic activity. The autonomic nervous system consists of a smaller number of cells which innervate the heart, blood vessels, glands, lungs, and viscera, and coordinate involuntary or vegetative functions, such as heart rate, respiration, and digestive activity.

The first class of depressant drugs is the narcotic analgesics. These include heroin, morphine, and other alkaloids of the opium poppy, in addition to their synthetic equivalents. Although they can cause fatal nervous system depression in high doses, narcotics produce only nominal sedation in therapeutic ranges and are used clinically to control pain. The second class is made up of the sedatives, hypnotics, and general anesthetics, which if given in progressively larger doses cause sedation, disinhibition, anesthesia, and complete depression of the central and autonomic nervous systems, including those centers in the brain stem that regulate consciousness, respiration, and cardiovascular activity. Among the many members of this class are phenobarbital and other drugs used primarily as sedatives. Also included are such hypnotics or sleeping medications as chloral hydrate, ether and other anesthetics, and ethyl alcohol.

Physical dependence and tolerance occur relatively soon after the administration of most narcotics and many sedatives, hypnotics, and general anesthetics. For this reason, physicians are all too familiar with heroin or barbiturate abusers who quadruple their intake of these drugs after only a few days of intravenous injection. The rapidity of this tolerance suggests to Dr. Jaffe that the adaptation processes which produce physical dependence probably begin with the first dose of these substances, and that, therefore, it is difficult to determine who is or is not dependent. The same difficulty exists with ethanol, but this drug differs from other sedatives, hypnotics, and general anesthetics and from narcotics in causing a less rapid form of physical dependence. Thus, tolerance develops relatively slowly with alcohol; it is only after months or years that people can increase the amount they regularly drink, and then only to two or three times their initial intake. Furthermore, although mild withdrawal symptoms, such as tremulousness, happen early in one's drinking history, the more dramatic manifestations of abstinence occur only after long periods of high-dose consumption of alcohol.[3]

In addition to these differences with other members of its class of chemicals, ethanol is unique in other aspects of its pharmacology. For one thing, it is a very small molecule with infinite water solubility. For another, it can be absorbed by passive diffusion along the entire gastrointestinal tract. This means that alcohol can be administered in enemas or given by mouth. When inhaled it also can be taken up through the air sacs of the lung and enter the circulation. And however it is absorbed, ethanol reguires no digestion. It is immediately ready to act as a fuel or a pharmacological agent.[4]

When taken by mouth, alcohol causes a warm sensation as it increases blood flow to the stomach. The drug also heightens the secretion of gastric acid through an excitation of nerve endings in the stomach, the release of certain chemical mediators, and the psychic stimulation that occurs when people who like ethanol contemplate taking a drink. This increase in gastric acid secretion in turn prompts a rise in the production of digestive enzymes within the pancreas. In spite of these actions, however, alcohol plays only a minor role in digestion and does not affect the appetite center within the central nervous system. Most people have adequate quantities of gastric acid and digestive enzymes and derive no benefit from the increase in these substances that is caused by alcohol, in spite of the fact that aperitifs and cocktails are employed for this purpose.

In most people, some 20 to 30 percent of orally ingested ethanol is absorbed by the stomach. The rest is mixed with gastric acid and copious amounts of mucus secreted by the stomach in self-defense. The drug then enters the small intestine, where the bulk of its absorption take place. The rate of this absorption depends on the alcohol concentration, the speed of its intake, the beverage ingredients and gastric contents with which it is mixed, and the intrinsic emptying time of the stomach. Milk and other protein-rich foods inhibit gastric emptying and hence can be taken before drinking to delay the absorption of alcohol. Conversely, the carbonation in champagne and drinks mixed with soda water enhances emptying and increases the intoxicating effects of these preparations.

In the stomach or the small bowel, alcohol diffuses readily through the gastrointestinal lining and into the bed of blood vessels beneath. Most of the drug then travels to the liver via the portal vein, where it either is metabolized or enters into a host of biochemical processes which are discussed in the next chapter. The remaining ethanol then joins the general circulation and is distributed throughout body fluids and tissues, including the placenta, in direct proportion to their water content. This preferential distribution favors organs like the brain which have a high amount of water as well as a good blood supply. Alcohol also appears in urine, saliva, sweat, and expired air in fixed ratios compared to its concentration in blood. Since these ratios vary little from person to person, expired air, urine, saliva, and other secretions can be used to calculate the BAC.

Ease of collection makes expired air the sample most commonly employed to determine the blood alcohol concentration for medical or legal purposes. Subjects who are providing such samples first rinse their mouths to clear the ethanol contained in saliva and then exhale into a collecting system. The sample next is introduced into one of many devices which operate under the principle that alcohol, as it is being oxidized by certain chemicals, donates electrons and thereby acts as a reducing agent. One such device, the Breathalyzer, uses a piston apparatus to trap expired air which subsequently is passed through a solution of potassium dichromate. The ethanol in turn causes a change in the color of the dichromate solution which is compared photoelectrically with a control sample of the chemical.

After this color change has been quantitated it is multiplied by a factor corresponding to the fixed ratio of expired air to blood alcohol to determine the BAC. The blood alcohol concentration then is expressed in milligrams per one hundred milliliters, or milligrams percent. An example will show how the BAC is calculated. One ounce of 100 proof distilled liquor, which is 30 milliliters, is the equivalent of 15 milliliters of 100 percent alcohol. This 15 milliliters contains approximately 15 grams, or 15,000 milligrams of pure ethanol. If this is consumed by a 150-pound or 70-kilogram man, whose body weight is from 60 to 70 percent water, it is diluted in 50 liters, or 50,000 milliliters of fluid. As a result, the BAC of an average person who has consumed a one-ounce highball, a four-ounce glass of wine or a twelve-ounce can of beer is roughly 30 milligrams percent.

Even when present in higher concentrations, alcohol has an insignificant effect on blood vessels, including the coronary arteries that supply the heart. Because of this, alcohol cannot increase coronary blood flow and has no direct use in the treatment of people with coronary artery disease. Yet alcohol does cause a dilation of the skin vessels as a result of its depressant action on the central nervous system. This enhanced cutaneous blood flow, like the increased flow to the stomach that occurs in the presence of alcohol, creates a pleasant sensation of warmth. But this sensation is misleading, for heat is lost rapidly from the skin and the internal temperature falls as a result. Furthermore, with large amounts of alcohol, the temperature-regulating center of the central nervous system also becomes deactivated. Thus, taking alcoholic beverages to keep warm is both irrational and potentially dangerous.

In spite of its actions on the circulation, alcohol has only minor effects on the normal heart. Indeed, blood pressure, pulse, cardiac output, and the force of contraction of heart muscle do not change significantly after a moderate dose. Chronic administration can bring harmful changes, however, and even at acutely high dose levels, cardiac function may fail due to depression of the vasomotor center in the central nervous system. Yet this failure usually happens only after the brain's respiratory center has been affected. Decreased respiratory function, therefore, is the terminal event in many alcohol overdoses, and in most cases patients stop breathing before their hearts stop.

In the kidney, ethanol acts to increase urine output. Part of this diuresis is due to the large quantities of fluid included in alcoholic beverages, but the drug also suppresses release of the anti-diuretic hormone produced by the pituitary gland. This suppression occurs only when the BAC is rising, so most chronic drinkers are not dehydrated by alcohol itself but because they frequently vomit, have diarrhea, and lack other liquids in their diet. However, occasional drinkers who drink heavily during the evening often feel thirsty the next morning. This usually relates to the fact that they have smoked and exercised strenuously, thereby losing some of their body water in sweat. At the same time, they have not replaced the fluids lost during ethanol ingestion by drinking water before going to bed.

In addition to its action in suppressing anti-diuretic hormone, alcohol affects a few other parts of the endocrine system. These parts include the adrenal glands and the testes, both of which produce the major male sex hormone, testosterone. Testosterone synthesis is depressed by ethanol, a fact of great significance to male heavy drinkers who may become physically feminized and less sexually assertive by relative testosterone lack in the presence of female sex hormones which normally exist in small amounts within the body. Women also manufacture some testosterone, and although the depression of testosterone production by ethanol does not appear to make females more feminine by allowing their female sex hormones to predominate, it may decrease their sexual assertiveness by reducing testosterone levels. This finding is compatible with the observation that alcohol limits sexual functioning during acute intoxication and may help explain the passivity and sexual disinterest of many chronic drunkards.

In contrast to its depression of testosterone synthesis, ethanol produces a prompt increase in blood levels of other hormones manufactured by the adrenal glands and released during stress. These include cortisol, and epinephrine and norepinephrine, which are commonly known as adrenalin and noradrenalin. These latter two hormones, called catecholamines, are released by nerve endings throughout the body as well as by the adrenals and serve to relay information within the autonomic nervous system. Their increased circulatory concentration may be responsible for the dilation of the pupils, the slight rise in blood pressure, and some of the feeling of excitation which occurs during the early stage of alcohol ingestion. Similarly, their subsequent depletion, like that of cortisol, may cause a sense of depression after drinking stops.

Since increased catecholamine levels are associated with excitation, alcohol and other members of its class were once considered stimulants. Yet this apparent stimulation results not from an activation of one part of the central nervous system but from the operation of other portions which are depressed and, therefore, disinhibited by the drug. The cerebral cortex, that part of the brain concerned with perception, thought, memory, judgment, and other advanced mental functions, is not thought to be stimulated directly by alcohol. Instead, like other anesthetics, the drug exerts a depressant action on a more primitive area of the nervous system, the reticular activating system. This network of nerve cells, which is located in the brain stem, serves as a switchboard to integrate the activities of the central nervous system. When ethanol depresses the reticular activating system, the higher cortex apparently is released from the integrative process and those functions governed by the cortex are altered as a result.

These changes in mental activity are accompanied by alterations in sensory and motor functions. Spinal cord reflexes, such as the knee jerk which occurs in response to a physician's hammer, are at first enhanced as they are freed from inhibition. Yet as intoxication progresses, this phase of disinhibition is succeeded by a general depression and a diminution in spinal cord activity. Paralleling this is a progressive slowing in the electroencephalogram, which measures brain wave activity. This slowing may not be appreciated by the person drinking alcohol, whose sense of well-being and decreased anxiety make him or her feel capable of near perfect mental and physical performance. But onlookers usually sense the depression, and study after study has demonstrated in animals and humans alike that all but the most familiar and ingrained behavioral responses are impaired by alcohol.

The degree of this impairment correlates roughly with blood alcohol levels. At a BAC of 30 milligrams percent, for example, or after taking a one-ounce shot of distilled spirits, many people feel sedated and relaxed, while at a BAC of 50 milligrams percent they may evidence hyperactive reflexes and mild euphoria. At 100 milligrams percent, uncoordination is common. At 150 milligrams percent, reflexes are hypoactive and motor activity often is clumsy. At 200 milligrams percent, or after drinking eight one-ounce shots, most people stagger. At 300 milligrams percent, most are stuporous. BACs of 400 milligrams percent are associated with deep anesthesia. Death then may ensue with only a slight rise in the blood alcohol level.

The relatively slight difference between the intoxicating, anesthetizing, and lethal doses of ethanol underscores the fact that the margin of safety is lower with alcohol than with many sedative, hypnotic, and general anesthetic drugs. Thus, a person can tolerate five or ten times the therapeutic dose of sedatives such as diazepam, the trade name for which is Valium®, or Librium®, which is chlordiazepoxide, and not reach their anesthetizing dose. Similarly, most compounds used today as anesthetics induce loss of sensation and unconsciousness at levels far below their lethal dose. Since the lethal dose of ethanol is so close to the anesthetic dose, alcohol is both a dangerous drug in general and a hazardous general anesthetic, notwithstanding the therapeutics of Hippocrates or the hundreds of Hollywood cowboys who have endured surgical procedures with whiskey bottles at their lips.

Although the correlations between BACs and behavior are considered accurate enough for legal purposes, they do not always square with performance. For example, some inexperienced drinkers constitute a menace on the highway at alcohol levels well below the legal minimum for driving under the influence. Other chronic drinkers, on the other hand, can negotiate traffic with BACs of 150 milligrams percent, so great is their adjustment to ethanol. This adjustment is called tolerance, of course. Although it develops more slowly and to a lesser extent with alcohol than with other sedatives, hypnotics, and general anesthetics, and with narcotics, it is noteworthy nevertheless.

Investigators have tried to understand tolerance in terms of ethanol metabolism, reasoning that if a person detoxified the drug more rapidly after years of drinking, he or she would require higher doses to achieve the same initial effect. Traditionally, alcohol detoxification has been thought to occur through one metabolic pathway in the liver. In this so-called cytoplasmic oxidation pathway, the drug is oxidized in the presence of the enzyme alcohol dehydrogenase to acetaldehyde, which in turn is oxidized in the presence of acetaldehyde dehydrogenase to acetic acid. The acetic acid then enters the normal cycle of carbohydrate metabolism and is broken down to water and carbon dioxide, releasing energy in the process.

The enzyme alcohol dehydrogenase is ubiquitous in man

and varies little from person to person. Because of this, investigators have assumed that the rate of ethanol metabolism is constant among people. Yet this assumption conflicts with scientific studies, discussed in Chapter 6, which have demonstrated small but significant differences in rates of metabolism among individuals and perhaps even among ethnic groups. Furthermore, the assumption is incompatible with the idea of metabolically determined tolerance, for there is no way in which an individual can increase the amount of alcohol dehydrogenase in his or her liver and thereby increase ethanol metabolism.

Because of this incompatibility, Charles Lieber and his colleagues have investigated hepatic alcohol metabolism and have proposed an alternate metabolic pathway. This they call the microsomal ethanol oxidizing system. According to Dr. Lieber, the enzymes of the microsomal system can be induced, that is, increased in number and activity, if they are exposed to certain chemicals over prolonged periods. Alcohol is but one of these chemicals. Thus the microsomal enzymes that metabolize ethanol in the liver are responsible for the detoxification of other sedatives, hypnotics, and general anesthetics, as well as a multitude of other drugs.

Dr. Lieber believes that the cytoplasmic oxidation system accounts for the bulk of ethanol metabolism within the liver, especially in light and moderate drinkers. The percentage of alcohol that is detoxified by the microsomal system is very small in these people, somewhere around 5 percent. But the microsomal enzymes can contribute to upwards of 50 percent of ethanol metabolism if enough of the drug is ingested over a long and as yet undefined period by chronic heavy drinkers. Presumably this period is required for alcohol to induce hepatic microsomal enzymes.[5]

Dr. Lieber also states that the activity or inactivity of the microsomal ethanol oxidizing system accounts for the many interactions of alcohol and other sedatives, hypnotics, and general anesthetics. These interactions are either additive, in that ethanol and another drug produces a numerically combined action, or synergistic and antagonistic, in that the effects achieved by such a combination are either greater or less than the sum of the two parts. A simple additive interaction is seen in light drinkers who use sedatives like secobarbital, or Seconal®, to help them sleep. These persons may experience mild sedation if they combine a therapeutic dose of secobarbital with a small nightcap. But if they increase their ethanol consumption to combat insomnia, the additive effects of the alcohol and Seconal® may make them comatose.

In contrast, synergistic and antagonistic interactions occur in heavy drinkers who are affected markedly by sedatives like secobarbital when they are intoxicated acutely by ethanol, yet scarcely feel the effects of these chemicals when their drinking is chronic and are even more resistant when it stops. When these people start drinking and have not yet induced their microsomal enzymes, the microsomal system has a limited capacity and is employed exclusively for the detoxification of alcohol, allowing concentrations of other chemicals to mount in the blood. As the heavy drinkers continue drinking, their microsomal systems increase in activity and can be used to metabolize other drugs, lowering their blood concentrations in the process. When these individuals stop drinking, their microsomal enzymes, now induced by exposure to ethanol, are devoted to the rapid detoxification of other compounds because they need no longer metabolize alcohol.[6]

Beyond its biochemical significance and its use in explaining the interactions of ethanol and other compounds, the implication of the microsomal pathway proposed by Dr. Lieber is that the rate of alcohol metabolism, and hence tolerance to the drug, may vary among individuals depending on their exposure to alcohol. This variation cannot be explained on the basis of differences in the amount and activity of alcohol dehydrogenase among people, since the enzyme is ubiquitous in man and seems to vary little from person to person. Thus, as of this writing, Dr. Lieber's is the most credible explanation of the variation in rates of ethanol metabolism among drinkers.

Such variation has been demonstrated by many investigators, including the psychiatrist Jack Mendelson, who has shown that heavy drinking patients at the Boston City Hospital cleared alcohol from their blood faster than did temperate subjects.[7] Dr. Fenna and his fellow investigators at the University of Alberta have described the same phenomenon and also have shown that Eskimos and Canadian Indians seem to detoxify ethanol more slowly than whites and may remain intoxicated longer as a result.[8] Charles Lieber has criticized the design of this study, noting that in it hospitalized Indians were compared to healthy whites.[9] Furthermore, Lynn Bennion and Ting-Kai Li of the Phoenix Clinical Research Section recently conducted a comparable study of whites and American Indians and failed to confirm the Canadian results. Yet like their counterparts at the University of Alberta, Drs. Bennion and Li did demonstrate that chronic heavy drinking can accelerate the rate of metabolism of alcohol as well as other compounds, and that this effect is more pronounced among Indian subjects. Since these subjects were found to have the same form of liver alcohol dehydrogenase as the whites, the recent study from Phoenix lends further credence to Dr. Lieber's theory.[10]

Additional support is offered by the fact that ethanol metabolism can be altered acutely among patients by agents other than alcohol, again suggesting an individual metabolic variation. The rate of ethanol metabolism can be increased very slightly by injections of insulin, for example, and decreased during starvation. Similarly, Leah Lowenstein and other investigators at Boston City Hospital have demonstrated that intravenous infusions of the fruit sugar, fructose, can lower blood alcohol concentration by 43 percent compared to the values obtained by salt water or glucose infusions. The authors hypothesize that fructose or its metabolites may accelerate the dissociation of the complex formed by alcohol dehydrogenase and the enzymatic cofactor NAD, or nicotinamide adenine dinucleotide, making more of the enzyme available for ethanol detoxification. They note that "the practical benefit of intravenous infusions of fructose may lie in the reduction of morbidly high concentrations of alcohol in the blood of patients in emergency wards where sobering up, prior to the treatment of other complications, may be advantageous."[11]

Yet as generations of drinkers have discovered, there never

has been nor does there now exist a practical outpatient procedure to significantly lower the BAC. The stimulant caffeine in coffee may counteract some of the depressant effects of ethanol, as might a confrontation with the police, but neither of these methods rid the body of the drug. Furthermore, neither vigorous exercise, cold showers, nor oxygen inhalations can speed alcohol metabolism. Multivitamins and thyroid hormones are also useless, while diabetics taking regular insulin injections still do not clear alcohol from their blood much faster than nondiabetic individuals. Thus the fact that ethanol metabolism varies somewhat among individuals and can be altered by experimental procedures has limited clinical application at present.

Because of this, and in keeping with the traditional alcohol dehydrogenase model of metabolism, a fixed amount of ethanol is thought to be detoxified at a fixed rate. The rate of this detoxification is calculated at approximately 15 milliliters or 15 grams of absolute alcohol per hour in the average person. This 15 milliliters is equivalent to 30 milliliters or one ounce of 100-proof distilled spirits, which also contains 15 grams of ethanol. In the hypothetical 70 kilogram or 150-pound man, whose body weight is from 60 to 70 percent water, the 15 grams is diluted in 50 liters of fluid, so that the BAC is lowered at an hourly rate of 30 milligrams percent, the equivalent of a one-ounce highball. Thus, if one were to take only one drink per hour at a cocktail party, he or she would usually have a blood alcohol level of zero milligrams percent at the end of each hour.

This estimate of fixed rate metabolism is considered adequate for legal purposes and can be used by physicians to compute when an intoxicated person's blood alcohol level will return to zero. Yet the concept does not help doctors understand tolerance, which, if it is not linked to different rates of ethanol metabolism among individuals, must be due to other factors. Currently the most widely accepted theory is that, through poorly understood mechanisms, the central nervous system adapts to the actions of alcohol. Neurologists think that ethanol, like other depressants, causes a reduction in nervous system activity so that progressively higher doses of alcohol are required to produce a given effect. Psychologists call this phenomenon behavioral tolerance and believe that drinkers consciously or unconsciously learn to live with their drug and to compensate for the malcoordination it causes.

To illustrate behavioral tolerance, subjects can be given rapid intravenous infusions of ethanol and become intoxicated at, say, blood levels of 200 milligrams percent. If this blood level is maintained over several hours, the subjects appear to become sober even though the alcohol in their blood remains at a potentially intoxicating dose. If they then are given another rapid infusion, so that the BAC is doubled to 400 milligrams percent, the subjects again appear intoxicated. Yet if this level is again held constant for several hours, the subjects again appear sober, even though their blood now contains a substantial amount of ethanol.

This tolerance cannot be explained in terms of absorption, inasmuch as the subjects receive the drug intravenously and exhibit the same blood alcohol levels. Neither can it be explained in terms of excretion or metabolism, since the concentrations of ethanol in the blood of the subjects remains fixed, and since, as we have noted, metabolic rates vary only slightly among individuals and virtually neglible amounts of alcohol are excreted by the body. Thus, at the present time, tolerance can be explained only on the basis of cellular adaptation within the nervous system and the conscious or unconscious manifestation of this adaptation in terms of behavior.

Intimately related to this theory of tolerance is the abstinence state associated with ethanol. This state is so universal among depressant drugs that it is called by Jerome Jaffe the "general depressant withdrawal syndrome."[12] The basic principle underlying this syndrome is that those body systems, including the central and autonomic nervous systems, whose activity is suppressed by the administration of depressant drugs, are released at the time of drug withdrawal. Heroin and other narcotics, for example, cause the pupils to constrict and slow down the gastrointestinal tract, while abstinence from them brings diarrhea and pupillary dilation. Similarly, alcohol, barbiturates, and other sedative, hypnotic, and general anesthetic agents suppress epileptic seizures and other signs of nervous system activity during their administration and are associated with a higher incidence of seizures during withdrawal.

In an effort to explain these withdrawal manifestations, Dr. Jaffe has postulated that depressant drugs cause both a reduction in nervous system activity and a central nervous system sensitization to neurochemical agents, including epinephrine and norepinephrine.[13] This sensitization cannot be observed as long as the nerve cells are bathed by alcohol or other depressants, but when drugs are removed, the neurons are exposed to the catecholamines, and demonstrate markedly increased activity which is termed rebound hyperexcitability. This pattern is paralleled by blood levels of epinephrine and norepinephrine which initially rise when ethanol is given, fall during chronic administration of the drug, and then rise precipitously when it is withdrawn. It also corresponds to the agitated behavior that characterizes the alcohol abstinence syndrome.

Another explanation for the phenomenon of rebound hyperexcitability has evolved out of research into the effects of alcohol and other depressants on sleep. The most pronounced effects involve REM sleep, that part of the sleep cycle that is associated with disinhibition of the nervous system. During REM sleep, subjects experience vivid dreams and nightmares and also exhibit quickened pulses, penile erections, muscle twitches, and rapid eye movements, or REMs. This state, which occurs periodically during sleep, seems to be essential for normal functioning, and subjects deprived of REM sleep experience hallucinations and perceptual alterations. Alcohol and other depressants also suppress REM sleep in normal subjects, and although REM returns toward a normal level in chronic drinkers, apparently as a form of compensation, it occurs at a much greater frequency during withdrawal.

From these findings, Irwin Feinberg and E. V. Evarts have proposed that there is an inherent biological need or pressure for REM sleep which is suppressed by alcohol. The two psychiatrists also feel that when the suppression ends in abrupt abstinence, very high REM levels ensue as a result of the now nonopposed compensatory process. These high levels in themselves are not sufficient to intrude upon normal consciousness and cause perceptual disturbances, but when accompanied by increased nervous system irritability they can cause severe withdrawal effects.[14] Yet regardless of its severity, whether withdrawal occurs at all depends entirely on abstinence from ethanol and not on concurrent illnesses or nutritional deficiencies, as physicians once thought. Such abstinence need not be absolute, for withdrawal symptoms can be precipitated by a relative decrease in the BAC. Furthermore, withdrawal does not relate entirely to the duration of drinking or the dosage of alcohol.

Indeed, hangovers, which may be the mildest manifestation of the abstinence state, occur often after little more than an evening's intoxication. These forgettable experiences differ from person to person, but in general they encompass symptoms attributable to increased release of the catecholamines, epinephrine, and norepinephrine. These symptoms include irritability, headache, increased heart rate, dizziness, nausea, and vomiting. Hangovers also are characterized by bloodshot eyes and facial flushing, both of which reflect blood vessel dilation. In addition, sleep disturbance is common, often involving early morning awakening in the midst of a vivid dream and not knowing whether one is dreaming, and then tossing fitfully for the rest of the night. Each hangover victim has his or her variation from this familiar pattern, but electroencephalographic brain wave studies have confirmed that the waking coincides with and may be caused by a burst of REM which has been suppressed during the early hours of sleep as alcohol is metabolized, only to return in force during the early morning and confuse dream with reality.

Although some hangover symptoms seem to relate directly to ethanol withdrawal, others do not. For example, certain people experience headaches and a malaise which may be caused either by the known toxic effects of congeners contained in alcoholic beverages or by an idiosyncratic intolerance to them which is not, strictly speaking, an allergy. The fatigue which follows overactivity during drinking may also be important, as may be the food ingested or the nicotine and other chemicals absorbed in cigarette smoke. Similarly, some hangovers are characterized more by mood changes than by physical discomfort. These mood changes may relate to guilt over intoxication and its many implications. They also may or may not correlate with the varying catecholamine levels which occur with drinking and during withdrawal.

Since these and other factors may contribute to hangovers, some people may find their mornings after more tolerable if they change their eating, drinking, and smoking behavior the night before. However, when hangovers are primarily a withdrawal manifestation, as seems to be most often the case, little of their sting can be lessened by drinking beverages like vodka which are low in congeners or by substituting young white wine for the more aged red. No objective benefit can be gained by not mixing drinks, either, since the severity of most hangovers relates to the total amount, not the components, of ingested alcohol.

Most hangovers are equally impervious to special diets or health foods. Exercise is good for assuaging guilt and improving cardiovascular function, and since otherwise healthy people are not weakened by brief periods of intoxication, there is no contraindication in most persons to vigorous exercise after drinking alcohol. Like exercising, inhaling extra oxygen may give one the sensation of doing something good for his or her body. Yet as we have noted, neither can affect the rate of ethanol metabolism which is what causes the hangover in the first place. Even aspirin is contraindicated because of its corrosive effect on the gastrointestinal tract. Probably the most rational regimen against hangovers is to take small doses of analgesics with antacids and mild sedatives like Valium® and Librium® and to resist the impulse to terminate abstinence with more alcohol.

Clearly, since most hangovers are manifestations of an abstinence syndrome, their only true antidote is the proverbial hair of the dog. The trouble with this remedy is that the dog chases his tail, to mix metaphors, and in many but not all cases, the longer one forestalls the onset of withdrawal by continuing to drink the more severe will be his or her ultimate abstinence symptoms. Some individuals can manage these symptoms by themselves or with the help of private physicians and drying-out centers. Others lack such environmental supports and become conspicuous because they must use public facilities. These people usually run out of money, are robbed and beaten, or become sick with incidental or, more often, alcohol-related illnesses. They then are brought by the police or ambulance into public hospitals to undergo what most doctors now recognize as archetypal alcohol withdrawal.

This stereotyped abstinence syndrome was first described by Maurice Victor and Raymond Adams in a series of chronic heavy drinkers admitted to Boston City Hospital.[15] According to the two neurologists, the most common withdrawal manifestation that occurs during admission for another medical or surgical problem is a state called acute alcoholic tremulousness in medical parlance and, in the language of the streets, "the whips and the jangles." Patients with this problem usually have severe hangovers around 12 hours after the cessation of heavy drinking. Their eyes are bloodshot, their heads quake, their hearts race, they cannot eat or sleep, and they startle at the slightest stimulation. Many of these symptoms respond to sedation, and the external tremulousness usually subsides after a few days. Yet patients often report a persistent inner shakiness and are likely to seek relief in the bottle after being discharged.

After the hangover and acute tremulousness, the most frequent form of the alcohol abstinence syndrome is called transient hallucinosis by Drs. Victor and Adams. This condition is characterized not only by tremulousness but also by misinterpretations of sensory impressions, so that patients usually mistake visual or auditory stimuli; for example, they may overhear people talking and think that their names are being called. In addition to these sensory illusions, the patients also experience hallucinations in which they see or hear things that are entirely the products of their imaginations. The onset of these hallucinations, like the tremulousness, is generally around 12 hours after the onset of abstinence. Fortunately, the perceptual alterations usually pass in a few days.[16]

A variation on this theme is acute and chronic auditory

hallucinosis. The central feature in this illness is the occurrence of auditory hallucinations in people who are otherwise oriented to reality. The hallucinations almost always are vocal in nature, with voices that discuss the patients in a maligning or threatening fashion. The patients often respond as if the voices were real, and some even may attempt suicide if it is suggested. Only gradually do most patients realize that their hallucinations emanate from themselves. A few never achieve this realization and go on to develop organized paranoid delusions and other symptoms reminiscent of schizophrenia.

Another manifestation of withdrawal is called alcoholic epilepsy, or "rum fits." This condition is characterized by generalized seizures, involving involuntary shaking of the entire body, which occur from 12 to 48 hours following the end of drinking and from which patients remain free unless they begin the cycle of drinking and abstinence again. These seizures occur singly or in short bursts and are accompanied by an increased rate of breathing which leads to disturbances of the body's acid-alkali balance and to falling blood levels of magnesium, a mineral whose deficiency elevates the excitability of the nervous system. Doctors once thought that drinkers who had such seizures had underlying epilepsy, but electroencephalographic studies have demonstrated that this type of seizure can be duplicated only by withdrawing experimental animals or human subjects from alcohol. Nevertheless, patients with a history of previous withdrawal seizures should be treated prophylactically with the anti-convulsant drug, diphenylhydantoin, or Dilantin®, when they begin withdrawal.

The final and most dramatic aspect of the abstinence syndrome is a state of profound central and autonomic nervous system overactivity, disorientation, and disturbed perception. Physicians refer to this state as delirium tremens or the DTs; on skid row it is known as "the shakes and the horrors." The DTs almost invariably occur from 72 to 96 hours after the cessation of drinking and are often seen in chronic heavy drinkers who are hospitalized for surgery or serious illness. These patients become extremely restless, agitated, and unable to sleep. They thrash in bed, pick at their sheets, and sweat so profusely that they require many liters of intravenous fluids and minerals to remain in salt and water balance. Often the patients carry on incoherent conversations, shout demands at nonexistent people, or recoil from onrushing automobiles. They also may experience vivid hallucinations in which animal subjects, including pink elephants, are changed to small or giant size. Yet patients with delirium tremens also have lucid moments from time to time, indicating that many of their higher cerebral functions are intact and that they suffer primarily from a misinterpretation of reality.

In most cases the DTs end peacefully after several days. Patients then fall into a deep sleep which may last as long as 48 hours and generally is followed by little or no memory for events of the delirious period. Yet sometimes the delirium persists for months or abates and then recurs. Furthermore, in from 5 to 15 percent of patients, the DTs end fatally. Doctors once believed that such deaths were due not to delirium tremens as such but to intercurrent illness or nutritional problems. Yet although these factors were implicated in two-thirds of a series of 100 patient studies by Maurice Victor and Raymond Adams, one-third of the series died of extremely high temperatures and cardiovascular collapse without any identifiable underlying cause.[17]

Previously physicians like J. J. Smith, who is discussed in chapter 6, have attributed these deaths to exhaustion of the adrenal glands as manifested by depletion of cortisol and catecholamines. Yet these substances are not reduced in all patients, and their administration does not alter the course of the DTs. Furthermore, although people undergoing delirium tremens generally are dehydrated and deficient in body minerals, replacement of sodium, potassium, magnesium, and other salts does not reverse their condition. Post-mortem examinations fail to reveal structural changes in the cardiovascular and nervous systems, and at present medical science cannot explain why a certain percentage of patients with the DTs die.

One compelling thought is that delirium tremens is literally a living nightmare. This was first suggested by the French physician Charles Lesegue in his article, "Alcoholic Delirium Is Not a Delusion, It Is a Dream," which was published in

1881.[18] Since that time many investigators have been struck by the sleeplessness and profound central and autonomic nervous system excitation associated with the DTs. Recent studies by Ramon Greenberg and Chester Pearlman have revealed that patients entering delirium tremens have 100 percent REM patterns on the electroencephalogram. Increased REM levels are seen in all stages of withdrawal from ethanol, but it may be that certain persons with abnormally excitable nervous systems and generally poor health sustain some other insult before alcohol abstinence, and thus are overwhelmed by REM rebound during withdrawal.[19]

Given this possibility, many doctors sedate drinkers in severe withdrawal with drugs that do not suppress REM sleep, hoping that their patients can discharge their REM pressure in sleep rather than delirium. This treatment is compatible with the medical approach to all depressant abstinence states. As described by David E. Smith and Donald Wesson, this approach involves substituting long-acting preparations for their short-acting counterparts and then gradually decreasing dosages to prevent wide fluctuations in blood levels, thereby making withdrawal less dangerous and more comfortable. Two examples of this technique are the detoxification of heroin abusers with methadone and the withdrawal of abusers of the short-acting barbiturate, secobarbital, using the long-acting barbiturate, phenobarbital.[20]

Ethanol has no direct pharmacological equivalent as do these other drugs, but alcohol abstinence can be eased by sedatives like Librium® or Valium®. At the same time, tremulousness and other peripheral manifestations of catecholamine excess can be treated with the drug, propranolol, whose trade name is Inderal®. For all their usefulness, however, these preparations are not antidotes for heavy drinking. They cannot prevent withdrawal seizures, overcome nutritional deficiencies, or treat the seemingly inevitable medical problems associated with chronic abuse of alcohol.

5. FORGETFULNESS OF THINGS PAST

> *Watching Bernie carefully, I said nothing for a while. The jovial twinkle in his eyes faded, and he began to scowl in a bewildered fashion, like a little kid in a strange part of town. Because he was unable to hold recent memories more than a few seconds, everything was strange to Bernie. He seemed to live in the instantaneous present, which he interpreted either by suggestions or by incongruous images from his distant past. Filling his mental gaps with confabulation, he was almost content. Sorrow and bitterness, I reflected, were based on memory of the past.*
>
> *"What were we talking about?" I asked after a minute.*
> *"I'm just sitting here," he replied. "I haven't said nothing."*
>
> JOHN HEJINIAN, *Extreme Remedies* (1974)

The withdrawal syndrome we have described differs depending on the duration of drinking, the health of the drinker, and the circumstances in which drinking and abstinence occur. To an even greater extent, variability is seen in the medical complications associated with consumption of alcohol. Some of these complications are thought to stem from the direct toxicity of ethanol, a poison that inflames human tissues in dilute form and destroys them in higher concentrations. Others seem to happen because the drug affects enzyme systems within certain cells or alters metabolic processes throughout the body.

For the most part, the direct effects of alcohol appear to be dose related. Most of these effects are also cumulative, in that one must ingest a given amount of the drug over a certain length of time. Yet this cumulative effect may produce different changes in different people, and often it is difficult to determine whether dose or duration of drinking is more important. Since science is not certain about the relative importance of these two factors, the best advice we can offer drinkers is that, at present, the product of the two factors probably determines whether one will or will not encounter medical problems with ethanol.

While some of the medical problems we will discuss relate to the direct toxicity of alcohol, others result indirectly from the interaction of ethanol and other drugs. In the previous chapter, we described these interactions as being either additive or synergistic and antagonistic, and discussed the probability that they relate to the state of the microsomal enzyme oxidizing system spelled out by Charles Lieber. We illustrated all three forms of interaction through examples involving the combination of ethanol and other sedatives, hypnotics, and general anesthetics. Yet the interactions also occur when alcohol is ingested with compounds outside of its pharmacological class. For example, additive interactions are seen when people pour ethanol and aspirin into a sensitive stomach. Synergistic and antagonistic interactions, on the other hand, are commonly reported among patients taking anticoagulant drugs, such as dicumarol or Coumadin®, which are given to inhibit the clotting of blood. An enhanced anticoagulant effect often follows acute alcohol intoxication, presumably because ethanol has not yet induced dicumarol metabolism. In contrast, chronic alcohol abuse is associated with a diminished Coumadin® effect.

A final form of interaction relates more to an interference with ethanol metabolism than to the impact of alcohol in the detoxification of other drugs. This interference does not affect the microsomal ethanol oxidizing system described by Dr. Lieber but instead involves the cytoplasmic oxidation system which is thought to account for the bulk of alcohol metabolism in most people. The agent that most dramatically interferes with cytoplasmic oxidation is disulfiram or Antabuse®. Originally developed to toughen rubber and treat worm infestations, disulfiram has been found to inhibit the enzyme acetaldehyde dehydrogenase and thereby prevent the conversion of acetaldehyde, the first breakdown product of ethanol in cytoplasmic oxidation, to acetic acid. Acetaldehyde is extremely toxic, so much so that several scientists believe it is responsible for many of the medical complications of drinking. As it mounts in the blood, this chemical can cause confusion, nausea, vomiting, abdominal cramping, facial flushing, and a dangerous fall in blood pressure.

These symptoms, which are considered typical of an Antabuse® reaction, result when very small amounts of alcohol are ingested by persons taking disulfiram. The drug, therefore, can be administered to create unpleasant associations with ethanol and prompt people not to drink. Patients taking Antabuse® in even moderate quantities must be warned what to expect if they concurrently drink alcohol. In addition, they and other patients should be advised that the interaction of ethanol and certain other compounds can lead to minor disulfiram-like reactions. These compounds include chloramphenicol or Chloromycetin®, an antibiotic; chlorpropamide or Diabenese®, an oral agent used to lower blood sugar; and metronidazole or Flagyl®, a chemical used to treat genital infections caused by *Trichomonas vaginalis*, a protozoan parasite.

The incidence of major and minor Antabuse® reactions, as a fraction of the total number of interactions involving alcohol and other drugs, has increased proportionally with the growth of the pharmaceutical industry. Yet another and even larger group of medical problems associated indirectly with ethanol is less modern. These problems seem to result from nutritional deficiencies which can occur when the drug alcohol is consumed to the absolute or relative exclusion of vitamins, minerals, and other essential food substances.

Although they cross all social and economic lines, such complications are generally seen in public hospital patients who do not eat when they drink either because they cannot afford food, because their appetites are assuaged by the calories in alcoholic beverages, or because they learn that not eating can enhance intoxication. These persons lead lives characterized by trauma and physical neglect in some instances. As a result, determining the contribution of nutritional deficiency or life style to their health is extremely difficult. And since the same people may consume high doses of alcohol over a long duration, it is equally difficult to determine whether their medical complications are directly or indirectly related to alcohol.

Most of the medical complications and withdrawal symptoms associated with ethanol have been studied in these patients, just as many assumptions about heavy drinking have been drawn from them. Yet although public hospital patients are highly visible and have provided the medical profession with valuable insights, the studies of Don Cahalan and other investigators demonstrate that these patients represent a small percentage of the people who drink and have problems related to alcohol. This means both that other people have such problems and that the problems may be magnified in public patients. Because such patients drink heavily and are in poor health, they often appear with full-blown illnesses, whereas in most people the effects of ethanol are subclinical. Thus, it is difficult to generalize from experience with public hospital patients. All we can say with confidence is that they and other less obviously ill individuals should be regarded as points on a spectrum of disease.

This reservation reflects our inability to assess completely the medical impact of alcohol. We do know that ethanol alters every organ system in the body and that many of these changes are disruptive. In spite of this, however, we are uncertain whether ethanol is good or bad for a given drinker. Charles Becker believes that regular high dose alcohol consumption over a ten-year period reduces the average person's life span by an equal amount.[1] Yet teetotalers also turn out to have shortened life expectancies, while recent studies suggest that moderate drinkers live longer than either chronic heavy drinkers or abstainers. This may be because moderate drinkers enjoy better health or because their drinking behavior reflects a more adaptive social or psychological attitude. And although few medical authorities have made the suggestion, the longer lives of moderate drinkers also may be due to alcohol.

In spite of these uncertainties, the biological consequences of drinking are both scientifically interesting and of importance to drinkers and their families. Therefore, we consider it appropriate to describe these consequences in some detail, stressing that although microscopic and biochemical changes occur after all drinking, they may be personally, socially, and medically insignificant. Current research is demonstrating that many of these changes are in fact dose-related and not due primarily to nutritional or life style factors. However, we cannot say yet who will or will not manifest alcohol-related illness. Nor can we help drinkers predict if or when small alterations will become significant enough to express themselves as disease.

For example, in all drinkers ethanol irritates the mucous membranes that line the gastrointestinal tract. It will sting the lips and, when swallowed in undiluted form, causes a characteristic burning of the mouth and throat. The drug then reaches the stomach, where it disturbs the integrity of mucous-secreting cells, increasing their vulnerability to gastric acid. Alcohol also enhances gastric acid secretion and, by doing so, helps activate the digestive enzyme pepsin, which further irritates the stomach mucosa and can cause small erosions. These few events cause an inflammation of the stomach which is called gastritis. Most people are unaware of this condition or ignore their mild symptoms. But in its more severe forms, especially when erosions predominate, the gastritis may be a source of nausea and vomiting, pain, or bleeding.

Another condition that is associated with drinking is peptic ulcer disease. Peptic ulcers are large erosions which extend through the stomach lining into the underlying muscle layer and occasionally perforate the wall of the gastrointestinal tract. The exact etiology of peptic ulcer disease is uncertain, but in most people it is thought to relate to an increased secretion of gastric acid and a vulnerability to the acid's effects. There is a higher incidence of new peptic ulcers among drinkers than among nondrinkers, presumably because ethanol enhances gastric acid secretion and damages the stomach mucosa. Alcohol is also known to retard the healing of ulcers in people who already have them. As a result, patients are advised to discontinue drinking if they have peptic ulcer disease.

As alcohol passes from the stomach into the small bowel, where most of it is absorbed, the drug causes an inflammation and swelling of the intestinal surface. This inflammation is rarely associated with erosion of the intestinal mucosa because gastric acid is neutralized and pepsin is inactivated by the alkaline environment of the intestine. But the swelling can block ducts draining the pancreas, which has been stimulated to produce protein and fat-splitting enzymes by the concurrent secretion of gastric acid. Unable to reach the gastrointestinal tract where they ordinarily act, the pancreatic enzymes have no recourse but to digest the organ that has produced them. This may lead to a condition called pancreatitis which is accompanied by nausea, vomiting, and stabbing pain radiating from the front of the abdomen to the back.

Occasionally the pancreatic stimulation is so great that enzymes burst from the organ into the abdominal cavity. The enzymes then may eat into blood vessels, cause intra-abdominal bleeding and lead to cardiovascular collapse. Fortunately, such hemorrhagic pancreatitis is relatively rare, and those few drinkers who develop pancreatitis usually only suffer a form of the disease which is characterized by swelling of the pancreas. But if those who have acute pancreatitis continue drinking, they may develop a chronic relapsing condition in which their organs are autodigested, replaced by scar tissue, and unable to produce insulin or digestive enzymes. This disorder is called pancreatic insufficiency. It is treated by the administration of supplemental enzymes and insulin.

Alcohol has a profound effect on the pancreas, but the liver remains its principal target. Long regarded as the seat of the soul, the liver was demoted in status by Plato, who placed the higher emotions above the diaphragm and the baser appetites, including love of poetry and music, below. Medicine has since stripped the liver of these functions but nevertheless considers it an indispensable organ. As if in recognition of this indispensability, the liver, to a point, is capable of self-regeneration. In health it is occupied with the synthesis of protein from dietary amino acids, the metabolism of fat and carbohydrate, the manufacture of factors that aid in blood clotting, and the detoxification of drugs and nitrogen-containing compounds, including ammonia, which are produced by colonic bacteria or ingested in the diet.

Ethanol is toxic to the liver because it is metabolized exclusively within that organ. We have noted that this metabolism occurs through two different pathways, one of which, in the presence of the enzymes alcohol dehydrogenase and acetaldehyde dehydrogenase, involves the conversion of alcohol into acetaldehyde and acetic acid. Since this process is oxidative, hydrogen ions are generated. These ions in turn accumulate in the liver, where they interfere with the chemistry of the hepatic cells. In an effort to rid themselves of the excess ions, the cells shunt them into metabolic pathways of several other substances, often with harmful results.

According to Charles Lieber, one such pathway is the process whereby amino acids, which are derived from the breakdown of proteins, are transformed into an intermediate compound called pyruvate and then into the simple sugar glucose. This process, which is termed gluconeongenesis, normally results in a rise in the blood sugar level and is a part of the body's response to stress. However, in the presence of hydrogen ions from ethanol, the pyruvate is converted into lactic acid instead of glucose. The lactic acid then accumulates in the blood, changing the body's acid-alkali balance and causing in a few extreme cases a condition called lactic acidosis. Like other forms of acidosis, this condition is characterized by progressive depression of the central nervous system, manifested as agitation, stupor, and ultimately death.[2]

Lactic acid accumulates even in heavy drinkers who do not have an acidosis, and as it does so it is transported to the kidney. There the substance may interfere with the excretion of uric acid, an inevitable by-product of normal cell turnover. In persons whose metabolism of uric acid may only have been subtly abnormal, the unexcreted uric acid can crystallize in body tissues, especially in joint spaces, where it produces pain, swelling, and extreme tenderness to the touch. This condition, which is called gout or gouty arthritis, has been associated historically with rich foods and heavy drinking. Hogarth prints have not inaccurately pictured rotund English port fanciers with toes that are swollen with gout. With an understanding of how alcohol can increase lactic acid levels and thereby disturb uric acid production, we can appreciate how gout, a hereditary condition of these and other people, is aggravated by ethanol.

Even more dramatic than these actions of alcohol is its impact on carbohydrate metabolism. When carbohydrates are ingested, they are broken down by enzymes in the intestines into several simple sugars, including glucose. The glucose then is absorbed and passes via the bloodstream to cells throughout the body. Normally, insulin, a hormone made by the pancreas, helps deposit the glucose in the cells, where it is metabolized to create most of our energy. The excess glucose is then transported to the liver, where it is stored in the form of a complex sugar called glycogen.

In normal people, blood glucose is kept at a fairly constant level through several mechanisms. One is the production of insulin by the pancreas and its release in response to the elevated blood levels of glucose. Other mechanisms are the conversion of hepatic glycogen into glucose or the creation of glucose from dietary amino acids or from protein which is broken down in the body. When normal people lower their intake of glucose, as occurs between meals or during a period of fasting, the latter two mechanisms maintain a constant blood sugar level. Conversely, when normal people eat heartily, insulin prevents glucose from mounting in the blood. A condition called hyperglycemia results from an abnormally high blood glucose level, while hypoglycemia occurs when there is too little glucose in the blood.

Hypoglycemia takes many forms, one of which is associated with ethanol. Called alcoholic hypoglycemia, this condition is seen in some chronic heavy drinkers who are extremely malnourished. Since starvation has depleted the glycogen stores in their livers, they cannot mobilize this source of glucose to raise their levels of blood sugar. And their increased levels of hepatic hydrogen ions prevents them from making glucose out of amino acids via gluconeogenesis. Because of these two factors, the drinkers have no reserve supply of glucose. Although they can gain immediate energy from ethanol, their blood sugar levels fall when they do not eat.

Receptors in the central nervous system, which is nourished exclusively by glucose, sense this fall and stimulate the release of epinephrine and norepinephrine. The catecholamines could induce the formation of glucose from glycogen and amino acids in normal people. But in these malnourished drinkers, the stimulation cannot restore blood sugar levels and serves only to increase perspiration, tremulousness, heart rate, anxiety, and other manifestations of catecholamine excess. Drenched in sweat, their hearts racing, these patients may pass out or sink into a fatal coma unless sugar is given to reverse the symptoms. Fortunately, most moderate drinkers never experience alcoholic hypoglycemia and have no need for extra sugar. But glucose can be life-saving in heavy drinkers with alcoholic hypoglycemia.

An alternate problem is alcoholic hyperglycemia, a condition that is seen in some well nourished rather than starved ethanol abusers. In such persons, whose epinephrine and norepinephrine levels are increased by ethanol intake, the conversion of glycogen to glucose within the liver produces a rise in blood sugar. Normally insulin would assist the cells throughout the body in utilizing this glucose and thereby would lower the blood level. Yet these few heavy drinkers either have pancreatic insufficiency or are insulin resistant, a state relatively common in middle-aged persons, so they cannot appropriately lower their blood glucose levels.

The hyperglycemic state that results is well tolerated over a short period of time by most people, who complain only of sluggishness and a sick feeling. But it is dangerous in diabetics, who lack or have a profound resistance to insulin in the first place. Thus, certain diabetics who cannot regulate their blood sugar levels well and wish to drink heavily are caught in a difficult, if not untenable position. If they ingest food along with alcohol, they may become hyperglycemic. Yet if they do not eat, hypoglycemia may result.

In severe diabetics, profound hyperglycemia may be accompanied by diabetic ketoacidosis. This condition occurs when, because of insulin lack or resistance, the body's cells cannot use glucose. Deprived of this source of energy, the cells turn to an alternate system, the oxidation of fats. These fats in turn are broken down to ketone bodies, acidic substances which accumulate in the blood and cause an injurious acid-alkali imbalance. Although diabetic ketoacidosis is not caused by alcohol, it can be aggravated in diabetic drinkers.

As will be discussed, the more these people burn ethanol, the less they metabolize fat. The fat then accumulates, providing a source of ketones.

A related condition, called alcoholic ketoacidosis, occurs in the absence of diabetes. Seen primarily in women for reasons which are poorly understood, this condition occurs when ethanol and hypoglycemia combine to raise catecholamine levels. The catecholamines in turn spark the conversion of fats into ketone bodies, causing a ketoacidosis. The acid-alkali imbalance caused by ketones may be increased by a concurrent lactic acidosis, the mechanism of which is described above. Diabetic ketoacidosis is treated with insulin, which pushes glucose into cells and allows the body to burn sugar instead of fat. Patients with alcoholic ketoacidosis have ample supplies of insulin but need glucose to restore normal carbohydrate metabolism.

Just as ethanol profoundly influences carbohydrate metabolism, so does it affect the metabolism of fats. Fat normally serves as a major energy source within the liver, but the plentiful hydrogen ions which result from the breakdown of alcohol suppress the oxidation of hydrogen ions from fats. The unmetabolized fats are allowed to accumulate in the liver, while at the same time, the excess hydrogen ions from ethanol are being diverted directly into the synthesis of other fatty substances. And when alcohol is ingested in large quantities, it can spark the release of hormones which mobilize fat from stores throughout the body and move it towards the liver.

According to Dr. Lieber, the liver has several ways of dealing with this excess fat. One way is to store the fat within the liver cells, as will be discussed further. Another is to wrap the fat in layers of protein, creating so-called lipoproteins which are water soluble and hence can be released into the blood. This process is paralleled by an increased production of cholesterol within the liver. Since both the lipoproteins and the cholesterol are synthesized by the enzymes of the microsomal ethanol oxidizing system described by Dr. Lieber, these substances are increased in number during prolonged periods of heavy alcohol consumption. They then are delivered into the blood.[3]

Thus in contrast to the popular notion that ethanol decreases fats in the blood stream, it actually leads to a rise in the blood levels of cholesterol and other lipoproteins. These two substances have been implicated in atherosclerotic cardiovascular disease, or "hardening of the arteries," as it is popularly known. Atherosclerosis is a condition in which plaques containing lipoproteins and cholesterol are formed within the walls of blood vessels, including the coronary arteries that supply the heart, resulting in heart attacks, stroke, or a compromise of blood flow to the limbs. The rise in blood levels of cholesterol and lipoproteins is small but detectable in all drinkers and may or may not be medically significant. Yet since the rise may contribute to atherosclerosis, patients with heart problems are at some risk from drinking. Furthermore, in those people who have a genetic predisposition to high blood cholesterol and lipoproteins and therefore to more atherosclerosis, alcohol is thought to exacerbate their underlying disease.

A final way for the liver to dispose of excess fat is to convert it into ketone bodies, as we have mentioned. The ketones, which are water soluble, can be released into the blood, causing a ketoacidosis. As noted above, ketones are found in both diabetic and alcoholic ketoacidosis. In diabetic ketoacidosis, they occur because the body cannot obtain energy from glucose and instead oxidizes fat and thereby creates ketones. Patients with alcoholic ketoacidosis also cannot properly metabolize glucose. Because they have increased hepatic fat stores, these patients produce a large amount of ketones.

Although alcoholic ketoacidosis is an uncommon condition, its existence emphasizes the significance of ethanol in the metabolism of fats and carbohydrates. This significance is underscored by recent studies which demonstrate that as little as one night of moderate drinking can double the amount of fatty acids in the blood of healthy subjects. Along these lines, Charles Lieber and his colleagues have shown that the substitution of alcohol for dietary carbohydrate or the addition of ethanol to the regular diets of nondrinkers will lead to fat deposition in the liver in only two days.[4] Dr. Lieber has produced the same findings in laboratory rats and baboons, which, like the human subjects, never reach intoxicating blood levels during the studies.[5]

This state of fat accumulation is called alcoholic fatty liver or hepatosis. Inflammation is not a feature of fatty liver, and the condition is not linked with symptoms other than the sense of pressure and fullness which is caused by a large liver displacing other organs in the abdominal cavity. Furthermore, hepatosis is completely reversible, assuming that patients stop drinking at an as yet unquantified point. But if they maintain a prolonged high dose ethanol consumption, some may progress to a condition called alcoholic hepatitis which is far more severe.

Hepatitis is a nonspecific term used to denote an inflammation of the liver which usually is accompanied by death of liver cells. It may be caused by viruses or drugs, including alcohol. Most cases of hepatitis are unrecognized because of their mildness, but patients admitted to hospitals with the disease usually feel quite sick and manifest fever, fatigue, aching joints, abdominal pain, a rise in enzymes reflecting damage to and destruction of liver cells, and some indication of hepatic insufficiency. Ethanol abusers do not differ from other hepatitis victims in their clinical presentation, but when they are undernourished and afflicted by other disorders, they may have a more severe illness. And even when it is diagnosable only by laboratory tests, alcoholic hepatitis often accompanies or serves as a precursor to cirrhosis, or chronic liver disease.

The term cirrhosis comes from the Greek word *kirrhos,* meaning tawny, a reference to the color of livers in people with the disease. Cirrhosis applies to all forms of chronic liver disease characterized microscopically by widespread loss of liver cells and their replacement by scar tissue. An important early result of the loss of these cells is a decrease in the liver's manufacturing function. With this decrease, the organ is no longer able to synthesize protein. When this situation is combined with malnutrition, it leads to wasting of the muscles of the arms and legs. The patients' abdomens then swell with large livers infiltrated with fat and with fluid, called ascites, which leaks from blood vessels because protein loss lowers the osmotic pressure of the blood. The patients ultimately come to resemble persons suffering from kwashiorkor, or protein deficiency. In addition, their livers cannot make clotting factors, giving them an increased tendency to bleed.

This defect in the manufacture of protein and clotting factors is paralleled by a loss of the liver's detoxifying function. This in turn leaves patients extremely sensitive to the effects of ethanol and other drugs which are metabolized by the organ. Males also cannot detoxify estrogens, the female sex hormones that are found in both sexes. When this condition is coupled with an underproduction of testosterone, the male sex hormone, they may become feminized with atrophy of the testicles, proliferation of breast tissue, loss of body hair, and impotence. The liver furthermore becomes unable to metabolize bilirubin, a pigment resulting from the turnover of red blood cells, which backs up in the blood stream and lends a yellow color to the skin and eyes which is called jaundice.

While this is occurring, scarring disrupts the pattern of capillary blood flow in the liver. This tends to increase pressure in the blood vessels that supply the organ, including the portal vein draining the intestines. The resultant portal vein hypertension shunts blood and ammonia and waste products by the liver and its now meager detoxifying mechanisms and into the body's general circulation, where the ammonia and waste products act to enhance central nervous system depression, through a process which is called hepatic encephalopathy. Ascites production is increased as fluid is squeezed out of the liver. At the same time, the portal hypertension causes a backup of blood throughout the abdominal circulation, swelling the neighboring spleen and creating venous shunts, called varices, which carry blood by the liver. Among the veins used for this purpose are the hemorrhoidal veins inside the anus, which may become distended and burst. Other varices are created in the esophagus, where the esophageal veins may rupture because of increased portal vein pressure and flood the esophagus and neighboring stomach with blood.

Many cirrhotic patients in hepatic failure die because of massive gastrointestinal bleeding from the esophagus or anus, but vigorous medical therapy can overcome acute exacerbations of their illness. Mechanical devices are available to compress varices, for example, and surgical procedures can reduce portal vein pressure. At the same time, blood products can be administered to offset bleeding and bolster the body's clotting mechanisms. Patients in hepatic coma also may improve when blood and bacteria, both of which contribute to ammonia production, are purged from the bowel, and when dietary protein is reduced. In addition, salt and water can be withheld to ease fluid retention, and ascites may respond to diuretic therapy.

Yet even with these measures, cirrhosis follows an inexorable course unless treatment is aimed at its underlying cause. Certain forms of the disease are partially reversible, including one which follows viral hepatitis, another which results from copper deposition in the liver, and a third seen among South African natives who ingest large amounts of iron. But the most common form of the disease seen in Western Europe and the United States, Laennec's cirrhosis, which follows chronic heavy drinking, is irreversible. It can be arrested, but only with complete abstinence from alcohol.

So close is the relationship between ethanol and Laennec's cirrhosis that E. M. Jellinek once devised a formula whereby the incidence of alcoholism within a community could be calculated from records of deaths attributed to cirrhosis.[6] Unfortunately, cirrhosis is often an autopsy diagnosis, and Dr. Jellinek's formula singled out cities like San Francisco, whose aggressive coroners' offices perform a large number of autopsies on public hospital patients, search for cirrhosis, and report a higher incidence of this condition than do other areas. Dr. Jellinek's formula is not regarded today as a very accurate method for measuring alcoholism. Yet it is employed by some to approximate the incidence of this condition, and its use underscores the fact that cirrhosis is associated closely with alcohol.

In spite of this close association, however, only 10 percent of persons known to be alcohol abusers carry the diagnosis of chronic liver disease. This circumstance has been used for years to buttress the claim that cirrhosis relates more to malnutrition than to ethanol. Yet kwashiorkor or severe protein deficiency, which can lead to fatty liver, does not cause cirrhosis, and cirrhosis has not been seen among concentration camp survivors. That not all chronic heavy drinkers have been proven to have cirrhosis may reflect the fact that their illness is not clinically apparent and demonstrable only by liver biopsy, or that they have been examined too early in the course of their disease.

The current hypothesis that chronic liver disease is an inevitable consequence of long-term alcohol abuse is supported by the work of Charles Lieber and his colleagues with baboons. When these animals, whose livers closely resemble those of humans, are given alcohol as part of or in addition to otherwise normal diets, they develop hepatosis, hepatitis, and cirrhosis which cannot be induced solely by malnutrition.[7] Comparable studies cannot be performed in human subjects for ethical reasons, but the studies of Dr. Lieber and years of clinical experience suggest that alcoholic hepatosis, alcoholic hepatitis, and alcoholic cirrhosis are caused more by the direct toxicity of ethanol than by faulty diets, and that all three conditions are part of a spectrum that should be called alcoholic liver disease.

Since this spectrum seems to relate more to drug toxicity than to diet, drinkers should not rely on vitamins, minerals, or other substances to offset the hepatic effects of ethanol. Yet the liver does regenerate to a certain extent, and alcoholic fatty liver is a reversible condition. Because of this, physicians have recommended that even moderate drinkers curtail their ethanol consumption for a few days each week or a week each month to allow their livers to return to normal. This recommendation is theoretically sound and may be clinically correct. Equally correct is the position that patients with nonalcoholic hepatitis should refrain from drinking to let their livers rest, while patients with alcoholic hepatitis or cirrhosis should abstain from ethanol forever.

Abstinence is also recommended for a comparatively rare condition called alcoholic muscle disease, or alcoholic myopathy. This disorder occurs in some chronic heavy drinkers who sustain either a diffuse weakness or decreased strength in the large muscles of their thighs, making it difficult for them to climb stairs or rise from a chair. Persons with alcoholic myopathy generally have elevated blood levels of certain enzymes which are released by damaged muscle tissue, while biopsies reveal their muscle cells to be laden with fat. Fortunately, this disorder often resolves with the cessation of drinking and rarely is crippling. But the outcome is less optimistic and the consequences more severe when alcoholic myopathy involves the muscle of the heart.

Doctors have long known that ethanol in small amounts has little effect on the hearts of normal persons, and the only associations between alcohol and cardiac problems have been assumed to be nutritional. One such association was noted in Quebec, where a number of drinkers developed irregularities in heart function which ultimately were linked with the cobalt that local brewers were using to stabilize the foam in their beer. A second association is with beriberi, a well-known type of nutritional heart disease. Beriberi takes two forms, one that is characterized by such neurological manifestations as weakness, muscle wasting, and a pins-and-needles feeling in the hands and feet, and another in which the heart enlarges and pumps blood less effectively. Both types of beriberi were seen first in Asians eating polished rice from which vitamin B_1, or thiamine, had been milled. During World War II they were witnessed in Japanese prisoner of war camps, and, thereafter, were reported in alcohol abusers in the United States.

These chronic drinkers were generally older persons whose diets were shown to be deficient in many vitamins, including B_1. In recent years, however, the clinical picture has emerged of relatively younger and more healthy drinkers, usually men, who have no history of cardiac problems but experience symptoms of heart failure of insidious and occasionally explosive onset and do not respond to thiamine. Their failure involves all heart chambers and results in a decreased cardiac output which is compromised severely during exercise. X-rays show their hearts to be large, flabby, and inefficient. Blood studies reveal elevated enzymes reflecting destruction of cardiac muscle, or myocardium. Post-mortem microscopic examination discloses fat accumulation and cell death without evidence of atherosclerosis or other common types of heart disease.

These same findings have been demonstrated by George

Burch and Thomas Giles in laboratory rats fed normal diets supplemented with ethanol.[8] Similarly, Lawrence Gould and his colleagues have shown that alcohol, although seemingly harmless in light drinkers with normal hearts, can decrease cardiac function in patients with pre-existing heart disease.[9] From these and other studies has evolved the increasingly strong suspicion that ethanol is a direct myocardial depressant capable of producing clinical and subclinical forms of heart muscle injury, or cardiomyopathy. Abstinence, along with bed rest, is the only treatment for this illness, and moderation is advisable for all persons with nonalcohol-related heart disease.

Abstinence or moderation are also recommended for patients with disturbances of their heart rhythm, which are called arrhythmias. This is because ethanol is known to interfere with the conduction system which transmits electrical impulses between the various cardiac chambers and thereby regulates the rhythm of the heart. This interference is insignificant in the great majority of drinkers, although characteristic changes in the electrocardiogram, a device which records cardiac rhythm, may be produced by only a few drinks. Yet some persons whose conduction systems are already scarred by atherosclerosis may develop serious arrhythmias from a single cocktail, if only as a result of the effects of catecholamines in disturbing the heart's rhythm and accelerating its rate.

In addition to its impact on the heart, ethanol in large amounts is associated with disorders of all three major components of the blood, or hematological system. These components include red blood cells, which contain the hemoglobin essential for oxygen transport; white blood cells, which fight infection by engulfing and digesting invasive microorganisms; and platelets, which are needed for blood clotting. Many of the adverse hematological effects of alcohol are due to its direct depressant action on the bone marrow, the site of red cell, white cell, and platelet production. Another reason is the inadequate dietary intake of certain vitamins and minerals. These include iron, which is used in hemoglobin synthesis; vitamin B_6 or pyridoxine, which stabilizes red cell membranes; vitamin B_{12}, abnormalities of which are associated with pernicious anemia; and folic acid, an enzyme cofactor which participates in many metabolic processes.[10]

Folic acid is abundant in leafy vegetables and meat, substances that alcohol abusers may go without. In addition, ethanol seems to interfere with the absorption and utilization of the vitamin. The net effect of these several factors is that red cells are manufactured within the bone marrow in distorted form and decreased quantity in drinkers who are folic acid deficient. This leads to an anemia, or red cell deficiency, which is termed megaloblastic because of characteristic red cell deformities. Another form of anemia associated with alcohol, called sideroblastic, is related to pyridoxine deficiency and results in abnormalities in the storage of iron. Added to this may be a decreased iron ingestion which leads to inadequate red cell production.

These so-called combined alcoholic anemias are frequently accompanied by abnormal destruction of red blood cells through the process of hemolysis. Such hemolysis occurs in part within the blood stream, where irregularly shaped red blood cells produced by the bone marrow burst apart. If they survive this, the cells may be caught up in the reticular network of the spleen, which increases in size in patients with cirrhosis and portal hypertension. Of course, the same patients are subject to many forms of gastrointestinal bleeding, which is a common source of red blood cell loss.

The action of ethanol on white blood cells is also due to a combination of loss, destruction, and decreased production. Like red blood cells, white cells are manufactured in the bone marrow and are subject to alcohol's depressant effect. Similarly, folic acid deficiency leads to megaloblastic changes in the white cells, which in addition may be trapped in the spleen or lost from bleeding. The net effect is to decrease the number of leukocytes which can be called upon to resist infection. The white blood cells of alcohol abusers also seem less able to digest certain bacteria.

Furthermore, ethanol depresses the activity of the cells that line the respiratory tract. These cells secrete mucus, which traps bacteria and other substances, and also contain cilia, hair-like projections that sweep back and forth in unison. This sweeping motion creates a so-called mucociliary blanket which forces foreign substances trapped in mucus toward the mouth, where they can be swallowed or expectorated. The mucociliary blanket can be paralyzed directly both by alcohol and by the nicotine in cigarettes. When such paralysis occurs, microorganisms are allowed to invade the respiratory tract. Pneumonia and other respiratory tract infections may result from this invasion, especially in persons whose lung tissue has been damaged by prolonged cigarette smoking. The smoking which many chronic heavy drinkers engage in, coupled with ethanol's actions on white blood cells and on the mucociliary blanket, make these drinkers particularly vulnerable to respiratory disease.

A final common hematological abnormality in alcohol abusers is a decrease in the platelet count, which is called thrombocytopenia. This decrease results in part from bone marrow depression, in part from folic acid deficiency, and in part from the platelets being sequestered in the spleen. Healthy persons may have a fall in their platelets after heavy drinking, and Charles Lieber and his coworkers have demonstrated a mild decrease in platelets in nondrinkers who have been administered ethanol in small amounts along with normal diets.[11] Fortunately, this decrease in platelets is clinically insignificant in most drinkers and is reversible. But when accompanied by liver disease in certain patients, it predisposes to potentially life-threatening bleeding.

If gastrointestinal bleeding were not enough, some chronic heavy drinkers also experience disorders of the nervous system. The most common of these disorders in the entire drinking population are ethanol intoxication and the subsequent withdrawal syndrome. The next most frequent from a hospital standpoint are neurological diseases consequent upon alcoholic cirrhosis and portal hypertension, in which toxic substances are shunted by the liver and reach the central nervous system. Also seen commonly in hospitals are the effects of head trauma in heavy drinkers. These run the gamut from simple concussions and loss of consciousness to the punch drunk syndrome, dementia pugilistica, which in boxers, and presumably in drinkers, relates to the number of knockouts they have sustained.

Other common results of head trauma are collections of blood localized within organs or tissues, which are called hematomas. Epidural and subdural hematomas are so named because they result from tears in blood vessels which lie either between the skull and dura, the membranes covering the brain, or between the membrane and the brain itself. The hematomas can occur acutely after injury to the skull or accumulate gradually, and in either case they may be manifested clinically in a number of ways. Since they generally, but not always, are one-sided, they may spark so-called focal seizures in which patients involuntarily move only parts or one side of their bodies. These convulsions are quite different from the generalized seizures seen in alcohol abstinence and should prompt investigation of their underlying cause.

Along with hematomas and other problems related to trauma, some alcohol abusers also suffer from nutritional disorders of the nervous system. The most common of these is a condition which is characterized by numbness, tingling, muscle weakness, depressed reflexes, and a burning sensation in the hands and feet, and is called alcoholic peripheral neuropathy. Noted throughout history in heavy drinkers, this condition today is equated with degeneration of cells in the peripheral nervous system, which includes nerve tissue existing outside of the brain or spinal cord. Peripheral neuropathy is seen in beriberi and other disorders of malnutrition. Vitamin B_1 deficiency is felt to contribute to the condition among ethanol abusers, and alcoholic peripheral neuropathy may respond to replacement of thiamine and other vitamins.

The Wernicke-Korsakoff syndrome is the most dramatic nutritional disorder seen among drinkers with peripheral neuropathies. Although this condition is now regarded as a syndrome, it once was thought to be two separate entities. The first was Wernicke's disease, described by the German neurologist Carl Wernicke in 1881 in three patients, two of whom were chronic inebriates and one of whom was a young seamstress with persistent vomiting following the ingestion of sulphuric acid. Albeit for different reasons, all these patients were physically wasted due to malnutrition. All three also demonstrated a confusion characterized by disorientation, apathy, and inattentiveness. In addition, they could not walk heel-to-toe and, instead, lurched from side to side like stereotyped inebriates. This disorder of balance is called ataxia.

Furthermore, the three patients had profound ocular disturbances. They manifested nystagmus, rhythmical oscillations of the eyeballs, and had gaze paralyses which resulted in their eyes being locked in certain positions. Later patients also complained of episodes of transient partial blindness in which spots would interfere with their vision. Called retrobulbar neuropathy, this problem was thought to be due to abnormalities within the optic nerve which conveys visual images to the brain from the retina. It and the other ocular disorders often responded to proper nourishment, leading Dr. Wernicke to suspect that the clinical entity, which he called hemorrhagic polioencephalitis, was a nutritional disease.[12]

Six years later, the Russian psychiatrist Sergei Korsakoff described a unique mental disorder which was accompanied by signs of peripheral neuropathy in 44 patients, 30 of whom were alcohol abusers. A few of these patients were as completely confused as were those of Dr. Wernicke in the early stages of their illness, but after clearing somewhat they and the others still manifested a disturbance in learning and memory out of proportion to defects in other areas of cognitive functioning. The patients could handle reality from moment to moment, but manifested a retrograde amnesia in which they could not recall in proper sequence events well established before the onset of their illness. Even more striking was an antegrade amnesia in which they could not assimilate new information, including details of their interviews with Dr. Korsakoff.

As part of this disturbance, the patients seemed unable to grasp the significance of their situation. They also demonstrated a process called confabulation in which they tended to amplify experiences and fabricate obviously false details in an apparent effort to fill in gaps in their memory. Like Dr. Wernicke, Dr. Korsakoff noted that some of his patients improved with nourishment, and because of its association with peripheral neuropathy, he called the condition psychosis polyneuritica. Later, doctors changed this to Korsakoff's psychosis or the amnestic-confabulatory syndrome.[13]

The close relationship of Wernicke's disease and Korsakoff's psychosis was not appreciated by the physicians or by their immediate followers. Eventually, however, clinicians saw in their patients an overlap of symptoms and recognized these as different aspects of the same brain disease. Many of the patients did not survive their illness, and post-mortem studies revealed bilaterally symmetrical and consistently localized degeneration in the central nervous system, including several parts of the cerebral cortex which are associated with memory. Degenerative lesions were also found in the cerebellum, which governs coordination, impressing neurologists with the pathological similarity between Wernicke-Korsakoff syndrome and alcoholic cerebellar degeneration, a more permanent condition characterized by ataxia. The same lesions were found in the optic nerve, where they caused retrobulbar neuropathy, and throughout the peripheral nervous system.

After its anatomy was clarified, doctors focused on the probable cause of the Wernicke-Korsakoff syndrome. Many had been struck by the similarity between the peripheral neuropathy seen in the syndrome and that observed with beriberi, especially since patients complained of burning hands and feet in both conditions. Then, during the Japanese occupation of Asia in the 1930s, malnourished patients were said to have many of the problems pointed out by Drs. Wernicke and Korsakoff, including retrobulbar neuropathy. American prisoners of war demonstrated the disease in the 1940s, at which point the pathological lesions originally seen in patients were reproduced in laboratory animals who were given diets deficient only in vitamin B_1.

Later, post-mortem studies of patients with the Wernicke-Korsakoff syndrome were conducted by Maurice Victor, Raymond Adams, and George Collins. From these studies and their extensive clinical investigations, the three neurologists concluded that although alcoholic peripheral neuropathy probably stems from a lack of several vitamins, the Wernicke-Korsakoff syndrome, along with alcoholic cerebellar degeneration, retrobulbar neuropathy, and other conditions, is, like beriberi, a disease of thiamine deficiency. The conditions are severe, as evidenced by the fact that Drs. Victor, Adams, and Collins found a mortality rate of 11 percent in their patients, 20 percent of whom also suffered attacks of delirium tremens. Yet many other patients regained reasonably good health, if not full functioning. Of all their residual problems, the most common was the amnestic-confabulatory state first described by Dr. Korsakoff.[14]

Physicians and patients alike have been struck by the correlation between drinking and memory defects, and it now appears that the Korsakoffian state is but the extreme end of a continuum. At the other end is the simple memory lapse, a blurring of details which can occur after only a few cocktails and may return to focus after abstinence ensues. Somewhere between this and the amnestic-confabulatory state is the blackout, a condition seen in chronic ethanol abusers in whom the memory for long time periods may permanently be lost. This condition, known medically as alcoholic amnesia, occurs most frequently with rising blood alcohol levels and does not require unconsciousness, although patients with the problem may not remember being conscious at all.

Alcoholic amnesia was once attributed to clinical or subclinical hypoglycemia, but Ralph Ryback believes that the condition results from a direct interference with memory. He divides memory into three phases corresponding to different patterns on the electroencephalogram. These include immediate memory, which is seen with nervous system activity lasting a few seconds and is so fleeting one must reinforce it with a scratch pad; short-term memory, in which the immediate memory is translated into memory traces stored within the central nervous system; and long-term memory, in which memory traces laid down previously are called upon.

Ethanol, according to Dr. Ryback, affects all three phases, yet disrupts short-term memory most of all. Thus, at a cocktail party, the drug produces an inattentiveness which prohibits the formation of distinct memory traces. During the blackout, however, no memory traces are deposited and events can never be recalled. The amnestic-confabulatory state is similar in that the brain's storage and retrieval mechanisms are malfunctioning and the patient can only handle a very limited input. As a result, he can neither lay down new memory traces nor recall previous information properly.

Another condition associated with alcohol abuse is called state dependent learning. This condition, in which information learned in a drugged state can best be remembered when the subject is again drugged, was first observed experimentally in dogs who were conditioned to act in certain ways while drugged and could respond appropriately again only under the drug's influence. A similar phenomenon is common among heavy drinkers who forget hiding places where they have secreted alcohol or money while sober but recall them when they become intoxicated. Like alcoholic amnesia, state dependent learning is thought by Dr. Ryback to be caused by the direct toxic effect of ethanol upon the central nervous system.[15]

Although controlled studies have never verified this toxicity in humans, many physicians believe that the drug or its breakdown products, acetaldeyde and acetic acid, are as harmful to the central nervous system as they are to other organ systems. Direct support for the view derived from the fact that alcohol can cause local anesthesia by destroying peripheral nervous tissue. Influential support, by contrast, comes from clinical observations of central nervous system damage in patients who have ingested the other alcohols used since Prohibition to denature ethanol. As mentioned earlier, these alcohols include isopropyl alcohol, which is approximately two times as strong as ethanol, and methyl alcohol, which is converted to formaldehyde and formic acid in the body. These meta- ˈbolic derivatives of methyl alcohol can cause blindness, depression, and irreversible anatomical changes in the nervous system. Interestingly, since methanol is metabolized by the same enzyme system as is ethanol, patients who have consumed the drug are given ethyl alcohol. The alcohol is then detoxified preferentially, preventing the breakdown of methyl alcohol until other steps can be taken to remove it from the body.

Support for the argument that ethanol is directly toxic to

brain tissue may also be inferred from the fact that chronic heavy drinkers display an abnormally high incidence of premature dementia. In fact, for centuries venereal diseases and heavy drinking have been the most common causes of adult mental deterioration. According to Charles Wells, the term dementia is derived from the Latin *dement,* or mad, and refers to a clinical state comprised of failing memory and loss of other mental faculties due to progressive degenerative disease of the central nervous system. Dementia is also called chronic brain syndrome in contrast with delirium, or acute brain syndrome, which may be reversible through various measures, including abstinence if alcohol is involved. The chronic condition may or may not be associated with impairment of other neurological functions, such as speech or sensation. Generally dementia is characterized in its early stages by disinterest, impaired judgment, lability of mood, lack of concern for social mores, and misconceptions which may progress to paranoid delusions. These then lead to total loss of intellectual faculties, followed by accelerated physical deterioration and death.[16]

From an anatomical point of view, the diagnosis of dementia implies diffuse disease of the central nervous system and more specifically the cerebral hemispheres, the seat of higher mental functions. This diffuseness can be confirmed at autopsy, which usually reveals cerebral atrophy, an actual loss of brain tissue which many feel may be due directly to alcohol in certain patients. But the brains of some long time ethanol abusers often show more than atrophy. Frequently old scars are found, presumably related to trauma. The traces of the Wernicke-Korsakoff syndrome and similar conditions also may be present, along with other evidence of chronic brain disease.

The central nervous system damage seen in some older drinkers certainly is alarming, but even more worrisome is a constellation of abnormalities currently being described in infants born to mothers who have consumed large amounts of ethanol. Kenneth Jones and David Smith, who first drew attention to this constellation, call it the fetal alcohol syndrome. According to the two pediatricians, infants with the syndrome are physically and psychologically retarded as a result of severe and permanent brain dysfunction. Some actually undergo ethanol withdrawal following delivery, while others are born with defective hearts, deformed limbs, and other birth defects. Although these defects are nonspecific, Drs. Smith and Jones believe that they occur much more commonly in the offspring of heavy drinking mothers than in other children and may affect from one-third tó one-half of such infants. The two pediatricians consider the fetal alcohol syndrome as serious as the set of abnormalities associated with the sedative drug thalidomide.[17]

In support of their position, investigators at other facilities have reported on several cases of the fetal alcohol syndrome. Similarly, studies conducted at the University of British Columbia have demonstrated that even moderate doses of ethanol administered to laboratory animals during pregnancy are linked with birth defects in rats and chicks. These defects seem to relate to the dose consumed by the mothers, since increases in blood alcohol concentration correlate highly with the severity of abnormalities in their offspring. At the same time, malnutrition does not appear to be implicated, inasmuch as the defects are seen in the offspring of animals maintained on supplemental vitamins and Metrecal®. Researchers have not yet determined when the defects occur during pregnancy, whether they result from chromosomal or structural alterations, or what the relevance of these animal studies is to human patients. But it does seem clear that both human and animal babies somehow are susceptible to the toxic effects of alcohol.

Since such toxicity has been described so frequently in infants and adults, the question of whether ethanol has primarily a direct or an indirect effect appears moot to many physicians. What is indisputable is the fact that alcohol is an extremely powerful drug, one that probably would not be approved for prolonged consumption or for use during pregnancy by the Food and Drug Administration if it were introduced today by a pharmaceutical company. Alcohol occupies an apparently immovable social place because of its caloric yield and its sedative, hypnotic, and general anesthetic properties. Although it is a poor general anesthetic and only a relatively good sedative, ethanol still is employed for these purposes and as a multi-duty medicine in those parts of the world that do not have access to more modern pharmaceuticals. But as pointed out by Charles Becker, in advanced countries its only appropriate therapeutic uses are as a germicidal agent, a stimulant of gastric acid secretion for diagnostic purposes, a cooling substance, a vehicle for other drugs, a local anesthetic, and a part of the treatment of poisoning due to methanol.[18]

6. THE DISEASE CONCEPT OF ALCOHOLISM

Mankind, ever in pursuit of pleasure, have reluctantly admitted into the catalogue of their diseases, those evils which were the immediate offspring of their luxuries. Such a reserve is, indeed, natural to the human mind; for of all deviations from the paths of duty, there are none that so forcibly impeach their pretentions to the character of rational beings as the inordinate use of spiritous liquors.

THOMAS TROTTER, *An Essay, Medical, Philosophical and Chemical, on Drunkenness and its Effects on the Human Body* (1804)

It is a historical irony that ethanol, the world's first wonder drug, should now be considered unsuitable as a therapeutic agent. Yet such reversals are common in medicine, and alcohol's fall from grace seems especially merited. In the first place, as we have emphasized, the drug confers few physical benefits upon its users. Second, it has a high potential for abuse. And third, its high dose consumption has been linked with a host of health problems. Given the current weight of scientific evidence, few people would deny that ethanol abuse is a source of illness. However, it is less universally acknowledged that such abuse is itself a disease.

Whether or not one accepts this idea depends on one's disease concept. The word disease comes from the Latin *dis,* meaning apart from or lack of, and *ease,* which means freedom from labor or pain. Many people think of disease simply in terms of its etymological roots, that is, as a dis-ease. Others, however, prefer a more formal definition. Thus, the *Random House Dictionary* describes disease, along with sickness and illness, as a "condition of an organ, part, structure, or system of the body in which there is incorrect function resulting from the effects of heredity, infection, diet, or environment."[1] In *Stedman's Medical Dictionary*, disease is "an interruption or perversion of function of any of the organs; an acquired morbid change in any tissue of an organism, or throughout an organism, with characteristic changes caused by specific microorganismal alterations."[2]

Whatever definition seems apt, implicit in one's disease concept is some notion of therapy. Such therapy may be symptomatic, in that one aims to assuage the manifestations of illness; specific, in that one tries to treat the underlying pathology; or preventive, in that one attempts to alter the conditions that lead to a disturbance. Specific and preventive therapies are generally thought to be more sophisticated than symptomatic measures because they are presumably derived from greater understanding of a given medical situation and attend to more basic problems. Yet what is called sophisticated one day may be deemed superficial the next, since therapies historically have stemmed less from scientific understanding than from one's social, religious, or philosophic concepts of disease.

For example, the Egyptians and other early peoples regarded disease as a passive process in which the entire individual was controlled by supernatural powers. Even Hippocrates, who rejected Egyptian spiritualism, upheld the traditional view that illness was an imposed condition. On the one hand, he refused to call epilepsy the "sacred disease," as it had been referred to for centuries, and correctly identified it as a malfunction of the central nervous system. Yet at the same time, he argued that human maladies were caused by a predetermined inequity of the various humors—blood, phlegm, black bile, and yellow bile—which governed the mind and body. Hippocrates' endorsement of wine was due largely to its resemblance to blood, which he considered the strongest humor, and to its hypothetical action in increasing the excretion of less desirable humors in the urine.

Galen carried Hippocrates' theories further by contending that human temperament reflected a humoral imbalance. Thus, he categorized people as sanguine, or buoyant; phlegmatic, or sluggish; choleric, or quick-tempered; and melancholic, or sad. Galen believed that men and women were born with a certain character type which could be altered only to a limited extent by pharmacological preparations. Implicit in his therapeutics, like those of Hippocrates, was the notion that disease is primarily an involuntary situation over which patients and physicians have little control.

The Jews and the Romans accepted this belief in part but were more impressed than the Greeks with the willfullness of human behavior. They also tended to view conditions like drunkenness as deviant in that they departed from social norms. The word deviance, which is derived from the Latin *de*, for away from, and *via*, for road, was essential to Roman jurisprudence. According to Berton Roueché, some Romans, including the jurist Domitius Ulpianus, viewed public inebriation and other forms of deviant behavior as medical, rather than legal, problems. But the majority view was articulated by Seneca, who stated that "drunkenness is nothing but a condition of insanity purposely assumed, and, therefore, a crime."[3]

The Christian church considered inebriation not a crime against the state or a departure from social standards, but a sin against God. This sin was both voluntary, in the sense that it was committed consciously by individuals endowed with reason, and involuntary, in that it stemmed from man's basic unworthiness. Inherent in the Christian concept of disease was an irreconcilable conflict between freedom and predestination. This was best expressed in the idea that man knew no sickness before his expulsion from the Garden of Eden, and, henceforth, was destined to suffer because of original sin.

In accordance with this image of mankind fallen from grace, the early Christian approach to chronic inebriation was rather gentle, with the clergy attempting to redeem drunkards through spiritual ministrations and to correct their humoral imbalance with galenicals. Yet the church became less lenient during the Dark Ages, when deviance was once again viewed as a form of possession, and it employed more extreme measures to rid patients of their personal devils. As detailed in the *Malleus Mallefacorum,* or *Hammers Used Against Those Presumed to be Witches,* these included interminable incarceration, chemical purges, prolonged beatings, and other techniques alleged to cleanse the soul.

These techniques were eschewed in the thirteenth century by Thomas Aquinas, who felt that the soul could not be possessed and argued that behavioral disorders were due to a deficient use of reason. According to Aquinas, this deficiency could occur if a person's passions were so fervent as to interfere with the reasoning process. Another possibility was that reason could not prevail because of improper bodily functioning. The Swiss physician Paracelsus agreed with Aquinas. He too modified the Christian disease concept and, anticipating Sigmund Freud by five centuries, suggested in his book, *Diseases Which Deprive Man of His Reason,* that sexual factors played a role in what he termed mental disease.

Reason had its greatest proponent in the person of René Descartes. Compromising a devotion to Catholicism with his mathematical interests, the French philosopher viewed the body and other parts of the physical world as mechanistic and entirely divorced from the mind, the only bridge between the two being the intervention of God. In his writings, Descartes contended that emotion was a physiological process and that control of the expression of emotions by chemicals would control the emotions themselves. Yet he is remembered less for this integrative and rather modern thought than for establishing a dualism of the mind and body which divides physiology and psychology to this day.

Although the mind and body dichotomy has continued to impede our understanding of illness, Descartes and other Renaissance thinkers deserve credit for freeing medicine from the demonology of the Dark Ages. They were the spiritual predecessors of Pinel, the French physician who removed the chains from psychiatric patients at Bicêtre in 1793. Several years later, the Italian Vincenzo Chiarugo wrote a three-volume work, *A Treatise on Insanity,* in which he described for the first time the psychological basis of personality. His work was well received in England, where Thomas Trotter became the first doctor to describe excess drinking as a disease.

Dr. Trotter's American counterpart was Benjamin Rush.

Both physicians believed in the salutary effects of moderate quantities of fermented beverages but feared the ascendance of distilled spirits. Both also considered it their responsibility, and that of society, to care for alcohol abusers, and both suspected that drunkenness was not entirely an unconstrained condition. Working almost alone in their respective countries, Drs. Trotter and Rush argued for humane treatment of inebriates and succeeded in persuading medical and lay readers to develop special institutions for drunkards, whom they called alcoholics, from the word *alcoholismus,* which was coined by Magnus Huss. The first such institution in the United States, the Washingtonian House for the Fallen, was opened in Boston in 1841.

Shortly after the word alcoholism was introduced, the superintendents of those institutions devoted to its treatment formed an organization which came to be known as the American Medical Association for the Study of Inebrity. This association was not affiliated with the American Medical Association. It had its own periodical, *The Journal of Inebrity,* and its members also contributed to *The British Journal of Addictions,* which was launched in 1892. Papers submitted to these publications were short on science, but they shared a humanitarian desire to help patients with alcoholism. Basic to their appeal was the belief that alcoholics, as such patients were called, were sick people who should not be punished because they were not wholly responsible for their actions. This theory was captured in the medical association's slogan: "Intemperance is a Disease."

Although accepted by the medical association, the disease concept of alcoholism was not popular among the public or the medical profession as represented by the AMA. One reason for this was that alcoholics were still viewed as sinners by most people, including physicians. Another was that the disease concept ran counter to the American temperance movement, which had declared its prohibitionistic tendencies by that time. Most of the prohibitionists viewed chronic inebriation not as an illness but as a sign of spiritual weakness. Even those who saw alcoholics as sick people insisted that their sickness was self-inflicted. The prohibitionists also felt that the disease concept gave drunkards an excuse to continue drinking and thereby minimized personal responsibility.

Prohibition was a paradigm for the moral and criminal models of alcoholism, and with repeal, the disease concept once again came to the fore. This time, however, it was advanced not only by the superintendents of institutions for inebriates but also by increasingly large numbers of academic physicians. Many of the latter group were associated at one time or another with the Yale University Laboratory of Applied Physiology, which later evolved into the Center of Alcohol Studies at Yale, and most recently at Rutgers University. In addition to providing basic alcohol research, the center has sponsored summer workshops and publishes *The Quarterly Journal of Studies on Alcohol.*

The failure of Prohibition promoted the disease concept, but its resurgence resulted primarily from increased understanding of the biological nature of disease. This understanding began in the Renaissance and reached a climax during the late nineteenth century, when Louis Pasteur elucidated the role of bacterial microorganisms in infection. Pasteur's discoveries were reinforced by Joseph Lister, a British surgeon who showed that antiseptic agents could decrease operative morbidity and mortality. He was followed by Rudolph Virchow, a German pathologist who disclosed cellular abnormalities in infectious states and instituted the first sanitation system in Berlin.

Eventually, Pasteur's germ theory replaced both the humoral notions of Hippocrates and the Christian belief that illness resulted from a failure of will power. It also provided the intellectual springboard for medical advances which have demonstrated that not all illnesses are due to infection. Yet in spite of these advances, the infectious disease model remains deeply entrenched in the public and professional mind, so much so that *Stedman's Medical Dictionary* still speaks of disease primarily in terms of "microorganismal alteration." This entrenchment, which was reinforced by the introduction of antibiotics, has hindered the efforts of some scientists who hope to move to a more modern disease concept. But it is understandable that early investigators who were eager to comprehend alcoholism tried to fit it initially into the prevalent infectious model of disease.

These investigators actually were anticipated by Benjamin Rush, who speculated that excessive drinking was either a hereditary condition or a contagion. Yet Dr. Rush never tested his hypotheses, and it remained to twentieth-century scientists to subject them to experimentation. Most of these experiments were naïve efforts either to isolate infectious agents from alcohol, to treat heavy drinkers with germicidal agents and later with antibiotics, or to briefly expose light drinkers to chronic inebriates in the hope that they would pick up new drinking patterns. Needless to say, an infectious component of ethanol never was isolated. Alcoholism failed to respond to antimicrobial medications, and the transmission of heavy drinking patterns could not be demonstrated after brief exposure to drunkards, although researchers did verify that such habits could be learned.

As the infectious model of alcoholism was falling into disrepute, investigators were becoming increasingly impressed with the idea that alcoholism might be a genetic disorder. The science of genetics grew out of the work of the Austrian abbot Gregor Mendel, whose experiments in plant hybridization during the latter part of the nineteenth century shed light on the inheritance of familial qualities. But even before Mendel's discoveries, Dr. Rush and other medical leaders were struck by the high incidence of heavy drinking among family members, and surveys conducted during the nineteenth century by superintendents of institutions for inebriates showed that 50 percent of their patients had one or more parents who were alcoholics as well. This association was thought to reflect the infectious nature of alcoholism until investigators failed to transmit drinking patterns from heavy to moderate drinkers. Then came Mendel's work and the subsequent identification of diabetes mellitus and other forms of genetic illness. At this point the investigators sought to demonstrate a relationship between alcoholism and heredity.

One of the most lengthy lines of research has involved efforts to develop strains of animals with a genetic preference for ethanol. Over the past 30 years investigators have discovered that animals do not consume alcohol voluntarily in nature, and are difficult to train to drink in the laboratory. In the 1930s and 1940s, R. J. Mardones and his colleagues tried to develop a laboratory animal model for drinking but failed in their attempt.[4] Yet in 1959, the team of G. E. McClean and D. A. Rogers finally succeeded in training mice to take ethanol by means of psychological conditioning. They then produced a strain of inbred mice which consumed two-thirds of its daily fluid intake in the form of 10 percent alcohol.[5]

Although intriguing, the work of Drs. McClean and Rogers is difficult to evaluate for two important reasons. First, their mice drank ethanol only in small concentrations and may have done so not out of genetic necessity but to satisfy caloric needs. Second, the animals' preference for alcohol was very slight and did not hold up when they were offered other choices. Finally, although such preference can be induced by psychological conditioning, just as physical dependence can be caused by repeatedly injecting ethanol into rats, spontaneous preference for alcohol over other liquids remains unknown in animals other than man.

Another major objection to animal studies is that their relevance to humans is uncertain. To achieve such relevance, contemporary researchers have turned to human subjects. One area of inquiry has involved determining the incidence of known hereditary characteristics, such as blood type and eye color, among moderate and heavy drinkers, with the assumption that if a given characteristic appears more frequently among inebriates, the genetic blueprint for both the characteristic and drinking behavior may be carried on the same gene. Called genetic marker studies, these investigations have been conducted in several countries using a wide variety of hereditary physical parameters. One study by Robert Cruz-Coke demonstrated an association between color blindness and cirrhosis in patients in an alcoholism treatment center.[6] Yet efforts to replicate these results have been unsuccessful, and no one has proven that heavy drinkers have a higher incidence of known hereditary characteristics than the population at large.

Another line of genetic investigation has involved correlating drinking patterns among chronic inebriates and their families. One such study was reported in 1957 in Stockholm by C. Amark, who interviewed alcoholic patients and their parents and siblings and found an increased rate of alcoholism among the brothers and fathers of alcoholics compared with the general population.[7] Four years later, Martin Bleuler performed a similar study of male drunkards in New York City, with their counterparts in Zurich, Switzerland, serving as controls. He found that 22 percent of their siblings and 13 percent of their half-siblings were heavy drinkers. Interestingly, the persons at greatest risk of being alcoholics in this study were not immediate family members but spouses, 29 percent of whom were found to drink as heavily as their husbands.[8]

The conclusions reached by Dr. Bleuler underscore the difficulty of drawing firm conclusions from most family studies. This difficulty has traditionally stemmed from two factors. In the first place, these studies are rarely comparable since they differ in their definition of who is or is not an alcoholic. Second and more important, merely showing that family members exhibit similar behavior patterns does not prove that such patterns are genetically transmitted if the family members are exposed to similar conditions. Thus, the controversy between nature, or genetics, and nurture, or environment, has contaminated these investigations, and although scientists since Benjamin Rush have observed that alcohol abuse tends to run in families, the demonstration of a genetic component in alcoholism has awaited more sophisticated research tools.

One such tool is the twin study technique in which scientists compare identical with fraternal twin pairs where at least one partner has been under investigation for a particular disease. The professed validity of this approach is based on the assumption that monozygotic, or identical, and dizygotic, or fraternal, twins differ only in respect to genetic makeup, and that environment is as similar to members of dizygotic as it is to monozygotic pairs. Given this assumption, investigators have reasoned that genetic disorders will be concordant, or occurring in both members of the pair, more often among identical than fraternal twins.

The first major alcoholism twin study was accomplished in

1960 by L. Kaij, who retrospectively examined 174 male twin pairs, at least one partner of which was registered at a Swedish Temperance Board because of a conviction for problem drunkenness. Dr. Kaij interviewed 90 percent of the subjects himself and determined zygosity by several methods, including photograph analysis, interviews with neighbors who had trouble telling twins apart, and blood typing. He also measured levels of alcohol abuse by his own standards, and established that 54 percent of his monozygotic subjects and 32 percent of his dizygotic subjects showed concordance in their drinking behavior.[9]

Although suggestive, this and other twin studies have suffered from the difficulty of diagnosing the condition called alcoholism, the problem of determining zygosity, and the fact that such studies have not been performed on twins raised separately. In addition, the assumption that identical and fraternal twins share the same environmental influences is arguable, and critics of twin studies have shown that monozygotic twins spend more time together and are related to in a more similar fashion by family members and other persons than are dizygotic twins. Twins are a genetically selected population as well, and although twin studies have suggested a hereditary factor in ethanol consumption, it is difficult to generalize from the few studies completed so far.

Generalizations are equally difficult to derive from the studies conducted on adopted children and half-siblings raised apart from their biological relatives. The first major work of this sort was conducted in 1944 by A. Roe and P. Burks, who studied the records of a child placement agency in New York and located 36 males whose fathers exhibited heavy drinking behavior and its consequences, such as arrests for disorderly conduct or drunk driving, and who were placed in foster homes early in their lives. The investigators then compared the fate of these subjects with 25 foster children of normal parentage. They found that the adopted children of alcoholics experienced slightly more adjustment problems in adolescence and early adulthood. Yet they did not drink more heavily at any time in their development.[10]

Perhaps the most thorough adoption study was conducted

in the 1960s and 1970s by Donald Goodwin and his colleagues. This group looked at 55 Danish men who had been separated from their biological parents; one of the parents, in 85 percent of cases the father, carried a hospital diagnosis of alcoholism. These subjects were then compared with two control groups. One of the groups had no family history of alcoholism, and the other members had parents who had been hospitalized for psychiatric problems other than alcoholism. Dr. Goodwin and his coworkers found that the total amount of psychological disturbance was similar between subjects and controls, but that 40 percent of the subjects had at the same point in their lives sought treatment and 15 percent, hospitalization, largely for alcoholism. This compared with 24 percent and 3 percent, respectively, of the controls.

Dr. Goodwin's group was quick to point out that environmental factors could not be excluded from their study, since many of the subjects spent the first weeks of their lives with their real mothers and may have received less desirable placement during adoption proceedings because of their family backgrounds. Yet the investigators felt that these facts did not detract from the genetic component of alcoholism which they had suggested. They concluded that "it seems certain that individuals do differ in their genes for key enzymes in the liver and brain and that such genetic differences may underlie alcohol metabolism, differences of adaptability of nerve cells, and differing personality patterns."[11]

This conclusion seems justified, and many investigators today believe that alcoholism has a genetic component. Yet merely demonstrating the presence of such a component does not prove that it is the cause of alcoholism or explain how the component might be included in the etiology of the disorder. Dr. Goodwin and his colleagues tried to overcome this objection by suggesting that genetically transmitted differences in ethanol metabolism, central nervous system sensitivity to alcohol, or personality formation might contribute to the condition. They thus implied that alcoholics differ from other drinkers not only in how much they drink but also in some inherited disorder of metabolism which governs their drinking behavior.

The theory that disordered metabolism exists among alcoholics has been one of the most popular and persuasive in alcoholism research for years. Implicit in the theory is the idea that alcoholism is beyond the control of patients because the seeds of the disorder are planted quite literally before they are born. Also implicit is the notion that excessive drinking is an expression of physiological rather than psychological needs. Alcoholism, according to this model, therefore is a disease which can be understood in terms of altered physical functioning and can be treated with drugs, hormones, or nutrients like other illnesses can.

Once the metabolic theory of alcoholism was introduced, investigators immediately tried to fit it into the conceptual structures that had been suggested for other metabolic disorders. The first such attempt involved viewing alcoholism as an immunological or allergic disease. The science of immunology grew out of the discovery that the body produces substances called antibodies when challenged by bacteria, pollen, and other foreign substances. When these substances, which are called antigens, are met by large amounts of antibody, symptoms result from the subsequent immunological reaction. These symptoms may amount to no more than a runny nose in patients with hay fever or may progress to anaphylactic shock in persons sensitized to penicillin. Such anaphylaxis is characterized by collapse of the cardiovascular system.

Since such reactions occur only in a few patients, and since people obviously differ in their response to drugs, investigators reasoned that some persons might have allergic disorders which make them more sensitive than others to alcohol. This sensitivity was described first as a compelling enjoyment of ethanol and later as an inability to detoxify the drug and resist its intoxicating properties. The major proponent of this latter view was William Silkworth of Towns Hospital in New York, who declared in the 1930s that alcoholism was "a form of anaphylaxis" which resulted from an inborn allergy to alcohol and led inexorably to its abuse.[12]

Dr. Silkworth's theory was taught to and accepted by many of his patients, the most famous of whom was Bill W., the cofounder of Alcoholics Anonymous. Dr. Silkworth's belief in the allergic basis of alcoholism thus became a basic tenet of Alcoholics Anonymous and remains a philosophic cornerstone of that organization. Yet neither anaphylactic reactions to ethanol nor anti-alcohol antibodies in animals or humans exposed to ethanol have been reported. Furthermore, no one has been able to curb excessive drinking through agents which presumably could block or suppress an immunological response to alcohol.

Although proof was never put forward to explain alcoholism as an allergic disorder, ample evidence has existed to suggest that the consequences of alcohol abuse, and perhaps such abuse itself, are related to nutritional deficiencies. This has led to a series of laboratory experiments which culminated in 1942 when R. J. Mardones and his colleagues demonstrated that rats maintained on a diet deficient in B complex vitamins increased their intake of ethanol and water over water alone when offered the two solutions and decreased their consumption when B vitamins were restored. Initially the investigators assumed that thiamine was the missing ingredient that induced the animals to drink ethanol. However, when the rats seemed unaffected by supplemental vitamin B_1, Dr. Mardones and his coworkers postulated the presence of an unknown factor. Yet this factor was never identified, and later research revealed that rats preferred sugar and water to alcohol and water. Dr. Mardones and his colleagues then conceded that their rats probably drank ethanol and water in preference to water because it contained more calories.[13]

One offshoot of Dr. Mardones's efforts was the so-called genetrophic theory of Roger J. Williams. In the 1940s, Dr. Williams proposed that in certain people "genetic blocks" led to the diminished production of one or more enzymes. This underproduction resulted in an impaired ability to utilize one or more nutritional elements, which led in turn to an increased need for these elements and a subsequent use of ethanol to satisfy heightened nutritional requirements. Dr. Williams later argued that alcohol weakens the brain's appetite center, causing an increased appetite for ethanol, and advocated the use of multivitamin preparations in treating alcoholics.[14] Such preparations did remedy some of the nutritional problems associated with alcohol abuse, but because Dr. Williams was unable to show that they affected drinking patterns, his theory has never been held in high regard.

Another line of thought is that alcoholism is a disorder of the endocrine system. Representative of this thinking was J. J. Smith, who, in 1949, noted the similarity between delirium tremens and Addison's Disease, a condition characterized by insufficiency of the adrenal glands. Confirming in the laboratory that chronic heavy drinkers did in fact have reduced levels of the adrenal hormone, cortisol, Dr. Smith postulated that these patients suffered from primary adrenal hypofunction which led to a craving for ethanol. He also recommended treating the DTs with ACTH, the pituitary hormone that regulates adrenal hormone synthesis, administering cortisone to induce sobriety.[15] Yet neither recommendation proved fruitful, and Dr. Smith's endocrinological theory was discarded.

Although alcoholism is not thought to be an adrenal problem, many persons have compared it with diabetes mellitus, another endocrine disorder. The main reason for this comparison is that people equate their own inability to "handle" ethanol with a diabetic's difficulty in metabolizing sugar. Because of this parallel, some patients with alcohol problems have suspected that they suffer from a biochemical defect comparable to that in diabetes. In fact, both ethanol abuse and diabetes do alter sugar and fat metabolism, and because of this, several scientists have supported the popular idea that alcoholism is an inherited metabolic condition. The difference between heavy and moderate drinkers, they have stated, is that the former have an inborn error of metabolism, manifested by the lack of an as yet undetermined hormone, which makes them either unable to detoxify ethanol or uniquely susceptible to its effects.

The idea that alcoholism might stem from an inborn error of metabolism is supported by several studies which seem to document individual and perhaps even ethnic variations in the metabolism of ethanol. For example, Jack Mendelson has demonstrated that heavy drinking patients can clear alcohol from their blood slightly faster than temperate subjects.[16] Dr. D. Fenna and his colleagues have described the same phenomenon and have also stated that Eskimos and Canadian Indians appear to detoxify ethanol more slowly than whites and may remain intoxicated longer as a result.[17]

An analogous but not comparable ethnic variability in sensitivity to drink has been described by Philip Wolff in Oriental adults and infants who experience facial flushing, increased heart rate, and other phenomena after low dose consumption of ethanol. Dr. Wolff determined that the incidence of flushing was accompanied by a similar distribution among the infant's parents and also noted that Mongoloids reported more symptoms of intoxication than Caucasians. He concludes that

> the greater alcohol sensitivity was not limited to vasodilation of the facial vessels, but extended to other physiological systems and particularly to those under autonomic nervous system control. Whether these findings are related to the etiology of alcoholism is open to question. But the vascular response to drinking and the associated subjective symptoms of intoxication expressed by Mongoloids may well prevent many of them from consuming even moderate quantities of alcohol. [18]

Because of its important implications, several investigators are trying to duplicate Dr. Wolff's research. Similar efforts have been made to confirm the findings of Dr. Fenna, but so far these efforts have not been successful. In fact, Lynn Bennion and Ting-Kai Li recently reported a lack of variation in ethanol metabolism among whites and American Indians, although they did show that chronic heavy drinking could accelerate the rate of metabolism of alcohol in both groups.[19] This latter finding can be explained entirely on a nongenetic basis by Charles Lieber's demonstration that drinking may cause a proliferation of liver enzymes which are used in the detoxification of ethanol and other drugs. Thus at present no one has proven that people differ in their metabolism of alcohol before they start drinking. And even if such differences do exist, they hardly prove that alcoholism derives from an inborn error of metabolism.

Furthermore, no evidence exists that alcoholism is primarily an endocrine disorder like diabetes. The hormones that chronic inebriates allegedly lack have never been isolated, and such persons have not been dissuaded from drinking by injections of insulin or other hormones. Indeed, the main reason people have continued to compare the two conditions is their conviction that alcoholism, like diabetes, might be genetically predetermined and, therefore, an involuntary disease.

The scientific drawback of this stance is that it unfairly favors the role of nature over nurture in the etiology of alcoholism. Few people today doubt that genetic and metabolic factors contribute somewhat to alcoholism, yet there really is little evidence that alcoholism is primarily or solely a physiological disorder. Research is now being conducted to determine the physical differences that may underlie ethanol metabolism and its action on the central nervous system, and this research could lead to new biological approaches in the treatment of alcoholics. Yet interest in this research should not lead us to underestimate the tremendous importance of environmental influences in determining drinking behavior.

This importance has been stressed most strongly by Sigmund Freud and other psychoanalysts, who introduced the revolutionary idea that behavior has meaning and can be understood. In the psychoanalytic model, chronic inebriation is seen as a sympton of intrapsychic disturbance and not a primary biological illness. Yet the Freudians' emphasis on early life experiences in influencing later action may imply a kind of psychological determinism. This determinism is compatible with the notion that symptoms and the expression of psychopathology in adults is somewhat inevitable, if not actually a disease.

The early Freudians focused on the role of primitive impulses in shaping drinking behavior. They were most impressed with the regressive, infantile nature of alcoholics and felt that these patients used ethanol to gratify needs for nurturance, to deal with latent homosexual strivings, and to resolve conflicts over passivity and dependence. Dr. Freud also noted the similarity between alcoholics and abusers of other drugs, as did Sandor Rado, who wrote in 1926 that addicts are persons who have a disposition to react to the effects of alcohol, morphine, or other drugs in a specific way, namely in such a way that they try to use their effects to satisfy the archaic oral longing which is a sexual longing, a need for security, and a need for the maintenance of self esteem.[20]

Along these lines, Otto Fenichel stated that

those persons become drug addicts for whom the effect of the drug has a specific significance. For them it means the fulfillment, or at least the hope of fulfillment, of a deep and primitive desire, more urgently felt than are sexual or other instinctual longings in normal persons. The specific elation from alcohol is characterized by the fact that inhibitions and limiting considerations of reality are removed from consciousness before the instinctual impulses are, so that a person who does not dare to perform instinctual acts may gain both satisfaction and relief with the help of alcohol. Thus the superego has been defined as that part of the mind that is soluble in alcohol.[21]

Amplifying the work of the early psychiatrists, Karl Menninger argued that many alcoholics were depressed people who used ethanol to deal with their depression. In 1938, Dr. Menninger maintained that

alcoholics have a powerful urge to destroy themselves because of guilt and a need for punishment caused by personally unacceptable aggressive impulses. Alcoholism performs two psychological functions: it is a form of gradual self-destruction, satisfying the need for punishment; and at the same time, it is a mechanism used to avert or escape an even greater form of self-destruction.[22]

By the latter, Dr. Menninger meant suicide.

An additional insight into the alcoholic personality was offered by Robert Knight, who observed that many alcoholics have difficulty dealing with their sense of inferiority as well as their aggressiveness and competitiveness. In 1940, Dr. Knight depicted the person most likely to become an alcoholic as one in whom

there is repressed but still active craving for loving maternal care. There is also a strong aggressive need, suppressed by circumstances to the extent that it comes to expression only in verbal form. Alcohol does a lot for these needs. It permits the young man to act as aggressively as he really feels, without forcing him to assume full responsibility for his actions. It also permits him to satisfy his dependent cravings without forcing his sober consciousness to become aware of them.[23]

A simpler explanation of these previous formulations is offered by Harold T. Blane, who has introduced the mnemonic "Three D's of Alcoholism." The first D is dependency, which allegedly leads either to overtly dependent drinkers who stay with their families or to covertly dependent ones who seek the fellowship of the tavern. Depression, the second D, results in drinkers from an unsuccessful wish for maternal love during childhood and manifests itself either as active violence or passive turning of angry impulses against the self. The third D is denial of both drinking problems and underlying dependency. Dr. Blane also stressed that many alcoholics are unable to tolerate frustration, control impulses, or reconcile feelings of worthlessness with omnipotent fantasies.[24]

In their works, Dr. Blane and the analytic psychologists have succeeded in developing powerful explanations of adult behavior. Yet these explanations, which have proven so useful from a clinical standpoint, have not been so helpful to researchers who have attempted to isolate an alcoholic personality and predict which young people will develop drinking problems. One reason for this is that the psychoanalytic formulations generally do not distinguish between pre- and post-drinking personalities. Another reason is that the traits identified retrospectively in alcoholic patients are also seen to a greater or lesser degree in many other troubled adults and, therefore, are not specific for the condition called alcoholism.

One prospective attempt to determine the contributions of intrapsychic processes and early environmental influences to adult drinking patterns was conducted by William and Joan McCord. The McCords' research involved 510 boys of lower socioeconomic backgrounds who participated in the Cambridge-Somerville Youth Project. One-half of these boys were selected because of disturbed home environments and potential social maladjustment, while the other half were comparably age- and class-related. Originally selected and observed in the 1930s, both groups of boys were followed to adulthood. Of the 510 subjects, 29 of the maladjusted sample and 22 of the so-called normals became alcoholics as defined by arrest records for public drunkenness and contact with social agencies, including Alcoholics Anonymous.

Significantly, those boys who became alcoholics did not differ from the nonalcoholics in terms of nutrition or genetics. They also did not seem to demonstrate more of the characteristics that the McCords expected to encounter in terms of Freudian theory, such as dependence and passivity, which the McCords tried to measure by observing the way in which the children played and interacted. However, these subjects did seem to differ in that their homes were marked by more parental conflict, less emotional support on the part of the parents, and an inadequate specification of the male role.

This led the McCords to speculate that the alcoholics' backgrounds caused conflicts over dependency and independence, in addition to confusion over self-image. The alcoholics seemingly tried to resolve this conflict during childhood by maintaining a facade of independence and aggressive masculinity. As adults, they used ethanol as an outlet which allowed them to become dependent on a drug rather than on other people and yet appear independent. Eventually, however, their self-images collapsed and their repressed needs emerged.[25]

Studies like that of the McCords have shown that there is no specific alcoholic personality nor any single definable set of circumstances that necessarily predisposes to alcoholism. Thus today's psychoanalytically-oriented therapists are concerned less with attempting to predict who will or will not become alcoholic than with trying to understand intrapsychic and interpersonal dynamics within the structure of Freudian theory. Modern depth psychologists continue to appreciate the importance of unconscious impulses while emphasizing the ego and its mechanisms of mastery, adaptation, and defense. They are increasingly willing to view behavior as the resultant of a number of forces, including the cultural, physiological, and psychological, which contribute to the richness of every personality.

At the same time, most depth psychologists subscribe to the

traditional Freudian view that alcoholism is a final common pathway of a variety of conflicts. As a corollary to this, they do not consider alcoholism as a specific state that can be isolated within an individual as can many physical illnesses. Most psychoanalytically-oriented therapists are concerned less with heavy drinking than with its meaning to a particular patient and his family. Since these therapists view human functioning as an integrated, dynamic process, they disagree with those who claim that alcoholics are no different from other people except for their alcoholism. They also refuse to focus on heavy drinking to the exclusion of the entire personality. Their objective, then, is to understand and individualize the needs and problems of patients through the process of psychotherapy.

In most cases, the psychotherapeutic process means bringing some unconscious material to light, helping patients accept their feelings, fears, and defenses, and aiding their psychological growth by providing them with a wider repertoire of behavior. Thus when persons enter treatment, they can learn to perceive their conflicts and appreciate the energy they expend in dealing with them. Alcoholics, for example, can see the stereotyped nature of their responses to people and situations, as well as the strife they keep reexperiencing in their lives. In many instances, this will prompt them to relieve stresses and reduce their reliance on ethanol.

The therapeutic process has been shown to be a corrective emotional experience for many individuals. It is particularly valuable for patients, including alcoholics, who can incorporate insight and affective learning into their psychological development. However, the goals of psychoanalytically-oriented psychotherapy are more limited for psychotic patients who are bombarded by seemingly bizarre thoughts and have a harder time testing reality. Psychotherapy also has had only limited success with so-called psychopaths, persons with character disorders who do not perceive themselves as patients or appreciate the social consequences of their behavior.

Of course, psychotherapy places certain requirements on its patients. It generally is a long process that demands that people be able to delay some gratifications. In its usual outpatient form, this process involves people in a therapeutic relationship for only one or a few hours each week, a situation that has not been specifically modified to suit certain conditions, including alcoholism. This situation may be adequate for some patients, but it may not be sufficient to meet others' needs. For these persons, dealing with problems in psychotherapy seems more difficult than dealing with them with ethanol.

In an attempt to increase their therapeutic impact, several practitioners who were seeing individual patients during the 1940s and 1950s developed a psychoanalytically-oriented group therapy. Their work was paralleled by that of educators from the National Training Laboratories in Bethel, Maine, who were impressed with the power of the group as an educational tool. Eventually the therapists and educators shared their experience and popularized the intrinsic properties of the group. These properties include the stimulation of emotional release in a tolerant, supportive setting; an instillation of hope as one observes growth in one's self and in others; an acknowledgement of the universality of one's feelings and failures; and an enhancement of self-awareness and acceptance through the process of confronting one's self in the presence of others.

Such confrontation has been aided by several new group techniques. One technique is psychodrama, a form of therapy in which several participants act out impromptu dramas in front of the group and rapidly engage their own and others' feelings. Another is transactional analysis, in which people learn to conceptualize life as a series of games in which they play the roles of child, parent, and adult. Other techniques include Gestalt therapy, in which individuals plunge into heated dialogues with themselves in front of the group, and encounter groups, in which people explore how they feel about one another and try to achieve intense emotional experiences in a group setting. These and other techniques have won attention for being innovative, but they all rely on the concepts of group dynamics spelled out in the 1950s. In addition, although some groups take on a collective identity which is described as greater than the sum of their parts, participants generally experience the groups less as entities unto themselves than as vehicles to assist them in their own therapy.

Like psychoanalytically-oriented individual therapy before them, group therapies have been applied to many types of patients, including those who have problems with alcohol. Some alcoholics have entered groups composed only of alcoholics, while others have formed groups with a mixed patient population. Similarly, some groups have focused almost exclusively on drinking, while others have dealt with the meaning of drinking and its relationship to underlying problems. A variation of the latter approach has been developed by Claude Steiner, a transactional analyst from San Francisco, who has identified several styles of alcoholic behavior. In his article, "The Alcoholic Game," Dr. Steiner defines alcoholism as a series of transactions engaged in with the purpose of obtaining interpersonal advantage. He also describes somewhat whimsically the ground rules for certain games played by alcoholics. These include the aggressive game, "Drunk and Proud of It"; the psychosocially self-damaging game, "Lush"; and the tissue-damaging game, "Wino."[26]

Group techniques have achieved a remarkable therapeutic impact and have broadened the base of psychotherapy. However, in the final analysis they have met with the same measure of success and failure with alcoholics as have individual therapies. This is understandable as they share the same patients and limitations. Yet group effectiveness can be maximized by the process suggested by I. D. Yalom of Stanford University. Dr. Yalom believes that alcoholics require more attention from the person leading a group than do other patients. In between scheduled group sessions, he uses mailed agendas and resumés of previous meetings to maintain contact with patients, allows them to call on him, and permits them to engage in other activities with group members.

The fundamental belief shared by Dr. Yalom and many psychotherapists is that drinking and other forms of behavior can best be changed through alteration of intrapsychic and interpersonal dynamics.[27] They are not concerned with merely treating people for such diagnosed conditions as schizophrenia, mania, anxiety, depression, or even alcoholism, although they recognize that such conditions do exist. Furthermore, although they often prescribe drugs for these conditions, the therapists esteem the psychotherapeutic process. Purists among them might even say that psychoactive substances impede therapy by suppressing anxiety.

In contrast, some therapists and many medically-oriented physicians value pharmacological approaches as much as or more than they do psychotherapy. The reasons for this preferance naturally vary from person to person, and in some cases drugs are blindly prescribed. Yet in most instances the pharmacological approach reflects a synthesis of physical and psychological theories of alcoholism and other disorders. This synthesis was first suggested by René Descartes, who believed that emotions are the expression of psychological processes which can be controlled by chemical agents. In recent years, Descartes's belief has been supported by demonstrations of the biological basis of behavior and the development of compounds to treat psychiatric problems. Some of these compounds are relatively nonspecific, whereas others are applicable only to clearly defined disorders. Today both types are used either alone or as adjuncts to individual or group psychotherapy.

Among the compounds employed for this purpose are antipsychotic agents such as chlorpromazine or Thorazine®, the antimanic-depressive drug lithium carbonate, antidepressants such as amitryptilene or Elavil®, and anti-anxiety drugs like Librium® or Valium®. These chemicals have been shown to be effective in treating the disorders for which they are prescribed, and many therapists have reported relief of disorganized thinking and other symptoms in drinkers taking the drugs. Yet even with such improvement, it is difficult to demonstrate consistent success in terms of decreased alcohol consumption. From a pharmacological standpoint, this may be because the compounds are never totally effective for a given condition, because the condition is misdiagnosed, or because the condition and the drinking that accompanies it are not closely allied.

Another pharmacological approach incorporates the use of

hallucinogenic compounds like lysergic acid diethylamide, or LSD. Here the goal has not been to treat a specific psychiatric disorder but to facilitate emotional release, aid in the recall of memory, or provide an intense spiritual experience which might obviate one's dependence on ethanol. Psychiatrists who first employed hallucinogens for these purposes claimed impressive results in the 1950s and early 1960s. Yet interest in the hallucinogens waned a few years later, after several investigators demonstrated that the drugs were ineffective in the treatment of alcoholism. Because of professional discouragement over the hallucinogens and their potential for abuse, the drugs seldom are used in the treatment of alcoholism today.

Other compounds which are prescribed by physicians include sedative, hypnotic, and general anesthetic substitutes for ethanol. As we have said, ethyl alcohol has no direct pharmacological equivalent. However, other compounds in its class do have comparable qualities and can be used in its place. Among these compounds are Valium® and Librium®, which ease alcohol withdrawal symptoms and are given on a long-term basis because they are less harmful than ethanol. Marijuana, which acts as a sedative and hypnotic agent in low doses, also is substituted for alcohol by some people who consider it a safer substance. Marijuana may be prescribed more frequently in the future as a replacement for alcohol unless it proves to have significant toxicity.

A final pharmacological approach to alcoholism stems from the desire to provide a specific chemical that will prevent people from drinking. The compound used most commonly for this purpose today is Antabuse®, the generic name of which is disulfiram. As mentioned in the previous chapter, disulfiram is a chemical that prevents the breakdown of acetaldehyde to acetic acid and thus causes an increase in acetaldehyde levels in persons who take the drug and simultaneously ingest ethanol. The elevated acetaldehyde levels in turn lead to severe Antabuse® reactions. Such reactions are so frightening and physically unpleasant that some people are readily dissuaded from drinking alcohol.

Disulfiram was introduced into clinical medicine in 1948 and shortly thereafter was employed in alcoholism treatment.

Today it is used in three basic fashions. One approach, called aversive conditioning, involves giving the compound to patients who can be taught to associate drinking with adverse disulfiram effects. Another method involves prescribing Antabuse® to patients who are motivated to take the drug by their desire to stay sober. Since one must not take disulfiram for several days before drinking to avoid a reaction, the drug assists these people in their day-to-day decision not to drink. A third approach involves imposing Antabuse® on patients and on persons in the criminal justice system as as a condition of parole.

Disulfiram is known to be effective in preventing drinking if people take the compound, although some psychotic individuals and persons who are given the drug under court order may continue to drink. As Charles Becker points out, voluntary acceptance of Antabuse® by a patient implies that both the patient and his or her doctor agree on a diagnosis. Such an acceptance also allows the patient and physician to concentrate on the reasons for drinking while sobriety is prolonged by disulfiram.[28] Antabuse® is particularly useful with people who feel more in control when they have access to a powerful external agent, and are able to make a ritual out of taking the drug. Some patients do well when the chemical is given to them on a regular basis by spouses, parents, physicians, and other authority figures. Others seem to profit most when they themselves control the administration of Antabuse®.

In spite of its effectiveness with these people, disulfiram and comparable newer compounds have several limitations. Antabuse® reactions with alcohol can be harmful, for example, and clinical experience indicates that the chemical has its own toxicity. Thus, some patients taking disulfiram and not drinking have repeated dermatological disorders, drowsiness, and impotence, while others have become psychotic when they have combined Antabuse® with other medicines. Another limitation of disulfiram is that it is an all-or-none proposition. That is, patients taking Antabuse® cannot moderate their drinking; if they use disulfiram, they simply cannot drink at all.

The prohibitionistic connotations of Antabuse® appeal to

people who are awed by alcohol and are willing to employ extreme countermeasures to combat its abuse. Many of these individuals equate ethanol with narcotics and subscribe to what might be called the pharmacological theory of alcoholism. According to this theory, certain persons share an inherent susceptibility to alcohol and soon after initial exposure become altered on a cellular level by the drug. This alteration, which is hypothesized to occur primarily but not exclusively in the central nervous system, leads to a biochemical need for ethanol, which in turn causes increased alcohol consumption. Tolerance and physical dependence then result, all because of a biological predisposition on the part of the drinker and his helplessness in the face of alcohol.

The pharmacological theory of alcoholism is an underpinning of some popular notions of alcoholism and is accepted by certain physicians. Nevertheless, in recent years even its most ardent proponents have admitted that ethanol is not so compelling as the pharmacological theory implies. Furthermore, they have recognized that physical dependence develops slowly to alcohol, and that some people can overcome such dependence rather easily, indicating that the drug is not all-powerful. It is also known that although dependence may be self-perpetuating, in that fear of withdrawal may lead alcoholics to avoid abstinence, this cannot explain why people become dependent in the first place. This knowledge has led the great majority of investigators interested in alcoholism to adopt a compromise position in which pharmacological, physiological, and psychological factors are all felt to play a role in its etiology.

Although many professional bodies have adopted this compromise position, several influential lay groups have maintained an essentially physical and pharmacological viewpoint which stresses biological vulnerability to the tremendous power of ethanol. Two of these groups have worked together in a complementary fashion since the 1930s and are largely responsible for current popular opinion about alcoholism. One is the National Council on Alcoholism, a volunteer agency devoted to providing treatment referrals, public education, and political lobbying for its viewpoint. The other organization is pointedly nonpolitical but has had an even greater impact. It is Alcoholics Anonymous, known throughout the world as AA.

Alcoholics Anonymous was cofounded by Bill W., a former stockbroker from New England who first was admitted for alcohol detoxification at the Towns Hospital in New York City in 1933. There he met William Silkworth, proponent of the allergic theory of alcoholism, who told him that his drinking had become an obsession that condemned him to drink against his will. Unconvinced, Bill W. left the hospital and resumed drinking. Later he encountered a former drinking acquaintance who had recently returned to America after having been treated for alcoholism in Switzerland by Carl Jung. As Bill W. understood his friend's story, Dr. Jung had told the friend, after months of therapy, that he could not profit from continued psychiatric treatment. His only hope was to return to the United States, join a religious group, and achieve a spiritual experience that might help him terminate his dependence on ethanol.

Carl Jung's position was crucial to the philosophic foundation of Alcoholics Anonymous. Along with the other early psychoanalysts, Dr. Jung acknowledged the parallels between heavy drinking and infantile longings. Yet he added a less secular component, emphasizing that the drinker's desires were comparable "with the spiritual thirst of our being for holiness, expressed in medieval language as the 'Union with God.' " The antidote for ethanol, Dr. Jung felt, was not insight therapy but spiritual illumination. As he wrote to Bill W. in 1961, long after Alcoholics Anonymous was established, " . . . you see, alcohol in Latin is *spiritus,* and you use the same word for the highest religious experience as well as the lowest poison. The helpful motto is: *spiritus contra spiritum.* "[29]

Taking Dr. Jung's advice, Bill W.'s friend joined the Oxford Group, a religious association with roots both in Christian fundamentalism and in the abstinence-oriented Washingtonians. The Oxford Group was founded by Frank Buckman, a Lutheran minister who promised salvation through five "life changing" stages. These included the stages of confidence, in which rapport was to be established between a previously initiated "changer" and the person to be changed; confession, in which changed persons confessed at group meetings attended by potential changers to faults overcome since joining the group; conviction, through which unchanged persons became more aware of their sins and acknowledged that they were powerless to solve their problems; conversion, in which through spiritual experience the unchanged became changed and promised to follow God's teachings; and continuance, through which the changed led changed lives and tried to alter others' lives as well.

Bill W.'s friend went through these stages and, in due course, set out to change Bill. Bill W. resisted initially, but in 1934 he entered Towns Hospital to dry out again. There, Dr. Silkworth impressed him for the first time with his allergic theory of alcoholism and what Bill W. later was to call "the nature of our illness: the obsession of the mind and spirit that compels us to drink and the allergy of the body that condemns us to go mad or die." Yet Bill W. rejected Dr. Silkworth until he finally became desperate. Then, while lying in a hospital bed, sick and depressed, he suddenly underwent a spiritual conversion in which he felt at one with the universe, at peace with himself, and at home with his God.[30]

Bill W. feared that he might be psychotic during this experience, but Dr. Silkworth assured him this was not so. Grasping for an explanation of what had happened, Bill W. read a copy of *The Varieties of Religious Experience* by William James. In this book, James states that spiritual illumination is possible only after one has experienced "deflation at depth." Bill W. felt that he had reached this point, which he called "low bottom," and had achieved illumination. Reading on, he found a passage which was to serve as a continuous source of inspiration: "The crisis of self-surrender is the throwing of our conscious selves at the mercy of powers which, whatever they may be, are more ideal than we are actually, and make for our redemption. Self-surrender has been and always must be regarded as the vital turning point of the religious life."[31]

Shortly after reading this passage, Bill W. joined the Oxford Group. He then moved to Akron, Ohio, where he met a drunken surgeon, Robert S., and accomplished his first conversion. Later the two left the Oxford Group and, in 1935, formed an organization devoted solely to the rehabilitation of alcoholics. According to David McDuff, Bill W. and Dr. Robert S. adapted the Oxford Group's five life changing steps for their own purposes. Thus, the "changer" in Oxford Group language became the "sponsor" in the terms of Alcoholics Anonymous. Similarly, the act of confession, which was called the "sharing of witness" by the Oxford Group, evolved at AA meetings into the recounting of drinking histories which were called colloquially "drunkalogues." At the same time, the founders of Alcoholics Anonymous expanded upon the moral absolutes of the Oxford Group to create a "Program of Recovery" which is known as the "Twelve Steps." These famous steps, whose language is borrowed from that of the Oxford Group, were spelled out in the book, *Alcoholics Anonymous*, which was published in 1938.[32]

As the Twelve Steps suggest, Alcoholics Anonymous since its inception has been a blend of group dynamics, self-help methods, prohibitionistic thinking, and fundamentalist philosophy. Henry Tiebout has stated that the steps induce the alcoholic to renounce his inflated self-image and infantile wishes in favor of God and the group ego. This act of surrender, which is comparable to conversion in the Oxford Group vernacular, is considered crucial by Dr. Tiebout because through it a person comes to tolerate frustration and to accept himself and others. It also allows him to resolve his conflicts over dependence and independence by being dependent on the group in place of alcohol.[33]

The importance of this group dependency is stressed by Hans Tochs, who describes Alcoholics Anonymous as a social movement. According to Dr. Tochs, such movements constitute "efforts by large numbers of people to solve collectively problems which they feel they have in common." Social movements offer the hope of self-improvement within the context of a philosophic system which is agreed upon by members. The movements also demand a rejection of any theories that threaten their ideological structure. Thus personal change can come only with group conformity.[34]

The group to which a prospective AA member pledges

himself is an association of self-acknowledged deviants. Usually there exist two kinds of deviant associations: those such as Weight Watchers, which attempt to conform to societal standards, and those such as Gay Liberation, whose members seek to influence society to respect their behavior. Alcoholics Anonymous since its inception has stressed that society is correct in its fear of ethanol and has defined its members as deviants. At the same time, it has offered them acceptance and has asked society to be accepting only of those alcoholics who have achieved reform.

Deviance, in AA thinking, is the equivalent of disease. Although the notion of alcoholism as an allergy shared by individuals with an innate sensitivity to liquor was discounted by medical spokesmen shortly after Dr. Silkworth proposed it, Bill W. and Dr. Robert S. clung to this concept and adopted, either wholly or in part, every other proposal that alcoholism is a genetic or metabolic illness which, therefore, is as immutable and irremediable as original sin. To reinforce this irremediability, the leaders of Alcoholics Anonymous declared that the disease of alcoholism could be arrested or placed in remission. It could also exist in a recovered state, but it could never be cured. Recovery, arrest, or remission could not be achieved through individual effort or psychiatric intervention, they claimed, but only by group participation, continued abstinence, and the help of a higher power.

Although this emphasis on spiritualism is obvious, Bill W. and Dr. Robert S. publicly played down their religious beliefs to encourage a wider membership. At the same time, they tried to avoid the mistakes made by the Washingtonians. Thus, they adopted a rigid ideology, kept their membership anonymous to broaden its appeal, and forbade any organizational involvement in politics. The AA leaders felt that such involvement had been a major factor in the decline of the Washingtonians. Instead of dissipating the energies of their group as had their predecessors, they sought to increase its longevity and effectiveness by focusing on the single goal of recovery from alcohol.

Bill W., Dr. Robert S., and their followers were not immediately successful in their endeavor. There were only two dozen

AA members in 1938, when *Alcoholics Anonymous* was published, but in 1941, an article about the organization appeared in the *Saturday Evening Post,* and its membership quickly expanded. Chapters sprang up in most American cities and soon were linked by the *Grapevine,* a newsletter which was launched during World War II. By 1960, AA claimed an active membership of 500,000 in the United States, with one hundred foreign chapters. Since then these ranks have been joined by the members of Al-Anon, an educational and therapeutic program for the spouses of alcoholics, as well as comparable organizations for their children, which are called Al-Atots and Al-Ateen.

The tremendous growth of Alcoholics Anonymous has occurred because AA is both a persuasive social movement and a successful therapeutic tool. Members of Alcoholics Anonymous equate such success with a cessation of drinking, and most people who have studied Alcoholics Anonymous estimate that it has helped hundreds of thousands of people achieve temporary and, in many cases, permanent abstinence. This help has been free in most instances, making AA, along with its auxiliary organizations and the multitude of self-help groups based on its model, the cheapest therapy for alcoholism now available.

Alcoholics Anonymous is also the most readily accessible form of therapy. Members of the organization are on hand around the clock to assist drinkers and their families. AA also places members in hospital emergency rooms and other locations frequented by alcoholics. Furthermore, in most areas Alcoholics Anonymous and its auxiliary organizations sponsor a great number of open meetings, many of which are devoted to special interests. Sessions are conducted in a variety of foreign languages, for example, and in many cities there are groups for men only, for women, for homosexuals, and for others. Although these groups do not focus on interpersonal dynamics, they afford many of the benefits of group therapy. In fact, AA's all-embracing nature seems to meet the needs of many patients more than does psychotherapy.

Whether this makes Alcoholics Anonymous the most efficacious therapeutic model remains to be determined. The organization does not keep records, and although AA's therapeutic successes are well known, its failures are not. The fact is that many drinkers avoid Alcoholics Anonymous or drop out after only one or a few meetings. Some people simply do not see themselves as alcoholics or never hit bottom, as Bill W. assumed all alcoholics did. Others are unable to tolerate AA's spiritual emphasis and group orientation, let alone its requirement of abstinence. Furthermore, Alcoholics Anonymous has little appeal on skid row or among upper social circles. Since its inception, the organization has registered its major impact on people from the middle and lower middle levels of society.

This is appropriate, since surveys such as those of Don Cahalan and his colleagues have shown that these latter persons report the greatest number of drinking problems. The only drawback from a scientific point of view is that AA, like the National Council on Alcoholism, which often seems to act as its unofficial legislative arm, has derived and disseminated a very limited idea of alcoholism from its experience with a selective patient population. It also has discouraged arguments against or alternatives to the concept of alcoholism as a disease.

Indeed, only one individual has done as much as Alcoholics Anonymous to advance the disease concept. He was E. M. Jellinek, who began his work at the University of California, San Francisco, and later became a member of the Yale Center for Alcohol Studies. Early in his career, Dr. Jellinek limited his definition of alcoholism to physical dependence, which he equated with an unquenchable craving for ethanol. His concern with this craving, which he blamed for the loss of control seen among alcoholics, stemmed in large part from the results of a questionnaire circulated among AA members in the *Grapevine*.

This questionnaire listed 43 symptoms considered representative of alcoholism by the leaders of Alcoholics Anonymous and believed in implicitly by the organization's members. Those members who received the *Grapevine* were assumed to have had the symptoms and were asked only to indicate at what age the symptoms occurred. One hundred and fifty-eight responses were collected by Alcoholics Anonymous and turned over to Dr. Jellinek for analysis. He rejected group responses and the few which came from women as being potentially unrepresentative. Thus, from the responses of less than 100 men, Dr. Jellinek formulated a sequential scheme for what AA considered the inevitable downhill course associated with dependence on ethanol.

According to this scheme, alcoholism consists of four phases. It begins with a "prealcoholic" phase in which the prospective alcoholic, who presumably drinks for social reasons, experiences not intoxication but relief from anxiety. This relief becomes more and more attractive to the drinker, who becomes habituated or psychologically dependent on the drug. He then forswears socially motivated drinking in pursuit of a diminution of tension. The more he drinks in this fashion, the more he develops tolerance to alcohol.

As tolerance increases, it ushers in the "prodromal" phase. This phase allegedly takes from six months to several years to develop, and is characterized by the onset of blackouts and of five symptoms. These symptoms include surreptitious drinking, preoccupation with ethanol to the exclusion of other pleasures, guilt feelings over one's drinking behavior, avoidance of references to alcohol in social discussions, and increasing consumption of ethanol.

This prodrome then leads to a "crucial" phase which is marked by physical dependence and loss of control. Such dependence in turn results in the 22 symptoms familiar to members of Alcoholics Anonymous. These are rationalizing of the drinking behavior, increasing social pressure on the alcoholic because of his drinking, grandiose behavior, increasing aggressiveness, persistent remorse, periods of total abstinence, changes in drinking patterns, loss of friends, loss of jobs, alcohol-centered behavior, loss of outside interests, reinterpretation of interpersonal relations, marked self-pity, plans for or attempts at geographic escape, changes in family habits, emergence of unreasonable resentments, protection of alcohol supply by storing and hiding, neglect of nutrition, decrease in sexual drives, regular morning drinking, alcoholic jealousies, and, often, the first hospitalization for the physical sequelae of chronic heavy drinking, including withdrawal.

According to the AA beliefs analyzed by Dr. Jellinek, during the crucial phase the alcoholic may try to limit intoxication to the evening hours. But inevitably he fails in this attempt and progresses to the fourth, or "chronic" phase. The cardinal symptom of this phase is the onset of "benders," periods of prolonged daytime drunkenness during which social, professional, and family obligations are neglected. The chronic phase is also characterized by twelve other symptoms. They include marked ethical deterioration; impairment of thinking; alcoholic psychosis; drinking with persons of a lower social level; recourse to methanol, isopropyl alcohol, and other ethanol substitutes; indefinable fears; tremors; psychomotor inhibition; obsessive thinking; development of vague religious desires; and failure to rationalize symptoms, the low point which reflects the hopelessness of alcoholism and its resistance to any form of therapy except that employed by AA.[35]

Dr. Jellinek's formulation was published widely and bestowed great medical prestige upon Alcoholics Anonymous. Yet critics were quick to note that his conclusions amounted to little more than a codification of symptoms previously agreed upon by his subjects. Dr. Jellinek seemed to realize the limitations of his methodology, for soon he abandoned the technique of reaching respondents through the *Grapevine* and instead interviewed 2,000 AA members in depth. These interviews formed the basis of his later formulation, which was summarized in 1960 in his work, *The Disease Concept of Alcoholism.*

Dr. Jellinek devoted much of his book to a review of the evolution of the religious, social, and philosophical thinking about alcoholism. Noting that some people were calling the disease concept a new approach, he explained that the concept actually dated back to the superintendents of institutions for inebriates. He then stated that alcoholism was a disease both because it satisfied many dictionary definitions and because "a disease is what the medical profession recognizes as such." Admitting that for most investigators, including himself earlier in his career, alcoholism was synonymous with physical dependence on ethanol, he declared that this view was too exclusive and, therefore, broadened his previous definition to include "any use of alcoholic beverages that causes any damage to the individual or society or both." He next advanced a formulation of five species of alcoholic identified with Greek letters to arouse fewer adverse connotations among students and patients with the disease.[36]

The first species, "alpha" alcoholism, Dr. Jellinek described as a purely psychological dependence upon the effects of ethanol to relieve bodily or emotional pain. Drinking in this form of alcoholism is "undisciplined" in that it contravenes social rules but does not lead to loss of control or inability to abstain. "The damage caused by this species of alcoholism may be restricted to the disturbance of interpersonal relations," Dr. Jellinek wrote.

> There may be interference with the family budget, occasional absenteeism from work and decreased productivity, and some of the nutritional deficiencies of alcoholism, but not the disturbance due to withdrawal of alcohol. Nor are there any signs of a progressive process. The relief of bodily pain or emotional disturbance implies an underlying illness, and thus, the "undisciplined" use of alcoholic beverages may be regarded as a symptom of the pathological condition which it relieves. This species of alcoholism cannot be regarded as an illness per se.[37]

"Beta" alcoholism, according to Dr. Jellinek, is that species in which such medical complications as peripheral neuropathy, gastritis, and cirrhosis occur without either psychological or physical dependence. The reason for the prolonged heavy drinking required to produce the complications may be social pressure or poor nutritional habits. The damage produced by beta alcoholism naturally includes the physical consequences of drinking, as well as impaired productivity and family problems. Yet withdrawal symptoms are not common and, as with "alpha" alcoholism, a progression of symptoms is not thought to occur.

Dr. Jellinek believed that such progression was most characteristic of "gamma" alcoholism, that species characterized by tolerance, altered cellular metabolism, withdrawal symptoms, and loss of control. Dr. Jellinek saw gamma alcoholism as the result of an advance from psychological to physical dependence. This in turn led to the marked behavior changes spelled out in his earlier formulation, as well as to profound damage to health, interpersonal relations, social standing and financial affairs. According to Dr. Jellinek:

> Gamma alcoholism is apparently the predominating species of alcoholism in the United States and Canada, as well as other Anglo-Saxon countries. It is what members of Alcoholics Anonymous recognize as alcoholism to the exclusion of all other species. Of course, they use loss of control and craving as the criteria par excellence but these necessarily include the other characteristics of gamma alcoholism mentioned above. As I have said before, Alcoholics Anonymous have naturally created the picture of alcoholism in their own image, although at least 10 to 15 percent of their membership are probably specimens of alpha alcoholism who conform in their language to the AA standards. I base this statement on the fact that in a sample of slightly over 2,000 AA members I have found 13 percent who never experienced loss of control. More likely than not only a small percentage of those with alpha alcoholism would seek the help of Alcoholics Anonymous, and almost none of those with beta alcoholism. The latter may be seen most frequently in general hospitals.[38]

"Delta" alcoholism Dr. Jellinek thought to be similar to the gamma type in that both involve tolerance, altered cellular metabolism, and the presence of withdrawal symptoms. However, in place of loss of control, this condition is characterized by inability to abstain. Delta alcoholics apparently are as unable to accept abstinence as are gamma alcoholics, but they can modulate their input, that is, they are capable of controlled drinking. Dr. Jellinek considered such persons rare in Anglo-Saxon countries but common in France, Italy, and other wine-producing areas. Their incentive to drink arises from cultural acceptance of such practices, and since these individuals do not experience social or psychological misfortune, they are unlikely to involve themselves with organizations like AA.

The fifth and final species outlined by Dr. Jellinek was "epsilon" alcoholism. Also called dipsomania or periodic alcoholism, this species is characterized by an overall pattern of sobriety punctuated by recurrent but brief drinking bouts or sprees. Spree drinkers can cause considerable harm to themselves and others, yet only occasionally do they lose self-control. Dr. Jellinek did not describe epsilon alcoholics more fully than this in his book on the disease concept. As to the causes of the condition, he did not say.

Nor did Dr. Jellinek comment on the many other so-called species of alcoholism, other than to note that "all the remaining 19 letters of the Greek and if necessary, other alphabets are available for labelling them." His major point was that representatives of all species share a disorder which is not entirely self-inflicted. Social pressure induces drinking, according to Dr. Jellinek, and in Anglo-Saxon countries alcoholism, along with drinking, is a social institution. Furthermore, many people have personality traits that limit their freedom of choice and predetermine their drinking behavior. In these people, as well as in others, ethanol is a compelling substance which can cause the physiological changes characteristic of a disease.[39]

7. BEYOND THE DISEASE CONCEPT

To assert that alcoholism is a disease runs the risk of obscuring the probable truth that it may be a symptom of a number of quite separate conditions; it also tends to direct the public to medical practitioners who, with their tradition of requiring the patient to be the passive recipient of treatment, may perpetuate errors. Thus it is possible that some forms of alcoholism are not diseases of individuals but of society; some may drown themselves in alcohol as lemmings drown themselves in the sea, and both may be responding to social rather than personal cues. Some forms of alcoholism should properly be grouped with other killing conditions such as obesity, smoking, and possession of high-powered motorcycles. Looked at in this way it may be bad psychology to call these persons "sick" and to be squeamish about such terms as "immaturity," "lack of wisdom" and "self-indulgence" when they are manifestly justified. Such terms as "self-indulgent" or "unreliable" may be objective descriptions, to be sharply distinguished from moral judgments such as "shameful," "wicked," etc. Addicts need someone who will call a spade a spade in a realistic fashion without adopting a punitive, moralistic or superior attitude. They know their weaknesses only too well and do not regard them as an illness, though they may secondarily bring illness. Certainly excesses of any sort may lead to illness or even to death, but we should guard against labeling everything which may shorten life as a disease, and the person who deliberately incurs risk as necessarily sick.

P. D. Scott, "Offenders, Drunkenness, and Murder" (1968)

Many works have been milestones in the history of alcohol, but none has had a greater impact than *The Disease Concept of Alcoholism.* One reason for this impact was that E. M. Jellinek's book expressed the growing belief among physicians and other people that alcoholism was some sort of illness. Many of these persons already had been exposed to Dr. Jellinek through his lectures and earlier writings, most of which were disseminated by Alcoholics Anonymous and the National Council on Alcoholism. Thus when his book was published in 1960, it was greeted enthusiastically by an audience already receptive to his ideas.

Another reason for the impact of *The Disease Concept of Alcoholism* was that the book increased E. M. Jellinek's audience by providing the medical profession with a definition of alcoholism as a disease. This was actually a dual definition, since Dr. Jellinek described all drinking problems as manifestations of alcoholism while singling out gamma alcoholism as the predominant American species. This dual definition contains somewhat incompatible ideas and has tended to divide investigators into two camps, the one favoring a broad approach to alcoholism and the other, a narrow approach. Nevertheless, Dr. Jellinek's definition of alcoholism supplied a model which could be used for diagnostic purposes. Integral to this model was an etiology that encompassed innate physical, psychological, and pharmacological factors; a treatment approach based on abstinence; and an invitation to doctors to regard alcoholism as being within their province, that is, as a disease.

Comparable definitions were proposed by other groups around the time that *The Disease Concept of Alcoholism* was published. One of the first came from the World Health Organization, which, in 1954, defined alcoholism as "a chronic behavioral disorder manifested by repeated drinking of alcoholic beverages in excess of the dietary and social uses of the community and to an extent that interferes with the drinker's health or his social or economic functions."[1] This definition properly regarded ethanol consumption as a cultural issue and resembles Don Cahalan's concept of problem drinking and our own idea of alcohol abuse. Yet its use is limited because the definition does not discuss many aspects of the alleged disease.

While the World Health Organization stressed social factors, the American Medical Association was more concerned with the possible biological causes and pathological consequences of alcoholism. The AMA defined alcoholism in the late 1950s as

an illness characterized by preoccupation with alcohol and loss of control over its consumption such as to lead usually to intoxication if drinking is begun; by chronicity; by progression; and by a tendency towards relapse. It is typically associated with physical disability and impaired emotional, occupational, and/or social adjustments as a direct consequence of persistent and excessive use of alcohol.[2]

The American Psychiatric Association combined both the broad and narrow approaches to alcoholism when it included the condition in its *Diagnostic and Statistical Manual of Mental Disorders,* the standard by which all psychiatric patients are diagnosed today. According to the *Manual,* the diagnostic category of alcoholism "is for patients whose alcohol intake is great enough to damage their personal health, or their personal or social functioning, or when it has become a prerequisite to normal functioning." The *Manual* lists several specific states under this general category of alcoholism. These include alcohol addiction, which "should be diagnosed when there is direct or strong evidence that a patient is dependent on alcohol"; episodic excessive drinking, which is defined as being intoxicated as often as 4 times yearly; and habitual excessive drinking, which involves being intoxicated more than 12 times a year.[3]

In its *Diagnostic and Statistical Manual,* the Psychiatric Association lists these specific states and the general category of alcoholism under the subheading of personality disorders. This group of disorders also embraces sexual deviations, dependence on other drugs, and certain character types, such as hysterical, antisocial, and obsessive-compulsive characters. Personality disorders are marked "by deeply ingrained maladaptive patterns of behavior that are perceptibly different in quality from psychotic and neurotic symptoms," according to the *Manual.* Personality disorders also are differentiated from other subheadings, including delirium, or acute organic brain syndrome, and dementia, or chronic organic brain syndrome, which are associated with abuse of ethanol.[4]

Alcoholism thus is considered a deeply rooted disorder of personality by the American Psychiatric Association. This classification rightfully stresses how important drinking can become to a person but artificially distinguishes between the personality style of the alcoholic and the results of prolonged heavy drinking. Furthermore, by separating out alcoholism from the neuroses and psychoses, the Psychiatric Association's labeling system reinforces the thought that alcoholics are different from other people only in their drinking behavior.

Under this system, alcoholism can be listed as a primary diagnosis in patients who evidence that kind of personality disorder. Yet the *Manual* also advises that when harmful drinking seems to coincide with or result from another state, such as a neurosis or psychosis, it should be listed as a secondary diagnosis. Thus a person might be described as having a personality disorder, alcoholism-type. Alternatively, he or she could be identified as manifesting an anxiety neurosis with alcoholism as a consequence. Or the individual might be described as a schizophrenic and also carry the diagnosis of alcoholism.

The labeling system used by the American Psychiatric Association represents a political compromise. On one hand, it is compatible with the psychoanalytic idea that alcoholism is a final common pathway of many conditions and not a specific disease entity. On the other, the system furthers the argument of Alcoholics Anonymous and the National Council on Alcoholism that alcoholism should usually be considered a primary diagnosis. Yet, as a compromise, the system falls short of the wishes of the lay organizations, which would have preferred that alcoholism be granted independent subheading status and not be included with drug dependence as a disorder of personality.

The Psychiatric Association wanted to increase public and professional awareness of alcoholism by placing it in the *Diagnostic and Statistical Manual.* The same position was taken by the American Medical Association, which distributed literature on alcoholism and passed a resolution urging that alcoholics receive the same services as other patients, and the American Hospital Association, which recommended that general hospitals admit alcoholics for the conditions spelled out in the *Diagnostic and Statistical Manual,* and not hidden behind labels such as gastritis, cirrhosis, and other physical problems related to prolonged ethanol consumption.

These actions helped change the attitudes of many physicians. However, the professional organizations were not entirely successful in obtaining treatment for alcoholics, in part because of prejudice against alcoholics prevalent among the general public as well as among doctors. Another reason was that physicians did not agree about a single definition of alcoholism or were unconvinced by the disease concept. Reflecting the general medical attitude toward alcoholics, a poll conducted in 1965 by the National Council on Alcoholism revealed that one-third of doctors, including psychiatrists, refused to treat alcoholics. Two-thirds of American hospitals did not accept patients with the primary diagnosis of alcoholism during the same year.

Contrary to this resistance on the part of physicians, the disease concept of alcoholism received new support from the legal profession. This support was prompted by a genuine desire to help alcoholics in some instances. In others, however, it stemmed more from frustration with alcoholics and from awareness of the expense and futility of the criminal justice approach to their condition. As we have noted, criminal justice methods have resulted from the traditional view that alcoholism is either a sin or a civil offense which should be controlled by religious or criminal sanctions. Laws endorsing this view were propagated before and after Prohibition, when state and federal governments favored the punishment of drunks over their rehabilitation. As a result, after World War II, the most common reason for incarceration in the United States, and the cause of two-thirds of all arrests in major cities, was public intoxication.

Lawyers and jurists in the 1950s and 1960s were convinced that arrests were not the answer for alcoholism. At the same time, they agreed with the increasingly popular idea that the criminal justice approach should be superseded by a medical model. Yet the lawyers and jurists also appreciated the inherent size and inertia of our health care system and realized that health professionals might not be willing to assume responsibility for patients who carried the diagnosis of alcoholism until changes were made in the legal status of this condition. They therefore tried to influence legislation and update laws to reflect the concept that alcoholism is a disease.

According to Judge Samuel Kirbens, this effort was given initial impetus in the 1962 case of *Robinson* vs. *California,* in which the California Supreme Court decided that the defendant could not be punished for his dependence on heroin. The court based this decision on the Fourteenth Amendment of the U. S. Constitution, which forbids the states from depriving American citizens of life, liberty, or property without due process of law. The court also invoked the Eighth Amendment prohibition of cruel and unusual punishment. Previously, only the due process provision had been applied to abusers of alcohol and other drugs, but since *Robinson,* these persons cannot receive criminal penalties for behavior resulting from a disease.[5]

While the *Robinson* case affirmed that alcoholics should not be punished for their illness, other cases have been concerned with the association between alcohol and criminal responsibility and have raised the question of whether alcoholism might be regarded, like insanity, as a defense to a criminal charge. The first such case occurred in 1865 when the Supreme Court of New Hampshire allowed that alcoholism was available as a defense to the charge of murder. More recently, in the 1967 case of the State of *Wisconsin* vs. *Freiberg,* the defendant, who was charged with failure to support his child, claimed the disease of chronic alcoholism prevented him from maintaining employment and thereby supporting his family. The court in this case agreed that the defense was valid, although the defendant was convicted for other reasons. However, in general the courts have continued to hold alcoholics responsible for murder and other major offenses while allowing for the decriminalization of alcoholism in terms of public intoxication and related crimes.

The campaign for decriminalization began in Washington, D.C., in 1964, following the arrest of a derelict named Walter Bowles for drunkenness. Bowles was immediately picked out of a drunk tank by interested attorneys to be a test case, but the prosecution avoided the issue by dropping the charges in this and three other cases until the Circuit Court of the District of Columbia refused to allow it to do so. The fifth case involved DeWitt Easter, a homeless alcoholic who had been arrested approximately 70 times for public inebriation and other problems stemming from his drinking behavior. As attention was drawn to Easter's case by the media, another test case was initated by filing a *habeas corpus* petition in the District

Court of North Carolina on behalf of a derelict named Joe Driver. The defendant in this case had over 200 arrests to his credit and had spent two-thirds of his adult life in jail.

In both cases the legal challenge to the public intoxication statutes was based on the principle that criminal sanctions may be applied only to voluntary actions. The attorneys for Driver and Easter argued that their clients were alcoholics whose ethanol consumption was compulsive and who could not avoid being seen in public because they could not afford to drink in private. This argument was rejected by the lower courts, but in 1966, the District of Columbia Circuit Court held that an alcoholic's intoxication is involuntary and hence is not punishable. At the same time, the North Carolina Circuit Court decided that jailing a derelict for drinking constitutes cruel and unusual punishment in keeping with the decision in *Robinson* vs. *California.*

Georgia followed the lead in these landmark cases, and there and in the District of Columbia judges began committing alcoholics to the care of health, rather than police, agencies. But society was logistically unprepared for the *Easter* and *Driver* decisions. Only 50 hospital beds were available for intoxicated patients in Washington, D.C., for example, although more than 9,000 persons were declared to be alcoholics by the courts. Similarly, in Atlanta, where 55 percent of all arrests previously were for drunkenness, the local hospitals and clinics were flooded with court referrals.

Such chaos set the scene in 1967 for the Supreme Court's *Powell* decision. In this case, an uneducated laborer and inebriate named Powell had been jailed for public intoxication in Texas and appealed the conviction on the grounds that he could not help appearing drunk in public because he drank out of necessity and could not afford a home. By a five to four vote, the Supreme Court turned down this appeal, noting that Powell was not homeless or otherwise unable to avoid public places when intoxicated. Yet five of the nine justices agreed that alcoholism is a disease, that an alcoholic drinks involuntarily as a result of his illness, and that a truly homeless alcoholic could not confine his drinking to a private place and therefore could not be convicted rightfully for public inebriation.

At the same time, the Supreme Court used the *Powell* case to criticize both the government and the medical profession. Thurgood Marshall, for example, stated that because of the lack of treatment facilities which existed in 1967, it was necessary to arrest alcoholics if only to let them detoxify themselves in jail. Justice Marshall considered this situation far from ideal and agreed that a change in the legal status of alcoholism and the social approach to it was desirable. Yet he and the other justices let it be known that they would not engage this issue until the federal government provided a framework for dealing with alcoholism on a national level, until the states furnished medical and psychiatric treatment for alcoholics, and until professionals agreed upon a definition of alcoholism as a disease.

Although the Supreme Court drew attention to the fact, the lack of a governmental framework for dealing with alcoholism had been evident for many years. Indeed, no federal health, welfare, or rehabilitation statutes explicitly referred to alcoholism prior to 1966. Laws were concerned with the issue only within the broader context of mental health, and it was not covered as a separate entity under the National Mental Health Act of 1948, which authorized an expansion of community mental health services.

The first federal appropriations for such services were made a year later, and in 1949, the National Institute of Mental Health was established as a subdivision of the National Institutes of Health to provide research and training. In 1963, Congress passed the Community Mental Health Centers Act, which authorized treatment services on a community basis for many disorders, including alcoholism for the first time. National Institute of Mental Health programs were extended, and in 1966, the organization spawned a National Center for the Prevention and Control of Alcoholism which was headed by Jack Mendelson.

The first federal statute to deal directly with alcoholism came in the same year. It was the 1966 Highway Safety Act, which required reports to the Congress on the effects of alcohol on traffic accidents. During the next year, in response to these reports, the federal Department of Transportation issued standards for highway safety which the states were required to meet in order to qualify for federal highway construction funds. These standards compelled the states to have specific tests available for determining blood alcohol concentrations, to define as under the influence of ethanol a person with a BAC in excess of 100 to 150 milligrams percent, and to enact provisions making it either unlawful or presumptive evidence of illegality to have a BAC in excess of that amount. As a result, those states that had not already established laws against driving while intoxicated did so, and today all fifty states also have adopted implied consent laws.

The Economic Opportunity Act of 1967 was the first federal statute to contain provisions for the treatment of alcoholics. In 1968, Lyndon Johnson became the first American president to legitimize the disease concept and, to avoid the problems that occurred after the *Easter* and *Driver* decisions, urged Congress to pass an Alcohol Rehabilitation Act which made limited funds available to the states for treatment programs. The Community Mental Health Centers Act was amended during the same year to provide some grants to facilities for alcoholics, and plans were formulated for the country's first comprehensive statute on alcoholism.

Although many people contributed to the development of this statute, certain individuals deserve major credit. They include members of the National Council on Alcholism, who campaigned across the country for new legislation, and Senator Harold Hughes of Iowa, who was its chief proponent in Washington. Senator Hughes was the highest elected official to discuss his drinking problems in public during the late 1960s, and since then he has devoted much of his time to Alcoholics Anonymous. More than any single person since E. M. Jellinek, he put alcoholism in the spotlight and won acceptance for the concept of alcoholism as a disease.

The Comprehensive Alcohol Abuse and Alcoholism Prevention, Treatment, and Rehabilitation Act, which also was known as the Hughes bill, was approved by Congress in 1970 and signed into law by President Richard Nixon. This historic statute acknowledged that the disease of alcoholism is a public health problem which should be removed from the criminal justice system. To facilitate this removal and provide for a public health approach, the act established a National Institute on Alcohol Abuse and Alcoholism, the successor of the National Center for the Prevention and Control of Alcoholism. The act empowered the new agency to administer all alcoholism programs assigned to the Department of Health, Education, and Welfare, and to coordinate federal activities in this field. It also created a National Advisory Council on Alcohol Abuse and Alcoholism to assist in developing a national policy.

Alcoholics Anonymous and the National Council on Alcoholism hoped that the National Institute on Alcohol Abuse and Alcoholism would become a separate institute of the National Institutes of Health and not be housed within the National Institute of Mental Health. The organization reasoned that more federal funds would be available for the new agency if it were granted separate institute status. They also resented the connotation that alcoholism was a mental health problem and felt that abstinence and self-help principles would be furthered if the new agency were independent. However, in spite of their wishes, the Institute became part of the National Institute of Mental Health until the mid-1970s, when the latter organization was incorporated into the federal Alcohol, Drug, and Mental Health Administration. Within this new framework, the National Institute on Alcohol Abuse and Alcoholism, the National Institute on Drug Abuse, and the National Institute of Mental Health are given equal status.

Under the leadership of Morris Chafetz, the National Institute on Alcohol Abuse and Alcoholism quickly established itself as an aggressive agency. It assumed the research, education, and training functions of its predecessors almost overnight and by 1971 had presented a new set of priorities in the *First Special Report to the U. S. Congress on Alcohol and Health.* These priorities included providing help to alcoholic employees, rehabilitating public inebriates, reducing alcoholism among American Indians, delivering comprehensive services to all alcoholics, treating people identified through traffic safety programs, and preventing alcohol abuse and alcoholism.

Although outlined by the federal government, these priorities were intended to become the responsibility of the states. The Comprehensive Act of 1970 required the states to develop community-based treatment programs in order to receive their share of federal funds, although it did not contain specific guidelines for the programs. To overcome this deficiency, in 1971, the National Commission on Uniform State Laws, which is made up of representatives appointed by state governors, drew up a Uniform Alcoholism and Intoxication Treatment Act. In its preamble, the Act declares that alcoholics and intoxicated persons should not be subjected to criminal prosecution because of their consumption of alcoholic beverages. It then describes how states and communities should set up a continuum of treatment and rehabilitation services for alcoholics.

The Uniform Alcoholism and Intoxication Treatment Act has been the model by which many states have moved from a criminal justice to a medical approach to alcoholism. The first state to do so was Hawaii, which, in 1968, abolished the crime of public intoxication and instituted a civil commitment and detoxification procedure in place of its previous policy of arrest and incarceration. North Dakota, Connecticut, Florida, Massachusetts, California, and Colorado followed suit, and communities across the country began diverting alcoholics into their public health systems during the early 1970s. This action has not always been successful, as will be seen in the next chapter. Yet, by and large, inauguration of the ideas contained in the Uniform Act has improved services for alcoholics and signified the acceptance of the concept of alcoholism as a disease.

Although the Uniform Act has had these effects, in 1971, the country still lacked a definition of alcoholism that was acceptable to the medical profession. This problem had been spelled out by the Supreme Court in its *Powell* decision four years earlier, but physicians did not respond immediately to the court's challenge. In fact, the first response came from the National Council on Alcoholism, which hoped to satisfy the Supreme Court and help doctors diagnose alcoholism by creating guidelines by which the condition could be identified.

The National Council wanted these guidelines to be as specific as the Jones criteria which were introduced earlier in the century to select those signs and symptoms that were diagnostic of rheumatic fever. The National Council also intended to overcome the limitations of other diagnostic systems by basing the diagnosis of alcoholism as much as possible on physical examinations, laboratory data, and the reports of patients and their families. Therefore, in 1971, it convened a group of physicians which was called the criteria committee of the National Council on Alcoholism.

This committee, of which Richard Shore was a member, was chaired by Samuel Kaim, director of the Staff for Alcoholism and Related Disorders of the Veterans Administration. It included over a dozen doctors representing medical schools, research institutes, treatment centers, and governmental agencies, including the National Institute on Alcohol Abuse and Alcoholism. Given their diverse backgrounds, these physicians naturally differed in their understanding of alcoholism and in their interpretation of various data. Yet they were able to agree that alcoholism is a pathological dependence on ethanol. Furthermore, the representatives all felt that diagnostic criteria would be helpful in promoting the early detection of dependence, preventing under- and overdiagnosis, providing uniform standards for research, and assisting in the treatment of persons with drinking problems.

These criteria, which ranged from withdrawal symptoms to surreptitious drinking, were divided into two so-called data tracks. Track one contained physiological and clinical data, and track two contained behavioral, psychological, and attitudinal data. Both tracks were then separated into three diagnostic levels, the first obligatorily linked with alcoholism, the second frequently indicative of alcoholism, and the third representing only a potential association with the condition. In addition to these diagnostic levels, the criteria for both tracks were divided into major and minor components in terms of their presumed severity, as is the case with the Jones criteria.[6]

The diagnostic criteria conceived by the committee convened by the National Council on Alcoholism were published in 1972. Since then, the criteria have been disseminated by the media and by medical educators. They have been praised for their completeness, their usefulness in case finding and research, and their impact in prompting physicians to treat alcoholism and alcohol-related problems. Although necessarily a compromise between different viewpoints, the criteria have satisfied the Supreme Court's objective of defining alcoholism quantitatively and qualititatively as a disease.

In spite of this fact, however, the criteria are fraught with problems. They are not written in readily understandable language, for example, and are almost overwhelming in their complexity. By using the diagnostic level approach, the criteria arbitrarily segment the life experiences that make up alcoholism. And by dividing these segments into behavioral and physiological tracks, they help perpetuate the mind-body dualism that separates medicine and psychiatry.

Furthermore, the criteria reflect a biological slant and say too little about the intrapsychic, interpersonal, and social factors which relate to alcoholism. This is understandable, since the criteria were created by physicians. But the biological slant limits the criteria's usefulness and points out the difficulty of trying to fit a multifaceted phenomenon such as alcoholism into a narrow system like that of the Jones criteria. And as noted by Charles Becker, Robert Scott, and Robert Roe, the criteria may lead doctors who suspect alcoholism to overlook other reasons for the physical complaints of their patients and to ignore the psychological problems that may underlie drinking behavior.[7]

Beyond these specific complaints, criticism of the diagnostic criteria really should be directed at the disease concept upon which they are based. Both the criteria and the concept overvalue the results and underplay the causes of behavior. Thus they define pathology in terms of physical dependence on ethanol as well as upon such symptoms as large livers and gulped drinks. This may be helpful to physicians, but it loses sight of the psychological meaning of what people do.

At the same time, the criteria and the disease concept share the reductionistic idea that, at any given moment, a person is or is not an alcoholic. This is a static notion which tends to freeze drinkers at points along a spectrum of experience and does not encourage a dynamic view of alcoholism. Indeed, it fosters a bookkeeping approach in which one's status as an alcoholic depends on a tabulation of the symptoms one has or has not accumulated in the course of his or her disease.

This cumulative notion may be conceptually handy, but it is both arbitrary and simplistic from a scientific standpoint. The stigmata of physical dependence admittedly are more conspicuous among certain heavy drinkers, yet such dependence is neither irreversible nor limited to hardened alcoholics. As we have noted, subtle withdrawal symptoms are seen in many drinkers, while the cellular changes attributed to ethanol can occur after only a few drinks and may or may not accumulate over time. Jerome Jaffe has emphasized that it is meaningless to differentiate among drinkers on the basis of physical dependence because the biological changes that cause such dependence probably begin with the initial ingestion of alcohol. As if in recognition of this fact, the Committee on Alcoholism and Drug Dependence of the American Medical Association recently stated that "there is no exact point in time when it can be said that heavy drinking becomes alcoholism. The transition from excessive drinking, as a manifestation of psychological dependence, to alcoholism, which also implies tolerance and physical dependence, is too subtle and insidious to be clearly defined."[8]

Even if we could separate out alcoholics on some quantitative basis, their so-called illness would not meet most rigorous disease definitions. Alcoholism does not satisfy the *Random House Dictionary* requirements of being "a condition . . . in which there is incorrect function resulting from the effects of heredity, infection, diet or environment."[9] Nor can it be called a condition "with characteristic changes caused by specific microorganismal alteration," as *Stedman's Medical Dictionary* would have it.[10] Admittedly, alcoholism does qualify as an illness if one uses Dr. Jellinek's broad description of a disease as being any condition that the medical professions recognizes as such. But alcoholism is far too pervasive a problem to be decided upon solely by physicians. Because of the social, political, and economic connotations of the disease concept, many sectors other than the medical should have a voice in defining disease.

This is especially true because alcoholism does not fit any known disease model. Billions of dollars have been spent to determine its etiology, but the precise causes of alcoholism are unknown. In brief, we suffer from a plethora of theories and a paucity of facts about the causes of dependence on ethanol. We have made progress in understanding this dependence and have developed drugs like Antabuse® which can enforce abstinence. We have also witnessed the change from a criminal justice approach to a medical model in dealing with alcoholism. However, we must not forget that our knowledge is incomplete, that medications like disulfiram do not work for all people, and that there are serious limitations with the medical model.

One limitation is that the model implies that physicians can deal with the basic causes of alcoholism, which is seldom the case. Another is that the model identifies the alcoholic as a patient for whom the hospital is an appropriate place of treatment; this isolates him from his family and culture and does not attend to the importance of environmental factors. The medical model also stresses the helplessness of patients instead of their self-determination. This tends to undervalue their sense of responsiblity and may lead to a therapeutic zealousness which interferes with civil liberties.

Such zealousness is the target of Thomas Szasz. Dr. Szasz believes that drinking is a habit and that the value placed by an individual on his or her habit should determine whether it is good or bad. Historically, society has decided that some forms of drinking are evil or criminal and thus has infringed upon individual rights. This infringement was widened when society decided that drinking was not only bad but also an illness, for this decision led to the supplanting of church or police intervention with civil commitment and involuntary treatment procedures. According to Dr. Szasz, the individual has even less legal defense against these procedures than if he committed a crime.

This change may have been well intentioned, Dr. Szasz notes, and in some ways it has had a salutary effect. Nevertheless, the upshot is deprivation of personal liberties in the name of medical help. If our ultimate aim is a society where individuals are self-disciplined, rather than controlled by external authority, we cannot expect to advance towards that goal by proliferating laws for the coercive medical control of an ever-increasing variety of behaviors, among them the use of alcoholic beverages.[11]

Although we share Dr. Szasz's concern about imposing treatment on anyone, we feel that the Uniform Alcoholism and Intoxication Treatment Act adequately safeguards the rights of patients. Borrowing from the act, many states have taken steps to prevent the confinement of psychiatric patients, including alcoholics, unless they are a danger to themselves or other persons. Thus Dr. Szasz's writings, which date from before such steps were taken, must be put in historical perspective. At the same time, we must remember that much of the impetus for imposing treatment on alcoholics stemmed from the popular belief that alcoholism is an inevitably progressive disorder caused and characterized by loss of control.

As we have noted, the basis for this belief is rooted in AA precepts and in E. M. Jellinek's early work on the four phases of alcoholism. Dr. Jellinek's four steps and their 43 attendant symptoms are ingrained in the folklore of alcoholism, yet no one has confirmed their existence. In fact, the studies of Don Cahalan and others have indicated that drinking does not follow an inexorable course, be it downhill or around corners, and that alcoholics who at one time might even meet the diagnostic criteria of the National Council on Alcoholism do not necessarily progress in their drinking behavior. The famous four steps have also proven useless in predicting behavior from a clinical standpoint, and the only persons who still subscribe to Dr. Jellinek's formulation are the members of Alcoholics Anonymous, from whom the steps and symptoms were originally derived, and the public that has been educated by them.

Scientific support has come, however, for the contention that many people drink to relieve anxiety. In the 1960s the team of John Tamerin, Sheldon Weiner, and Jack Mendelson obtained extensive psychological profiles on hundreds of subjects and determined that drinkers of all sorts, including alcoholics, seek in their drinking a decrease in anxiety and depression and an increase in sociability and self-esteem. Moderate drinkers may in fact achieve these results and presumably are more likely to drink to, but usually not beyond, the point at which such results are achieved. Chronic alcoholics report similar gratifications in the early stages of drinking, yet as their alcohol consumption continues, they manifest more anxiety and depression than they did before drinking. They also appear less sociable and suffer a drop in self-esteem.[12]

Why then do they continue drinking? From the loss of control perspective, one reason might be a physiological craving for ethanol. Yet such craving, a cornerstone of the disease concept, has never been verified and may well have been disproved. In 1966, for example, John Merry took a large number of alcoholics and for 18 days gave them drinks so strongly flavored that the subjects could not tell when the drinks contained alcohol. Dr. Merry found that as many subjects reported a craving for the non-alcoholic solution as they did for the one containing ethanol.[13] In 1972, K. Engle and T. Williams repeated Dr. Merry's work and learned that the only increased report of craving came from those subjects who were told, falsely, that there was alcohol in their drinks.[14] These investigators concluded that suggestion and psychological factors were important in the craving issue, not the pharmacology of ethanol.

Theoretically, if some sort of pharmacological craving does exist, alcoholics placed in a setting with unrestricted access to alcohol should consume large amounts of the drug. Yet this was not the case with the subjects of experiments conducted recently by Nancy Mello and Jack Mendelson. In these experiments, subjects could receive ten milliliter doses of whiskey any time they wished. After five days of drinking, their requests were infrequent, and most subjects demonstrated that they could either take alcohol or leave it alone.[15]

Also integral to the loss of control perspective is the theory that people continue drinking to avoid withdrawal. If this were true, one might expect that alcoholics offered unlimited ethanol would maintain a fairly constant blood alcohol level to forestall the onset of abstinence symptoms. Yet Drs. Mello and Mendelson, who investigated this possibility in drinkers in a ward setting, found that it was not the case. The BACs of their subjects fluctuated widely, and occasionally the subjects stopped drinking for days at a time, even though doing so meant the onset of withdrawal symptoms. Rather than gulping drinks and appearing desperate, the subjects exhibited a great deal of self-control.[16]

Controlled drinking was also demonstrated in a recent study by Alfonso Paredes and his colleagues. This study was conducted on 30 alcoholics with an average of 12.5 years of heavy drinking, 24 of whom reported that they regularly experienced loss of control. On a hospital ward setting, these subjects were offered unlimited quantities of ginger ale and 95 percent ethanol and demonstrated controlled behavior in that they drank in an area designated for drinking, began and ended drinking at times designated by the researchers, displayed no disruptive activity, and conformed to a predetermined period of two weeks of abstinence prior to and after the period of drinking. Three of the 30 subjects left the study before its completion, but the majority manifested purposeful drinking in the research setting and experienced no subjective loss of control.[17]

One limitation of these two studies is that they were conducted in artificial hospital environments. Yet we and others have observed controlled drinking in a variety of natural settings. On skid row, for example, it is customary for residents to sip fortified wines throughout the day and rarely become incapacitated. In business circles, it is common for executives to drink heavily at luncheons, before board meetings, and after such meetings are held. However, because the executives are able to function during these moments their colleagues willingly tolerate their involvement with alcohol.

A third and classic example of controlled drinking is seen in the French laborers who may drink up to three liters of wine a day and never appear intoxicated. These laborers may develop delirium tremens during hospitalization for nonalcohol-related problems, proving that they are physically dependent on ethanol. Yet their families and friends may never have suspected the degree of their dependence. According to E. M. Jellinek, the French call this common condition *alcoolisation,* or *l'alcoolisme sans ivresse,* or alcoholism without drunkenness. Indeed, the presence of this condition in France led Dr. Jellinek to identify delta alcoholism as that species that is characterized by inability to abstain rather than by loss of control.[18]

Thus it seems from both street and laboratory experience that the loss of control perspective, with its inherent ideas of physiological craving and the need to forestall withdrawal symptoms, is less a personal imperative than a self-fulfilling prophecy. It provides an excuse to the person who needs to continue drinking, a weapon for AA members who wish to frighten him into abstinence, and an explanation for those who view alcoholism primarily in terms of pharmacology. Yet there is limited scientific support for the loss of control perspective. Some people may increase their alcohol intake to offset anxiety after prolonged heavy drinking, but one sip of ethanol does not lead to another through loss of control.

If loss of control is not the reason, why then do people continue to drink in the face of increased discomfort? Nancy Mello offers two possible reasons other than avoidance of withdrawal and physiological craving. One reason, she states, is that alcohol may disturb short-term memory to such an extent that alcoholics cannot remember the eventual consequences of heavy drinking and recall only its immediate, pleasurable effects. As a corollary to this, it is possible that their positive recollections of drinking experiences may relate to state-dependent learning in some as yet unexplained way. The end result is that many of those alcoholics who report being depressed and anxious when interviewed while they are drinking perceive of themselves as having had the opposite feelings when questioned after they sober up. Drinking thus may have a salutary effect on the memories of these alcoholics. Seeking quick relief from painful feelings, they may consciously or unconsciously drink to forget.[19]

Another possibility offered by Dr. Mello, is that alcoholics are rewarded several ways for their drinking behavior. The idea of behavioral rewards comes from learning theory, a school of psychological thought which, in contrast to psychoanalytic theory, has evolved more from laboratory experiments than from clinical experience. Its founder was the Russian physiologist Ivan Pavlov, while in recent years it has been identified with B. F. Skinner and other behavioral psychologists.

Basic to learning theory are the ideas of operant conditioning and the conditional response. Such responses are conditioned in the sense that the organism learns to react in a certain way to both an initial stimulus and to a condition associated with it. Operant conditioning derives from the principle that if behavior is positively reinforced, the organism will tend to repeat it. By contrast, behavior can be extinguished if it is not reinforced or if it takes on a negative connotation. From the ideas of operant conditioning and the conditioned response have evolved two major theories of alcoholism. The first theory holds that alcoholism is a conditioned response in that people come to associate ethanol with pleasurable sensations or a diminution of discomfort. The second theory states that alcoholism is drinking behavior that is repeated because it is reinforced.

The possibility that alcoholism might be a conditioned response was explored in the experiments of Jules Masserman and K. S. Yum. In 1946, these investigators created a conflict situation by training cats to open boxes to obtain food and then subjecting the animals to blasts of compressed air when the boxes were opened. The cats thereafter avoided the boxes, even to the point of starvation, until they were given ethanol and started to open the boxes again.[20] Several years later, John Conger trained a group of rats to approach a food area, and another to avoid electric shock. After an injection of alcohol, the pull away from the shock was weaker, while the move toward the food was not stronger. These experiments were interpreted to suggest that ethanol tends to blunt a response based on fear, rather than to enhance the response to a pleasant situation.[21]

The idea of alcoholism as reinforced behavior was proposed by J. A. Dollard and N. E. Miller. These investigators stated that alcohol results in a temporary reduction of fear and conflict and that the attempt to decrease these states with ethanol, followed by the discomfort of withdrawal, produces an addictive cycle.[22] Nancy Mello and other behaviorists are in basic agreement with this model. They feel that alcoholics learn to relieve anxiety through drinking and that this relief becomes its own reinforcement. The relief also crowds out other behavioral responses to stress because it is so rapid. However, as chronic drinking causes other problems, anxiety recurs and prompts drinking again.

A common objection to learning theory is that the results of long-term ethanol consumption seem unrewarding and therefore should extinguish drinking behavior. Yet this objection can be answered in several ways. In the above model, for example, drinking is seen as a self-perpetuating phenomenon. Furthermore, the relief provided by ethanol is described as a strong positive reinforcement. The strength of this reinforcement relates to the fact that it is a clear and immediate gratification, one that offsets the vague and distant effects of heavy drinking.

Although learning theory stresses the strength of certain reinforcements, it also emphasizes that behavior is neither preordained nor immutable but can be modified. Such behavioral modification has become an important therapy in the field of alcoholism. It generally involves the use of positive or negative reinforcement techniques to ingrain or extinguish learned responses and thereby change behavior.

Aversive conditioning, a form of negative reinforcement, was introduced in the treatment of alcoholism in the 1930s. During that period, investigators showed cards containing labels of liquor bottles to patients while simultaneously giving the patients electric shocks. The investigators then paired the shocks with the actual bottles as well as the sight, smell, and taste of their contents. After several weeks of this aversive conditioning, the patients lost their desire to drink and subsequently remained abstinent up to a year.

Since this early work, behavioral therapists have reported comparable success through a variety of aversive techniques. Some still use electric shock with patients. Others give their patients Antabuse® and alcohol and make them vomit. Still others combine these techniques with films of alcoholics in delirium tremens and videotapes of the patients themselves as they drink and become sick. Although such methods seem undignified, when entered into voluntarily by patients they often bring impressive results.

By contrast, positive reinforcement has involved the giving of rewards for desirable behavior. Such behavior might include regular attendance in treatment, a decreased incidence of police problems, or improved health. The rewards afforded patients have included praise from therapists, increased responsibility as a therapeutic group member, or tokens that can be used to purchase food and cigarettes. Admittedly, positive reinforcement is best suited to hospital settings, where outside influences can be minimized. Yet positive reinforcement also can be used during office visits, and when continued reinforcement can be provided through programs that provide detoxification, counseling, social activities and other services, some patients have been able to sustain changes in their drinking behavior for years.

While some therapists have tried to develop programs that offer continued reinforcement, others have focused on the association between alcohol and anxiety which is so fundamental to learning theory. These therapists have assumed that patients might not be prompted to drink so much if they could learn to relax and thereby lower their anxiety levels or if they were desensitized to stressful interpersonal situations which cause their anxiety levels to rise. From this assumption have evolved techniques designed to accomplish desensitization or relaxation and a concommitant reduction in anxiety.

The desensitization techniques are the same as those used to treat phobias. They involve exposing patients to thoughts about and pictures or sound tapes of stressful situations, such as cocktail parties or business meetings, which normally are associated with anxiety and heavy drinking. Gradually this exposure is increased, while the patient is taught to relax in these settings. The therapy is considered successful when patients can tolerate the formerly stressful situations in reality.

Relaxation techniques, on the other hand, aim for a more

general decrease in tension and anxiety. Although some merely attempt to teach muscle relaxation, many of these techniques relate to the fact that the autonomic nervous system and the physiological functions it governs, such as heart rate, blood pressure, and brain wave activity, can be brought under semi-voluntary control. Acquiring such control has been an objective of Yoga, meditation, and other ancient Eastern disciplines. It also is the goal of modern biofeedback methods utilizing devices that monitor autonomic functions and relay this information to patients. The patients in turn use the information to achieve states of deep relaxation and moderate their drinking behavior.

Essential to these methods is the belief that heavy drinkers can and should be taught to temper their alcohol consumption without necessarily becoming abstinent. The goal, then, is controlled drinking, the intentional modulation of the quantity and duration of alcoholic beverage consumption which is practiced by the overwhelming majority of Americans. Such a therapeutic endpoint would have been considered heretical at best 15 years ago, when *The Disease Concept of Alcoholism* was published. But in recent years, demonstrations that controlled drinking is possible for some alcoholics, coupled with increased sophistication in the techniques of behavioral modification, have led some therapists to attempt to modify, rather than abolish, drinking behavior.

In 1962, for example, D. L. Davies reported that seven out of 93 chronic drunkards had become social drinkers after participation in a hospital-based detoxification, behavioral modification, and aftercare program. After one year, Dr. Davies claimed, three of the seven subjects drank between one and three pints of beer each evening; three intermittently drank beer, wine, and whiskey; and one had stopped drinking because of peptic ulcer disease.[23] Dr. Davies's report initially was denounced by therapists who called abstinence the only answer for alcoholism and insisted that if these seven individuals were capable of social drinking they could not be alcoholics in the first place. But later reviewers indicated that the seven met Dr. Jellinek's criteria.

After Dr. Davies broke the therapeutic ice, other investigators reported comparable success in developing social drinking patterns in former drunkards. This success was recorded most often in middle and upper middle class clients who seem more attracted and amenable to behavioral modification than other persons. In one study, Kenneth Mills and his colleagues used electric shock to shape such patterns in 13 subjects.[24] Similarly, M. and L. Sobell followed 70 male alcoholics through treatment and found that some of them could be taught to drink socially in a ward environment.[25]

Larry Meredith of the Bureau of Alcoholism of San Francisco's Community Mental Health Services has developed a prototype program which employs desensitization and relaxation techniques, and positive and negative reinforcement in combination with group process and insight psychotherapy. According to Dr. Meredith, a recent study has revealed that after one year 16 percent of participants in this program had remained abstinent. Fifty-one percent were still drinking but were drinking far less than when they began the program. Even more important, these drinkers reported significant improvement in such areas as increased psychological well-being, decreased physical symptoms, greater feelings of self-esteem, and fewer feelings of anxiety and depression. These data suggest that, in contrast to traditional beliefs, abstinence is not always a prerequisite for sobriety.[26]

This position is held by Mansell Pattison, who, in 1966, reviewed the abstinence versus social drinking debate and came to several conclusions. First, he noted, abstinence is neither a necessary nor a realistic goal of treatment in all instances, and in many cases controlled drinking can be induced or spontaneously realized. Second, abstinence need not be a sign of therapeutic success, any more than lack of abstinence need be a sign of failure. Third, abstinence is not synonymous with mental health, since people who stop or alter their alcohol consumption do not always improve the quality of their life experience. And fourth, when behavioral modification and other therapies succeed, they seem to do so not because they help alcoholics return to earlier, more moderate drinking patterns, but because they teach them an entirely new attitude towards ethanol.[27]

The conclusions reached by Dr. Pattison are shared by a new self-help group which offers a therapeutic and philosophic alternative to Alcoholics Anonymous. Called Drinkwatchers, this group rejects the disease concept of alcoholism. Drinkwatchers also disputes the goal of life-long abstinence sought by members of AA. As one of its leaders, Ariel Winters, is quoted as saying, "I am a cured alcoholic, not an 'alcoholic in remission.' I have regained my self-respect by throwing off the feeling that I was a diseased person. I am not. I have learned to drink moderately and there is now a stability to my life and a joy in living that wasn't there before."[28]

The claims of Drinkwatchers have been contested by Alcoholics Anonymous. Similarly, many therapists have expressed doubts about the effectiveness and the applicability of controlled drinking treatment programs. These doubts are based primarily on the widespread experience that most alcoholics are unable to modify their drinking to the point that it is no longer a problem. Yet such experience is not universal, and there may well be more drinkers who are capable of modification than are known to traditional treatment programs or to AA. Furthermore, new techniques should be encouraged if they can increase our understanding of drinking problems.

One approach which is achieving wide popularity is called conjoint, couple or family therapy. Family therapy grew out of interest in psychoanalytically-oriented group techniques. It also envolved from the work of behavioral therapists who, in the 1940s and 1950s, began treating the families of disturbed children as well as the children, who previously had been singled out as the patients in therapy. Eventually these therapists and their followers stopped isolating individual patients and instead focused on the couple or the family unit, viewing its problems either as the expression of neurotic interactions among family members, in the psychoanalytic model, or as responses to stress within the family structure, in keeping with behaviorist theory.

Essential to family therapy is the observation that couples and families function symbiotically. This relationship has been emphasized by Peter Steinglass, Sheldon Weiner, and Jack Mendelson, in a description of what they call a systems approach to alcoholism. These investigators define a system as "a set of objects together with a relationship between objects and between their attributes." They see the family as a social system with interdependent parts whose behavior affects the function of other parts. So interdependent are these parts, they argue, that in spite of intrafamily feedback and homeostatic mechanisms, drinking problems may represent the malfunction of the system as a whole.

According to the investigators, the systems approach highlights a question that must be asked by all therapists treating alcoholics:

> Is the identified patient's drinking behavior an emergent symptom signaling the appearance of stress and strain within the family, or is the drinking part of an ongoing pattern of interaction between family members that helps to stabilize the family system? In other words, in a malfunctioning system, the stress or strain created by conflicts within the system may be expressed through the drinking behavior of one member of the system. Clinically, such a family would typically have one member who represents a drinking problem arising after numerous years of nonalcoholic functioning. In such instances, the drinking might be viewed as an attempt to relieve the stress within the system (an escape valve), or an attempt to alter some of the behavioral programs of the system which are not functioning adequately.
>
> The alternate possibility is that the drinking is an integral part of one of the working programs within the system. In such an instance, drinking might serve to satisfy unconscious needs of both partners in the marriage, might cement clear cut role differentiation of power distribution within the family, might provide a scapegoat for aggression within the family, and might express culturally learned attitudes towards alcohol. Whatever possibility proves more important, the systems approach argues against the probability of a unidetermined explanation of alcoholic behavior and would predict that research geared toward the discovery of such an element would not be fruitful. Second, it suggests that the basic unit of clinical research be shifted from the individual alcoholic to the individual drinking system.[29]

This systems approach is integral to the technique used in couple and family therapy. These techniques are based on the belief that the alcoholic is not "ill" in contrast to his or her "well" spouse, but that the family system is under stress. As a corollary to this, family therapists do not attack drinking per se, realizing that it reflects an imbalance and that sudden abstinence on the part of one member of a couple may precipitate psychological problems in the other member. Steve Wolin, for example, does not hospitalize alcoholic spouses alone, but instead admits husbands and wives to a hospital ward where he can observe their interactions. He even allows them to drink, knowing that this more closely approximates their real behavior. Dr. Wolin's goal, like that of other family therapists, is to clarify relationships, improve communication, reduce the blaming of others for one's faults, and assist families in solving problems by means that are more creative and adaptive than alcohol.[30]

One striking aspect to family therapy is that it focuses on the meaning of drinking within the nuclear family as the smallest unit of society. The next conceptual step is to study drinking in extended families and then to broaden this investigation to include so-called "associated others." This phrase is used by social scientists to describe groups of people who are not related by blood or marriage but by links like geographical location or place of employment. Such links are the interest of Mansell Pattison, who has devised a scheme which he calls social systems psychotherapy. According to Dr. Pattison, this approach represents the natural progression from the individual to the group as an object of treatment. The approach has been incorporated into therapeutic community techniques, such as Synanon, which are used with alcoholics. It also is essential to hospital milieu therapy and to the community mental health movement with its emphasis on treating the entire community.[31]

Dr. Pattison's interest in large social groups is shared by a number of sociologists and anthropologists. These investigators acknowledge the significance of biomedical research in explaining certain aspects of alcoholism but emphasize that alcohol is a cultural artifact. They also stress the fact that the form and meanings of drinking alcoholic beverages are defined differently from culture to culture. Because of this, the social scientists have concentrated on the various uses of ethanol in different societies.

Donald Horton was perhaps the first sociologist to propose that alcohol is used primarily for its anxiety-reducing properties. He drew this conclusion in part from prevalent psychological concepts and in part from his observations in the 1940s of primitive people who are constantly exposed to natural dangers. Such dangers seem to induce fears and tensions that may prompt drinking, according to Dr. Horton. Today tensions may emanate more from interpersonal conflicts and confusion about social roles than from natural occurrences. Nevertheless, Dr. Horton feels that both primitive and advanced people drink to reduce anxiety.[32]

Robert F. Bales has accepted this premise but is also concerned with how culture itself affects anxiety. In his view, the amount of drinking among a given people depends on three factors: the sort of attitudes toward drinking that the culture produces, the degree to which the culture operates to bring about an inner tension or need for adjustment, and the degree to which the culture provides alternative means of self-satisfaction. Dr. Bales feels that Jewish ritual drinking is conducive to moderation because it is integrated into Jewish culture. In contrast stands the convivial drinking of the Irish, which serves no religious purpose and is not a fully accepted part of Irish society.[33]

Another anthropological view is offered by E. M. Lemert, who believes that drinking of the heavy sort constitutes deviant behavior. Dr. Lemert draws a distinction between what he calls primary and secondary deviance. Primary deviance, he states, is behavior that causes an individual to be labeled as a deviant in the first place. Secondary deviance, on the other hand, is that kind of behavior that is produced when someone is placed in a deviant role, such as that of a "wino" or skid row resident. Labeling persons as deviants thus perpetuates deviance because so-called deviants tend to act as expected. Denied access to alternatives, they join deviant groups and become even more alienated from society, refusing even to leave skid row.[34]

A somewhat different approach to the interaction of social norms and deviance is included in the anomie theory of Robert K. Merton. Anomie is a term derived from the Greek word for lawlessness which in sociological parlance refers to a condition characterized by a breakdown or absence of social norms. Dr. Merton uses the term to describe the disparity between culturally accepted goals and the means of attaining them, a disparity that is accentuated by the emphasis on success and achievement as measured by social rank and material possessions which is so prevalent in American society. At the same time, he notes that institutionalized channels of access for achieving these objectives are not evenly distributed. According to Dr. Merton, "It is the disjunction between culturally induced high aspirations and socially structured obstacles to the realization of these aspirations which is held to exert distinct pressure for heavy drinking and other forms of deviant behavior."[35]

Dr. Merton's anomie theory of deviance was afforded its most thorough test in the tri-ethnic study conducted in the early 1960s by Richard Jessor, Theodore Graves, Robert Hanson, and Shirley Jessor. This study was an attempt to account for the different rates of occurrence of heavy drinking and other kinds of alleged deviance among three ethnic groups—Anglo-Americans, Spanish Americans, and American Indians—within a small rural community in southwestern Colorado. Although the residents of this community offered their own explanations for the difference in rates, the investigators felt that the answer might lie in the three ethnic groups' cultural expectations, social position, and access to desired objectives, as well as their attempts to realize these objectives through either deviance or conformity.[36]

According to Dr. Jessor's group, their three-part study provided some degree of support for their hypothesis. The Anglo-Americans, for example, were found to have the greatest expectations, the highest social position, and the most readily available channels of access to achieving desired objectives. They also demonstrated strong social controls to conform and little pressure to adopt deviant behavior. These findings were consistent with the fact that the Anglo-Americans made the slightest contribution to deviance rates within the community.

The situation was more complex with regard to the other two ethnic groups. In terms of pressure toward deviance, the

American Indians actually occupied a somewhat more favorable social position than did the Spanish Americans, at least when opportunity was defined as socioeconomic status, income, or material possessions. However, with respect to controls, the Spanish had less anomie because of their close family structure and involvement with the Catholic church. Thus, despite an equal or even greater pressure toward deviance, the Spanish Americans were subject to stronger social controls than the American Indians. These findings were consistent with the fact that the Indians contributed most to deviance rates within the community, with the Spanish Americans intermediate between them and the Anglo-Americans.[37]

The investigators recognized the limitations of their study, not the least of which was the fact that it took place within a small rural community. They also acknowledged that they had not dealt with all of the factors that may lead to heavy drinking. Nevertheless, certain conclusions can be drawn from the tri-ethnic study. First, the study demonstrates the importance of expectations in prompting behavior. Second, it emphasizes that sociological and psychological variables profoundly affect heavy drinking and other forms of deviance. This conclusion is supported by the work of Don Cahalan, who applied the tri-ethnic model to a small study of drinking patterns in Hartford, Connecticut, and described in *American Drinking Practices* and *Problem Drinkers* six variables comparable to those discussed by the researchers from the University of Colorado. To reiterate, these variables include individual attitudes toward drinking, environmental support for heavy drinking, impulsivity and nonconformity, alienation and maladjustment, unfavorable expectations, and looseness of social controls.

A third conclusion reached by Dr. Jessor and his colleagues is that the deviance rates of the three ethnic groups they studied related less to ethnicity than to social position. The investigators felt that if Anglo-Americans were put in the same place in the opportunity structure as the American Indians, their deviance rates might be comparable. This view departs from the belief that deviance and drunkenness are biologically determined traits inherent to American Indians. It implies that since drinking patterns are in large part culturally determined, treatment and prevention measures must be aimed not only at the individual but also as his or her society.[38]

The weight of evidence that drinking is culturally determined has impressed upon Don Cahalan the limitations of the disease concept of alcoholism. As he points out in *Problem Drinkers,* the concept of alcoholism as a physical entity is difficult to support from a scientific standpoint. Like the term deviant, it imparts a label that is impossible to shake and that detracts from an analysis of behavior and personality. The word alcoholism is clouded with prejudice and superstition. Many people who are called alcoholics refuse to accept the appellation, and those who apply it to themselves or others rarely know what it means.

As Dr. Cahalan states,

"To summarize, it would appear that the concept of alcoholism as a disease may have had the undesirable consequence of driving a wedge between the alcoholic and society, of providing the problem drinker with an alibi for failure to change his behavior, and of creating an atmosphere in which alcoholism becomes a stubborn disease to cure because it is perceived as possessing only the derelict or semiderelict or the incompetent who is incapable of control over his behavior. But if these limitations of the alcoholism as a disease concept are granted, what concepts are more likely to bring about better understanding and control of the misuse of alcohol?[39]

Dr. Cahalan advances a concept, problem drinking, which he considers superior. He defines problem drinking as we do drug abuse, namely as the repetitive use of beverage alcohol which causes physical, psychological, or social harm. The advantage of this redefinition, Dr. Cahalan believes, is that it substitutes a less emotionally loaded label than alcoholism. Implicit in the concept of problem drinking is the idea that such drinking constitutes one end of a spectrum and is not a distinct, easily defined condition. How this end is reached by some people and not others is described by Dr. Cahalan:

First, the culture must permit drinking, and heavy drinking at least occasionally, before the individual can get himself into a position to become a heavy drinker. Second, given that the culture is permissive of heavy drinking under at least some circumstances, the individual may become a heavy drinker under circumstances permitted him in his sex, age, ethnic, social class, and other roles. Third, an individual may find himself suddenly to be a problem drinker because of a change in his cultural environment; for example, he moves or marries or ages out of an environment permissive of heavy drinking, but still remains a heavy drinker.

Fourth, given that the individual may have formed a habit of heavy drinking which he discovers to have become maladaptive in his environment, he may continue as a heavy drinker under one or more of the following circumstances: (a) if his social adaptability is hampered by a highly impulsive tendency towards resorting to short-term gratifications, he may continue to drink heavily even in the face of social disapprobation; (b) if the gradient between his usual subjective condition when he is not drinking and the way he feels when drinking is a steep one (such as might stem from either a highly alienated, neurotic or depressive personality, or living under conditions of high subjective deprivation of the worthwhile things in life), he may continue to drink heavily because of the powerful reinforcements obtained from drinking and the lack of rewards from not drinking.

Fifth, given that the individual has become a heavy drinker to the point where it has occasioned problems for him in his environment, he may continue heavy drinking if that environment is modified to be more permissive (such as by his becoming separated from such significant others as his family, his work associates, and his cultural peers). However, he may cease heavy drinking if the environment continues to exert counter-pressure through the persons who are important in his life. Thus those with severe drinking problems are more likely to eliminate such problems if they maintain social ties which support them as persons and do not reinforce the problem behavior.[40]

The paradigm offered by Dr. Cahalan is a comprehensive amalgam of sociological thought and behavioral psychology. Unfortunately, however, it fails to incorporate psychodynamic formulations and makes little allowance for physiological factors or the pharmacology of alcohol. Thus while Dr. Cahalan's concept of problem drinking goes farther than many approaches, it is not the final answer to the alcoholism issue.

Nevertheless, we strongly agree with Dr. Cahalan's criticism of the disease concept of alcoholism and have several objections of our own. One objection, as we have noted previously, is that alcoholism does not qualify as a disease by traditional medical definitions. This is acceptable in some ways, since most definitions of disease are old-fashioned. Yet these definitions still are popular with the public, and the more alcoholism is equated with sickness, the harder it is to broaden its understanding.

Our understanding of alcoholism is also hindered by the many definitions that have been applied to it. We have described these definitions in this and other chapters to impress readers with the irreconcilable differences among the definitions and the difficulty in using any but the broadest of them. Professional and lay organizations have gone to great lengths to create narrow definitions which might identify patients with alcoholism. Yet none of these efforts has been entirely successful, and all have drawn attention from two important facts. The first is that alcoholism is not one but many conditions. The second is that treatment should be extended not just to a limited number of patients who meet the requirements for an alleged illness, but to all persons who have problems with alcohol.

Our final objection to the disease concept is that it makes little allowance for cultural differences in the perception of alcoholism. For example, the Tarahumara of Mexico and the Camba of Bolivia do not see themselves as alcoholics and have no words for alcoholism in their language, as we have indicated. The French, who have such words in abundance, consider alcoholism primarily in terms of health because impaired physical functioning is the most obvious complication of heavy drinking to Frenchmen. The Italians, who have few alcohol-related health problems, are more disturbed by public drunkenness. By contrast, the impoverished Irish tend to overlook intoxication but are very concerned when people squander their income on liquor and thus "drink up the land."

The point of these examples is that what one country calls alcoholism is not considered alcoholism in the next. This situation suggests the ultimate futility of trying to derive a narrow definition of alcoholism, especially one that is based on a disease model. Alcoholism should either be defined broadly or be replaced by the term problem drinking, provided that this term conveys more psychological and physiological connotations than were proposed by Dr. Cahalan. The concept of problem drinking is intentionally diffuse and nonmedical. It invites a multifaceted approach to the study of drinking and thus is the best available alternative to the disease concept of alcoholism.

8. DEALING WITH
PROBLEM DRINKING

Yes, death is at the bottom of the cup,
And every one that lives must drink it up;
And yet between the sparkle at the top
And the black lees where lurks that bitter drop,
There swims enough good liquor, Heaven knows,
To ease our hearts of all their other woes.

WILLIAM DEAN HOWELLS, *My Literary Passions* (1895)

In the previous two chapters, we have drawn certain distinctions between alcoholism and problem drinking, a term we use interchangeably with alcohol abuse. We have also contrasted the theories underlying these two abstractions. Recognizing these differences between alcoholism and problem drinking is essential if one is to understand the evolution of current thinking on the subjects and move to a viewpoint that unites them. Yet attention to such differences should not obscure the fact that, whatever one calls it, excessive drinking is a staggering social problem. Therefore, we begin this concluding chapter by emphasizing the extent of problem drinking and its substantial economic and social costs.

One estimate of the extent of problem drinking is found in the *First Special Report to the U. S. Congress on Alcohol and Health,* which was published in 1971. According to this document, in that year between 5 and 10 percent of the adult American population manifested drinking problems. This percentage amounted to approximately 10 million out of the 100 million or so adult drinkers in the nation. Although skid row residents were the most visible of these problem drinkers, they probably represented no more than 5 percent of the excessive drinking population, a fact that has been verified by many studies. Thus, the majority of problem drinkers in this country are not made up of grizzled "winos" but of respectable persons, like the readers of this book and the proverbial people next door.[1]

The *First Special Report* did not deal with the economic impact of problem drinking, but its successor, the *Second Special Report to the U. S. Congress on Alcohol and Health,* estimated these costs to be $25.37 billion in 1971. This estimate was derived from a study conducted for the National Institute on Alcohol Abuse and Alcoholism by R. Berry and his colleagues. In this study, the investigators analyzed six areas of social behavior that were known to be sources of great expense associated with ethanol. They then applied an economic yardstick to this behavioral data and came up with certain real and estimated costs.

According to Dr. Berry and his colleagues, the largest single area of economic cost, amounting to $9.35 billion, was the lost production of goods and services which could be attributed to the reduced productivity of adult male workers with drinking problems. This lost production was related to decreased job efficiency, absenteeism, faulty decision making, industrial accidents, impaired morale, premature death and disability, and the expense of the rehabilitation of persons within the public and private sectors. The economic cost of the lost production was estimated on the basis of observation of the difference in earning of families with and without adult male members who reported problems with ethanol. The estimate did not make allowances for the lost or reduced production of women, workers under 21 years of age, institutionalized alcoholics, or those on skid row.

The second largest area of cost was the $8.29 billion spent for alcohol-related health and medical problems. This figure was derived from literature on the relationship between ethanol and health care, data provided by alcohol treatment centers on hospital utilization by their patients, and field interviews. Of the $8.29 billion, $5.3 billion was estimated to have been allocated for hospital care, $0.9 billion for physicians' services, nearly $0.3 billion for drugs, and more than $1.5 billion for administrative expenses, patient education, professional training, and the construction of medical facilities. The $5.3 billion for hospital care was almost 20 percent of all hospital expenditures for adults in 1971, while the total spent for alcohol-related problems represented more than 12 percent of the nation's total $68.3 billion health expenditures. This percentage would have been higher if the estimate had included the economic cost of home accidents, drownings, and suicides associated with ethanol.

The third largest area of economic cost was that proportion of the expenses from various types of motor vehicle accidents which could be attributed to the abuse of alcohol. The estimate of this cost came to $6.44 billion. It was based on the number of accidents occurring in 1971 among drivers or pedestrians with BACs of 50 milligrams percent or higher, the minimum level at which the investigators considered ethanol to be implicated causally in the accidents. Using this rather severe criterion and data supplied by the National Highway Traffic Safety Administration, Dr. Berry determined that alcohol abuse contributed to 43 percent of the nonpedestrian traffic fatalities, a total of 19,000 deaths in 1971; 38 percent of the adult pedestrian fatalities, a total of 2,700 deaths; 14 percent of the personal injury accidents; and 6.8 percent of the property damage accidents. Thus about 40 percent, or 21,700, of the motor vehicle deaths were linked by the investigators with alcohol.

Expenditures for alcoholism diagnosis, treatment, rehabilitation, prevention, education, and research programs made up the fourth largest area of economic cost attributed to alcohol by Dr. Berry. These costs amounted to $0.64 billion in 1971, a figure that is only 10 percent of the amount lost due to motor vehicle accidents during the same period. The estimates of expenditures for treatment were derived primarily from reviews of the budgets of federal and state alcoholism agencies as well as the budgets of private projects and organizations, including AA and other self-help groups. Not included in the estimates were the contribution of the clergy, counselors, physicians, and other sources of aid for people with drinking problems.

The fifth largest area of economic cost involving ethanol was the $0.51 billion invested in the criminal justice system. This amount represented approximately 5 percent of the $10.5 billion expended by the police, courts, and criminal institutions in 1971. This figure of 5 percent was determined by reviewing the literature on alcoholism and criminal behavior, tabulating total expenditures for crimes, and then attributing to alcohol a certain percentage of the costs for these offenses. For example, excessive drinking was thought to be 100 percent associated with crimes like disorderly conduct, which cost $74 million in 1971. An association with ethanol was recorded in 64 percent of all murders, 41 percent of all aggravated assaults, and 34 percent of all forcible rapes, which cost $60 million in police and court costs alone. Nearly 35,000 persons were thought to have been incarcerated for these and other violent crimes associated with alcohol at a cost of $75 million. In addition, the modest amount of $25 million was assigned to the cost of crime prevention and alcoholism rehabilitation activities by the criminal justice system.

The sixth and final area of economic cost analyzed by Dr. Berry and his colleagues was the $0.14 billion for ethanol-related expenditures by the social welfare system. This total was comprised of two categories: social service costs and transfer payments. Transfer payments, which represent direct benefits to the needy in order to support persons whose jobs may have been lost because of alcoholism, were not listed as economic costs per se, although the administrative expenses for handling such payments were included. The social service costs were incurred in the areas of child welfare and special support. Such costs totaled some $135 million during 1971, a figure that is far less than the expenses of families of alcoholic patients which were not met by welfare.[2]

Even if upward adjustments are made in this and the other five economic areas analyzed by the investigators, the $25.37 billion total they derived from the six areas probably fell far short of the actual cost to society. These shortcomings occurred in part because many expenditures, such as personal and property losses due to fires in which drinking was implicated, did not fit into the six areas and therefore were not included in the study. However, a more important reason for the underestimation was that Dr. Berry and his coworkers were entirely unable to calculate certain costs. They had no available accounting tool to measure such phenomena as the number of work days missed by alcoholic employees, for example. They also could not sum the debts accrued by people who were diverted from presumably more productive activity by drinking, or estimate the tremendous present and future drain of the disturbed children of alcoholic parents on the economy.

Given these limitations, one might ask why such an elaborate and expensive study was undertaken. The likely reason is that the National Institute on Alcohol Abuse and Alcoholism hoped to use the research to impress lawmakers with the tremendous expense of alcoholism and imply that prevention and treatment would be less costly. This presumably would enable the Institute to compete more favorably with other agencies for federal funds.

The same tactic is used on every level of government. The objective is to simplify a problem so that it can be seemingly understood; this means that in Dr. Berry's study, alcohol was singled out and little attention was paid to the complexities of drinking behavior. Next, whenever possible human costs are translated into dollar terms which legislators can deal with and which appeal to many voters. This strategy is in keeping with the economic and political realities that governmental programs are subject to.

The main difficulty with this approach is that its financial slant detracts from more important human needs. Thus, Dr. Berry's study does not place a price tag on death or on the physical and psychological suffering of problem drinking patients and their families. Perhaps this price tag can never be fully estimated. Nevertheless, research that fails to account for it cannot accurately estimate economic or social costs.

Another drawback of the approach taken by Dr. Berry is that it isolates ethanol as an evil and itemizes only the liabilities associated with the drug. In fact, as summarized in the *Second Special Report to the U. S. Congress,* the study did not acknowledge alcohol's positive economic benefits. For example, it did not mention the billions of dollars spent by the alcoholic beverage industry in payrolls, shipping, manufacturing, advertising, distributing, and tax payments during 1971. Nor did it include the other billions received by tavern owners, liquor store proprietors, grocers, truckers, and other people whose livelihoods are somehow related to ethanol.

Furthermore, the study did not allow for alcohol's incalculable personal benefits. It correctly demonstrated how many homes are disturbed or destroyed by drinking but did not give equal time to the many lives that are enriched. This enrichment comes in many forms and fashions, since ethanol is used for a multitude of religious, cultural, and recreational purposes as we have emphasized. The drug is also employed as a nutrient and a medicine by millions of people, in spite of scientific evidence of its hazards. This suggests that alcohol is not only a multipurpose pharmacological agent, but also a social necessity.

The word necessary conveys the connotations of being essential or acting from a compulsion. In its most archaic sense, the term refers to rendering indispensable services, as was the case with servants who were called necessary women in Victorian England. This latter meaning is captured by Morris Chafetz in the title of his book, *Liquor: The Servant of Man.* In this work, Dr. Chafetz argues that ethanol enjoys a historically inevitable position. He claims that

> the desire for drink has been so keen, the quest for it so unremitting, and the use of it so continuous, that there can be little doubt about its importance to individuals and societies. There has always been—and will always be—a need for some agent by which man can alter his inner being in relationship to his environment.[3]

We do not know whether this need really exists, or whether it should best be regarded as a "conditioned social response," in the words of Charles Becker.[4] Yet we are impressed with the fact that alcohol has an enduring popularity and an apparently secure niche in our society. Of course, other substances today rival ethanol's position. Marijuana is increasingly popular among people of all ages, for example, while Valium® and Librium® are the largest selling prescription drugs in the United States. In addition, medical science may, and perhaps should, come up with a better means of internal alteration. But for the time being, the agent of choice is ethanol.

Given ethanol's entrenchment, how should we deal with the drug and with drinking problems? One approach is to deny that a need for alcohol exists, as was done during Prohibition in this country and is being attempted in the People's Republic of China today. As part of their cultural revolution, the Chinese have decided that they cannot afford the diversion of agricultural products into alcoholic beverage manufacture or the lost productivity of problem drinkers through a continuation of pre-Communist drinking practices. Although these practices were moderate for the most part, the Communist Chinese have imposed a rigid prohibition against drinking. At the same time, they virtually have eliminated the production, advertising, and distribution of beverages containing ethanol.

This prohibition has been possible in part because the Chinese have a tradition of temperance. Furthermore, the Communist government exercises almost total control over cereal grain allocation and the means of alcoholic beverage manufacture. Students of drug abuse are now looking to China to see if that nation can maintain an ethanol-free state. Such a state would seem to disprove Dr. Chafetz's notion of the need for intoxicating drugs. Yet if this form of prohibition is successful it may be due less to the lack of such a need than to the power of the government or to the possibility that the need for intoxication is filled, in China at least, by participation in revolutionary society.

In contrast to the Chinese, the Russians have a rather intemperate cultural heritage. They also appear to be impressed by the relative trade-off between the economic and social costs of ethanol and its benefits as a source of revenue. Therefore, the Russians recently have allowed a continuing but calculated level of alcoholic beverage production, advertising, and distribution. This has resulted, according to some sources, in the reemergence of alcoholism as a national issue. Although the Russians officially deny that problem drinking exists among their people, the Chinese have pointed to it as an example of Russia's drift toward Westernism. The Russians in turn have taken steps to punish ethanol abuse and to make alcoholic beverages that are weaker than vodka. Reportedly this is resulting in a decline in their drinking problems.

It probably is within the logistic, if not the legal, capacity of the United States to control ethanol in the Chinese or Russian fashion. But absolute control runs counter to our tradition of personal liberty and could precipitate a public reaction comparable to that seen during Prohibition. Furthermore, control to the point of prohibition would conflict with the apparent acceptance of alcohol and its positive and negative aspects which is implicit in our present advertising, production, and distribution of the drug. Rather than trying to ban ethanol, it might be more politically realistic to attempt to alter the balance of pleasure and problems associated with alcohol through the following proposals.

One recommendation concerns the production of alcoholic beverages. Although it is obvious that a person who wants to get drunk can do so with almost any preparation containing ethanol, most people realize that those beverages with a high alcohol content are disproportionately damaging from a social and biological standpoint. We therefore consider it appropriate to impose a graduated tax upon alcoholic beverages according to their ethanol content. This tax should be levied on both the producer and the consumer. Presumably, it would induce corporations to manufacture and individuals to purchase weaker beverages.

This approach, which would have delighted Benjamin Rush, is presently being considered by several Western countries, including Canada. It requires almost no public expense or bureaucratic proliferation, since mechanisms already exist to tax alcoholic beverage manufacturers and the people who buy their products. The approach represents no more an encroachment upon individual liberties than does any form of taxation. It offers the advantage of raising revenue while reminding producers and consumers alike that they are paying, in medical as well as economic terms, for a high alcohol content.

Our second proposal is also aimed at alcoholic beverage production. It pertains in particular to the fortified wines that are so popular among problem drinkers and so injurious to their health. Although this injury relates to the relatively high concentration of ethanol in these preparations and to the destructive life style of their drinkers, it also stems from the fact that the cheap wines are almost totally lacking in vitamins, minerals, and other nutrients, many of which are removed in the manufacturing process. The same wines are a source of great profit to manufacturers, and we feel that these manufacturers should assume some responsibility for the health of their customers.

One way to accomplish this would be for the wine makers to include certain ingredients, such as potassium, pyridoxine, thiamine, and folic acid, in their products. These ingredients should be added in doses sufficient enough to insure that chronic drinkers receive some sustenance. The cost of these additives would be infinitesimal in comparison to the money made from the sale of these beverages. At the same time, even a slight improvement in the nutritional status of heavy drinkers might substantially reduce the public funds spent for these patients in general hospitals and emergency rooms.

Another suggestion involves alcoholic beverage advertising. This area is crucial, given the impact of the advertising industry on drinking and other national pastimes, and could prove to be more meaningful than any other form of intervention. Basically, we urge that alcoholic beverage manufacturers and the advertising agencies they employ be required to modify their present practices. Television, magazine, and newspaper advertising of all alcoholic beverages might be prohibited, for example. Television advertising, at the very least, should be limited to certain hours. Advertisers also should be prevented from glamorizing drinking by associating it with success and seductiveness, and the peddling of pop wines to young people should be discouraged or disallowed.

America's alcoholic beverage manufacturers are currently

getting considerable public relations mileage out of their campaign to encourage responsible drinking. Yet this campaign represents only a tiny fraction of their advertising budget and should be greatly expanded at the expense of the manufacturers in such a fashion that the manufacturers are required to spend a larger proportion of their budget on the responsible drinking campaign. In addition to providing people with relevant and accurate information, this effort should include the labeling of alcoholic beverage containers with a statement regarding the dangers of excessive drinking which is similar to the Surgeon General's caution about smoking and health. Such a warning might not immediately change drinking practices, but it would update our official position about problem drinking and enhance public awareness of the issues associated with alcohol.

Our fourth recommendation deals with the distribution of alcoholic beverages. Earlier in this book we stated that this distribution is accomplished among the states either by licensed private distributors or through state-owned-and-operated networks. We feel that both systems are acceptable, although neither should be expected to seriously influence drinking behavior. Thus we would prefer that the systems make alcoholic beverages readily available while fulfilling their proper function of raising revenue. Like the funds generated through a graduated tax on ethanol, these revenues should be used for education, prevention, and treatment programs.

A fifth proposal involves further implementation of the Uniform Alcoholism and Intoxication Treatment Act. This act has limitations, but it offers the best available model by which the states can move from a criminal justice treatment of problem drinkers to public health programs. The act adequately demonstrates how to decriminalize public intoxication. It also provides excellent guidelines for establishing comprehensive treatment programs.

In spite of these attributes, the Uniform Act has not been adopted by enough states. And even those states that have approved versions of the act have been unable to implement their versions due to a lack of local or federal funds. Far too

often, state legislatures like those in California and Colorado
have abolished criminal justice programs without having
planned or financed adequate alternative resources for problem drinkers. This has forced public inebriates from jails into
other public agencies without necessarily improving the prog-
nosis for those people or enhancing the quality of treatment
for other problem drinkers and their families.

Our sixth suggestion concerns the issue of drunkenness
and criminal responsibility, which is not dealt with sufficiently
in the Uniform Act. The courts have skirted the same issue,
although in general they have not accepted the argument that
intoxication is a defense for involvement in major crimes. We
agree with the courts' position in this matter. Yet we also feel
that the legal profession should confront the issue of drunkenness and criminal responsibility in a more straightforward
way.

Ideally, this confrontation should occur at the national and
state legislative level. If this is not possible, however, the
courts must become involved. Their role might center on a
case in which intoxication, either acute or chronic, is used as
the defense against a criminal charge. Such a test case would
allow the courts to review medical and psychiatric research
relevant to the issue and to comment on the social applicability of these studies. Hopefully, the courts could outline those
circumstances under which drunkenness may be considered
a mitigating factor in criminal offenses. We trust that these
circumstances will be few, if any. Furthermore, because the
point cannot be overemphasized, we hope that the courts will
affirm that intoxicated persons are just as responsible as sober
individuals for their crimes.

As a corollary to this, we propose as our seventh recommendation that the states acknowledge the personal responsibility of drivers by passing stricter drunk driving laws. The
association between ethanol and driving accidents has been
exaggerated in certain instances, but there is no doubt that an
automobile in the hands of an impulsive, intoxicated person
is the true "Saturday Night Special" in our society. Most
United States laws allow a blood alcohol concentration that is
appreciably higher than that tolerated by European nations.

This BAC is also in excess of what many medical investigators consider reasonable and probably should not be allowed.

If and when new laws are enacted, they should be aggressively and uniformly enforced. Strict enforcement might not lead to a swift decrease in drunk driving accidents, since many of these events are caused by recalcitrant individuals who do not respond to ordinary legal sanctions and may require special programs which are discussed below. Yet other drivers may be dissuaded from drinking by knowledge of strict enforcement of the law, and adequate drunk driving legislation eventually should reduce accidents as effectively as have laws lowering the speed limit. In addition, such legislation will remind people that in this area, as in others, they are responsible for their use of ethanol.

Our eighth proposal involves the creation of special programs for those persons who habitually drive while intoxicated. These drivers constitute a special subgroup of people who mix drinking and driving. They tend to be young and male, as do many other drivers who drink, and generally are of lower socioeconomic status. But drivers in this subgroup differ from other young people in that they appear to have highly impulsive and assaultive behavior patterns which lead them to drink heavily and then drive with abandon. Most of them are not alcoholics in the sense that they are not physically dependent on alcohol, yet they often drive with BACs in excess of 200 milligrams percent. In addition, many of these drivers have previous arrest records and continue to drive after their licenses are suspended. They have little social consciousness and do not respond to traditional traffic safety programs.

This is unfortunate, for in many cities such programs are all that is offered them. Traditionally, these programs are designed to facilitate the early diagnosis and treatment of alcoholism, and in some instances they are successful. But too often problem drinkers refuse to see themselves as alcoholics or stop drinking. The impulsive young people described above are included in this category.

Because of the limitations of traditional traffic safety programs, Portland, Phoenix, and certain other cities are experimenting with so-called Alcohol Safety Action Projects. These are modeled after comparable Canadian efforts to identify assaultive drivers and channel them into intensive rehabilitation programs. Most cities have reported success in this endeavor, at least initially. However, the Canadians, who also felt optimistic about the Alcohol Safety Action Projects, have found that the percentage of persons with high blood alcohol concentrations who are arrested or involved in automobile accidents today is the same as when these intensive programs were started. Perhaps this percentage will go down as the programs are perfected and as we learn more about people who drive while intoxicated. Yet we fear that in the meantime revocation of drivers' licenses or incarceration may be the only recourse for impulsive people who drink and drive.

Our ninth proposal concerns the question of whether people should be reimbursed by society for their drinking problems. This question may sound improbable, coming as it does after other recommendations stressing personal responsibility for drinking behavior. Yet in recent months, plaintiffs in Denver, San Francisco, and other cities have brought complaints against their employers on the grounds that the plaintiffs became problem drinkers because of job-related stress and hence are entitled to disability compensation. Yugoslavia and other Communist nations have created bureaucratic networks containing review boards and treatment agencies to deal with the issue of problem drinking among workers. Sooner or later someone will suggest that similar networks be created here.

We have no objection to this plan, provided that it is conducted in a more demanding a fashion than now occurs with industrial accidents. By this we mean that plaintiffs should be required to prove that their employment led to drinking problems, or perhaps to other drug abuse, before they receive any compensation. We doubt that many people will be able to demonstrate such a cause and effect relationship, given the complexity of problem drinking and our limited understanding of it. Nevertheless, dealing with this issue may increase our understanding. It also should encourage employers to sponsor programs for persons whose drinking problems relate in some fashion to their jobs.

The creation of such programs for employees is our tenth suggestion. The great advantage of these programs is early case finding and identification. Problem drinking accounts for more Monday morning absenteeism than any other condition, and supervisor checks of unproductive workers and those who take large amounts of sick leave often turn up problem drinkers. Once identified, these individuals can be approached on the basis of their underproduction. They then can be induced to accept treatment because failing to do so may cost them their jobs.

Such treatment may amount to only counseling and referrals in small companies, whereas many corporations now sponsor full-scale rehabilitation efforts for employees. The federal government is particularly interested in the latter approach and now supports programs for alcohol and drug abusers among civilians and the military. Planned for the most part by people from Alcoholics Anonymous and the National Council on Alcoholism, these programs were formed in the early 1970s when the National Institute on Alcohol Abuse and Alcoholism was forced by the alcoholism lobby to limit case finding to people with drinking problems. But since then this goal has been questioned, and rather than isolating drinkers from other people, some programs have begun to treat all patients under the rubric of "troubled employees."

This is a positive step, since presumably it will involve more people in treatment. Another way to increase the effectiveness of these programs is to make them less paternalistic and extend them not only to workers, who can be persuaded into treatment, but also to management. "Troubled employees" programs should emphasize that problem drinking is no disgrace and is seen in all social classes. Employees should be guaranteed that they will not be penalized for seeking help. They also should be offered a variety of forms of treatment, including new therapeutic techniques like family therapy as well as traditional psychiatric assistance and AA.

"Troubled employee" programs will increase the accessability of treatment, but help for these problem drinkers will be available on a wide basis only after our eleventh recommendation, which calls for broader coverage for problem drinking in health insurance policies, is acted upon. This idea is endorsed by the American Medical Association, which has passed a resolution calling on private insurance companies and prepayment plans like Blue Cross and Blue Shield to remove their limitations on the extent of coverage afforded alcoholics. Similarly, the National Institute on Alcohol Abuse and Alcoholism has proposed public third-party payment mechanisms for the treatment of alcoholism. Yet these and other efforts have met resistance, and few patients today are adequately covered for the treatment of drinking problems.

Although far from ideal, the most comprehensive coverage is provided for federal employees. This coverage generally comes in two forms: the three dozen or so health insurance plans negotiated by the U. S. Civil Service Commission for federal workers and the CHAMPUS, or Civilian Health and Medical Program of the Uniformed Services, which covers servicemen and their families. These various plans all approach problem drinking as a mental health issue and therefore subject it to the same limitations as they do other psychiatric conditions. Thus the programs offer adequate hospital inpatient services but are less generous in support of emergency and intermediate services as well as outpatient care, the most essential service of all.

The situation is even less advantageous for most state employees. According to a recent survey cited in the *Second Special Report,* only six states—California, Illinois, Massachusetts, Minnesota, Washington, and Wisconsin—have adopted legislation that mandates that alcoholism be covered in group health insurance plans for persons employed by the state. Legislation is pending in another five states—Alaska, Michigan, Mississippi, Nebraska, and Maine—but most other states offer little to their employees. The only far-reaching program is in California, whose new occupational health insurance covers alcoholism as a primary diagnosis for state employees and their families. This program provides for six days of detoxification, 21 days in a general hospital or residential facility, and 45 outpatient visits per person, making California's the most advanced state employee insurance plan.[5]

Although the federal and state plans are suboptimal, even

less coverage is available for persons not employed by government. Many of these people depend on Medicare, which provides mandatory hospital insurance and supplemental medical insurance primarily for the elderly. Medicare does cover psychiatric services, including those for problem drinkers, but these are limited largely to hospital settings and contain grossly inadequate provisions for outpatient follow-up. Medicaid is supposed to fill this gap by offering federal funds to the states for caring for the blind and other categorically needy persons in addition to the medically indigent. Unfortunately, although these funds are available, some states lack facilities for the treatment of problem drinking while others refuse to use the money for this purpose. And even those that do offer treatment still overemphasize inpatient services.

Another approach advocated by recent administrations is the HMO, or health maintenance organization. The HMO was introduced by Kaiser Industries to provide medical care through a prepayment scheme for its employees on the West Coast during World War II. Since then, the Kaiser Plan has been expanded to offer services to other individuals and groups outside of the West, including governmental employees and members of labor unions. HMOs patterned after the Kaiser Plan now are springing up in many American cities, and should proliferate, thanks to new federal legislation which requires companies with twenty-five or more employees to offer HMO membership as an option to other forms of coverage. Kaiser and other HMOs should provide comprehensive alcoholism treatment for individuals, couples, and groups as part of their coverage but none now offer these prepaid services.

At present private insurance is the only option to no insurance at all for people who are not enrolled in HMOs, do not receive Medicare or Medicaid, or do not work in government. This coverage generally involves routine fee-for-service insurance obtained through private carriers, although prepayment plans are available through Blue Cross, which covers hospital services for the most part, and Blue Shield, which covers physicians' services. According to the National Institute on Alcohol Abuse and Alcoholism, a minority of the civilian population has private insurance which provides hospitalization for mental health problems, including alcoholism. At the same time, an even smaller number of people are reimbursed for visits to physicians' offices. Furthermore, few insurance plans specifically cover alcoholism, and those that do usually contain many restrictions.

Of course, the problem is far more severe for the millions of people in our country who have no insurance at all. The great majority of these individuals have ongoing health needs, including in many cases the need for treatment of difficulties related to ethanol. In addition, many of the uninsured are at great risk to develop drinking problems by virtue of their urban residence, national origin, and low socioeconomic status. Some of these persons refuse to seek professional assistance because they cannot pay for it. Although their total care would cost less if they were afforded early diagnosis and treatment, these people have no access to insurance and eventually become a significant drain on the economy.

We feel that the best way out of the current dilemma in health care financing is some form of comprehensive national health insurance. In spite of its potential cost, such insurance has been desired by a majority of Americans polled since the presidency of Harry Truman. National health insurance should guarantee broad coverage to all patients and should cover them for more than catastrophic illness. Although catastrophic coverage would help families with overwhelming medical debts and is an important first step, it is hardly adequate to meet the country's health needs.

Whatever form of national insurance is adopted, we hope that it will emphasize health and not be crisis-oriented. Most human afflictions are not acute surgical diseases which can be dealt with by a single intervention in the hospital, but are chronic medical and psychiatric disorders which like alcoholism require repeated outpatient visits. Although paying for these visits over many years is just as expensive as is meeting a single bill for hospitalization, most public programs and private insurance plans support only hospital care and surgical procedures, not outpatient medical and psychiatric care.

This preference has contributed in our country to over-utilization of hospitals and emergency rooms, unnecessary surgery, and inadequate long-term care.

Health insurance as it now exists also tends to underwrite the medical establishment and overlook other resources. For example, most insurance plans and programs pay only for services performed in institutions accredited by the American Hospital Association. This provision helps maintain good quality control, but it also discriminates against innovative facilities. Many of these facilities stress an experimental preventive medical approach and offer new ideas in areas such as alcoholism treatment where traditional therapies are less than universally successful. Many also incorporate the training of new types of health professionals and paraprofessionals, and physicians' assistants. National health insurance, if it truly is concerned with health, must be willing to pay for the services of these people and support the facilities in which they are employed.

The creation of comprehensive national health insurance would broaden the coverage afforded problem drinkers and allow us to improve their treatment. Yet to be truly effective, such treatment must not only be adequately financed, as should be the case under national health insurance, but also must be tailored to the specific needs of certain groups. Some of these groups, including "troubled employees" and persons who drive while intoxicated, have been discussed earlier in this chapter. Now, as our twelfth recommendation, we wish to propose new approaches to problem drinking as it exists among other groups, including the public inebriates who inhabit skid row.

To most persons who avoid it, skid row may seem like any other socially deprived area. Yet according to Jacqueline Wiseman, skid row really serves as "a reservation for the containment of undesirables and a unique asylum for the homeless man." The first such asylums were developed in the East and South at the close of the Civil War, when countless unemployed men, newly discharged from the Army, roamed the country. Later in the nineteenth century, the term skid row, which originally referred to streets down which logs were skidded, was introduced to describe the squalid neighborhoods of itinerant loggers in the Pacific Northwest. Today a skid row is found in every fairly large city in America.[6]

"Not only has Skid Row proved tenacious as a continuing urban pattern," Dr. Wiseman writes,

> but the area and its culture are strikingly similar from city to city and from time period to time period. In fact, the descriptions of Skid Row have been remarkably stable over the past 50 years: the filth and stench of the hotels, the greasy cheapness of the restaurants, the litter in the streets, the concentration of bars. This consistency overrides the changes in Skid Row demographic composition from itinerant workers to more stable local spot jobbers and retired men living on Social Security. The social silhouette of these men has not changed to any degree. They are pale, ill-kempt, living hand to mouth. Even the special jargon used by habitués of Skid Row is amazingly consistent. Equally consistent is the fact that the majority of Skid Row residents are men alone, without families, whose heavy drinking orientation outweighs efforts towards maintaining steady employment or improving living standards. In this way, Skid Row is different from other urban low income areas where some struggle to sustain family life and employment is attempted.[7]

Some of the men who live in skid row are there because they never have known a better place. Others are thought to be people with psychiatric disturbances which have forced them to descend the ladder of society. For a variety of reasons, most are poorly educated individuals with poor health and limited rehabilitation potential. They therefore patronize more than their share of jails, hospitals, welfare offices, and other public institutions, a practice that is called "making the loop" in street language. This had led to their also being labeled "visible multiple agency alcoholics," a bureaucratic eponym which reflects not only their habit of going from one facility to another but also the fact that they constitute an eyesore. In addition, these men are known as the "revolving door population" for two reasons. One is that they tend to reuse public resources. Another is that they go from resource to resource because the resources do not meet their needs.

The "revolving door population" is an expensive group: San Francisco has approximately 5,000 skid row residents, for example, each one of whom costs the city an average of $3,000 in public services a year. Yet although these costs are accrued primarily by the residents, part of the expense results from inept public and private actions regarding them. The most archaic of these has been the criminal justice approach to public inebriates which has been superseded by the Uniform Alcoholism and Intoxication Treatment Act and its medical model. Another example of ineptness has been the continued attempt by local governments to sweep "multiple agency alcoholics" under the rug of urban renewal. This has merely forced the alcoholics into other areas of their cities where they have helped create new skid rows.

Another approach has been to round up the residents and herd them out of town. In the nineteenth century, skid row residents were housed in institutions for drunkards. Similar institutions exist today at the periphery of some cities; in others, they have been augmented by rural rehabilitation farms. Although these farms have helped public inebriates in certain instances, most often the alcoholics return to skid row after discharge and resume drinking. Thus geographic dislocation fails because it does not treat the alcoholic within his community.

A final attempt has been to "improve" the residents of skid row. Here the efforts have been conducted primarily by the Salvation Army and the many storefront missions that are found in most cities. Blending AA precepts with their own religious orientation, these organizations have tried to interest "visible multiple agency alcoholics" in abstinence and spiritual revival. Their efforts have rarely been successful, however, since few public inebriates respond to religion or are amenable to abstinence. Although the missions may attract alcoholics by offering them food and shelter, their appeal falls off when they begin to sermonize.

A true therapeutic impact can only be registered on the "revolving door population" by providing services to members of this population on their own terms. The residents of skid row need nutritional meals, dietary supplements, occasional detoxification, health screening, medical attention, real beds, and warm clothing. They require a place to wash their clothes and to cash welfare checks without having to pay the same surcharge they must meet at local restaurants and grocery stores. Those few residents who want to stop drinking can profit from involvement in "dry" living groups whose members are also attempting to abstain. Other residents who wish to continue drinking should be allowed to do so in "wet" hotels.

These and other services can be furnished at a much lower cost than they now are in most cities. For example, although some public inebriates require intensive medical care, most who request routine detoxification can be cared for at non-hospital drying out centers in the community. Similarly, health screening, public showers, washing machines, recreational opportunities, and counseling services can be made available at inexpensive drop-in centers. Given the availability of relevant services, some skid row residents may cycle out of "the loop." Most will stay on skid row but their lives will be less destructive. Expensive public resources, such as jails and hospitals, will not be misused by the skid row population, which instead will use facilities that are better suited to their needs and do not function as revolving doors.

Another group of people with unique drinking problems is made up of American Indians. According to the *First Special Report to the U. S. Congress on Alcohol and Health,* the rate of alcoholism among Indians is twice the national average. This rate approaches 25 to 50 percent in many reservations and is associated with an awesome rate of health and social problems. These problems are complicated by the fact that many Indians do not accept the appellation of alcoholic or the disease concept of alcoholism. And when they do admit to being alcoholics, they consider themselves the victims of a white man's disease.[8]

This belief is understandable, since the white man first called the Indians alcoholics although he did not introduce them to ethanol. Alcoholism also may be thought of as the white man's disease because among Indians it is so resistant to the white man's remedies. For this reason, as well as the fact that drinking may serve functions in Indian culture which Anglo-Americans cannot appreciate, Indians should not be grouped together with other alcoholics. American Indians require special treatment and rehabilitation programs operated by their own people as part of a general effort toward self-determination and meeting individual needs.

Personal needs must also be addressed among women with drinking problems. Such problems have always been assumed to be rare among women, and the older literature on alcoholism describes the ratio between male and female alcoholics as being approximately eight or ten to one. Yet investigators like Don Cahalan reported a ratio of from two or three to one during the 1960s, while recent research suggests that the numbers of male and female alcoholics may be almost equal. This has led the National Council on Alcoholism to call women the "hidden alcoholics" of our society.

One reason drinking problems have remained less conspicuous among women is that women, who until recently have not been an important part of the labor force, were not accountable to employers. Another is that many husbands have denied that their wives drink heavily out of fear that such drinking might suggest that the husbands cannot control their wives. A third reason for the hidden nature of problem drinking among women is that throughout American history society has assumed that such problems could occur only among the undesirable. Thus female drunkards were required to wear a scarlet D for drunkard and were scorned by proper people in Puritan society. Only women of low social standing were allowed to operate taverns during colonial days, or to serve men in frontier saloons. And while thousands of so-called respectable women were finding solace in Lydia Pinkham's "Vegetable Compound," society was insisting that drinking, like cigarette smoking, was something "nice girls" didn't do.

Even today, people of both sexes apply a double standard to women drinkers. This fact is illustrated in a survey entitled *Drinking Behavior, Attitudes, and Problems in San Francisco* which has just been completed by Don Cahalan and Beatrice Treiman for the San Francisco Community Mental Health Services Bureau of Alcoholism. As part of this survey, Dr. Cahalan and his colleague asked males and females of three age groups for their emotional reactions to four vignettes of hypothetical drinkers, two of which involved women and two of which involved men. Of the two vignettes involving women, one described a woman who drank quietly alone at home and the other was of a working woman whose job performance was hurt by drinking. The vignettes involving males were of a similar nature. Dr. Cahalan found that both men and women of all ages rendered harsher judgments on the hypothetical female drinkers than they did on the men, even though the actual behavior was comparable for the two groups. According to Dr. Cahalan, establishing the presence of such a double standard is all the more significant because it occurred in one of the most liberal cities in America.[9]

Because drinking among women has been so disapproved of in our society, it has been poorly acknowledged and even more poorly understood. Many research efforts, such as E. M. Jellinek's early sampling of AA members, entirely excluded women. And more recent investigations of drinking patterns among women suffer from a lack of unanimity which is greater than that seen in research conducted among men. Some of these studies have stated that women alcoholics have rigid, domineering mothers. Others emphasize the correlation between problem drinking and depression.

Edith Lisansky, in the 1950s, found that female alcoholics reveal greater personality disorganization than do men. They also seem to drink for a greater variety of pathological reasons. Problem drinking among women is also associated with problems in living, Dr. Lisansky stated. Drinking problems and sexual promiscuity are related, although cause and effect cannot be determined. In addition, women generally start drinking later in life, move from moderate to heavy drinking more quickly, and manifest more health problems because of their age.[10]

These findings may have been relevant to the 1950s, but Don Cahalan and other investigators have demonstrated that drinking practices are changing among women today. Furthermore, we believe that as more women speak openly about their drinking, they will be seen to have the same range of drinking behavior and the same varied reasons for drinking as men. Certainly, the changes in women's drinking, and smoking, for that matter, must relate to altered roles and greater social emancipation. This means that female drinkers can no longer be shamed into abstinence or told to hide their drinking because it looks bad. Instead, they require treatment programs that address them as individuals. Hopefully, these programs can cut into the alarming rise in problem drinking among women. But we fear that such problems may be the price women must pay for their long overdue social emancipation, along with lung cancer and other difficulties heretofore encountered primarily among men.

Drinking is also occurring at an unprecedented rate today among young people. Many studies have confirmed this fact, which was highlighted in a recent article on drinking among youth in *Time* magazine. *Time* has noted that in 1970, a survey conducted in San Mateo County, California, revealed that 11 percent of the ninth grade boys had drunk some sort of alcoholic beverage during the year preceding the survey. By 1973, the number of boys who drank had doubled to 23 percent, while the percentage among twelfth grade boys rose from 27 to 40 percent over the same three-year period. Twelfth grade girls drank less, but they appeared to be catching up with their male counterparts. Thus, 29 percent of the girls said they drank 50 or more times in 1973, compared with only 14 percent three years earlier.[11]

According to *Time,* there also is evidence that increased drinking among the young is leading to more drug problems. An informal poll conducted by one school district, for example, revealed that if problem drinking was defined as being severely intoxicated at least once a month, 5 percent of senior high school students within the district in 1970 would fall into the problem drinker category. This figure had climbed to 8 percent by 1974, and the school district felt it would top 10 percent by 1975. At the same time, Alcoholics Anonymous has claimed that its chapters are seeing more and more young alcoholics. Some of these young people, the chapters report, are under 12 years of age.[12]

We doubt that these young drinkers are alcoholics even by AA standards, since few of them have been shown to be physically dependent on ethanol or to have embarked on a downhill course which will lead inexorably away from sobriety. Nevertheless, study after study has demonstrated not only that young people are drinking more at present but also that more of them are experiencing drinking problems. Perhaps these problems are inevitable, given the fact that adolescence is such a stressful period. Lacking the psychological maturity of their elders, the young are more vulnerable than adults to peer group pressure and more likely to drink to satisfy social demands. They also are more likely to experiment with ethanol and other drugs as a form of identification with adults or as a kind of rebellion.

Because of the vulnerability of youth, special measures must be taken to deal with problem drinking among the young. One such measure involves using the school as a place to identify all problems, including those with drugs; to bring these problems to the attention of students; and to provide adequate resources for counseling and therapy. In this scheme, the school comes to resemble a business or industrial plant, while the student is seen as a "troubled employee." Such "troubled student" programs have been established in several cities, and their success so far points to the fact that many students can be reached through their schools.

Another function which schools have always fulfilled is the development and reinforcement of socially acceptable attitudes. Thus, alcohol and drug education programs now are required in public elementary and secondary schools in all the states, albeit the legal requirements, the curriculum content, and the philosophic thrust of these programs vary from state to state. In some states, for example, the evils of ethanol are taught and the disease concept of alcoholism is stressed. In others, instruction is offered in the proven medical effects of illicit chemicals as well as legal alcohol.

The scare approach generally fails with students who know that ethanol is not simply an evil and cannot conceive of themselves as becoming alcoholics or suffering the medical consequences of heavy drinking. Yet didactic drug instruction also falls short of the mark since many young people know as much or more about pharmacology as do the people who lecture them. Even when students are less knowledgeable, the information they take away from the classroom may be different than what is expected. Thus, when a doctor outlines the scientific facts about alcohol and marijuana to a classroom, some students come to appreciate that the compounds are not nearly so dangerous as other people profess them to be.

Given this situation, drug education programs should be more practical than they presently are. Seymour Halleck confronts this issue as follows:

> It would be useful for programs to begin by acknowledging that the abuse of legal substances, including those prescribed by physicians, is probably a greater problem for our society than abuse of illegal drugs. Prescription drugs such as amphetamines, barbiturates, and tranquilizers are massively overused in our society. It must be noted that these drugs do not alleviate specific diseases and have little medical purpose other than helping people tolerate the stress of everyday life. Yet they are prescribed more frequently than any other class of legal drugs and create more problems than any illegal drug.
>
> If the drug problem is viewed from a broad perspective, a crucial ethical question for our society is which drugs, if any, make life better? Most drugs provide the user with a pleasant experience, for the moment. Increasingly, there may also be drugs which expand human awareness and provide people with new insights. Whether one uses tobacco, alcohol, marijuana, amphetamines, or heroin, he is searching for something, occasionally for greater awareness but usually for stimulation or relaxation, for a temporary respite from the tedium and stresses of everyday life. If we agree that man is entitled to a certain degree of artificial stimulation or relaxation, it is important to know what drugs do this most effectively and with the greatest safety."[13]

In addition to being more pragmatic and providing accurate information, alcohol and drug education programs should engage young people on an emotional and attitudinal level. They also should acknowledge that the young will experiment with drugs, and furnish principles through which people of all ages can learn, as the liquor industry would have it, to drink responsibly. Morris Chafetz has defined responsible drinking in the following fashion: "The decision as to whether or not to use the drug ethanol is properly a personal and private choice to be made by each individual. However, should the desire be to drink, that individual assumes a responsibility not to destroy himself or others. That, in the broadest sense, is responsible drinking."

"Fundamental to responsibility is a strong positive self-image or respect for oneself and his well being," according to Dr. Chafetz:

> This in turn results in the assumption of responsibilities and obligations towards others. In trying to teach responsible drinking, it is important to keep in mind that the mere dispensing of information is insufficient to bring about any behavioral changes or induce a sense of responsibility. Factual information must be internalized and used in a context of personal motivation in order to have a lasting effect.[14]

To enhance a sense of responsibility, the National Institute on Alcohol Abuse and Alcoholism offers several drinking guidelines. It points out, for example, that it is not necessary to drink; that drinking does not confer adult status, maturity, or masculinity; and that problem drinking is neither a perversity nor a character defect, but a problem that is particularly common among people as they struggle through adolescence, marriage, parenthood, and other life stages. Responsible drinking, according to the Institute, depends on many factors, including the early development of healthy attitudes within a family environment, prevention of high intoxicating ethanol levels by restricting beverage consumption, and recognition that drinking is dangerous when used to solve personal problems. Responsible drinkers make sure that alcohol improves social relationships rather than impairing them. Responsible drinkers enjoy ethanol as an adjunct to activities rather than as an activity unto itself. Above all else, they make certain that human dignity is served with the use of alcohol.[15]

These guidelines for responsible drinking are appropriate and applicable to young people and adults. However, although they are being incorporated by school districts into alcohol and drug abuse education programs, the guidelines are not being followed by many people. This seems to be due less to deficiencies in education than to the fact that such education cannot compete with the attitudes of parents and the distorted material that is broadcast by the media about ethanol and other drugs. The underlying theme of this material is "Better Living Through Chemistry," to quote the Du-Pont Corporation's slogan. Its message is that chemicals should be used to solve problems in our society.

This message actually is as old as alcohol itself, and knowing the many ways in which the drug has been used and abused throughout history, we hardly are surprised that responsible drinking is not more commonplace today. Nevertheless, recent experience has impressed us with the difficulty of trying to encourage responsible drinking and to prevent and treat drinking problems on a local level. We therefore wish to end this book with a brief discussion of what happened when problem drinking was dealt with in one particular community.

The community in question is San Francisco, which has the greatest per capita number of problem drinkers and drug abusers in America. Although San Francisco long has been a haven for such people, the city offered few services for them in 1968, when Dr. Richard Shore, co-author of this book, became director of the Bureau of Alcoholism, a division of San Francisco's Community Mental Health Services, which itself is a part of the Department of Public Health. At that time there were no public detoxification facilities to serve the alcoholics who were treated at San Francisco General Hospital for medical problems. There also were no psychologically-oriented inpatient treatment programs, although the city operated a chronic medical care facility, the Laguna Honda Hospital and Rehabilitation Center. And there were no public halfway houses, drop-in centers or outpatient clinics to serve the residents of skid row.

By contrast, San Francisco did have several private resources for problem drinkers. One local hospital maintained a clinic for private patients, for example, and many psychiatrists and other mental health workers included alcoholics in their practices. The city also could boast of over 100 AA groups, including groups for blacks, Orientals, and other minorities; and half of the local Alcoholics Anonymous membership was made up of women, in contrast to other cities where women numbered only one-third. In addition, the Salvation Army was quite active in the city, and there were several private halfway houses. Yet for all these private services, there was no coordination of individual efforts and no continuum of public and private care.

San Francisco was not unique in these respects, for few cities in the United States offered extensive public services or were organized in their approach to problem drinking. Seattle had an exceptional public education program; Portland had created a progressive rehabilitation plan for public inebriates; and one area in Philadelphia had developed a program that could have become a model had it not required alcoholics to leave the community as part of their treatment. Detoxification units stressing cooperation between the police and physicians were also underway in New York and St. Louis, although these were lacking in aftercare. But no city had taken these ideas and combined them into a comprehensive program.

The members of the Bureau of Alcoholism attempted to do this in San Francisco within the guidelines established by the Uniform Alcoholism and Intoxication Treatment Act and the community mental health model described by Gerald Caplan. This model provides for the prevention of many problems, including problem drinking, on three levels. These include primary prevention, which involves reducing the likelihood that people in a given community will experience a given problem; secondary prevention, which involves reducing the prevalence of the problem and preventing further disability by early case finding, diagnosis, and treatment; and tertiary prevention, which involves the treatment of patients in whom the problem is already apparent.

According to Dr. Caplan, success on all three levels entails a combination of administrative action and personal interaction. Administrative action refers to reducing preventable stress, providing services to assist patients facing stress, or assisting communities in developing such services. This can be accomplished by changing customs, laws, and regulations by the types of governmental reform we have suggested. Personal interaction represents an attempt to alter the emotional forces in an individual's environment or the way in which he or she solves problems by direct intervention with that person or with the people around her or him. This can be accomplished by many techniques, including medical treatment, self-help groups, counseling, and psychotherapy.

Dr. Caplan's dual approach is predicated on the belief that patients, not vested interests or institutions, must be the focus of education, prevention, and treatment programs. This requires that services be designed to treat the needs of people as their needs exist in a community. The services should also be farsighted as well as comprehensive. This means that the community should not favor tertiary prevention, the results of which are personal and immediate, out of proportion to primary and secondary prevention and their potential long-term gains.[16]

In accord with Dr. Caplan's model, the Bureau of Alcoholism hoped to stress primary and secondary prevention as well as to treat people already identified as alcoholics. The members therefore deemphasized the word alcoholism, which they considered an ill-defined and often end-stage diagnosis, in favor of the broader and more hopeful term problem drinking. Their goal was not only to treat the inebriates seen at San Francisco General but also to reach, educate, and care for a much wider but less visible variety of individuals. These included American Indians and other minorities, drunk drivers, employed problem drinkers, women, youth, gay people, and other groups, in addition to the residents of skid row.

The Bureau members wanted to involve the entire community in a comprehensive network of services. They therefore tried to coordinate a continuum of private and public resources which would include prevention and education, early case finding and diagnostic services, hospital and nonhospital detoxification, halfway houses and other after-care efforts, and outpatient therapy for individuals, couples, and families. The members sought to include preexisting facilities in this continuum whenever possible, although they initiated new programs for problem drinkers when necessary. Finally, they tried to gain community input by creating a city-wide alcoholism advisory board in which minorities, physicians, educators, patients, members of private and public agencies, and other people were represented.

During the early 1970s, the Bureau achieved many results. It created the advisory board, for example, and contracted with several private programs to provide specific services and thereby fill gaps in the continuum of care. At the same time, the Bureau shored up faltering city projects and expanded the services afforded problem drinkers. One major accomplishment was the development of a model detoxification unit at San Francisco General Hospital under the direction of Charles Becker. Another was the creation of a novel intermediate care and outpatient program at Laguna Honda Hospital under the leadership of Larry Meredith.

Members of the Bureau also developed or supported resources for the previously mentioned target groups. A problem drinking program was started for public employees, and comparable programs in private industry were assisted by the Bureau. In addition, outreach and education efforts were directed at students, homosexuals, and ethnic groups. A residential facility was created by and for former alcoholics in San Francisco's Tenderloin district with the assistance of Jeffrey Ordover, while a therapeutic community and a counseling, recreation, and social center were established on skid row. Finally, plans were made for more self-help facilities and a large center which was designed to meet the needs of public inebriates for food, health, and shelter and to reduce the number of visits by these patients to San Francisco General Hospital. These and other proposals were drawn up in 1973 by Dr. Ordover and Carolyn Dobson as part of a Five Year Comprehensive County Plan.[17]

The Bureau's plan was approved in 1974 by the National Institute on Alcohol Abuse and Alcoholism. However, along with similar proposals from four other cities, it never was funded. This apparently occurred because the National Institute had experienced severe budgetary cutbacks and could not assist even those programs that it intended to develop as models. Although Presidents Nixon and Ford still spoke about dealing with problem drinking, they and Congress would not or could not do so.

During this period, the Bureau was supported on a continuing basis by the State of California and the City of San Francisco. Most of this support came from federal and state mental health monies. Some also resulted from the California legislature's adoption of a medical approach to public intoxication and its mandate to provide limited funds for local treatment programs. Yet although the city and state paid for some services for problem drinkers, they were unable or unwilling to provide additional support to the Bureau when its proposal to the National Institute on Alcohol Abuse and Alcoholism was not funded. Again, budget restrictions were the main reason for this setback. Yet it also seemed that the state and city, as is the case throughout the country, preferred to support tertiary facilities such as general hospitals rather than innovative service centers for public inebriates which might cost far less in the long run.

Another difficulty was the divisiveness of representatives of community groups and private treatment programs who were members of the alcoholism advisory board. These members were unable to collaborate with one another and instead competed for patients and for treatment funds. Early in the advisory board's history, a split emerged between those representatives of treatment programs who were concerned with the meaning of drinking as a symptom and whose who categorically demanded abstinence. This split widened when the latter individuals argued against the city's investing in any treatment efforts other than those sponsored by self-help agencies. Such polarization, which occurs at the local, state, and national level, illustrates the inherent disadvantage of involving vested interests in social action programs.

The same interests have presented obstacles to moving from the narrow disease concept of alcoholism to the broad approach of problem drinking. This is unfortunate, for the broad approach offers the advantage of looking at the whole person, not just his or her drinking behavior. The broad approach is also more compatible with the goals of primary and secondary prevention since it encourages the assistance of persons before they develop advanced problems. In addition, this approach is potentially more fruitful than that of the alcoholic beverage industry and of certain therapists who call alcoholism a disease, isolate alcoholics from other drinkers, and focus on tertiary treatment without understanding the reasons for problem drinking and its prevalence in our society.

We trust that a broad approach to problem drinking will be adopted in the future. And although our experience in San Francisco has been sobering, it has not blinded us to the fact that much has been and will be done about drinking problems. Future progress depends, we believe, on two major factors. The first of these, the political, requires the development and implementation of a realistic public policy regarding alcohol and alcohol-related problems. It also awaits the growth of a spirit of tolerance and cooperation in which all concerned people can contribute to public policy.

The second factor, the scientific, entails several research needs. From a clinical standpoint, we must determine what kind of treatment works best for the many types of problem drinkers we have described in this book, and why. In terms of education, we need more information on what and how young people should be taught about ethanol and other drugs. Medical research must increase our knowledge of alcohol and its effects on the mind and body, while biochemical investigations should outline the role of ethanol metabolism in the genesis of drinking problems.

Perhaps the most important contribution can come at the interface of psychology, sociology, and anthropology. From this combined point of view, we must examine our own culture to learn why we employ alcohol so often as a panacea while other cultures can solve their personal and social problems with less destructive drinking. We also need to understand how certain cultures have been able to integrate the use of ethanol within a framework of reason and moderation, thereby combining the best of Appollonian and Dionysian traditions. Hopefully, the application of such understanding will foster responsible drinking, minimizing the problems and maximizing the pleasures of alcohol.

NOTES

Chapter 1. The Triumph of Dionysus

1. Berton Roueché, *The Neutral Spirit: A Portrait of Alcohol* (Boston: Little, Brown, 1960), p. 21.

2. *Ibid.*, p. 5.

3. André Simon, *Wines of the World* (New York: McGraw-Hill, 1968), pp. 12–13.

4. Philip Wagner, "Wines, Grape Vines, and Climate," *Scientific American*, 230, no. 6 (1974): 106–107.

5. *Ibid.*, p. 108.

6. Simon, *Wines of the World*, p. 245.

7. Kurt Schlesinger, "The Meaning of Ritual in the Passover Ceremony," in *The Psychoanalytic Study of Society*, Volume VII (New Haven: Yale University Press, 1976).

8. Mark Keller, "The Great Jewish Drink Mystery," *British Journal of Addictions*, 64 (1970): 287–296.

9. Charles Snyder, "Culture and Jewish Sobriety," in David Pittman and Charles Snyder, *Society, Culture and Drinking Patterns* (New York: Charles Wiley and Sons, 1962), pp. 188–225. Also in Charles Snyder, *Alcohol and the Jews: A Cultural Study of Drinking and Sobriety* (New Haven: Yale Center of Alcohol Studies, 1955), pp. 25–96.

10. E. R. Dodds, *The Greeks and The Irrational* (Berkeley: University of California Press, 1951), pp. 2–8.

11. Edith Hamilton, *The Greek Way* (New York: Norton, 1942), pp. 213–218.

12. Robert Graves, *The Greek Myths* (Baltimore: Penguin Books, 1955), pp. 103–108. Also in Thomas Bulfinch, *Bulfinch's Mythology* (New York: Random House, 1967), pp. 131–135.

13. Graves, *ibid.*, p. 107.

14. Salvatore P. Lucia, *A History of Wine as Therapy* (Philadelphia: Lippincott, 1963), pp. 36–37.

15. Georgio Lolli, Emilio Scrianni, Grace Golder, and Pierpaolo Luzzatto-Fegiz, *Alcohol in Italian Culture: Food and Wine in Relation to Sobriety Among Italians and Italian Americans* (New Haven: Yale Center of Alcohol Studies, 1956), pp. 19–41.

16. Roland Sadoun, Georgio Lolli, and Milton Silverman, *Drinking in French Culture* (New Brunswick: Rutgers Center of Alcohol Studies, 1956), pp. 19–41.

17. David Mandelbaum, "Alcohol and Culture," *Current Anthropology*, 6 (1965): 281–293.

18. *Handbook of South American Indians, Volume Two* (Washington: U. S. Bureau of American Ethnology, 1946), pp. 394–455.

Chapter 2. A Noble Experiment That Failed

1. Roueché, *The Neutral Spirit*, p. 21.

2. R. F. Bales, "Attitudes Toward Drinking in the Irish Culture," in Pittman and Snyder, *Society, Culture*, pp. 157–187.

3. Morris Chafetz, *Liquor: The Servant of Man* (Boston: Little, Brown, 1965).

4. *Ibid.*, p. 79.

5. Gerald Carson, *The Social History of Bourbon* (New York: Dodd, Mead, 1963), p. 37.

6. Ruth Benedict, *Patterns of Culture* (Boston: Houghton Mifflin, 1934), pp. 78–98.

7. Advertisement for Lydia Pinkham's "Vegetable Compound." Cited by Charles McCabe, *San Francisco Chronicle*, May 18, 1973.

8. Stanley Baron, *Brewed in America: A History of Beer and Ale in the United States* (Boston: Little, Brown, 1962), p. 184.

9. Benjamin Rush, "An Inquiry Into the Effects of Ardent Spirits Upon the Human Mind and Body," in Yarnell Henderson, *A New Deal for Liquor: A Plea for Dilution* (Garden City: Doubleday, 1934), pp. 5–26.

10. *Oxford English Dictionary*, 3d. ed., s.v. "teetotaler."

11. Joseph Gusfield, *Symbolic Crusade: Status Politics and the American Temperance Movement* (Urbana: University of Illinois Press, 1969), pp. 30–33.

12. Milton Maxwell, "The Washingtonian Movement," *Quarterly Journal of Studies on Alcohol*, 2 (1950): 410–451.

13. Andrew McLaughlin, *Satire as a Weapon Against Prohibition: 1920–*

1928, doctoral dissertation, Department of History, Stanford University.

14. Andrew Sinclair, *Era of Excess: A Social History of the Prohibition Movement* (New York: Harper and Row, 1964), pp. 61–62.

15. McLaughlin, *Satire.*

16. Sinclair, *Era of Excess,* p. 117.

17. *Ibid.,* pp. 135–149.

18. *Ibid.,* p. 394.

19. Franklin D. Roosevelt, "Proclamation on the Amendment of the Repeal of Prohibition, December 6, 1933." Cited by Henderson, *A New Deal for Liquor,* p. 118.

Chapter 3. American Drinking Practices and Problems

1. Carson, *The Social History,* p. 222.

2. Charles McCabe, *San Francisco Chronicle,* 18 May 1973.

3. Samuel M. Kirbens, "Chronic Alcohol Addiction and Criminal Responsibility," *American Bar Association Journal,* 54 (1968): 817–930.

4. *Ibid.*

5. *First Special Report to the U. S. Congress on Alcohol and Health* (Washington: U. S. Government Printing Office, 1971), p. 48.

6. James Maas, *Driving While Intoxicated: Problems, Programs, and Proposals* (San Francisco: Public Health Department Research Paper, 1973).

7. *Ibid.*

8. Baron, *Brewed in America,* pp. 322–336.

9. "Wine: Selling the New Mass Market," *Business Week,* 67, no. 8 (1974): 64–70.

10. *Ibid.,* p. 66.

11. Arpad Haraszthy. Cited by Simon, *Wines of the World,* p. 698.

12. David Daiches, *Scotch Whiskey: Its Past and Present* (New York: MacMillan, 1969), p. 120.

13. Joel Fort, *Alcohol, Our Biggest Drug Problem* (New York: McGraw-Hill, 1974), p. 97.

14. *First Special Report,* pp. 9–15.

15. *Ibid.,* p. 17.

16. D. Cahalan, I. H. Cisin, and N. M. Crossley, *American Drinking Practices: A National Study of Drinking Behavior and Attitudes* (New Brunswick: Rutgers Center of Alcohol Studies, 1969), pp. 1–18.

17. *Ibid.,* pp. 18–70.

18. *Ibid.,* pp. 71–99.

19. *Ibid.,* pp. 125–183.

20. *Ibid.,* pp. 184–210.

21. Don Cahalan, *Problem Drinkers* (San Francisco: Jossey-Bass, 1970), p. 22.

22. *Ibid.,* pp. 18–34.

23. *Ibid.,* pp. 35–62.

24. *Ibid.*, pp. 63–95.
25. *Ibid.*, pp. 96–133.

Chapter 4. To Dream But Not to Sleep

1. Jerome H. Jaffe, "Drug Addiction and Drug Abuse," in L. Goodman and A. Gilman, *The Pharmacological Basis of Therapeutics* (New York: Macmillan, 1970), p. 276.
2. *Ibid.*, p. 277.
3. *Ibid.*, p. 278.
4. Charles Becker, "The Clinical Pharmacology of Alcohol," *California Medicine*, 113, no. 3 (1970): 37–45.
5. Charles Lieber, "Liver Adaptation and Injury in Alcoholism," *New England Journal of Medicine*, 288, no. 7 (1973): 356–362.
6. Charles Lieber, personal communication.
7. Jack Mendelson, "Biological Concomitants of Alcoholism," *New England Journal of Medicine*, 283, no. 1 (1970): 24–32, and 283, no. 2 (1970): 71–81.
8. D. Fenna, L. Mix, D. Schaefer, and J. A. L. Gilbert, "Ethanol Metabolism in Various Racial Groups," *Canadian Medical Association Journal*, 105, no. 9 (1971): 472–475.
9. Charles Lieber, "Metabolism of Ethanol and Alcoholism: Renal and Acquired Factors," *Annals of Internal Medicine*, 76 (1972): 326–327.
10. Lynn Bennion and Ting-Kai Li, "Alcohol Metabolism in American Indians and Whites," *New England Journal of Medicine*, 294, no. 1 (January 1, 1976): 9–12.
11. L. M. Lowenstein, R. Simone, P. Boulter, and P. Nathan, "Effect of Fructose on Alcohol Concentrations in the Blood of Man," *Journal of the American Medical Association*, 213, no. 11 (September 14, 1970): 1899–1951.
12. Jaffe, "Drug Addiction," p. 276.
13. *Ibid.*, p. 281.
14. I. Feinberg and E. V. Evarts, "Some Implications of Sleep Research for Psychiatry," in *Neurobiological Aspects of Psychopathology* (New York: Grune and Stratton, 1969), pp. 334–391.
15. M. Victor and R. D. Adams, "The Effects of Alcohol on the Nervous System," in *Metabolic and Toxic Diseases of the Nervous System* (New York: Association for Nervous and Mental Diseases, 1953), pp. 526–535.
16. *Ibid.*, p. 539.
17. *Ibid.*, p. 545.
18. Charles Lesegue, "Le Delire Alcoolique N'est pas un Delire, Mais un Reve," *Archives of General Medicine*, 88 (1881): 513–536.
19. R. Greenberg and C. Pearlman, "Delirium Tremens and Dreaming," *American Journal of Psychiatry*, 124, no. 2 (1967): 37–46.
20. D. E. Smith and D. Wesson, "A Conceptual Approach to Detoxification," *Journal of Psychedelic Drugs*, 6, no. 2 (1974): 161–168.

Chapter 5. Forgetfulness of Things Past

1. Charles Becker, personal communication.

2. Charles Lieber, "The Metabolism of Alcohol," *Scientific American*, 234, no. 3 (March, 1976): 25–33.

3. *Ibid.*

4. E. Rubin and C. Lieber, "Alcohol-Induced Hepatic Injury in Non-Alcoholic Volunteers," *New England Journal of Medicine*, 278, no. 16 (1968): 869–876.

5. E. Rubin and C. Lieber, "Fatty Liver, Alcoholic Hepatitis and Cirrhosis Produced by Alcohol in Primates," *New England Journal of Medicine*, 290, no. 3 (1974): 128–135.

6. E. M. Jellinek, *The Disease Concept of Alcoholism* (New Haven: College and University Press, 1960), pp. 37 and 40.

7. Rubin and Lieber, "Alcohol-Induced Hepatic Injury," p. 131.

8. G. E. Burch and T. D. Giles, "Alcoholic Cardiomyopathy," *American Journal of Medicine*, 50, no. 2 (1971): 141–146.

9. L. Gould, M. Zaber, A. DeMartino, and R. F. Gomprecht, "Cardiac Effects of a Cocktail," *Journal of the American Medical Association*, 218, no. 12 (1971): 1799–1802.

10. Edward Eichner, "The Hematological Disorders of Alcoholism," *American Journal of Medicine*, 54 (1973): 621–630.

11. J. Lindenbaum and C. Lieber, "Hematological Effects of Alcohol in Man in the Absence of Nutritional Deficiency," *New England Journal of Medicine*, 281, no. 7 (1969): 333–338.

12. Carl Wernicke, *Lehrbuck der Gehirnkrankheiten fur Aertze and Studirende* (Kassel: Theodore Fischer, 1881), pp. 229–242. Cited by M. Victor, R. D. Adams, and H. Collins, *The Wernicke-Korsakoff Syndrome* (Philadelphia: F. A. Davis Co., 1971), pp. 2–3.

13. S. S. Korsakoff, "Disturbance of Psychic Function in Alcoholic Paralysis and Its Relation to the Disturbance of the Psychic Sphere in Multiple Neuritis of Nonalcoholic Origin," *Vesthik Psichiatrii*, 4, no. 2: 1887. Cited by Victor, Adams, and Collins, *ibid.*, pp. 4–6.

14. Victor, Adams, and Collins, *ibid.*, pp. 25–97.

15. Ralph S. Ryback, "The Continuum and Specificity of the Effects of Alcohol on Memory," *Quarterly Journal of Studies on Alcohol*, 32 (1971): 995–1016.

16. Charles E. Wells, *Dementia* (Philadelphia: F. A. Davis Co., 1971), p. 12.

17. Kenneth Jones and David Smith, "The Fetal Alcohol Syndrome," *Pediatrics*, 27, no. 5 (1974): 105–118.

18. Becker, "Clinical Pharmacology of Alcohol," p. 43.

Chapter 6. The Disease Concept of Alcoholism

1. *Random House Dictionary*, S.V. "disease."

2. *Stedman's Medical Dictionary*, S.V. "disease."

3. Roueché, *The Neutral Spirit*, p. 103.

4. R. J. Mardones, N. Segovia-Riquelme, A. Hederra, and F. Alcaino, "Effect of Some Self-Selection Conditions on the Voluntary Alcohol Intake of Rats," *Quarterly Journal of Studies on Alcohol*, 16 (1949): 425–437.

5. G. E. McClean and D. A. Rogers, "Differences in Alcohol Preference of Laboratory Mice," *Quarterly Journal of Studies on Alcohol*, 21 (1959): 691–695.

6. R. Cruz-Coke, "Color Blindness and Cirrhosis of the Liver," *Lancet*, 2 (1969): 1064.

7. C. Amark, "A Study in Alcoholism," *Acta Psychiatrica and Neurologia Scandinavia*, 70 (1951).

8. M. Bleuler, "Familial and Personal Background of Chronic Alcoholics," in Diethelm, ed., *Etiology of Chronic Alcoholism* (Springfield: Charles Thomas, 1955).

9. L. Kaij, *Alcoholism in Twins* (Stockholm: Almquist and Wiksell, 1960).

10. A. Roe and P. Burks, "The Adult Adjustment of Children of Alcoholic Parents Raised in Foster Homes," *Quarterly Journal of Studies on Alcohol*, 5 (1944): 370–391.

11. D. W. Goodwin, F. Schulsinger, L. Hermansen, S. Guze, and G. Winokur, "Alcohol Problems in Adoptees Raised Apart from Alcoholic Biological Parents," *Archives of General Psychiatry*, 28 (1973): 238–245.

12. William Silkworth, "Alcoholism as a Manifestation of Allergy," *Medical Review*, 1215 (1937): 249–251.

13. Mardones, *et al.*, "Effect of Some Self-Selection Conditions."

14. Roger J. Williams, *Alcoholism: The Nutritional Approach* (Austin: University of Texas Press, 1959), pp. 48–65.

15. J. J. Smith, "A Medical Approach to Problem Drinking," *Quarterly Journal of Studies on Alcohol*, 10 (1949): 251–257.

16. Mendelson, "Biological Concomitants."

17. Fenna, *et al.*, "Ethanol Metabolism."

18. Philip H. Wolff, "Ethnic Differences in Alcohol Sensitivity," *Science*, 175 (1972): 449–450.

19. Bennion and Li, "Alcohol Metabolism."

20. S. Rado, "The Psychic Effects of Intoxicants," *International Journal of Psychoanalysis*, VIII (1926): 16–17.

21. O. Fenichel, *The Psychoanalytic Theory of Neurosis* (New York: W. W. Norton, 1965), p. 379.

22. K. Menninger, *Man Against Himself* (New York: Harcourt, Brace, 1938), pp. 115–117.

23. R. Knight, *The Abnormal Personality* (New York: Ronald Press, 1948), p. 147.

24. H. T. Blane, *The Personality of the Alcoholic* (New York: Harper and Row, 1968), p. 161.

25. W. McCord and J. McCord, *The Origins of Alcoholism* (Stanford: Stanford University Press, 1960).

26. Claude Steiner, "The Alcoholic Game," *Quarterly Journal of Studies on Alcohol,* 30 (October, 1969): 920–938.

27. I. D. Yalom, "Group Therapy and Alcoholism," unpublished manuscript.

28. Charles Becker, personal communication.

29. Carl Jung, letter to Bill W., 30 January 1961. In Bill W., "When AA Came of Age," *Alcoholics Anonymous Comes of Age* (New York: Alcoholics Anonymous World Services, 1957), p. 13.

30. William Silkworth. Cited by Bill W., *ibid.,* p. 15.

31. W. James, *Varieties of Religious Experience* (New York: Macmillan, 1947), p. 410.

32. David McDuff, personal communication.

33. H. M. Tiebout, "The Act of Surrender in the Therapeutic Process," *Quarterly Journal of Studies on Alcohol,* 10 (1949): 48–58.

34. Hans Tochs, *The Social Psychology of Social Movements* (New York: Bobbs-Merrill, 1965), p. 5.

35. E. M. Jellinek, "Phases in the Drinking History of Alcoholics," *Quarterly Journal of Studies on Alcohol,* 7 (1946): 1–88.

36. Jellinek, *The Disease Concept,* p. 12.

37. *Ibid.,* p. 36.

38. *Ibid.,* p. 37.

39. *Ibid.,* pp. 39–40.

Chapter 7. Beyond the Disease Concept

1. "Diagnosis of Alcoholism," World Health Organization, 1974.

2. *Manual of Alcoholism* (Chicago: American Medical Association, 1968), pp. 5–7.

3. *Diagnostic and Statistical Manual of Mental Disorders* (Washington: American Psychiatric Association, 1968), pp. 221–226.

4. *Ibid.,* p. 119.

5. Kirbens, "Chronic Alcohol Addiction," pp. 817–930.

6. Criteria Committee, National Council on Alcoholism, "Criteria for the Diagnosis of Alcoholism," *Annals of Internal Medicine,* 77 (1972): 249–258.

7. Charles E. Becker, Robert A. Scott, and Robert L. Roe, *Alcohol As a Drug* (New York: Medcom Press, 1974), pp. 75–80.

8. Committee on Alcoholism and Drug Dependence, American Medical Association, "Alcohol and Society," *Journal of the American Medical Association,* 216 (1971): 6.

9. *Random House Dictionary,* 3d. ed., s.v. "alcoholism."

10. *Stedman's Medical Dictionary,* s.v. "alcoholism."

11. Thomas Szasz, "Alcoholism: A Socio-Medical Perspective," *Washburn Law Journal*, 6 (1967): 255–268.

12. J. S. Tamerin, S. U. Weiner, and J. H. Mendelson, "Alcoholics' Expectancies and Recall of Experiences During Intoxication," *American Journal of Psychiatry*, 126 (1967): 12.

13. John Merry, "The Loss of Control Myth," *Lancet*, 1 (1966): 1257–1258.

14. K. Engle and T. Williams, "Effects of an Ounce of Vodka on Alcoholics' Desire for Alcohol," *Quarterly Journal of Studies on Alcohol*, 33 (1972): 1099–1105.

15. N. K. Mello and J. H. Mendelson, "Experimentally Induced Intoxication in Alcoholics," *Journal of Pharmacology*, 173 (1970): 101–106.

16. *Ibid.*, p. 110.

17. Alfonso Paredes, William Hood, Harry Seymore, and Murray Golob, "Loss of Control in Alcoholism," *Quarterly Journal of Studies on Alcohol*, 34 (1973): 1146–1161.

18. Jellinek, *The Disease Concept*, pp. 17 and 36.

19. Nancy Mello, personal communication.

20. J. H. Masserman and K. S. Yum, "An Analysis of the Influence of Alcohol on Experimental Neuroses in Cats," *Psychosomatic Medicine*, 8 (1946): 26.

21. J. J. Conger, "The Effects of Alcohol on Conflict Behavior in the Albino Rat," *Quarterly Journal of Studies on Alcohol*, 12 (1951): 1–29.

22. J. A. Dollard and N. E. Miller, *Personality and Psychotherapy* (New York: McGraw-Hill, 1950).

23. D. L. Davies, "Normal Drinking in Recovered Alcohol Addicts," *Quarterly Journal of Studies on Alcohol*, 23 (1962): 99–104.

24. K. Mills, M. Sobell, and H. Schaefer, "Training Social Drinking as an Alternative to Abstinence in Alcoholics," *Behavioral Therapy*, 2:1071.

25. M. Sobell and L. Sobell, "Individual Behavior Therapy for Alcoholics," *California Mental Health Research Monograph*.

26. Larry Meredith, personal communication.

27. Mansell Pattison, "A Critique of Alcoholism Treatment Concepts," *Quarterly Journal of Studies on Alcohol*, 27 (1966): 49–71.

28. *San Francisco Chronicle*, 31 March 1975.

29. P. Steinglass, S. Weiner, and J. Mendelson, "A Systems Approach to Alcoholism," *Archives of General Psychiatry*, 24, no. 5 (1971): 401–410.

30. Steve Wolin, personal communication.

31. E. M. Pattison, "Social Systems Psychotherapy," *American Journal of Psychotherapy*, 17, no. 3 (1973): 396–409.

32. Donald Horton, "The Functions of Alcohol in Primitive Societies: A Cross-Cultural Study," *Quarterly Journal of Studies on Alcohol*, 4 (1943): 199–320.

33. Robert F. Bales, "Cultural Differences in Rates of Alcoholism," in R. G. McCarthy, ed., *Drinking and Intoxication* (New York: Free Press, 1959), pp. 263–277.

34. E. M. Lemert, *Human Deviance, Social Problems and Social Control* (Englewood Cliffs: Prentice Hall, 1967).

35. Robert K. Merton, *Social Theory and Social Structure* (New York: Free Press, 1957), p. 174.

36. Richard Jessor, Theodore D. Graves, Robert C. Hanson, and Shirley L. Jessor, *Society, Personality, and Deviant Behavior: A Study of a Tri-Ethnic Community* (New York: Holt, Reinhart and Winston, 1968), p. 407.

37. *Ibid.*, pp. 410–411.

38. *Ibid.*, p. 420.

39. Cahalan, *Problem Drinkers*, p. 151.

40. *Ibid.*, pp. 151–152.

Chapter 8. Dealing With Problem Drinking

1. *First Special Report*, p. 67.

2. *Second Special Report to the U. S. Congress on Alcohol and Health* (Washington: U. S. Government Printing Office, 1974), pp. 49–56.

3. Morris Chafetz, *Liquor: The Servant of Man* (Boston: Little, Brown, 1961), p. 67.

4. Charles Becker, personal communication.

5. *Second Special Report*, p. 94.

6. Jacqueline P. Wiseman, *Stations of the Lost* (Englewood Cliffs: Prentice-Hall, 1970), p. 3.

7. *Ibid.*, p. 4.

8. *First Special Report*, p. 55.

9. Don Cahalan and Beatrice Treiman, *Drinking Behavior, Attitudes, and Problems in San Francisco* (San Francisco: Public Health Department Publication, 1976), pp. 48–53.

10. Edith Lisansky, "Alcoholism in Women: Social and Psychological Concomitants," *Quarterly Journal of Studies on Alcohol*, 55, no. 7: 588–623.

11. "Alcoholism: New Victims, New Treatment," *Time Magazine*, 22 April 1974, pp. 75–77.

12. *Ibid.*, pp. 77–78.

13. Seymour Halleck, "The Great Drug Education Hoax," *The Progressive*, (1970).

14. Morris Chafetz, "Towards a National Policy on Alcoholism Services," National Institute on Alcohol Abuse and Alcoholism, working paper (1974), pp. 20–21.

15. National Institute on Alcohol Abuse and Alcoholism, working paper (1974), pp. 25–28.

16. Gerald Caplan, *An Approach to Community Mental Health* (New York: Grune and Stratton, 1961).

17. Jeffrey Ordover and Carolyn Dobson, *Five Year Comprehensive County Plan for San Francisco* (San Francisco: Public Health Department Publication, 1973).

INDEX

A.A., *see* Alcoholics Anonymous
Absenteeism, *see* Industry
Abstinence, 29–31
  among problem drinkers, 147, 168–70
  as criterion for treatment success, 96–97, 168–70
  syndrome, *see* Alcohol abstinence syndrome
Accidents
  and drinking, 43–44, 69, 189–92
  industrial, 181, 192–93
  traffic, 35, 43–44, 182
Acetaldehyde dehydrogenase, 4, 69–70, 83–84, 88, 105
Acid-alkali balance, 79, 88, 90
Adams, Raymond, 78, 80, 103
Addiction, *see* Dependence, physical
Addison's Disease, 122
Adolescents, *see* Youth
Adrenaline®, *see* Epinephrine
Advertising, 188–89
Aggression, 58, 125–26, 127
Al-Anon, 139
Al-Ateen, 139
Al-Atots, 139
Alcohol, 1–2
  absorption, 64, 74
  abstinence syndrome, 61, 63, 74–78, 163

abuse, 61–62
antagonism by disulfiram, 83–84
as a depressant, 66, 67–68
as a sedative, hypnotic and general anesthetic, 62–63, 69
as a stimulant, 67–68
chemistry, 1–3
consumption, 50–52
dehydrogenase, 69–70, 71, 72, 83–84, 88
dependence, *see* Dependence, alcoholic
detoxification, *see* Detoxification, alcohol
effects on
  autonomic nervous system, 62, 67, 74
  cardiovascular system, 65–66, 92, 97–98
  central nervous system, 62, 66, 72, 74, 100–106
  endocrine system, 66–67
  gastrointestinal system, 63–64, 94–95
  hematological system, 64, 65–66, 94–95, 98–100
  peripheral nervous system, 101–102
  respiratory system, 66, 99–100

impairment due to, 43–45, 68
See also Accidents
interactions with other drugs, 70–71, 83
intoxication, 189–90
medical contraindications against, 77, 85
medical indications for, 77–78, 85
metabolism of, 1–2, 64, 69, 71–73, 83–84, 122
racial differences in metabolism of, 25, 71–72, 122–23
safety action programs, 192
tolerance to, 63, 69
toxicity, 68–69, 82–83, 107–108
Alcohol Administration Act (1936), 38
Alcohol, Drug, and Mental Health Administration, 155
Alcoholic beverages
consumption
domestic, 50–51
foreign, 51–52
distillation, 18–19, 22–23
industry, 22, 27, 46, 47, 50
manufacture, 19–20, 22, 23–24, 187–88
See also specific beverages
Alcoholics Anonymous, 57, 121, 135–140, 193, 203
See also Alcoholism, treatments of
See also Al-Anon; Al-Ateen; Al-Atot
Alcoholism, 113
alpha, 143
as a disease, *see* Disease concept of alcoholism
beta, 143–44
costs of, 180–84
definitions of, 57–58
delta, 144–45
diagnosis of, 157–59
epsilon, 145
gamma, 144
indices, 57–60
l'alcoolisme sans ivresse, 164
legal status of, 150–57, 189–90
prevalence of, 180–81
research on, 52–60, 140–45, 182
species of, 143–45
stages of, 141–42
theories of
allergic, 120–21, 138
behavioral, 124–25, 127–28, 147, 165–67
cultural, 127–28, 147, 173–78
endocrinological, 122, 124
genetic, 115–19, 121–22

infectious, 114–15
intrapsychic, 124, 126, 127
learning theory, 165–67
metabolic, 119–20, 122–23
nutritional, 121–22
pharmacological, 131–35, 162–63
physiological, 124–25, 127–28, 162–63
psychoanalytic, 124, 127–28, 148–49
psychological, 124, 128
social, 174–76
treatments of
Alcoholics Anonymous, 137–40
aversive conditioning, 133, 166–67
behavioral therapy, 74
biofeedback, 168
community, 156, 172–73, 208–12
compulsory, 133
disulfiram (Antabuse®), 132–34
family therapy, 170–72
federal employees, 194
group therapy, 129–30, 140
industry, 181, 193, 195
inpatient, 152, 167
medical, 83–84
milieu therapy, 173
operant conditioning, 165
outpatient, 129, 196
pharmacological, 131–35
psychotherapy, 129–30
social rehabilitation, 168–69
social systems therapy, 171–72
vocational rehabilitation, 156
See also Problem drinking
Alienation, 56, 59
Allergic theory of alcoholism, 120–21, 138
Amark, C., 117
American
alcoholic beverage consumption, 50–51, 180–81
drinking practices, 52–60
drinking problems, 43–45, 180–81
American Council for Alcohol Problems, 40
See also Anti-Saloon League
American Drinking Practices, 52, 57–60, 175–78
See also Cahalan, Don
American Indian, 25–26, 40, 72, 174–75, 200–201
American Medical Association, 32, 39, 113, 147–48, 159, 194
American Medical Association for the Study of Inebriety, 113

American Psychiatric Association, 148–49
Amitryptilene (Elavil®), 131
Amnesia, alcoholic, 102, 104–105
Anemia, alcoholic, 99
Anomie, 174–75
Antabuse®, see Disulfiram
Anti-diuretic hormone, 66
Anti-Saloon League, 31–32, 40
Anxiety, 162, 166–68, 173
Apollo, 10, 11, 26
Aquinas, Thomas, 112
Aqua vitae, 19
Arnauld of Villanova, 18–19
Arrests, 183
    See also Crime
Association Against the Prohibition Amendment, 36
Ataxia, 102, 103
Ale, 10
Autonomic nervous system, 62, 67, 74
Aversive conditioning, 133, 166–67

Bacchus, 12
Bales, R. F., 21, 173
Barbiturates, 63
Baron, Stanley, 45
Becker, Charles E., 85, 108, 133, 158, 185, 210
Beer, 11, 14, 17, 32
    alcoholic content, 2
    history, 3–5, 27, 45–46
    manufacture, 3–5
Behavior therapy, see Alcoholism, treatments of
Benedict, Ruth, 26
Bennion, Lynn, 72, 123
Beriberi, 97, 101, 103
Berry, R., 181
Biofeedback, 168
Binge drinking, 57
Blackouts, 104, 141
    See also Amnesia, alcoholic Blacks
    alcoholic beverage consumption, 54
    drinking practices, 54–55
    drinking problems, 54
Blane, Harold T., 126
Bleuler, Martin, 117
Blood, see Hematological system
Blood alcohol concentration (BAC), 43–45, 65, 68, 190–91
Blue Cross, 194, 195
Blue Shield, 194, 195
Bootleggers, 35, 40
Bourbon whiskey, 24, 39, 49

Brain, see Central nervous system
Brandy, 19–20, 39
Breathalyzer®, 45, 65
Buckman, Frank, 136
Burch, George, 97–98
Burks, P., 118

Cahalan, Don, 52–60, 140, 147, 175–78, 201
California, 28, 46–48, 156, 190, 194
Calories, 1–2, 84
Camba, 16, 178–79
Canada, 187, 192
Caplan, Gerald, 208
Carbohydrates, 2, 69–70, 87, 89–92
Cardiomyopathy, alcoholic, 98
Cardiovascular system, 65–66, 98
    See also Alcohol, effects on
Catecholamines, 67, 75, 76–77, 80, 89–91, 98
    See also specific drugs (e.g. epinephrine)
Catholics, 55
Central nervous system, 62, 64, 66, 72, 74, 100–106
    brain syndromes, 101–107
    damage, 106
    dysfunction, 107
    See also Alcohol, effects on
Chafetz, Morris, 23, 155, 185, 206
Chiarujo, Vincenzo, 112
Chinese, 186–87
Chlordiazepoxide (Librium®), 69, 77, 81, 131, 132, 186
Chlorpromazine (Thorazine®), 131
Cholesterol, 91–92
Christians, early, 13–14, 111
Cirrhosis, alcoholic, see Liver
Civilian Health and Medical Program of the Uniformed Services (CHAMPUS), 194
Cocktails, 28–29
Codex Medicamentarium (French), 20
Cognac, 19–20, 49
Color vision, 116
Colorado, 156, 190
Community alcoholism treatment, see Alcoholism, treatments of
Community Mental Health Centers Act (1963), 154
Comprehensive Alcohol Abuse and Alcoholism Prevention, Treatment, and Rehabilitation Act (1970), 154–55, 156
Compulsory treatment, 133
Congeners, 3, 7, 19, 50

Conger, John J., 165–66
Controlled drinking, 8–9, 85, 162–64, 168–71
Cortisol, 67, 80
Cortisone, 122
Craving, 140
Crime, 189–90
   arests, 183
Cruz-Coke, Robert, 116
Cytoplasmic ethanol oxidizing system, 69–70, 83–84
   See also Liver

Daiches, David, 49
Davies, D. L., 168
Delirium, 61, 106
Delirium tremens, 79–80, 122, 167
   See also Alcohol abstinence syndrome
Dementia, 107
Denial, 126
Denmark, 119
Dependence
   alcohol, 61–63, 126–27
   drug, 61–63, 125
   physical, 61–62, 134, 158–59
   psychological, 56, 61, 134
Depression, 67, 125, 126
Descartes, René, 112, 131
Detoxification, 87, 94, 210
   alcohol, 69–70, 73, 105–106
   drug, 70–71
Deviance
   as related to problem drinking, 138, 173–78
   historical views, 110–13
   primary *versus* secondary, 149
Diabetes mellitus, 73, 115, 122–24
   See also Carbohydrates
Diagnostic and Statistical Manual of Mental Disorders, 148–49
Diazepam (Valium®), 69, 77, 81, 131, 132, 186
Dionysus, 10–11, 26
Diphenylhydantoin (Dilantin®), 79
Disease concept of alcoholism
   definition, 109–110
   history, 110–14
   shortcomings, 114–15, 178–79
   See also Jellinek, E. M.
Disulfiram (Antabuse®), 83–84, 132–34, 167
   See also Alcoholism, treatments of
Dobson, Carolyn, 210
Dodds, E. R., 10
Dollard, J. A., 166

Dram shop acts, 33, 40
Dreams, 75–76
   See also Rapid eye movement sleep
Drinking problems, *see* Problem drinking
Drinkwatchers, 170–71
Driver decision, 43–45, 152
   See also Alcoholism, legal status of; Intoxication, public
Drug
   abuse, 61–62, 125
   dependence, 61–63, 125
   interactions, 70–71, 83–84
   tolerance, 69, 70
   treatment, 81
   use, 185–86, 203–204
Drunkalogues, 137
Drunken driving, 35, 43–44, 182, 190–92
Drunkenness
   as a disease, 109–110, 112–13
   as deviance, 111
   involuntary, 111
   public, *see* Intoxication, public
DTs, *see* Delirium tremens
Duodenum, *see* Gastrointestinal system

Easter decision, 151–52
Economic Opportunity Act (1967), 154
Education, 54
Eichner, Edward, 217
Elavil®, *see* Amitryptilene
Endocrine system, 66–67, 73, 80, 94, 112
Endocrinological theory of alcoholism, 122, 124
England, 5, 12, 22–23, 42
English
   alcoholic beverage consumption, 22
   drinking practices, 22
   drinking problems, 23
Engle, K., 162
Environment, 59, 117–18
Enzymes, 121–22
   See also specific enzymes (e.g. Alcohol dehydrogenase)
Epilepsy, alcoholic, 79
Epinephrine (Adrenaline®), 75, 76, 89–90
Escape drinking, 57
Eskimos, 72, 123
Esophagus, *see* Gastrointestinal system
Estrogen, 94
Ethanol, *see* Alcohol
Evarts, E. V., 75–76

Family therapy, 170, 172
Fat, 2, 87, 90–93, 97
Federal Alcohol Administration Act (1936), 38–40
Federal employees, 194
Feinberg, Irwin, 75–76
Fenichel, Otto, 125
Fenna, D., 72, 123
Fetal alcohol syndrome, 106–107
First Special Report to the U.S. Congress on Alcohol and Health, 44, 50–51, 155–56, 180–81
Folic acid, 99, 100, 188
Fort, Joel, 50
France, 12, 13–15, 42
French, 179
    alcoholic beverage consumption, 14–15, 51
    drinking practices, 14
    drinking problems, 164
Freud, Sigmund, 112, 124
Fructose, 72

Gastritis, 64, 86
Gastrointestinal system, 63–64, 74, 86–90, 94–95, 99
Genetics, 115–19, 121–22
German
    alcoholic beverage consumption, 13–14
    drinking practices, 13–14
    drinking problems, 13–14
Germany, 13–14, 42, 51
Giles, Thomas, 98
Gin, 22–23, 49
Gluconeogenesis, 88, 89
Glucose, 72, 89–91, 92
    See also Carbohydrates
Glycogen, 89–90
Goodwin, Donald, 119
Gould, Lawrence, 98
Gout, 88
Graves, Theodore, 174
Greeks, ancient, 3, 4, 10–12, 111
    alcoholic beverage consumption, 10
    drinking practices, 11–12
    drinking problems, 10–11
Greenberg, Ramon, 81
Group therapy, 129–30, 140
Gusfield, Joseph, 30

Halleck, Seymour, 205
Hallucinosis, alcoholic, 78
Hallucinogens, 26, 132

See also specific drugs (e.g. Lysergic acid diethylamide)
Hamilton, Edith, 214
Hangover, 49, 76–78
    See also Alcohol abstinence syndrome
Hanson, Robert, 174
Hawaii, 156
Health maintenance organizations (HMO), 195
Hejinian, John, 82
Hematological system, 64–66, 83, 87, 94–95, 98–100
Hepatic, *see* Liver
Hepatitis, alcoholic, *see* Liver
Hepatosis, alcoholic, *see* Liver
Heredity, *see* Genetics
Heroin, 62, 63, 74, 81, 151
Highway Safety Act (1966), 154
Hippocrates, 12, 110
Homer, 10
Hoover, Herbert, 36
Hope, 4
Hormones, *see* Endocrine system
Horton, Donald, 173
Howells, William Dean, 180
Hughes, Harold, 154
Hyperglycemia
    alcoholic, 89–90
    diabetic, 90
Hypoglycemia, alcoholic, 89–90, 91

Implied consent, 45
Indeval®, *see* Propranolol
Industry, 181, 193, 195
Infectious theory of alcoholism, 114–15
Inpatient treatment, 152, 167
Insulin, 72, 73, 87, 89–91, 124
    See also Carbohydrates
Insurance programs, 195–97
Intestine, *see* Gastrointestinal system
Intoxication, 74
    public, 21, 42–43, 151–52, 189–90
    See also Alcohol intoxication
Intrapsychic theory of alcoholism, 124, 126, 127
Ireland, 20, 51–52
Irish
    alcoholic beverage consumption, 20–21
    drinking practices, 21, 179
    drinking problems, 21, 173
Israel, 8–9, 52
Italian
    alcoholic beverage consumption, 14

drinking practices, 14
drinking problems, 179
Italy, 13, 14, 51

Jabir Ibn Hayyan, 18
Jackson, Charles, 61
Jaffe, Jerome, 61, 63, 74–75, 159
James, William, 136
Jellinek, E. M., 57, 95, 140–145, 146–47, 202
Jessor, Robert, 174–75
Jessor, Shirley, 174–75
Jewish, 8–9, 34
   alcoholic beverage consumption, 8–9, 173
   drinking practices, 8–9, 173
   drinking problems, 173
Johnson, Lyndon, 154
Jones, Kenneth, 106–107
Jung, Carl, 135

Kaij, L., 118
Kaim, Samuel, 157
Kaiser Industries, 195
Keller, Mark, 9
Ketoacidosis, 92
   alcoholic, 91
   diabetic, 90–91
Ketones, 90–91, 92
Kiddush, 9
Kirbens, Samuel, 42, 150–51
Knight, Robert, 125
Korsakoff, Sergei, 102–104
   Korsakoff's psychosis, 103
Kwashiorkor, 94, 95–96

Lactic acid, 88
Lactic acidosis, 88, 91
Learning theory, 165–67
Learning theory of alcoholism, 165–67
Legal responsibility, 190
Lemert, E. M., 173
Lesegue, Charles, 80
Li, Ting-kai, 72, 123
Librium®, *see* Chlordiazepoxide
Lieber, Charles, 70–72, 88, 91, 92, 96
Life changes, *see* Oxford Group
Lippmann, Walter, 18
Lister, Joseph, 114
Liver, 90
   cells, 91, 93
   cirrhosis, alcoholic, 93–96
   enzymes, 69–70, 123

functions, 87, 94
   hepatitis, alcoholic, 93, 96
   hepatosis, alcoholic, 93, 96
   metabolism, 64, 70, 87–88, 91
   microsomes, 91
Loss of control, 68, 144, 147, 163
Lungs, *see* Respiratory system
Lowenstein, Leah, 72
Lydia Pinkham's Vegetable Compound, 26–27, 39
Lysergic acid diethylamide, 132

McClean, G. E., 116
McCord, Joan, 126–27
McCord, William, 126–27
McDuff, David, 137
McLaughlin, Andrew, 33
Magnesium, 79
Malleus Mallefacorum, 111–12
Mardones, R. J., 116, 121
Marijuana, 132, 186
Marshall, Thurgood, 153
Masserman, Jules, 165
Maxwell, Milton, 214
Mead, 3, 11
Medical model, 114–16, 147
Medical treatments, 83–84
Medicaid, 195
Medicare, 195
Meditation, 168
Mello, Nancy, 162–63, 164–65, 166
Men
   alcoholic beverage consumption, 52–53
   drinking practices, 52–53, 58
   drinking problems, 57–58
Mendel, Gregor, 115
Mendelson, Jack, 71–72, 122–23, 153, 162, 171
Menninger, Karl, 125
Meredith, Larry, 169, 210
Merry, John, 162
Merton, Robert K., 174
Metabolic theory of alcoholism, 19–20, 22–23
Metabolism, *see specific substances* (e.g. Alcohol)
Microsomal ethanol oxidizing system, 70–71, 91
   See also Liver
Milieu therapy, 173
Miller, N. E., 166
Moderate drinking, *see* Controlled drinking

Moonshine, 25, 35, 40
Motivation
    for abstinence, 133
    for drinking, 162
    for treatment, 133
Multi-agency alcoholic, 198–99
Myopathy, alcoholic, 96–97

Narcotics, 62, 74, 81, 205
    See also specific drugs (e.g. Heroin)
National Center for the Prevention and
    Control of Alcoholism, 153, 155
National Commission on Uniform State
    Laws (1971), 156
National Council on Alcoholism, 135,
    140–46, 150, 154–55, 157–58, 193
National Institute of Mental Health, 153,
    155
National Institute on Alcohol Abuse and
    Alcoholism, 155, 181, 184, 194,
    195–96
National Mental Health Act (1948), 153
National Temperance and Prohibition
    Council, 40
Nature-nurture conflict, 117, 124
Neuropathy, alcoholic peripheral, 101
Neurosis, 148–49
Nixon, Richard, 155, 210
Noradrenaline®, see Norepinephrine
Norepinephrine (Noradrenaline®), 67,
    75, 76, 89–90
    See also Catecholamines
Nutrition, 188
    in alcoholics, 2
    in relationship to alcohol-associated
        diseases, 84–86, 89–91
Nutritional theory of alcoholism, 121–22

O'Abernon, Lord, ix
Operant conditioning, 165
Ordover, Jeffrey, 210
Outpatient treatment, see Alcoholism,
    treatments of
Oxford Group, 135–37

Pancreas, see Gastrointestinal system
Pancreatitis, 87
Paracelsus, 112
Paredes, Alphonso, 163
Pasteur, Louis, 14, 15, 114
Pattison, Mansell, 169–70, 172–73
Pavlov, Ivan, 165
Pearlman, Chester, 81
Peripheral nervous system, 101

Pharmacological theory of alcoholism,
    131–35, 162–63
Pharmacological treatment, 131–35
Pharmacology, science of, 20
Phenothiazines, 131
    See also specific drugs (e.g. Chlorproma-
        zine)
Phylloxera vastatrix, 28, 47
Physicians
    attitudes towards alcoholics, 113–14
    role in treatment, 147, 149–50
Physiological theory of alcoholism, 124–
    25, 127–28, 162–63
Pittman, D. J., 213
Port, 19, 88
Powell decision (1967), 152–53
    See also Alcoholism, legal status of; In-
        toxication, public
Pregnancy, 106–107
Prevention, 208–211
Problem drinking, 61–62
    age associated with, 59
    attitudes towards, 58, 59
    belligerence associated with, 58
    consumption of alcohol in relation to,
        58
    costs of, 180–84
    definitions of, 57–58, 147–50
    demographic factors, 59
    financial problems associated with, 58
    indices of, 57–60
    job problems and, 58, 181
    medical problems and, 58, 181–82
    prevalence, 59–60, 180–81
    psychological issues, 59
    socio-economic factors, 59, 177–78
    sex associated with, 58
    urbanization, 59
    See also Alcoholism
Problem Drinkers, 57, 60, 175–76
Prohibition, 33–37, 114
Prohibition Party (1861), 31–32, 40
Prohibitionists, 31–33, 113–14
Propranolol (Inderal®), 81
Protein, 2, 88, 94
Psychoanalytic theory, 124
Psychoanalytic theory of alcoholism, 124,
    127–28, 148–49
Psychological theories of alcoholism, 124,
    128
Psychosis, 103, 128–29
Psychotherapy, 124–26, 128–30

Racial differences
    in drinking practices, 25, 70
    in metabolism of, 70–72, 122–23

Rado, Sandor, 124
Rapid eye movement sleep (REM), 75–76, 81
Rebound hyperexcitability, 75
  See also Alcohol abstinence syndrome
Revolving door population, 198–99
Responsible drinking, 168–69
Reticular activating system, 68
Robinson decision (1962), 151–52
  See also Alcoholism, legal status of; Intoxication, public
Roe, A., 118
Roe, Robert, 158
Rogers, D. A., 116
Rogers, Will, 36
Romans, 5, 12–14, 111
  alcoholic beverage consumption, 12
  drinking practices, 13
  drinking problems, 111
Roosevelt, Franklin D., 37
Roueché, Berton, 1, 3, 18, 38, 111
Rum, 23–24
Rush, Benjamin, 29, 30, 112–13, 115, 187
Russia, *see* Soviet Union
Ryback, Ralph, 104–105

S., Dr. Robert, 137–39
Saloons, 31–33, 41–42
San Francisco
  Community Mental Health Services' Bureau of Alcoholism, 169, 201–202
  community survey, 202, 207–212
Schizophrenia, 79, 131, 149
Schlesinger, Kurt, 8
Scotch whiskey, 20, 22, 24, 39, 49
Scotland, 20, 22
Scott, P. D., 146
Scott, Robert, 158
Second Special Report to the U.S. Congress on Alcohol and Health, 181, 185
Sedatives, hypnotics and general anesthetics, 62–63, 64, 70–71, 132
  See also specific drugs (e.g. Alcohol)
Seizures, *see* Epilepsy, alcoholic
Shore, Richard S., 157, 207
Silkworth, William, 120–21, 135–36, 138
Sinclair, Andrew, 32
Skid row, 197–98
Skinner, B. F., 165
Smith, Alfred E., 36
Smith, David E., 81, 106–107
Smith, J. J., 80, 122
Sobell, L., 169
Sobell, M., 169

Sobriety, 122
Social drinking, *see* Controlled drinking
Social rehabilitation, 168–69
Social systems therapy, 171–72
Social theory of alcoholism, 174–76
Soviet Union
  alcoholic beverage consumption, 186–87
  drinking practices, 186–87
  drinking problems, 186–87
Speakeasies, 35
State dependent learning, 105
Steiner, Claude, 130–31
Steinglass, Peter, 171
Suicide, 125, 182
Sweden, 118
Sylvius of Leyden, 22
Synanon, 173
Szasz, Thomas, 160–61

Tamerin, John, 162
Tarahumara, 16, 178–79
Taxation, 23–25, 39, 185, 187
Teetotalers, 29–30, 85
Temperance movement, 29–31, 40, 113–14
Testosterone, 67, 94
Thiamine, 97, 101, 104, 121, 188
Thorazine®, 131
Tiebout, Henry, 137
Toch, Hans, 137–38
Tolerance
  to alcohol, *see* Alcohol, tolerance to
  to drugs, *see* Drugs, tolerance to
  See also Dependence, physical
Treisman, Beatrice, 201
Tremulousness, alcoholic, 63, 78
Trotter, Thomas, 109, 112–13
Truman, Harry, 196
"Twelve Steps," 137
Twin studies, 117–18
  See also Genetics

Uniform Alcoholism and Intoxication Treatment Act (1971), 156, 161, 189–90, 199
Uric acid, 88

Valium®, *see* Diazepam
Victor, Maurice, 78, 80, 103
Violence, 126
Virchow, Rudolph, 114
Vitamins, 2, 97, 98–99, 103–104
  See also Thiamine

Vitis labrusca, 17
Vitis rotundifolia, 17
Vitis vinifera, 6, 12, 15, 16, 28, 47
Vocational rehabilitation, 156
Vodka, 49–50
Volstead Act (1919), 33–34, 37

W., Bill, 120–21, 135–39
Washingtonians, 30–31
  home for the fallen, 113
  social movement, 138–39
Weiner, Sheldon, 162, 171
Wells, Charles, 106
Wernicke, Carl, 101–104
  Wernicke's encephalopathy, 102
Wernicke-Korsakoff syndrome, 101–104, 106
Wesson, Donald, 81
Whiskey rebellion, 24–25
Williams, Roger J., 121–22
Williams, T., 162
Wilson, Woodrow, 33
Wine, 2, 5–17, 19–20, 27–28, 46–48, 188
Winters, Ariel, 170

Wisconsin decision (1967), 151
  See also Alcoholism, legal status of; Intoxication, public
Wiseman, Jacqueline, 197
Withdrawal, *see* Alcohol abstinence syndrome
Wolin, Steve, 172
Wolff, Philip, 123
Women
  alcoholic beverage consumption, 52–53, 59–60
  drinking practices, 52–53, 58
  drinking problems, 59
  special difficulties of, 54–55, 201–203
Women's Christian Temperance Union, 31–32, 40
Women's Organization for National Prohibition Reform, 36
World Health Organization, 147

Yalom, I. D., 130
Yeast, 3–4
Youth, 41, 44, 54, 126–27, 203–204
Yum, K. S., 165